Implicating Empire

Polly Kellogg
612 721-9408

Implicating Empire

Globalization and Resistance in the 21st Century World Order

Stanley Aronowitz and Heather Gautney, editors

Clyde W. Barrow • Peter Bratsis • Jeremy Brecher • Jeffrey Bussolini
Alex Callinicos • William DiFazio • Carmen Ferradas • David Graeber
Bruno Gullì • Michael Hardt • Cindi Katz • Andrew Light
Manning Marable • Peter Marcuse • Randy Martin • Antonio Negri
Michael Ratner • Corey Robin • William K. Tabb • Ellen Willis

BASIC
BOOKS

A Member of the Perseus Books Group

Copyright © 2003 by The Center for the Study of Culture, Technology and Work,
Graduate School and University Center of the City University of New York

Published by Basic Books,
A Member of the Perseus Books Group

All rights reserved. Printed in the United States of America. No part of this book may be reproduced in any manner whatsoever without written permission except in the case of brief
quotations embodied in critical articles and reviews. For information, address Basic Books, 387
Park Avenue South, New York, NY 10016–8810.

Designed by Brent Wilcox

Library of Congress Cataloging-in-Publication Data
Implicating empire : globalization and resistance in the 21st century world order /
    Stanley Aronowitz and Heather Gautney, editors ; Clyde Barrow . . . [et al.].
        p.   cm.
    Includes bibliographical references and index.
    ISBN 0-465-00494-6 (alk. paper)
    1. Globalization.   2. World politics.—21st century.   I. Aronowitz, Stanley.
II. Gautney, Heather.   III. Barrow, Clyde W.
JZ1318 .I47   2002
303.48'2—dc21

                                                                    2002011820

03 04 05 / 10 9 8 7 6 5 4 3 2 1

For the resisters

Contents

Part III: The Culture of
Globalization and Resistance

Preface and Acknowledgments

In the summer before the attack on the World Trade Center, the Center for the Study of Culture, Technology and Work at the CUNY Graduate Center, along with members of Left Turn, began planning the "Globalization and Resistance Conference" for November 2002. The impetus for this conference was to raise awareness and stimulate discussion on the broad range of social, cultural, environmental, and political issues related to globalization and its burgeoning resistance movement. The subject matter we sought to cover included the history of neoliberalism and its relationship to globalization; the role of the state and imperialism in the new world order; the social and ecological sustainability of capitalism; and alternatives to the current world system. Positioned as an educational and rallying mechanism for the public, the conference aimed to raise awareness of the issues related to globalization and to engage activists in discussions about their various campaigns and how to achieve them in the contemporary political climate.

September 11 fundamentally changed the tone and focus of the conference. The attacks on the Pentagon and the World Trade Center vastly increased the urgency and timeliness of the proposed discussions, necessitating a reorientation of the conference to include such topics as the effects of 9/11 on impending trade agreements and the world economy in recession, the political climate in the Middle East, terrorism and war, and the potential destabilization of the globalization resistance movement—all of which now occupy a central role in this book.

THE CENTER FOR THE STUDY OF CULTURE, TECHNOLOGY AND WORK

The Center for the Study of Culture, Technology and Work opened in 1988 at the Graduate School and University Center at the City University of New York. Since its inception, the Center has focused on fostering connections between intellectuals and activists, and on translating theoretical and conceptual work into practice. Toward these ends, the Center sponsors conferences, colloquia, and workshops in diverse areas including urbanism, education, technoscience, and the future of work. In addition to supporting the development of the Paolo Friere Institute, sponsoring *First of the Month* (an infrequent tabloid of politics and culture), and producing *Found Object* (a student-run journal dedicated to bridging the gap between academic and nonacademic work), it has undertaken several action research projects on problems of work and education in collaboration with Service Employees International Union (SEIU) Local 1199, Musicians Union Local 802, the three Library Locals of DC 37, and various other agencies.

ACKNOWLEDGMENTS AND DEDICATIONS

We would like to acknowledge the many organizations and individuals who contributed to the conference and to this volume, starting with our sponsors: Neil Smith and the Center for Place, Culture, and Politics, CUNY Graduate Center; Continuing Education & Public Programs, CUNY Graduate Center; Mike Davis; FREE CUNY; Left Turn; NY Open Society; and the Professional Staff Congress AFT.

We would also like to thank Rabab Abdulhadi, Tariq Ali, Marnie Archer, Robert Ausch, Barbara Bowen, Harriet Brown, Dennis Brutus, Chris Cage, Brian Campbell, Eric Canepa, Manuel DeLanda, Ariel Ducey, Norman Edelman, Rami El-Amine, Zein El-Amine, Laura Fantone, Silvia Federici, Johanna Fernandez, Judith Fulmer, Deborah Gambs, Barbara Garson, Susan George, Karen Gilbert, Steve Gorelick, Miriam Greenberg, Stefano Harney, David Harvey, Merilee Helmer, Doug Henwood, Agnieszka Kajrukszto, Jonathan King, Mansha Kinger, Eric Laursen, Michael Letwin, David Levine, Penny Lewis, Freddie Marrero, Lorna Mason, Michael Menser, Kim Moody, Ananya Mukherjea, Jeff Myers, Frances Fox Piven, Michelle Ronda, Rami Rothkop, Armand Samos, Stuart Schaar, Abby Schoneboom, John Schoneboom, Shana Siegel, Crystal Sylvia, Annie Vanesky, Alex Vitale, Will Weikert, Jami Weinstein, Rob Weissman, Irwin Wesley, Dominic Wetzel, and, of course, all of the authors whose work appears herein.

Many thanks as well to the activist groups that participated in the conference, either by presenting their work or by helping to organize: ACT UP!, Association for Union Democracy, Autonomedia, Brecht Forum, Colombia Action Committee, Critical Resistance, DC-Indymedia, the Democratic Socialists of America, the Green Party, Greenmap, Health GAP Coalition, Justice Action Coalition, Labor Notes, NY Direct Action Network, NYC Labor Against the War, NY-Indymedia, Rainforest Action Network, SUSTAIN, Teamsters for Democratic Union, and UNITE!

Finally, very special thanks to Vanessa Mobley, our editor at Basic, and to Bilal El-Amine, a long-time activist whose idea for the conference was the basis for this book.

For Heather, this book is dedicated to my mother Diane Gautney, and in loving memory to my father, Spencer Gautney. For Stanley, this book is dedicated to my students, without whom . . .

The Debate
About Globalization

An Introduction

STANLEY ARONOWITZ AND HEATHER GAUTNEY

Between the emergence of a mass anti–Vietnam War movement in 1966 and the September 11 attack on the World Trade Center and the Pentagon, the term *imperialism* acquired considerable, almost popular, legitimacy in the United States and Western Europe. Neither the decolonization struggles such as France's Algerian War nor Portugal's misadventures in Angola had dealt such a severe ideological blow to the democratic pretensions of the United States' and the West's foreign policy as had the war in Vietnam. The reason was fairly plain: Despite the dependent status of Puerto Rico, Guam, and a scattering of islands, colonization was never the American imperial style, and its claim to constitute a Great Exception to the European colonialism and imperialism was a recurring theme of American ideology. Vietnam dispelled the illusion that the United States, as the undisputed military and political leader of the "Free World," stood apart from the pattern of Western European imperialism. While the U.S. government claimed that its intervention was undertaken in order to defend the sovereignty of South Vietnam against a Communist invader—despite the region's admittedly corrupt government—most of the world and, in time, many of its own citizens came to believe that the intervention was an unwarranted interference in what was described by many as a "civil war."

The perception that the United States was, indeed, an imperial power was shared by the diverse groups and individuals who, as legatees of the Vietnam era, converged on Seattle in December 1999 to protest the "free trade" policies of the World Trade Organization (WTO). Most interpreted these policies as thinly veiled justifications for sweatshops, environmental despoliation, and union-busting capital flight from the basic industrial sectors of advanced capitalist societies. As the new century turned, the international global justice movement finally had legs—

for the first time since 1848, when Marx and Engels called upon "workers of all countries" to unite. The shock of seeing 50,000 demonstrators from unions as well as mainly student-based anti-sweatshop groups, feminists, and environmentalists—together with the surfacing of a significant youthful anarchist contingent that proclaimed anti-capitalism as its signature—was a tremor heard around the globe. Sympathizers and detractors alike took the magnitude of Seattle as a sign that the new century would certainly bring to birth a resurgence of "the movement" against corporate domination, if not capitalism itself.

Yet, given that protests brought to the surface the economic exploitation and political domination of industrially advanced countries as well as developing nations, and highlighted the role of international agencies, such as the World Trade Organization, the World Bank, and the International Monetary Fund, linked to the superpowers, especially the United States, the situation was more complex. The September 11 attack, preceded by the post–Cold War tragedies in Bosnia, Kosovo, and Rwanda where the United States and the European Union dawdled in the face of genocide and ethnic cleansing, altered the common view. Now seasoned anti-war activists and intellectuals alike entertained the idea that military intervention by the United States and its allies in the internal affairs of a sovereign nation-state might be justified to protect human rights and human lives. As early as the events in the former Yugoslavia, particularly the Serbian siege of the Bosnian city of Sarajevo, a new concept began to surface in international affairs: Human rights trump sovereignty. In the mid-1990s some human rights advocates urgently demanded that the West respond to the crisis by means of military intervention, if necessary. Inherent in this formula is the view that there are universal values that supersede the old 19th-century notion that the prerogatives of nation-states are inviolable, challenging both the liberal and the Marxist theories of imperialism.

And with the September 11 assault, erstwhile anti-imperialist forces were sharply divided between those who continued to insist that a U.S. military reprisal would simply extend its imperialist aims and those who argued that the right to self-defense is equally universal. The fact that no U.S. government could have survived its refusal to act failed to detain not only pacifists for whom no military response was valid but also those who maintained that America's imperial power vitiated its right to self-defense. On the other side, even if they did not sign on to Attorney General John Ashcroft's Patriot Act, which threatened to shred the constitution by denying due process to those suspected of terrorism, a constellation of longtime war opponents found themselves justifying the broad outlines of the Bush administration's aim to remove the Taliban government as well as the Al Qaeda forces of Osama bin Laden. As a result, neither the American bombings of Afghanistan nor the Bush declaration that the "war on terrorism" might call for wide-scale U.S. military offensives against the "axis of evil" (consisting of eight countries including Iran and Cuba, which had explicitly denounced terror as an instrument of foreign policy) evoked widespread protests in the United States. Clearly, the left was divided and we had entered a new era.

A SHORT HISTORY OF THEORIES OF GLOBALIZATION

To say that globalization is "not new" is an understatement. As soon as humans learned how to build ships that could navigate deep waters and withstand nature's furies, they began roaming the globe. In ancient Greece these voyages were usually bent in the service of conquest. Indeed, war has almost always been the partner of technical innovation. But in the 15th and 16th centuries, contrary to the common understanding that these wanderings were motivated by pure exploration, even the most curious seafarer needed resources and commercial motives. These were provided by monarchs, merchants, and corporations such as the East India Company in order to whet and satisfy the appetites of royalty, the growing merchant classes themselves, and the nascent manufactories that produced textile goods and tobacco products. They financed trips in order to discover sources of raw cotton, tobacco, and spices. In order to stabilize their access to these raw materials and to find an outlet to address growing unemployment and to dissipate religious dissent by offering opportunities for settlement, European states and 16th-century mercantilist interests acquired a taste for colonization. England, Holland, Spain, and Portugal, the leading mercantilist countries, engaged in vigorous exploration and territorial acquisition, particularly in the New World and in Africa where the slave trade had become a prime means of capital accumulation for Europe, as well as a source of labor for cotton and tobacco plantations in the Americas.[1]

The processes of capital accumulation and colonization ran like a red thread throughout the industrializing era. Although many historians mark the 19th century as the era of "nationalism" because it witnessed the emergence of the nation-state organized around the themes of the consolidation of new political identities and territories that signified the formation of geographically defined markets and currencies, from the Napoleonic conquests of the first two decades until the Franco-Prussian War in 1870 the century was marked by frequent bilateral international conflicts. And by the last quarter of the century, liberal and radical critics were heralding the epoch of modern imperialism. The term *modern* signified that mercantile interests no longer dominated globalization, nor was imperialism merely a policy of powerful capitalist states. Even early-20th-century liberal critics of imperialism such as J. A. Hobson and Joseph Schumpeter acknowledged that developed capitalist societies required access to global markets in labor and raw materials as a condition of their economic reproduction and growth.[2]

Following suggestions in the third volume of Marx's great work *Capital,* the Austrian Rudolph Hilferding argued that the sources of the globalization of capital lay in the inner logic of the system rather than in the greedy acts of large corporations, which, by the turn of the 20th century, dominated production and finance as well as governments and militaristic regimes. In broad strokes Hilferding's argument was that, owing to the concentration and centralization of capital in fewer hands, the epoch in which a large number of small capitalists in the industrial sectors competed with each other for relatively modest shares of the national market had given way to a new form, finance capital. Finance capital signifies the merger of industrial and banking capital—a merger that results from the deleterious manifestations of cutthroat competition: lower prices that drive marginal capitals from the field; lower rates of profits, even as the mass of profit increases due to technological innovation; and, perhaps most important of all, the rise of a powerful labor movement that places limits on the ability of capital to reduce wages and extend working hours in order to enlarge profits.[3]

This development takes place in stages: the rise of the modern corporation that replaces the individually owned enterprise; the enlarged role of banks and other financial institutions in the ownership and management of enterprises; and intensified labor struggles that expose the limits of the national market to maintain profit rates adequate for the reproduction of capital on an expanded scale. In addition to the search for raw materials to provide the engine for production, the new period of imperialism is marked by the massive export of capital, the internationalization of labor and the labor markets, and the expansion of capitalism to all corners of the globe by economic penetration, force, or both. To be sure, the vehicle for capital's global reach remains the nation-state. Hilferding believed that the emergence of huge financial combines would, in the wake of the appearance of labor as an organized political force, lead to what became known as "organized" capitalism. Capital's ability to rationalize itself by eliminating competition, granting social reforms to the underlying population, and making the state a source of political stability rather than conflict would eventually overcome the anarchy of capitalist production and the class wars that marked the 19th century.

But Rosa Luxemburg, a prominent Polish and German Marxist theorist, drew different conclusions from her study of the dynamics of modern capitalism. Her main contribution to the globalization debate was *The Accumulation of Capital*, published in 1913. Without exploring the complexity of her critique of Marx and her alternative theory of expanded reproduction, suffice it to say that Luxemburg derives her theory of imperialism from the ineluctable tendency of capitalism to accumulate on an expanded scale. Accumulated capital inevitably outstrips the limitations of the national market. Luxemburg writes:

> Imperialism is the political expression of the accumulation of capital in its competitive struggle for what remains still open in the non-capitalist environment. Still the largest part of the world in terms of geography, this remaining field for the expansion of capital is yet insignificant as against the high level of development already attained by the productive forces of capital; witness the immense masses of capital accumulated in the old countries which seek an outlet for their surplus product and strive to capitalise their surplus value, and the rapid change-over to capitalism of the pre-capitalist civilizations.[4]

The consequence, according to Luxemburg, is that with "their increasingly severe competition in acquiring non-capitalist areas, imperialism grows in lawlessness and violence, both in aggression against the non-capitalist world and in ever more serious conflicts among the competing capitalist countries. But the more violently, ruthlessly and thoroughly imperialism brings about the decline of non-capitalist civilizations the more it cuts the very ground from under the feet of capitalist accumulation."[5] A year later World War I broke out.

Hilferding's *Finance Capital* was published in 1909 and Luxemburg's tacit rebuttal of his "organized capitalism" thesis was published in 1913. World War I, in which two great alliances of capitalist states plunged the world into an unprecedented global conflict, apparently refuted Hilferding's predictions and confirmed Luxemburg's analysis. Shortly after the war's outbreak in 1915, Nicholai Bukharin published *Imperialism and World Economy*. Borrowing heavily from Hilferding's economic analysis, he parted ways politically by arguing that imperialism is marked by intensified "inter-imperialist rivalry" in which the older established powers are challenged by the upstarts; in this case, Britain, France, and, secondarily, Russia faced an insurgent alliance of Germany and the Austro-Hungarian empire. Bukharin argued that the chronic tendency of the rate of profit to fall and its concomitant, economic concentration, inevitably lead to imperialism and, as capitalism matures, to war. The likely outcome is revolution, which, Vladimir Illyich Lenin notes, would break out first in the defeated countries. Lenin's popularization of and amendment to Bukharin's thesis, *Imperialism: The Highest Stage of Capitalism*, addressed the consequences of imperialism. Written in 1916 at the very apex of the war's unprecedented destruction of human lives and natural resources, Lenin's pamphlet became a central document informing the postwar revolutionary upsurge in the defeated countries—Russia, Germany, and many components of the Austro-Hungarian empire. But the fundamental assumption of Lenin's theory is that modern imperialism signified the end of world capitalism. World capitalism had entered the era of its "general crisis," whose outcome was the emergence of a new social system.[6]

In the immediate aftermath of World War I, Lenin's prediction seemed to have been brilliantly vindicated. The defeated countries of Russia (which was forced by the revolution to leave the war "prematurely"), Hungary, and Germany all underwent revolutionary upheaval. That only the Soviet regime survived did not diminish the sense of foreboding in ruling circles of the leading capitalist countries. The interwar period was marked by a sharp turn to the right in many European countries and, until the second New Deal of 1935–1937, in the United States as well. American labor confronted the most severe state repression since the 1890s, and in the aftermath of the Great Steel Strike of 1919, which shook capital's confidence to its roots, thousands of immigrant workers associated with the left were deported during the infamous Palmer Raids. The fascists came to power, in part, as the most reliable bulwark against bolshevism, and many in the commanding heights of capitalist power readily concurred with this characterization. Even Roosevelt's National Industrial Recovery Act was interpreted by some as being consistent with the economic program of the fascists: a command economy in which the state plays a central role in controlling industrial and labor relations and in becoming a direct employer of labor.[7]

The Depression ushered in a new phase in the imperialist modus vivendi. While domestic investment slumped and, in the United States, virtually crashed, global investment rapidly grew, especially in capital export and raw materials. Leading U.S. corporations such as United States Steel and General Electric made substantial investments overseas, especially in Germany and Japan. American-, British-, and Dutch-based corporations invested heavily in raw materials as well. For example, in the search for cheaper sources of fuel and metals, even as tens of millions remained unemployed in the advanced capitalist societies, the 1930s witnessed the emergence of new oil-producing states in the Middle East, and Latin America and Africa became the site of a vast expansion of mining, particularly for gold and other precious metals. The American South, the nation's leading source of cotton, was left virtually destitute as Egypt and India expanded their production of raw cotton. Globalization became a zero-sum game.

World War II and its aftermath did not substantively alter the frantic search for cheap labor and raw materials. But it was an era of decolonization. The underlying populations led by incipient and frustrated middle classes in the British colonies—notably India and North, West, and Southern Africa—waged unremitting struggles for independence lasting some thirty years, after which the British empire in its characteristic form was destroyed. Similarly, the French, Dutch, German, and Portuguese colonies achieved their independence. But after the initial postwar decade and a half of reconstruction, European countries as well as the United States required sources of raw material and concomitant sites for capital export. A new form of globalization had to be developed to take account of the changed circumstances. What some have called the "new imperialism" emerged.

The "new imperialism" required that the leading capitalist countries, led by the United States, make clients of the independent third world and semi-peripheral states of Asia, Africa, and Latin America. Clientism was (and is) defined by the willingness of the banks and other financial institutions to lend billions of dollars to these states, but under severe restrictions. Clients were required to reduce or eliminate their social welfare programs such as health care, education, and laws establishing labor standards. They had to lower or abolish trade barriers and help facilitate capital investment through measures such as tax concessions, state financing of building plants and material infrastructure (roads as well as electrical and communications systems), monetary controls favorable to investors, and police forces to provide for security. As a result of such costs, they were now heavily indebted to these financial institutions. Default on the debt accompanied by devaluation of their respective currencies would inevitably imperil the regimes. In many instances this meant that the client states invested most of their resources to fund the military, whose object was less to keep the peace than to quell discontent. We have the examples of Argentina and Nigeria as key indicators of the contradictions of the new globalism.[8]

Here we must refer to the perspective of dependency theory, first developed in the 1960s by a number of Latin American Marxists and by Andre Gunder Frank, a European whose major reference is Latin America. Basing their writing on the work of Karl Polanyi and, indirectly, on Luxemburg, writers such as Ferdinand Cardozo (later the centrist president of Brazil), Walter Rodney, and Arrighi Emmanuel advanced the thesis that the so-called developing world was actually mired in planned underdevelopment. Political independence was chimerical so long as these countries were economically dependent upon the imperial societies and their financial institutions. In many countries lacking a middle class of entrepreneurs and larger capitalists, the landlords and the state, often in military guise, constitute a sort of comprador class that has neither interest in nor incentive for building the necessary conditions for genuinely independent, autarkic economic activity. Interestingly, after World War II, Brazil and Mexico made significant efforts to construct such economies, with some success. But eventually each was forced to give ground to transnational capital and to seek huge loans from the IMF and the World Bank to forestall economic collapse.[9]

Imperial globalization in a postcolonial environment entailed the creation, or rather the expansion, of international institutions charged with the tasks of stabilizing these regimes in the context of a new world order. The World Bank, the IMF, the WTO, and other global institutions have become crucial actors in steering the postcolonial states. Although they have been obliged to surrender some of their autonomy, nation-states do not disappear. Indeed, the economic gyrations became more pronounced in the 1980s and 1990s—as exemplified by the formation of the European Union and the subsequent adoption of a common currency, the Euro. Moreover, as the global economic crisis has deepened and capital has fled from the West to developing countries, we have seen a new phase emerge in which, beyond raw materials, the value of the peripheral and semi-peripheral sites for relatively cheap industrial labor has become crucial. Now the global division of labor is not only that between industrial production and agriculture but also that between two spheres of industrial production itself: the advanced societies in which labor, owing to its historical trade union and political power, still enjoys higher monetary and social wages (i.e., the social benefits enacted largely through government) and the developing societies where wages are low and benefits almost nonexistent.[10]

This altered situation is one of the sources of the emergence of the movements for global justice. In some cases, alliances between unions and environmentalists have posed new challenges to capitalist globalization; witness the famous Teamsters-Turtle alliance in Seattle and the growing protests before and after September 11 in Europe and, to a lesser degree, the United States. At the same time it must be acknowledged that attempts to organize independent labor unions not tied to ruling parties and governments are met with severe repression in the form of assassination or imprisonment of key leaders in places such as Guatemala and Indonesia, to cite only two well-known instances. Yet the movements aimed at curbing the power of capital and achieving political and economic democracy have gained new momentum in some countries, despite September 11.

The latest and perhaps most controversial theory of globalization, detailed in Michael Hardt and Antonio Negri's *Empire,* appeared in 2000 to considerable public discussion. Although acknowledging the key role of the United States in fostering the new economic and political arrangements, the authors define the new situation as more a network, consisting of the national governments of the Great Powers and the leading institutions of transnational capital. In this configuration nation-states have lost much of their salience, according to the authors. And they understand the "Human Rights" slogan, far from being a manipulative mantra of imperialism's self-justification, as a genuine effort to impose liberal democratic regimes on the client countries. "Human Rights" is a crucial means to shield the Empire from the turbulence associated with military dictatorships and the widespread corruption characteristic of client governments. Far from being a form of altruism, these measures may have some of the same objectives of the old imperialism. For if the "political and social climate" is filled with revolutionary violence and military repression, the climate for investment sours and capital simply refuses to enter or does not hesitate to pull out of the country and move to another. Still, some are already aware of Rosa Luxemburg's prognostication that as the former colonial world is developed, capital, which depends on underdevelopment, may eventually run out of outlets. The hope of its most enlightened sector is that capitalism can survive rough equality. Needless to say, the proposal to go beyond the theory of international rivalry among the imperial powers or to ignore another favorite in the previous theoretical paradigms—that the contradiction between advanced capitalism and the third world constitutes nothing less than a new global divide, in which the working class of the advanced countries share the booty derived from the unequal division of labor—has provoked criticism from many quarters.[11]

Yet, regardless of whether imperialism (old or new), third world oppression, or the thesis of Empire constitutes an adequate description and theoretical explanation for what is generally termed "globalization," there can be little debate that the new arrangements mean that no nation, no region, no alliance either of labor or of capital is stable. As the old Chinese proverb reminds us, we are "condemned to live in interesting times."

"human Rts." helps enable a stable investment climate,

EMPIRE TODAY

Terrorism and War

Although the contention that September 11 marked a turning point in world history has been widely disputed, it undoubtedly altered the discourse on globalization and the tenor of resistance worldwide. The attack and subsequent events not only spurred a wave of debates regarding U.S. imperialism and the right to "self-defense" but also called into question the national security of the United States and its role as an unassailable world superpower. Furthermore, the event threatened the stability of the world system and implicated globalization as a volatile and potentially destructive force. Following 9/11, the discourse on globalization necessarily shifted to discussions regarding terrorism, fundamentalism, and war, stimulating broad speculation on the entailments of the War on Terror, America's "permanent war." The U.S. government's renewed obsession with security raised concern over threats to civil liberties and the mounting xenophobia against persons of Middle Eastern and South Asian descent in the wake of a renewed American patriotism.

The first two chapters in this volume, Manning Marable's "9/11: Racism in a Time of Terror" and Jeffrey Bussolini's "The Wen Ho Lee Affair: Between Race and National Security," address the relationship between war and racism, drawing from both the discourse on September 11 and that regarding the nature of race relations in the history of war and conflict. While engaging in a comprehensive discussion of the social and historical conditions that gave rise to the event, Marable argues that 9/11 did not signify a radical departure from the program of contemporary politics but, rather, was an inflammation of currents already set in motion in the 1980s by Reagan and the U.S. program to establish a national security state. Marable reviews the development of the prison industrial complex and dramatic increases in prison populations, the erosion of trade unionism, and the assault on social welfare, all driven in part by "the ugly politics of race."

Marable elucidates the complex of race-oriented identity politics that emerged in the aftermath of September 11 and focuses on the African American community, caught in the contradiction between American patriotism and its own stark history as the object of an institutional racism that dates back to the early 17th century. He points out that "the African American is unquestionably a recognized member of the American national household, but has never been a member of the American family." The term *recognized* is key to his thesis; while African Americans have become an accepted part of American culture and are the dialectical counterpoint to the "whiteness" of the American identity, the *unrecognized* "terrorist Other" of Middle Eastern or South Asian descent—a perceived foreigner on American soil—continues to be seen as a threat to national security and the safety of the U.S. citizenry.

This problematic is also taken up by Bussolini, who cites sociologist George Simmel's concept of "the stranger." Only slightly dissimilar to Marable's assertion, Bussolini's "stranger" is a recognized presence in U.S. culture but remains outside America's self-image. Arguing against the conjecture that we have entered a new phase of history marked by the dissolution of the nation-state, Bussolini asserts that globalization is perhaps best understood as an amalgamation of forces that are *reshaping* the increasingly porous nation-state of the 21st century. He details the case of Wen Ho Lee, the Taiwanese American nuclear physicist who was incarcerated under suspicion of espionage, to demonstrate the relationship between national security and national identity, and the use of security to legitimize racisms already embedded in American culture. Bussolini explicates the character of the U.S. National Security State and its tendency to create new enemies (and resurrect old ones) to justify its aggressive use of intelligence operations and massive development and deployment of weapons worldwide. For both Marable and Bussolini, the U.S. security state serves as a conduit of fear, insecurity, and intimidation, aimed not only at the "enemy within" but also at the entire international community by way of the massive proliferation of its "defense" infrastructure.

National security and the threat to civil liberties within the post–September 11 United States are discussed at length by Michael Ratner in "Making Us Less Free: War on Terrorism or War on Liberty?" and by Corey Robin in "Fear, American Style: Civil Liberty After 9/11." Ratner and Robin utilize markedly different, but complimentary, approaches to the problem. Robin, in presenting his concept of "fear, American style," argues that repression in the United States is organized according to a division of labor between the state and civil society. For him, the state-sponsored erosion of freedom and civil liberties is supplemented by the considerable use and presence of fear in the realm of everyday life, of which the politics of race outlined by Marable and Bussolini are indeed a significant part. Ratner, on the other hand, focuses on the role of the state in oppressing civil liberties and analyzes the "new legal landscape" that emerged after September 11. The establishment of the U.S. Office of Homeland Security, significant increases in the investigatory and prosecutorial power of government agencies such as the FBI and CIA, expanded executive powers and the president's unrestricted discretion to declare war, and the construction of new crimes such as "domestic terrorism"—all point to a formal, juridical dissolution of civil liberties by way of both a "permanent war" abroad and a "war at home." Like Bussolini and Marable, Ratner and Robin characterize racial profiling and the censorship of information as constituents of an overall "silencing of dissent" that tears at the very heart of the country's hard-won civil liberties. They also criticize the false dichotomy between security and freedom in the discourse on civil liberties: Robin points out that these terms tend to measure freedom relative to state policy rather than according to their social and political consequences, and Ratner asserts that the fight to safeguard individual rights and the problem of national security are indeed part of the same struggle, one that must put forth a more significant challenge to U.S. foreign policy than is currently in sway.

The dissolution of the right to dissent is taken up by Heather Gautney in "The Globalization of Violence in the 21st Century: Israel, Palestine, and the War on Terror." Gautney explores the history and politics of the Israeli-Palestinian conflict and, like Marable, positions the Intifada as a legitimate liberation movement, which, she asserts, has been wrongly conflated with terrorism in contemporary political discourse. She intervenes in the aforementioned debates among members of the anti-imperialist left over the War on Terror and addresses questions regarding the legitimacy of certain forms of violent resistance and the problem of what constitutes "terrorism" and "self-defense"—an issue that has been severely complicated by the recent suicide bombings. For Gautney, the historical subjugation of the Palestinian people epitomizes a broader affront to the right to resist; she uses the conflict as a starting point to deliberate on the general character of contemporary warfare and what she terms the "globalization of violence": The failure of diplomacy, the overwhelming use and threat of force in modern conflict resolution, and the increased presence of new, nomadic forms of violent resistance all point to the emergence of a world order in which violence is progressively supplanting consent as a primary source of legitimate power. For her, the extensive use of force in conflict resolution not only undermines the potential for democracy but signals the emergence of a truly apolitical order.

Ellen Willis, in "The Mass Psychology of Terrorism," takes a unique approach to the problem of terrorism that differs significantly from that of many on the Left. Rather than rehearsing the typical geopolitical-economic analyses regarding 9/11 (the importance of which she does not deny), she adds a feminist-cultural critique of terrorism and fundamentalism. Against Marable's appeal that we distinguish Islam from Islamicists, Willis argues that the attack on the World Trade Center and subsequent events cannot be understood apart from the cultural context that gave rise to them, which necessarily includes religion as well as "the psychosexual dimension of politics." Counter to those who dismiss Samuel Huntington's "clash of civilizations" thesis, she identifies an alternative "clash of civilizations," citing the contradictions between *and* among the liberal, democratic movements of the last 200 years and patriarchal, authoritarian forms of social organization that have dominated world cultures for the last five centuries. Willis, however, moves beyond Huntington to identify the "clash of civilizations" within: The attack on the WTC was a materialization of the tensions, anxieties, and social-psychological antagonisms associated with the liberal program's threat to patriarchal and traditionalist culture, a contradiction that profoundly exists in the psyche of the West as well as in that of Islamic countries. Willis calls for a separation of church and state, and for more rigorous interrogation of the cultural forms—and the psychosexual tensions they ignite—that threaten human freedom.

This issue is also taken up by Bruno Gullì in "Beyond Good and Evil: A Contribution to the Analysis of the War Against Terrorism." Gullì addresses the events of September 11, and, against the "irrational, superstitious, and Manichean" explanations that have pervaded the discourse on the war against terrorism, he calls for—and puts forth—an enlightened, secular, and critical understanding of them. Gullì situates the event within the currents of world history beginning with the 20th century, marked by the West's assault on communism and its ongoing struggle against alternatives, especially those that speak to the possibility of *universal* freedom. He points out the continuity between the war against communism and the war against terrorism, which is really just another form of Western authoritarianism, yet one that now operates on a somewhat different plane, as a conflict *among* various fundamentalisms and wills to power. For him, September 11 was "nothing but a moment within a logic of violence that has ensnared the entire world" (and the United States, "an element within the motor of this logic"); he calls for a move beyond the now dominant "discourse on power" to a "discourse on freedom" and a move beyond the logic of good and evil as necessary conditions for emancipation from the violence endemic to the contemporary world climate.

Globalization, the State, and the Political Economy

This second section enters the core debates on globalization that inspired the title of the volume: implicating "Empire" and its merit as an adequate and accurate account of the contemporary global order. It reflects the divisions among globalization theorists, which tend to follow two distinct lines of thought: Some understand national sovereignty as the ultimate authority in international affairs, and globalization as simply a new form of imperialism, while others assert that a new regime and constituent power relations have emerged in which an imperial authority (i.e., Empire) trumps the sovereignty of nation-states. Theories regarding political strategy are similarly divided along these lines: Some argue for a global movement that reinforces national or local sovereignty, as exemplified by the program of the Association for the Taxation of Financial Transactions for the Aid of Citizens (ATTAC), a global activist organization focused on establishing democratic self-determination for local and regional economies, most notably through the mechanism of the Tobin Tax. Others argue for a globalized resistance that mirrors the form of social organization they seek to promote—namely, an anarchist-oriented position unbound by the state form, more organically allied through global networks and local affinity groups, and skeptical of reformist politics and strategy. The chapters in this section query debates regarding political power and space, and further interrogate formal and ideological manifestations of globalization and the neo-liberal program, such as transnational institutions and "free trade," the increasingly uneven distribution of wealth worldwide, the erosion of democracy, and the politics of labor in the global political economy.

In "Globalization and Democracy," Michael Hardt and Antonio Negri generate a new understanding of democracy in terms of their highly controversial concept of Empire, which asserts that in the contemporary global arrangement, a new imperial authority has emerged that supersedes the sovereignty of the nation-state and remains unbound by its form. Borrowed from the ancient Roman formulation, Empire is the combination of the three classical forms of government—monarchy, aristocracy, and democracy—into a single sovereign rule, yet it is this third element that is of particular concern in this chapter. Hardt and Negri review the modern conception of democracy, based on representational structures and the construction of "the people" as a unity, as an identity bound to the nation-state, but posit that in the contemporary age of Empire, the destabilization of national boundaries and "imaginaries" gives way to potentially new forms of democracy, beyond that which assumes a social contract and fixed national space. What follows is an explication of their concept of a democracy of the multitude and *counterpower*—the fusion and continuity of resistance, insurrection, and constituent power—aimed toward the realization of human freedom.

In "Global Capital and Its Opponents," Stanley Aronowitz implicates Hardt and Negri's *Empire* in the debate regarding the role of the nation-state in contemporary globalization and resistance. He begins with an explication of world affairs and demonstrates shifts in the global distribution of power—from the Cold War to the colonial period to the fall of the Soviet Union—and how these relate to patterns of global economic integration and the emergence of the neo-liberal program, with its accompanying institutional framework manifest in the triumvirate of the IMF, World Bank, and WTO. Aronowitz argues that, despite the conjecture that national sovereignty has been superseded by that of the "metastate," nations remain critical actors in the constitution of the global order. Contrary to Hardt and Negri's lack of "institutional perspective," he demonstrates the importance of social groups and institutions as mediators of regulation as well as resistance, and although he agrees that direct confrontation is indeed an appropriate form of protest, social movements must also test the mettle of existing institutions and "discover the limits of the old." Furthermore, given the lack of a legal and juridical definition of "global citizenship," the nation-state remains the primary regulatory force of societies, economies, and politics in world affairs, as evinced, perhaps most prominently, by the unilateralism of the Bush administration: Aronowitz asks, "Are we witnessing a new stage of international rivalry?" He closes with an analysis of the tensions between attempts at reform tied to the nation form and resistance movements that seek to transcend the boundaries of the nation and enact a global citizenship in the face of Empire, citing the failures of the former and the latter's need for a "persuasive and coherent" political program.

In "Over, Under, Sideways, Down: Globalization, Spatial Metaphors, and the Question of State Power," Peter Bratsis argues that Hardt and Negri, and other theorists of globalization, tend to rely on overly legalistic understandings of nationality and territoriality, and make use of "imprecise spatial metaphors" (such as "above") that erroneously dichotomize political space into an "inside" or "outside" national boundaries. Whereas some globalization theorists understand sovereignty in relation to formal (legalistic) territorial limits, Bratsis poses an alternative view that understands the space of the state as a social fact—as socially constituted. While spatial metaphors may be used to approximate perception and experience, their misuse creates an appearance that politics is determined from "outside" society itself, in the form of international legal mandates, the free market, and transnational institutions such as the IMF and the World Bank. Bratsis calls for a break from the level of appearances toward an understanding of political power and strategy that acknowledges how the nation-state is constituted by the people. He draws from Nicos Poulantzas to present the ancient conception of political space—the Greek *polis*—as a way of demonstrating the historical specificity of the fragmented space of modern capitalism, in which the nation-state is understood as the center of bourgeois power, and national identity, as a mechanism of control that is still very much alive, despite globalizing forces.

Alex Callinicos, in "The Anti-Capitalist Movement After Genoa and New York," provides an incisive analysis of the "anti-capitalist" globalization movement following September 11 and the G8 Summit in Genoa (in July 2001). For Callini-

cos, these events similarly raised critical issues for the movement, including the role
of violence (by the state as well as that waged against it) in the contemporary order;
the role of the state and imperialism; and the question of how to produce alternatives and enact systemic social change. He asserts that, despite the various setbacks
to the movement, these events demonstrated the need for a systemic critique of the
contemporary global system, and illuminated, perforce, the relationship between
capitalism and imperialism theorized by Marx and Engels more than a century ago.
Callinicos stresses the role of nationalist discourses and identities (highlighted by
the new American patriotism and the responses of national actors and "regional
powers" to the war on Afghanistan and the ongoing "war on terrorism"), but he
questions whether the nation-state is a viable conduit of democratic transformation
in the contemporary political-economic climate, and whether reform is a suitable
strategy, given the tendency of the state toward violence or cooptation.

Like Hardt and Negri, William DiFazio, in "Time, Poverty, and Global Democracy," highlights the failures of modern representative democracy in enacting global
freedom, yet he suggests that a mass participatory democracy must take into account
local and global economic and social disparities that preclude the participation of the
masses in their own historical development. DiFazio identifies two key factors central
to the democratic program: First, there must be a movement toward obtaining economic equality worldwide, and second, the structure of the everyday must be redefined so as to create time necessary for political participation. DiFazio reviews a broad
array of theoretical approaches to the problem of the global political economy and
democracy, and demonstrates how many of them tend to adopt a reductionist view
of globalization that does not address failures of both the neo-liberal program and the
liberal, pluralist versions of democracy. DiFazio calls for a revolutionary revamping of
the global order but suggests specific means of institutional reform, such as a reduction of the working day to allow more time for civil participation and the establishment of a living wage as a baseline of economic equality. In this regard, DiFazio
moves beyond the problem of political programs that tend to engage in systemic, revolutionary critique without posing practical alternatives and strategies for dealing
with urgent problems such as world poverty.

In "Race to the Bottom?" William K. Tabb interrogates the conceptualization
of free trade as a "race to the bottom"—a critique of globalization that focuses on
transnational corporations' tendency to relocate production sites to low-cost countries, thereby creating a highly competitive world labor market that gives way to decreased wages and job security as well as increased unemployment worldwide. For
Tabb, the "race to the bottom" thesis is a limited view of transnational capital and a
potentially dangerous one: In addition to the fact that transnational corporations
rarely employ labor from "the bottom," and that for many workers, especially those
in the global South, such new employment opportunities may provide a step up, the
"race to the bottom" logic has been used by some to justify the protectionist tendencies that have plagued the labor movement for decades. Tabb discusses the
changes in the U.S. labor movement under John Sweeney, in which "fair trade over

free trade" is being used as a means to move beyond protectionism toward understanding globalization as a potential conduit of worldwide worker solidarity. Tabb
points out that "[t]rade brings the workers of the world into a single labor market
as never before," thus creating new spaces for the labor movement in which to address contemporary class issues and the uneven global distribution of wealth.

The Culture of Globalization and Resistance

The culture of globalization in contemporary times is inextricably linked to many
of the problematics articulated earlier in the volume. This section, however, focuses
on the wide range of phenomena associated with how globalization and resistance
are understood, practiced, and lived. It covers critical issues regarding global environmental change; the shifting spaces of capital and its effect on particular places;
the transformation and, in some cases, dissolution of national identities and cultural forms; the ways in which the global economy is lived at the level of convention as well as in spaces of rupture; the effects of globalization on cultural institutions, such as health care, the family, and education; questions of world security,
the threat of global warfare, and the role of law enforcement and the military in the
scenes of everyday life; and, perhaps most important, cultures of resistance and
their relationship to political strategy.

In "Globalization Today," Jeremy Brecher distinguishes the character of "globalization from above" from that of "globalization from below": While the former is
driven by the neo-liberal imperative to integrate the global economy, the latter
emerged to counter the hegemony of transnational financial institutions that favor a
power elite. Brecher creates another critical distinction, however, by identifying a
shift in the practice of "globalization from above" toward a more destructive phase,
marked by increased militarization, worldwide recession, and increased economic inequality. Citing specific examples—from the Enron debacle to the collapse of the Argentine economy to the labor crisis of the Mexican maquila workers—he shows how
the global economy is failing to sustain itself by way of IMF-imposed austerity programs, profits based on "speculative fiction," and a labor market that feeds off of intensified competition and radical foreclosures on worker protections and job security
(a "race to the bottom"). Moreover, he identifies the emergence of a new unilateralism, spearheaded by the United States, that privileges national interest over international concerns and legal mandates. Brecher describes the culture of "globalization
from below," including the emergence of new grassroots organizational forms—social forums, advocacy networks, affinity groups—based on cross-national cooperation (often among seemingly disparate movements) and rooted in opposition to the
logic of competition put forth by proponents of "globalization from above." He
closes with a series of challenges to the movement regarding social and political strategy that reach to the very core of the debates on globalization and resistance.

In "Globalization, Trade Liberalization, and the Higher Education Industry,"
Clyde W. Barrow analyzes the impact of globalization and (partial) privatization of

the higher education industry over the last two decades. He reviews the history of the General Agreement on Tariffs and Trade (GATT) and the WTO, as well as the emergence of the General Agreement on Trade in Services (GATS), which is focused specifically on promoting trade liberalization in service industries. He explicates the character and course of multilateral trade liberalization in higher education services and the structural adjustment policies of the IMF and WTO (which privilege developed countries as suppliers) and their potential to transform higher education, as well as other traditionally public enterprises, into a private commodity traded on world markets. He cites changes in the culture and administration of educational services vis-à-vis the corporatization of education, and demonstrates how trade liberalization contributes to global inequality and effectively ignores the role of educational institutions in promoting equal opportunity, citizenship, democracy, and public service.

In "Geography Financialized," Randy Martin presents the concept of "financialization"—which, in his words, is "the incorporation of money management into daily life . . . [and] the idiom in which globalization is lived." For Martin, "financialization" is a regime of self-management and a form of colonization in which financial planning, neo-liberal policy, and their translation into uneven development are integrated into everyday life. Martin assesses the old geography of finance capital in which the first world consumed that which was produced by third world labor policed by despotic regimes; now, through mechanisms of micro-credit, the poor are lulled into indentured servantry by way of their integration into the system of finance capital. Financialization has thus transformed poverty into something other than lack; it is a new principle of association marked by the "complete delineation of persons according to their access to credit and category of risk." Martin cites the geographical interests of the poor as precariously located between globalization's claims to eliminate poverty and its dependence on it. Implicating venture philanthropy, he also criticizes the privileging of personal accrual of wealth and the pervasive "business makes history" mentality characteristic of the culture of contemporary globalization.

Andrew Light, Peter Marcuse, and Cindi Katz focus on the political ecology of globalization with differing, yet complementary, approaches. Whereas Marcuse emphasizes the effects of globalization and the "decentralized concentration" of corporate enterprise on urban space *and* place, Light is concerned with the development of a participatory environmentalism—among and within urban communities—as a potential solution to the increasingly insalubrious condition of the global environment. Marcuse and Katz alike pose critiques of global capital and its disengagement from particular places, whereas Light focuses on the problematic from the standpoint of resistance and promotes a re-engagement with the environment at the level of the everyday. Although Katz and Light diverge in terms of their theoretical approaches, they similarly propose and define new forms of trans-localism: Katz, as a means to address the detrimental effects of globalization on particular places, and Light, as a means to develop an urban environmental citizenship that may serve as a starting point for a more global awareness.

In "Globalization and the Need for an Urban Environmentalism," Light criticizes "anti-globalization" theorists, such as Vandana Shiva and Wolfgang Sachs, who identify globalization as constitutive of a "green imperialism" in which environmental issues that are deemed "global" are, in reality, focused on justifying the implementation of global policies that serve the interests of particular, often first-world locales. Citing Shiva's argument that globalization is a "political and not an ecological space," as well as her assertion that a truly democratic globalization would necessarily privilege the local, Light argues against the notion of a purely political globalization and points to its ecological dimension in which the world is understood as an integrated system with environmental concerns that transcend artificial, national boundaries. The heart of Light's chapter is his focus on ascertaining responsibility for global environmental problems that often appear beyond the scope of communities and individuals. While there is clearly a need for global or transnational initiatives, for Light, local milieux provide a critical starting point from which to wage an active, global environmentalism. Against the typical anti-urbanism among today's (and yesterday's) environmentalists, he promotes the development of a local, urban environmental citizenship as a vital conduit to a more sustainable environmentalism worldwide.

Cindi Katz, in "Vagabond Capitalism and the Necessity of Social Reproduction," poses similar recommendations for understanding the global ecology, but she attacks the problem from a theoretical standpoint markedly different from that of Light. Katz analyzes the effects of globalization and "vagabond capitalism"—the "irresponsible stalker of the world"—on social reproduction. In light of intensified capitalist accumulation, growing world inequality, and social disinvestments associated with the neo-liberal program, social reproduction has been progressively unhinged from capitalist production in the last three decades. The shifting of sites of production to lower-cost sites has effectively ignored the importance of social reproduction—the stuff of everyday life—which always occurs within specific locales. In a discussion similar to that put forth by Marcuse, Katz identifies the trend toward privatized means of sustaining social reproduction and the lack of commitment of states and governments to particular places, now that global capitalism no longer depends on any one place. She points out, however, that for people, place matters. She proposes the development of *topologies*—precise, ecological knowledges of particular places (including their mechanisms of social reproduction)—and *countertopologies* as means of waging resistance against vagabond capitalism. Countertopologies connect topological knowledge, and not only further illuminate what is known about particular places but, by warrant of their linkage, allow for knowledge of the spaces in-between, the shifting spaces of global capital.

In "On the Global Uses of September 11 and Its Urban Impact," Peter Marcuse analyzes the impact of September 11 on urban forms and urban life and, in the process, elucidates the social, political-economic, and spatial character of what he terms "really existing globalization" (i.e., Davos globalization, and not Porto Alegre). Similar to Katz, he draws attention to the decreasing dependence of global capital on place as evidenced by the movement toward "concentrated decentralization," a trend that was already in motion prior to September 11 but nevertheless was intensified by it. Moreover, he identifies how September 11 served to push the issue of security to the forefront of U.S. foreign and domestic policy, and to effectively ground it in the everyday. Behind the rhetoric of security, however, lies the impending expansion of U.S. economic and military power on a global scale. For Marcuse, "concentrated decentralization" occurs when businesses that once operated in core regions of the global economy, such as Wall Street, increasingly concentrate in locations that are in close proximity, but are indeed outside them. Such relocation patterns serve to augment the citadelization of urban spaces as corporate enterprise concentrates in walled, secured communities that employ physical, economic, and social barriers to entry *in the name of security*. Further, these patterns reinforce policies that direct public funds away from social welfare and toward the erection of a security infrastructure, a trend that was legitimized and intensified by the events of September 11. On the flipside is a systematic segregation and ghettoization of entire communities that Marcuse identifies as part and parcel of the growing inequality implicit in really existing globalization.

In "Argentina and the End of the First World Dream," Carmen Ferradás discusses the effects of the neo-liberal policies of global institutions, such as the IMF and World Bank, on the sociopolitical economy of Argentina, which she terms "a newly *submerging* society." Ferradas's piece not only indicates the failure of neo-liberalism to integrate individual states into a homogenous, global economy; it also demonstrates how such failures compromise the sovereignty of nation-states and, in some cases, radically alter entire social structures. She points out how the effects of such transformations can, in turn, give rise to new nationalisms and new forms of resistance that cross and sometimes unify traditional class boundaries, as is the case with the *piqueteros* and *caceroleros* in Argentina. In her analysis of the nationalism present in the Argentine resistance, Ferradas runs somewhat counter to those who claim that the Argentine resistance is intentionally positioned in opposition to global capital; while the nationalist fervor to which Ferradas refers is clearly based on a critique of the hegemony of the neo-liberal program, what remains unclear is whether the resistance is indeed connected to a broader trans-Latin or transnational movement, given that, according to Ferradas's account of the historical development of the Argentine identity, Argentina has historically set itself apart from other South American countries. In closing, Ferradas advocates for the development of transnational linkages despite her skepticism that the emergent resistance movement, and its ability to unify disparate social classes in Argentina, will be sustained over the long run.

David Graeber, in "The Globalization Movement and the New New Left," directly addresses professional intellectuals who put forth theoretical claims about social movements without truly being in touch with them. His concern is to clear up common misconceptions about the globalization movement and to suggest future directions for how the gap between activists and professional intellectuals might be bridged. He begins by reviewing the history of the globalization movement and addressing the most common criticisms of it: first, that the movement is against globalization; second, that it is geared toward violent resistance; and, third, that it has not engaged a coherent political program. In terms of the first criticism, Graeber identifies the movement as a "globalization movement" waged against the dominance of the neo-liberal program, which understands human historical development as a unidirectional process directed by a power elite and without democratic accountability. He reviews the history of the movement and the character of the future it envisions: a globalization that involves the opening of borders for the free flow of people, ideas, and information. Regarding the second critique, Graeber debunks the notion of the movement as violent and asserts that conflicts between globalization activists and the state are largely a result of the inability of police forces to deal with the movement's nontraditional modes of resistance, such as the street theater, festival, and "nonviolent warfare" of the Direct Action Network, Reclaim the Streets, various black blocs, and Ya Basta! among others. Addressing the criticism that the movement lacks a coherent political program, he details the struggles associated with the grassroots implementation of direct democracy, which includes the design and use of new organizational forms and, ultimately, a reinvention of everyday life. In closing, he suggests future directions in the spirit of what he terms "the intellectual equivalent of a gift economy," in which activists and professional intellectuals alike intermingle their respective knowledges in a gift-like exchange.

NEW QUESTIONS ABOUT GLOBALIZATION

The chapters in this volume capture some of the historical tendencies of globalization and resistance in the early-21st-century world order. Yet globalization also means that changes are occurring at what we believe to be an increasingly rapid pace. These changes include the following:

- Informed scientific opinion says that human intervention into nature may be more catastrophic than has been predicted. The world's water supply is in serious jeopardy, a problem that conventional science has linked to human population growth, sprawl, and overconsumption. Scientists are also expressing concern over the decline in biodiversity and rapid extinction of plant and animal species due to pollution, overfishing, deforestation, and the mishandling of genetically modified organisms. And they have continued to warn of the impending danger of global warming associated with the extensive use of fossil fuels and other nonrenewable energy sources in advanced industrial societies. At the most general level, these concerns raise the question of whether capitalism itself is sustainable.
- Contrary to those who thought that the end of the Cold War and the collapse of the Soviet Union would mean a reduction in ideological conflict and warfare, we are now seeing an intensification of both. President George W. Bush has declared a new Axis of Evil, consisting of Middle Eastern and

Asian nations, to replace communism, and war has become a permanent feature of our time. In the service of the new militarism, all other concerns, including poverty and constitutional protections such as civil liberties and civil rights—indeed, the right to dissent from official policy—are not only subordinate to the advancing war machine but have become suspect on patriotic grounds. And the labor movement is experiencing new threats to its independence, especially the right to strike as the American president threatens to abrogate its exercise on national security grounds.

• We are now beginning to see a trend in which social issues such as feminism and racial justice and even labor struggles that were once seated in advanced industrial societies are shifting to the global south. Societies that once operated under theocratic power are now being faced with a new liberalism. The UN World Summit on Sustainable Development, held in summer 2002 in South Africa, thrust environmental concerns to the front burner of its agenda. The American president refused to join other world leaders at the conference.

These developments confirm the central thesis of *Implicating Empire:* that globalization is not just another political, economic, or social issue. It is the context within which future struggles will be waged and future alliances forged.

NOTES

1. Immanuel Wallerstein, *The Modern World System* (New York: Academic Press, 1974).

2. J. A. Hobson, *Imperialism* (London, 1904); Joseph Schumpeter, *Imperialism and Social Classes* (New York: Harper and Row, 1961).

3. Rudolph Hilferding, *Finance Capital* (New York: Routledge, 1988).

4. Rosa Luxemburg, *The Accumulation of Capital* (New York: Monthly Review Press, 1951).

5. Ibid., p. 45.

6. V. I. Lenin, *Imperialism: The Highest Stage of Capitalism* (New York: International Publishers, n.d.).

7. V. J. Jerome, *The Peril of Fascism* (New York: International Publishers, 1934). This view was shared by the Socialist Party leader, Norman Thomas, but, of course, he did not follow the analysis offered by Jerome, a Communist Party theoretician. Reflecting CP policy at the time, Jerome held the Socialists complicit with early New Deal corporatism.

8. Sheryl Payer, *A Fate Worse Than Debt* (New York: Monthly Review Press, 1988).

9. Andre Gunder Frank, *Capitalism and Underdevelopment in Latin America* (New York: Monthly Review Press, 1967).

10. Robert J. S. Ross and Kent C. Trachte, *Global Capitalism: The New Leviathan* (Albany: State University of New York Press, 1990).

11. See Stanley Aronowitz, "Global Capital and Its Opponents," and Peter Bratsis, "Over, Under, Sideways, Down: Globalization, Spatial Metaphors, and the Question of State Power," both in this volume.

PART I

Terrorism and War

9/11

Racism in a Time of Terror

MANNING MARABLE*

I

It is still mourning time here in New York City. It has been weeks since the terrorist attack destroyed the World Trade Center towers, but the real tragedy remains brutally fresh and terribly real to millions of residents in this overcrowded metropolis. The horrific sight of thousands of human beings incinerated in less than a hundred minutes, of screaming people free-falling more than a thousand feet and plummeting to their deaths, is nearly impossible for anyone to explain or even to comprehend.

The criminals who obliterated the World Trade Center and part of the Pentagon attempted to make a symbolic political statement about the links between transnational capitalism and U.S. militarism. But by initiating acts of mass murder, any shred of political credibility of those who plotted and carried out these crimes was totally destroyed. There can be no justification, excuse, or rationale for the deliberate use of deadly force and unprovoked violence against any civilian population. This was not essentially an act of war but a criminal act, a crime against not only the American people but all of humanity. Those who committed these crimes must be apprehended and brought to justice under international law and courts.

....

*Earlier versions of this chapter were presented at the New York Law School "September 11, 2001: Causes, Responses, Long-Term Solutions, A Symposium," sponsored by the New York City Chapter of the National Lawyers Guild October 3, 2001; at the "Teach-in on September 11th," sponsored by Riverside Church, New York City, October 23, 2001; and at the "Globalization and Resistance Conference," City University of New York Graduate Center, November 16, 2001. No publication or distribution of this text is permitted without the prior authorization of the author, except for personal uses.

In the days immediately following the terrorist attacks, some elements of the American left, including a few black activists, took the sectarian position that those who carried out these crimes were somehow "freedom fighters." These "left" critics implied that these vicious, indiscriminate actions must be interpreted within the political context of the oppression that gave rise to those actions. In short, the brutal reality of U.S. imperialism, including America's frequent military occupation of third world countries, to some degree justifies the use of political terrorism as a legitimate avenue for expressing political resistance.

It is certainly true that the American left must vigorously and uncompromisingly oppose the Bush administration's militaristic response to this crisis, because the unleashing of massive armed retaliation will inevitably escalate the cycle of terror. However, progressives must also affirm their support for justice—first and foremost, by expressing our deepest sympathies and heartfelt solidarity with the thousands of families who lost loved ones in this tragedy. We should emphasize the fact that among the victims, over 1,000 labor union members were killed in the World Trade Center attack; that more than 1,500 children in metropolitan New York were left without a parent; and that the families of the hundreds of undocumented immigrants who perished in the flames of September 11 are unable to step forward to governmental authorities because of their illegal residence in the United States.

Although there was a generous outpouring of charitable donations to the victims' families after September 11, less attention has been given to the most disadvantaged workers whose lives or livelihoods were destroyed. Kitchen workers at the World Trade Center's Windows on the World, for example, have only $15,000 life insurance policies. Over 100,000 jobs were destroyed, along with hundreds of small businesses in the area.

However, our criticisms of the Al Qaeda group should not support their "demonization," and description as "cowards" or "evil doers," in the incoherent denunciations of President Bush. We can denounce their actions as criminal, while also resisting the Bush administration's and media's racist characterizations of their political beliefs as "pathological" and "insane." Bush's demagogical rhetoric only feeds racist attacks against Middle Eastern people and other Muslims here in the United States.

Perhaps one of the most effective criticisms would be to highlight the important differences between the sectarianism of Islamic fundamentalism, versus the rich humanism that is central to the Islamic faith. In the eloquent words of the late Muslim intellectual Eqbal Ahmad, Islamic fundamentalism promulgates "an Islamic order reduced to a penal code, stripped of its humanism, aesthetics, intellectual quests, and spiritual devotion." It manipulates the politics of resentment and fear, rather than "sharing and alleviating" the oppression of the masses in the Third World.

We must also make a clear distinction between "guilt" and "responsibility." The Al Qaeda group is indeed guilty of committing mass murder. But the U.S. government is largely responsible for creating the conditions for reactionary Islamic fundamentalism to flourish. During Reagan's administration, the Central In-

telligence Agency (CIA) provided over three billion dollars to finance the mujahadeen's guerrilla war against the Soviet Union's military presence in Afghanistan.
It also used Pakistan's Inter-Services Intelligence, or secret police, to equip and
train tens of thousands of Islamic fundamentalists in the tactics of guerrilla warfare.

According to one 1997 study, the CIA's financing was directly responsible for
an explosion of the heroin trade in both mujahadeen-controlled Afghanistan and
Pakistan. By 1985, the region had become, states researcher Alfred McCoy, "the
world's top heroin producer," supplying 60 percent of U.S. demand. Heroin addicts in Pakistan subsequently rose "from near zero in 1979 . . . to 1.2 million by
1985." Our Pakistani "allies" operated hundreds of heroin laboratories. The Taliban regime consolidated its authoritarian rule in the mid-1990s in close partnership with Pakistan's secret police and ruling political dictatorship. And the Clinton
administration was virtually silent when public executions, mass terror, and the
draconian suppression of women's rights became commonplace across Afghanistan.

As *The Nation* columnist Katha Pollitt observed, under the Taliban dictatorship, women "can't work, they can't go to school, they have virtually no healthcare,
[and] they can't leave their houses without a male escort." The Bush administration's current allies in Afghanistan, the so-called Northern Alliance, are no better.
As Pollitt notes, both fundamentalist groups are equally "violent, lawless, misogy-
nistic [and] anti-democratic."

One standard definition of *terrorism* is the use of extremist, extralegal violence
and coercion against a civilian, or noncombatant, population. Terrorist acts may be
employed to instill fear and mass intimidation, to achieve a political objective. By
any criteria, Al Qaeda is a terrorist organization. Most Americans have rarely experienced terrorism, but we have unleashed terrorism against others throughout our
history. The mass lynchings, public executions, and burnings at the stake of thousands of African Americans in the early twentieth century was home-grown, domestic terrorism.

The genocide of millions of American Indians was objectively a calculated
plan of mass terrorism. The dropping of the atomic bomb on Japanese cities during World War II, resulting in the fiery incineration of several hundred thousand
civilians, was certainly a crime against humanity. The U.S.-sponsored coup against
the democratically elected government of Chile in 1973, culminating in the mass
tortures, rapes, and executions of thousands of people, was nothing less than state-
financed terrorism. There is a common political immorality that links former
Chilean dictator Augusto Pinochet, Osama bin Laden, and former U.S. Secretary
of State Henry Kissinger: They all believe that political ends justify the means.

II

A consensus now exists across the American political spectrum, left to right, that
everything fundamentally changed in the aftermath of the September 11 attacks.

To be sure, there was an upsurgence of patriotism and national chauvinism, a desire to "avenge" the innocent victims of the Al Qaeda network's terrorism.

I would suggest, however, that these recent events are not a radical departure into some new, uncharted political territory but, rather, the culmination of deeper political and economic forces set into motion more than two decades ago.

The core ideology of Reaganism—free markets, unregulated corporations, the vast buildup of nuclear and conventional weapons, aggressive militarism abroad and the suppression of civil liberties and civil rights at home, and demagogical campaigns against both "terrorism" and Soviet Communism—is central to the Bush administration's initiatives today. Former president Reagan sought to create a "national security state," where the legitimate functions of government were narrowly restricted to matters of national defense, public safety, and provision of tax subsidies to the wealthy. Reagan pursued a policy of what many economists term "military Keynesianism," the deficit spending of hundreds of billions of dollars on military hardware and speculative weapons schemes such as "Star Wars." This massive deficit federal spending was largely responsible for the U.S. economic expansion of the 1980s. Simultaneously, the Soviet Union was pressured into an expensive arms race that it could not afford. The fall of Soviet Communism transformed the global political economy into a unipolar world, characterized by U.S. hegemony, both economically and militarily.

The result was a deeply authoritarian version of American state power, with increasing restrictions on democratic rights of all kinds, from the orchestrated dismantling of trade unions to the mass incarceration of racialized minorities and the poor. By the end of the 1990s, 2 million Americans were behind bars, and over 4 million former prisoners had lost the right to vote for life. "Welfare as we know it," in the words of former president Clinton, was radically restructured, with hundreds of thousands of women householders and their children pushed down into poverty.

Behind much of this vicious conservative offensive was the ugly politics of race. The political assault against affirmative action and minority economic set-asides was transformed by the right into a moral crusade against "racial preferences" and "reverse discrimination." Black and Latino young people across the country were routinely "racially profiled" by law enforcement officers. DWB, "Driving While Black," became a familiar euphemism for such police practices. As the liberal welfare state of the 1960s mutated into the prison industrial complex state of the 1990s, the white public was given the unambiguous message that the goal of racial justice had to be sacrificed for the general security and public safety of all. It was, in short, a permanent war against the black, the brown, and the poor.

The fall of Communism transformed a bipolar political conflict into a unipolar, hegemonic "New World Order," as the first President Bush termed it. The chief institutions for regulating the flow of capital investment and labor across international boundaries were no longer governments. The International Monetary Fund, the World Trade Organization, and transnational treaties such as the North American Free Trade Agreement (NAFTA) exercised significantly greater influence over the lives of workers in most countries than did their own governments. By the year 2000, fifty-one of the world's hundred wealthiest and largest economies were actually corporations, and only forty-nine were countries. The political philosophy of globalization was termed "neo-liberalism," the demand to privatize government services and programs, to eliminate unions, and to apply the aggressive rules of capitalist markets to the running of all public institutions, such as schools, hospitals, and even postal services. The social contract between U.S. citizens and the liberal democratic state was being redefined to exclude the concepts of social welfare and social responsibility to the truly disadvantaged.

A new, more openly authoritarian philosophy of governance was required, to explain to citizens why their long-standing democratic freedoms were being taken away from them. A leading apologist for neo-authoritarian politics was New York Mayor Rudolph Giuliani. In 1994, soon after his election as mayor, Giuliani declared in a speech: "Freedom is about authority. Freedom is about the willingness of every single human being to cede to lawful authority a great deal of indiscretion about what you do and how you do it." As we all know, the Giuliani administration won national praise for reducing New York City's annual murder rate from 2,000 to 650; violent crime rates also plummeted. But the social cost to New York's black, brown, and poor communities was far more destructive than anything they had known previously. The ACLU estimates that between 50,000 and 100,000 New Yorkers were subjected annually to "stop-and-frisk" harassment by the police under Giuliani. The city's notorious Street Crimes Unit functioned not unlike El Salvador's "Death Squads," unleashing indiscriminate terror and armed intimidation against "racially profiled" victims.

Many white liberals in New York City passively capitulated to this new state authoritarianism. It is even more chilling that in the wake of the September 11 attacks, *New York Times* journalist Clyde Haberman immediately drew connections between "the emotional rubble of the World Trade Center nightmare" and Amadou Diallo, the unarmed West African immigrant gunned down in 1999, with forty-one shots fired by four Street Crimes Unit police officers. "It is quite possible that America will have to decide, and fairly soon, how much license it wants to give law enforcement agencies to stop ordinary people at airports and border crossings, to question them at length about where they have been, where they are heading, and what they intend to do once they get where they're going," Haberman predicted. "It would probably surprise no one if ethnic profiling enters the equation, to some degree." Haberman reluctantly acknowledged that Giuliani may be "at heart an authoritarian." But he added that "as a wounded New York mourns its unburied dead, and turns to its mayor for solace," public concerns about civil rights and civil liberties violations would recede. Haberman seems to be implying that the rights of people like Amadou Diallo are less important than the personal safety of white Americans.

As the national media enthusiastically picked up the Bush administration's mantra about the "War on Terrorism," a series of repressive federal and state laws were swiftly passed. New York State's legislature, in the span of one week, created a new crime—"terrorism"—with a maximum penalty of life in prison. Anyone convicted of giving more than $1,000 to any organization defined by state authorities as "terrorist" will face up to fifteen years in a state prison. When one reflects that, not too many years ago, the United States considered the African National Congress to be a "terrorist organization," and that the Palestinian Liberation Organization is still widely described as "terrorist," the danger of suppressing any activities by U.S. citizens that support any Third World social justice movements now becomes very real.

At all levels of government, any expression of restraint or caution about the dangerous erosion of our civil liberties has been equated with treason. The anti-terrorism bills in the New York State Assembly were passed with no debate, by a margin of 135 to 5. And the U.S. Senate on October 12, 2001, passed the Bush administration's anti-terrorism legislation by 96 to 1. The militarism and political intolerance displayed in the Bush administration's response to the September 11 attacks created a natural breeding ground for bigotry and racial harassment. For the Reverend Jerry Falwell, the recent tragedy was God's condemnation of a secularist, atheistic America. The attacks were attributed to "the pagans, and the abortionists, and the feminists and the lesbians," according to Falwell, "the ACLU [and] People for the American Way." Less well publicized were the hate-filled commentaries of journalist Ann Coulter, who declared: "We should invade their countries, kill their leaders, and convert them to Christianity."

Similar voices of racist intolerance are also being heard in Europe. For example, Italian Prime Minister Silvio Berlusconi recently stated that "Western civilization" was clearly "superior to Islamic culture." Berlusconi warmly praised "imperialism," predicting that "the West will continue to conquer peoples, just as it has Communism." Falwell, Berlusconi, and others illustrate the direct linkage between racism and war, between militarism and political reaction.

Even on college campuses, there have been numerous instances of the suppression of free speech and democratic dissent. When City University of New York faculty held an academic forum that examined the responsibility of U.S. foreign policies for creating the context for the terrorist attacks, the university's chief administrator publicly denounced them. "Let there be no doubt whatsoever," warned CUNY Chancellor Matthew Goldstein, "I have no sympathy for the voices of those who make lame excuses for the attacks on the World Trade Center and the Pentagon based on ideological or historical circumstances." Conservative trustees of CUNY sought to censure or even fire the faculty involved. According to the *Chronicle of Higher Education*, hundreds of Middle Eastern college students have been forced to return home from the United States, due to widespread ethnic and religious harassment.

At UCLA, library assistant Jonnie Hargis was suspended without pay from his job when he sent an e-mail on the university's computers that criticized U.S.

support for Israel. When University of South Florida professor Sami Al-Arian appeared on television talking about his relationships to two suspected terrorists, he was placed on indefinite paid leave and ordered to leave the campus "for his [own] safety," university officials later explained. The First Amendment right of free speech, the constitutional right of any citizen to criticize the policies of our government, is now at risk.

Perhaps the most dangerous element of the Bush administration's current campaign against democratic rights has been the deliberate manipulation of mass public hysteria. Millions of Americans who witnessed the destruction of the World Trade Center are still experiencing post-traumatic anxiety and depression. According to the *Wall Street Journal*, during the last two weeks of September, pharmacies filled 1.9 million new prescriptions for Zoloft, Prozac, and other anti-depressants, a 16 percent increase over the same period in 2000. Prescriptions for sleeping pills and short-term anxiety drugs like Xanax and Valium also rose 7 percent. The American public has been bombarded daily by a series of media-orchestrated panic attacks, focusing on everything from the potential threat posed by crop-dusting airplanes being used for "bio-terrorism" to anthrax-contaminated packages delivered through the U.S. postal service. People are constantly being warned to carefully watch their mail, their neighbors, and each other. Intense levels of police security at sports stadiums, and armed National Guard troops at airports, have begun to be accepted as "necessary" for the welfare of society.

We will inevitably also see "dissident profiling": the proliferation of electronic surveillance, roving wiretapping, harassment at the workplace, the infiltration and disruption of anti-war groups, and the stigmatization of any critics of U.S. militarism as disloyal and subversive. As historian Eric Foner has recently noted,

> Let us recall the F.B.I.'s persistent harassment of individuals like Martin Luther King, Jr., and its efforts to disrupt the civil rights and anti-war movements, and the C.I.A.'s history of cooperation with some of the world's most egregious violators of human rights. The principle that no group of Americans should be stigmatized as disloyal or criminal because of race or national origin is too recent and too fragile an achievement to be abandoned now.

You cannot preserve democracy by restricting and eliminating democratic rights. To publicly oppose a government's policies, which one believes to be morally and politically wrong, is expressing the strongest belief in the principles of democracy.

We must clearly explain to the American people that the missile strikes and indiscriminate carpet bombings we have unleashed against Afghanistan peasants will *not* make us safer. The policies of the Bush administration have actually put our lives in greater danger; the use of government-sponsored terror will not halt brutal retaliations by the terrorists. The national security state apparatus we are constructing today is being designed primarily to suppress domestic dissent and racially profiled minorities, rather than to halt foreign-born terrorists at our borders.

Last year alone, 489 million people passed through our border inspection systems. Over 120 million cars are driven across U.S. borders every year, and it's impossible to thoroughly check even a small fraction of them. Restricting civil liberties, hiring thousands more police and security guards, and incarcerating innocent Muslims and people of Arab descent only foster the false illusion of security. The "War on Terrorism" is being used as an excuse to eliminate civil liberties and democratic rights here at home.

III

It has become popular to suggest that "everything changed" after the traumatic events of September 11. Yet what has *not* changed in the United States is the traditional connection between war and racism.

Because U.S. democracy was constructed on institutional racism, the government has always found it difficult to present a clear, democratic argument to advance its interests in the pursuit of warfare. Instead, it relies on and manipulates the latent racism and xenophobia at all levels of society. Usually, racism is used to target external enemies, such as "Japs" during World War II. But in general, whenever the United States mobilizes militarily and goes to war, white racism goes hand in hand.

Since September 11, America's domestic color line has been temporarily restructured and shifted in both interesting and disturbing ways. Thousand of people of Middle Eastern origin and descent have experienced varying degrees of harassment, including verbal and sometimes physical abuse. People who are coded or classified by appearance, dress, language, or name as Muslim or Arab have been rudely escorted off airplanes and Amtrak metroliners, and many have been detained without formal charges or access to attorneys. Anecdotal evidence suggests that a significant number, perhaps even the majority, of the people of color stigmatized for harassment as potential "terrorists" have not been "Muslims" or "Arabs" at all. In Seattle and other West Coast cities, dozens of Hawaiians, Central Americans, South Asians, and even American Indians have been subjected to verbal insults and harassment because they "appear" to be vaguely "non-American."

On the East Coast, many Sikhs and Hindus have been victimized, along with non–English language speakers and non-European undocumented immigrants. Most white middle-class Americans in the so-called heartland of the country, the Midwestern states, lack both the cultural capacity and the geopolitical awareness to make fine distinctions between "Muslims" and racialized others who happen to be non-Muslims.

The great exception to this phenomenon of new racialization in the time of terror appears to be the African American. People of African descent, having lived on the American continent since 1619, occupy a unique position in the construction of white American identity and national consciousness. State power was deliberately constructed to exclude black participation; but black labor power was absolutely essential in the economic development of the nation. Black culture, moreover, contributed the most creative and original elements, which defined American national culture and various forms of representation.

Thus the African American is unquestionably a recognized member of the American national household, but has never been a member of the American family. Yet there is a necessary dialectical connection here, linking the false superiority of whiteness as a political and social category in the United States to the continued and "normal" subordination of blackness. Without "blacks," whiteness ceases to exist as we know it. White supremacy has difficulty imagining a world without black people, but has no reservations about the indiscriminate mass bombing of Afghan peasants, or supporting an embargo against Iraq, which is responsible for the deaths of hundreds of thousands of Muslim children, according to international human rights observers.

The great sociologist Oliver C. Cox understood this contradiction, the subtle distinctions between white racism, social intolerance, and xenophobia. As Cox put it: "The dominant group is intolerant of those whom it can define as anti-social, while it holds race prejudice against those whom it can define as subsocial. In other words, the dominant group or ruling class does not like the Jew at all, but it likes the Negro in his place." In a time of political terror, the "terrorist" becomes the most dangerous Other, and is recognized by certain subhuman qualities and vague characteristics—language, strange religious rituals, unusual clothing, and so forth. The "terrorist Other" thus is presented to the white public as an uncivilized savage who has richly merited our hatred and must be destroyed to ensure our safety and the preservation of the "American Way of Life." Similar racist rhetoric of "terrorism" was undoubtedly used against Crazy Horse and Geronimo during the Indian Wars in the nineteenth century.

The contradiction that has always confronted black Americans during these periods of racist wars is whether or not to take advantage of this situation, to advance up the racial and political hierarchy. Check out the displays of American flags, for example, in the fronts of black businesses and middle-class suburban homes. On New York City subways, I've seen more black and Latino people wearing red-white-and-blue buttons, caps, and other patriotic paraphernalia following September 11 than in the past twenty years.

The media is now full of stories about the "new American patriotism," and you can be sure that people of color will be featured on center stage. Colin Powell, after all, is President Bush's secretary of state, and Condoleeza Rice is his national security adviser. The majority of the Congressional Black Caucus voted in favor of authorizing the use of U.S. military force against Afghanistan. Nevertheless, it is also true that African American activists and many black elected officials have been consistently the sharpest and most vocal critics of the war and the suppression of civil liberties, and have actively defended the rights of American Muslims. But I also suspect that the new xenophobia is viewed by some African Americans as not a bad thing, if jobs that had previously gone to non-English speaking immigrants now go to blacks. There is considerable hostility in cities such as Detroit and Houston between impoverished and working-class black urban neighborhoods and Muslim shopkeepers and small storeowners. Blacks voted overwhelmingly in 2000 for the Gore-Lieberman ticket, while at least 40 percent of Arab Americans supported Bush-Cheney, based in part on their opposition to Lieberman.

Part of the frustration the African American community feels is found in the complicated love-hate relationship we have toward our own country. That U.S. democracy was crudely constructed on the mountain of black bodies destroyed by centuries of enslavement, segregation, and exploitation is abundantly clear to us. Yet there is also the knowledge, gleaned from our centuries-old struggle for freedom, that the finest ideals of American democracy are best represented by our own examples of sacrifice. This was undoubtedly behind W.E.B. Du Bois's controversial editorial, "Close Ranks," which endorsed African American participation in the U.S. war effort during World War I. It is important to remember, however, that immediately after World War I, the "Red Summer of 1919" erupted, during which hundreds of African Americans were lynched, beaten, and even burned at the stake. We cannot overturn the structural racism against us if we accommodate or compromise with war and racism against others.

IV

The bombing campaign against the people of Afghanistan will be described in history as the "United States Against the Third World." The launching of military strikes against peasants does nothing to suppress terrorism, and only erodes American credibility in Muslim nations around the world. The question "Why Do They Hate Us?" can only be answered from the vantage point of the Third World's widespread poverty, hunger, and economic exploitation.

The U.S. government cannot engage in effective multilateral actions to suppress terrorism because its behavior illustrates its complete contempt for international cooperation. The United States owed $582 million in back dues to the United Nations but paid up only when the September 11 attacks jeopardized its national security. Republican conservatives have demanded that the United States should be exempt from the jurisdiction of an International Criminal Court, a permanent tribunal now being established at The Hague, Netherlands. And for the 2001 World Conference Against Racism, the U.S. government authorized the allocation of a paltry $250,000, compared to over $10 million provided to conference organizers by the Ford Foundation.

For three decades, the United States refused to ratify the 1965 United Nations Convention on the Elimination of Racism. Is it any wonder that much of the Third World questions our motives? To Third World observers, the carpet-bombing of the

Taliban seems to have less to do with the suppression of terrorism and more with securing future petroleum production rights in central Asia.

U.S. media and opinion makers repeatedly have gone out of their way to twist facts and to distort the political realities of the Middle East, by insisting that the Osama bin Laden group's murderous assaults had nothing to do with Israel's policies toward the Palestinians. Nobody else in the world, with the possible exception of the Israelis, really believes that. Even Britain, Bush's staunchest ally, links Israel's intransigence toward negotiations and human rights violations as having contributed to the environment for Arab terrorist retaliation.

In late September 2001, during his visit to Jerusalem, British Foreign Secretary Jack Straw stated that frustration over the Israeli-Palestinian conflict might create an excuse for terrorism. Straw explained: "[T]here is never any excuse for terrorism. At the same time, there is an obvious need to understand the environment in which terrorism breeds." Millions of moderate and progressive Muslims who sincerely denounce terrorism are nevertheless frustrated by the extensive clientage relationship between the United States and Israel, financed by more than $3 billion in annual subsidies. They want to know why the United States allowed the Israelis to relocate more than 200,000 Jewish settlers—one half of them after the signing of the 1993 peace agreement—to occupied Palestine. It is no exaggeration to say that to most of the world's 1 billion Muslims, Israel is an anathema, as the apartheid regime of South Africa was for black people.

How does terrorist Osama bin Laden gain loyal followers from northern Nigeria to Indonesia? Perhaps it has something to do with America's massive presence in—in fact, its military-industrial occupation of—Saudi Arabia. The *Washington Post* recently revealed that in the past two decades, U.S. construction companies and arms suppliers have made over $50 billion in Saudi Arabia. Today, over 30,000 U.S. citizens are employed by Saudi corporations, or by joint Saudi-U.S. corporate partnerships. And Exxon Mobil, the world's largest corporation, recently reached an agreement with the Saudi government to develop gas projects worth $20–$26 billion. Can Americans who are not Muslims truly comprehend how morally offensive this overwhelming U.S. occupying presence in their holy land is to them? Even before September 11, the United States regularly stationed 5,000–6,000 troops in Saudi Arabia. Today, that number probably exceeds 15,000 American troops. How would the U.S. government react if the PLO's close ally, Cuba, offered to send 15,000 troops to support the Palestinian Authority's security force? There is, to repeat, no justification for terrorism by anyone, anytime. But it is U.S. policies—such as blanket support for Israel, and the blockade against Iraq that has been responsible for the needless deaths of thousands of children—that help to create the very conditions in which extremist violence flourishes.

There is a direct linkage between the terrible events of September 11 and the politics represented by the United Nations World Conference Against Racism held in Durban, South Africa, only days prior to the terrorist attacks. The U.S. government in Durban opposed the definition of slavery as "a crime against humanity." It refused to acknowledge the historic and contemporary effects of colonialism, racial segregation, and apartheid on the underdevelopment and oppression of the non-European world.

The United States also polemically manipulated the charge of anti-Semitism to evade discussions concerning the right of self-determination for the Palestinian people. The world's subaltern masses represented at Durban sought to advance a new global discussion about the political economy of racism—and the United States insulted the entire international community. Should we therefore be surprised that Palestinian children celebrate in the streets of their occupied territories when they see televised images of our largest buildings being destroyed? Should we be shocked that hundreds of protest marches in opposition to the U.S. bombing of Afghanistan are being held throughout the world?

The majority of dark humanity is saying to the United States that racism and militarism are not the solutions to the world's major problems. Transnational capitalism and the repressive neo-liberal policies of structural adjustment represent a dead end for the developing world. We can end the threat of terrorism only by addressing constructively the routine violence of poverty, hunger, and exploitation that characterizes the daily existence of several billion people on this planet. Racism is, in the final analysis, only another form of violence.

In the House of Representatives, when the administration demanded authorization to use military force in Afghanistan, only California Democratic Representative Barbara Lee had the courage to vote no. She immediately was subjected to death threats and, in her own words, was "called a traitor, a coward, [and] a communist." But as Congresswoman Lee alone had the integrity to declare, "As we act, let us not become the evil that we deplore." To resist the reactionary mobilization toward war, we must have the principled courage of Barbara Lee.

To stop the violence of terrorism, we must stop the violence of racism and class inequality. To struggle for peace, to find new paths toward reconciliation across the boundaries of religion, culture, and color, is the only way to protect our cities, our country, and ourselves from the violence of terrorism. Because without justice, there can be no peace.

2

The Wen Ho Lee Affair

Between Race and National Security

JEFFREY BUSSOLINI

GLOBALIZATION, EMPIRE, AND SECURITY

While naïve formulations of globalization hold that it is a generalized process of sweeping away borders in an increasing circulation of goods, capital, and people, it is clear enough that this is not a smooth or unidirectional process. Far from resulting in an automatic overriding of the nation-state, globalization is, instead, resulting in its reshaping and redefinition. In some respects the state takes on novel roles, and in others it intensifies roles it has long held. Nor has the increasing porosity of nation-states resulted in diminished anxieties about national security and national identity; quite the contrary, in fact. Hence, while global flows of capital and of people are indeed significant and augmenting, nationalisms, anxieties about ethnic mixing and ethnic cleansing, and paranoia about security and safety have by no means been swept aside. Certainly in the wake of September 11 there can be little doubt that the nation-state and its military apparatus remain decisive forces affecting world affairs and the relations between people. In terms of this dynamic of globalization and nationalism, the Wen Ho Lee episode is very telling, as it ties into matters of national secrets, national loyalty, ethnicity, and, especially, turn-of-the-millennium national security.

Further, the controversy surrounding Lee plays on the central element of U.S. empire: nuclear weaponry. While of course complexly related to U.S. economy and society, the nuclear bomb is the preeminent symbol of U.S. global dominance post–World War II. The bomb fits neatly, if troublingly, into the narrative that says the United States essentially won the war and "saved the world for democracy." Of course, this narrative covers over the tremendous contributions and sacrifices made by a number of other nations, not the least of them by the Soviet Union; but such a messianic story is necessary to present the United States as intrinsically peace-loving, just, and democratic in order to deflect attention away from its economic imperialism after the war and from the atrocities it committed during the war—namely, the atomic bombings of Hiroshima and Nagasaki. A vast portion of the U.S. industrial and technological infrastructure in the last six decades has remained exclusively dedicated to the development and production of new weapons, and the role of this "permanent war economy" in the economic life of the nation can scarcely be underestimated.[1]

Thus in a 1990s moment when the situation in world power was markedly changing and globalization seemed increasingly to be the order of the day, the fate of Wen Ho Lee was directly about the ongoing status of U.S. empire. If talk of the "end of the Cold War" and of the "peace dividend" seemed for some years to threaten the existence of the massive U.S. National Security State that proliferated in the Cold War, Lee's treatment showed clearly that this bureaucracy, and the nationalist fears and preoccupations on which it fed, would not go gentle into the good night of trade as the primary factor determining relations between states. Certainly it was hasty to proclaim that states themselves had been superseded by global economic flows, as national security remains a major issue and a major anxiety. In addition, certain tensions continue to act against a simple push toward globalization, such as conflicts between military-industrial capital tied to the nation-state and finance capital that favors liberalization.

THE WEN HO LEE AFFAIR

The case of wrongly accused nuclear-code physicist Wen Ho Lee, described by the U.S. government as one of the most damaging spies in national history, is both shocking and informative in a number of respects illustrating the operation of the U.S. National Security State and the continued change in and anxiety over the ethnic composition of the U.S. population. The "manufacture" of the case itself, and the speed and hysteria with which it caught on, are indicative of significant forces (in terms of bureaucratic and political inertia) and of the nationalistic and xenophobic attitudes prevalent in U.S. society. Although the history and national narrative of the United States revolve around immigration and migration, and in terms of current policy the United States remains a major country of immigration, there is nonetheless a strong isolationist and eurocentric contingent in U.S. political and cultural life that hearkens to the Aryan dream of a white fortress America. This American nationalism is by no means new, but it is represented in contemporary garb by people like Pat Buchanan, who continuously returns to the same tired and troubling themes of the decline of the white race and the dilution of the Christian church in America. In a recent diatribe, Buchanan even went so far as to say that America's current cultural crisis and weakening of vigor are due to the nefarious effects of "critical theory" in the country (a reference that allowed him to cast aspersions on those "troublemaking Communist Jews" who came here after

World War II and deigned to criticize the "market democracy" of the United States).[2] Hence the controversy and the blunders surrounding Wen Ho Lee are not only about the institutionalized paranoia and the bureaucratic operation of the U.S. national security organizations, they are also centrally about the ethnic self-image of the country, and about the *de facto* status of the U.S. population versus the representational and ideological narrative of Americanness, which only partially and poorly pays heed to this *de facto* situation.

It is crucial that we examine the Wen Ho Lee Affair (by which I mean the particular set of accusations, actions, and reactions undertaken with respect to Lee) in terms of its close ties to the operation of the National Security State and in light of the latter's fears about national vulnerability, construal of enemies in terms of the national interest, and acceptance versus suspicion of domestic populations depending upon this index of international threat. The fact that those of certain backgrounds and perceived ethnicities (mostly European, but also African) are relatively directly accepted within the fuzzy envelope of "American," while those of other ethnicities—Wen Ho Lee, for instance—are held in a kind of "permanent foreigner" status despite having been naturalized or even born in the United States, illustrates the unfolding of this national-identity tension. It is also crucial that we approach the Wen Ho Lee Affair from the tradition of Foucault-style "writing the history of the present," given that this controversy immediately preceded the paranoid security response to the September 11 attacks.[3] The way that "those of Middle Eastern descent, Arabs, and terrorists" are now held up as the locus of suspicion and potential national threat was presaged by the way that the People's Republic of China (PRC) and its reputed army of spies in the United States were vilified a few years ago. At that time, security briefings in Los Alamos warned that the presence of so many Chinese restaurants in town was a sure sign of espionage activity.[4]

RACE IN THE CASE

One of the most shocking, and least deniable, elements of the Wen Ho Lee Affair is the direct and disturbing way that race and racial profiling were major elements in the generation and propagation of the case. Initial announcements about flaws in the case amounted to serious allegations about the acquisition of advanced U.S. nuclear weapons designs by the People's Republic of China, which was said to be due to certain espionage, and which therefore led to hasty conclusions about "Chinese" scientists within the national security infrastructure. Upon closer scrutiny in the unfolding of the case, none of the claims of the initial story would stand up. In fact, the Chinese had not obtained all the most sophisticated designs of U.S. weapons, and had certainly not tested an exact copy of any one of them. There was simply no evidence of the massive espionage originally claimed, let alone a smoking gun or lighted trail leading directly to a number of Chinese American scientists working as sleeper agents for the PRC. Despite the fact that these major suspicions were dispelled somewhat early in the affair, the suspicion against Wen Ho Lee persisted, and he continued to be subjected to suspicious treatment himself. Even as the doom-and-gloom stories of Chinese nuclear theft dissolved under inspection, the specter of the slight and mysterious Taiwanese American man who worked at the heart of the bomb industry continued to haunt the national imagination.

Of course, allegations of treason and espionage have historically provoked the most intense kind of legal and cultural response. These are special crimes as they seem to endanger the country itself and all the citizens of it. Such sentiments and such crimes are at issue, for instance, in the case of Damiens the Regicide, whose brutal treatment at the hands of the state was detailed by Foucault in *Surveiller et punir*—for Damiens had acted against the sovereign and therefore against the symbol of the state itself.[5] Foucault described how Damiens was singled out for a special kind of brutal public torture, which was supposedly commensurate with the egregious act he had committed against the king/state. In addition, the public spectacle of his torture by hot pincers, burning sulfur, boiling oil, drawing and quartering, and the like was intended to serve as a symbolic warning to all who would dare to attack the power and integrity of the state. In this connection, it is notable that Paul Robinson, the Cold-Warrior president of Sandia National Laboratories, disingenuously claimed that Wen Ho Lee had directly endangered the safety and security of the entire U.S. population. He testified not only that the detonation of such a thermonuclear weapon could kill millions of people in a city but also that the federal judge overseeing the case, James A. Parker, faced a "you-bet-your-country decision" in determining whether or not to let Lee be freed on bail before the trial. The appeal to nationalist paranoia and high Cold War themes is unmistakable in Robinson's pronouncements.[6]

Curiously, just days before this testimony Secretary of Energy Bill Richardson, one of the most vitriolic actors in the prosecution of Lee, visited Robinson and Sandia National Laboratories and announced that the hundreds of anticipated layoffs and budget cuts there would not in fact take place.[7] Here we see clear evidence not only of crooked politics but also of the national security infrastructure acting to ensure its survival and continuation. A Los Alamos nuclear weapons physicist, Richard Krajcik, testified that the Lee tapes were the "Crown Jewels" of U.S. nuclear research. Here, too, the concern with national pride and safety is readily evident. In summing up the government's case against Lee's bail on December 13, 1999, Assistant U.S. Attorney Robert Gorence outdid himself when he said: "I assert to the court that the risk of his liberty pending trial is so enormous [because] . . . the 'community' in this case is 270 million persons that face a degree of peril by virtue of what he did." This overzealous prosecutor literally stated that Lee endangered every citizen and resident of the United States through his supposed crime against the state.

Treason is an exemplary crime in the sense that it immediately draws into question who is loyal and who is antagonistic, who is a member of one's community and who is a foreigner. The spy is the very figure of the enemy of the state. Thus many significant controversies surrounding supposed treason have revolved around questions of ethnicity. In France, Captain Dreyfus of the army, who was a Jew, was accused of divulging guarded defense secrets to Germany. The accusations against him—seemingly based on a lack of evidence, as in Lee's case—spoke volumes about a French society in continued crisis over the role of Jewish citizens and lingering uncertainty about their "Frenchness." In this liminal position within French society but not entirely within the French national imagination, French Jews were like the "strangers" described by Georg Simmel in his famous essay "The Stranger." Here he used the situation of Jews in Europe over several centuries as an example of people who are in neither the in-group nor the out-group, but hover in between. For Simmel, then, the stranger is not entirely foreign or new or unrecognized but, rather, someone who lives within a given society and has a function and a space there, yet who remains somewhat foreign, somewhat distant, and not entirely incorporated into the self-image and full acceptance of the society at hand.

Several decades later the United States experienced parallel anxieties over whether or not, or to what degree, Jews were in fact American. In this increasingly anti-communist society, Jews were portrayed as stalwarts of the communist cause, and as potential "enemies within." It was in such circumstances that the hysteria surrounding Julius and Ethel Rosenberg was generated and propagated. The Rosenbergs were portrayed as exactly the kind of nefarious traitor enemy who cuts to the quick of the nation, thereby illustrating the profound tensions over membership in American society and nation. It is the "stranger" status of such figures that leads to such extreme action against them: Not purely and simply the Other or the enemy, they are those who are said to have deceived and taken advantage of a society to gain its benefits while at the same time betraying it. Hence they are treated in the same draconian manner as Damiens the Regicide.

The case of Wen Ho Lee, whom the FBI threatened with execution through references to the Rosenbergs and their fate, arose later still, at a time when the United States was experiencing another kind of anxiety about the status of its ethnic makeup and national picture. Millions of Chinese Americans are living in the United States; but in their case, too, there is a lingering ambiguity in the national conception as to whether or not, or to what degree, they are "American." Chinese Americans work in every sector of U.S. society and live in every state, yet there is still a political and cultural uneasiness about the role of Chinese in the United States. The accusations against Wen Ho Lee and the pictures created of him by the government and by the media were predicated upon exactly this kind of ambiguity about the membership and belonging of Chinese in the United States. Lee, a naturalized U.S. citizen who had devoted his scientific life to the U.S. defense industry, was still held to be so suspicious and so mysterious because he was Chinese, because of his face and ideas about his demeanor.

Racial profiling—which is extensively used in the United States, from the New Jersey Highway Patrol to the Los Angeles Police Department to the Federal Bureau of Investigation and the Customs Service—bears upon groups about whom there is an ongoing anxiety in U.S. society. It is widely known that the majority of people in prison are African Americans and Latinos, yet it is also widely known (despite racist conservative protestations to the contrary) that most crimes are not, in fact, committed by members of these groups. On the contrary, what the makeup of the prison population reflects is structural racism in the criminal justice system and racist suspicions at the core of dominant U.S. culture. No studies have ever indicated that racial profiling fulfills any constructive or useful function in law enforcement; indeed, it has been challenged at many levels. Yet it remains central to the *modus operandi* of all law-enforcement agencies in the United States. Sociologically, this says a great deal about dominant conceptions of who is "American" and which people are respected and considered "normal" (i.e., accepted) members of society. Not responding to actual threats or well-defined situations, these techniques of profiling are, rather, extended practices of disciplining large segments of the U.S. population that have a somewhat liminal or "stranger" position in the nation and national conception.

Racial profiling was at the crux of the Wen Ho Lee Affair. In articles published in March 1999 alleging that advanced and critical secrets of the U.S. nuclear weapons research program had been stolen, the *New York Times* irresponsibly and erroneously announced that this deed had been carried out by a Chinese American computer scientist at the Los Alamos National Laboratory. This fairy tale turned out to be entirely fabricated, based on no evidence whatsoever; but as a paroxysm of U.S. security paranoia, it fit perfectly into the ongoing dynamic by which U.S. nationhood is defined in opposition to prominent external enemies and the domestic populations that are cast as the agents of these enemies. In like fashion, after the Japanese attack on Pearl Harbor, President Roosevelt signed Executive Order 9066 authorizing the internment of Japanese Americans in concentration camps, with no regard to the citizenship or loyalty of those interned. It became undeniably clear in the unfolding of the Wen Ho Lee Affair that he had been selected as a suspect and as a target solely and simply on the basis of his ethnicity—or, rather, perceived ethnicity. The fact that Lee is *Taiwanese* American, having been born and raised in Taiwan before being naturalized as a U.S. citizen, was apparently disregarded. Why Lee would aid the People's Republic of China with nuclear arms that the PRC repeatedly threatened to use against Taiwan, where many of his family members and friends still live, is a crucial question indeed. Nonetheless, Lee was soon singled out by racist, paranoid investigators. Robert Vrooman, former head of counterintelligence at Los Alamos and a former CIA case officer, made this assertion in the Federal Court: "Agent [Robert] Messemer's statement that the individuals selected for investigation were chosen because they fit a 'matrix' based on access to W-88 [warhead] information and travel to the PRC is false. Dozens of individuals who share those characteristics were not chosen for investigation." In explaining why these dozens of others were overlooked while Lee was scrutinized, Vrooman said in no uncertain terms that "[i]t is my opinion the failure to look at the rest of the population is because Lee is ethnic Chinese."[8] Such a forthright comment from someone so intimately familiar with the investigation leaves little doubt that racial profiling was the driving force behind both the investigation and the maltreatment of Lee.

The accusations against Lee were particularly curious given the complete absence of evidence linking him to the supposed breach of security. Vrooman said that he had "worked on this case since June 23, 1995. I know that there is not one shred of evidence that the information that the Intelligence Community identified as having been stolen by the Chinese came from Wen Ho Lee, Los Alamos National Laboratory, the Department of Energy or from a DOE office." In short, evidence was lacking not only against Lee but against any part of the Department of Energy as well! In light of this gaffe, Vrooman noted again that "it can be said at this time that Mr. Lee's ethnicity was a major factor" in the undeserved scrutiny and blame that he received.

In addition to explaining that Lee had been singled out based on his ethnicity, Vrooman and others questioned the assumption as to whether a transfer of U.S. secrets to China, if it occurred at all, was likely to have been carried out by ethnic Chinese—thereby undermining the very foundation for racial profiling in such espionage investigations. In his statement, Vrooman added the following comment:

> The contention that the Chinese target ethnically Chinese individuals to the exclusion of others, therefore making it rational to focus investigations on such individuals, was not borne out by our experience at Los Alamos, which was the critical context for this investigation. It was our experience that Chinese intelligence officials contacted everyone from the laboratories with a nuclear weapons background who visited China for information, regardless of their ethnicity. I am unaware of any empirical data that would support any inference that an American citizen born in Taiwan would be more likely than any other American citizen [to engage in espionage for the PRC].

In explaining the lack of any link between Chinese Americans and the intelligence services of China, Vrooman refuted any rational presumption on the suspicion of domestic Chinese populations in the United States. In effect, he was saying that there are no grounds on which to regard Chinese American scientists as "strangers" (in the sense that Simmel described), and he was calling attention to the way that suspicions of them are indices of national anxieties in U.S. society (as opposed to sound government practice).

Vrooman was not alone in criticizing the security rationale for racial profiling in the Lee case. Charles E. Washington—who had been head of all counterintelligence for the Department of Energy, the government agency that oversees all nuclear research in the United States—also cast serious doubts on the accusations against Lee and the way that they were derived. At the same time, he refuted the notion that Chinese Americans are "strangers" who live in the United States but owe allegiance to China:

In the counterintelligence training I have received and in my counterintelligence experience, I am unaware of any empirical data that would support a claim that Chinese Americans are more likely to commit espionage than other Americans. Further, I know of no analysis whatsoever that has been done as to whether American citizens born in Taiwan would be more likely to commit espionage for the People's Republic of China.[9]

Like Vrooman's comments, this statement from someone so prominent within the national security bureaucracy was damning to the case brought against Lee, showing demonstratively that what was really at issue here was deep concern over the ethnic composition of U.S. society and the status of the U.S. empire.

As there was no justification for focusing on Chinese Americans in this nuclear espionage investigation, and indeed the dire allegations made about Chinese nuclear theft were refuted wholesale, the only remainder of the case seems to have been an intense paranoia about Chinese Americans working at the heart of the U.S. defense industry. Despite the fact that Lee's life, in terms of his home, his favorite activities (cooking, fishing, reading nineteenth-century European literature, listening to classical music), his family, and his daily routine, closely resembled that of many other scientists with whom he worked at Los Alamos, he was held out for a special kind of suspicion and lingering doubt. In effect, Lee was treated as Simmel's "stranger," and was freighted with a kind of permanent foreigner status despite his U.S. citizenship and his career-long dedication to national defense. The fact that other scientists at Los Alamos or at other national laboratories who are also naturalized U.S. citizens, but who are from European countries such as Germany and Italy, are not viewed in the same "strange" and "persistently foreign" light, while yet other researchers from, for instance, India or Pakistan are viewed with the same kind of uncertainty as Lee, indicates an underlying tension in American society about the ethnic self-image and ideology of the nation. Although the American population includes large numbers of Asians who live and work throughout the society, the history, government, and mass culture of the nation remains largely eurocentric and white in its ethnic valence. Of course these representations and institutions are in flux, but the fact that they are changing highlights and fuels anxieties over what new forms of ethnic self-imagination and national picture will emerge in the United States. Within this dynamic, the Wen Ho Lee Affair is a pivotal event in the adjustment of the U.S. imagination to include Chinese Americans and in the still-present resistance against this adjustment.

The controversy surrounding Lee is of course not an isolated one in the history of the United States. The kind of racism underlying the wild claims against him is but a continuation of anxieties about the Chinese that have long troubled U.S. society. The Chinese Exclusion Acts of 1882, which formally prohibited Chinese people from becoming U.S. citizens and remained in force well into the 20th century, stand as a reminder of this country's long-standing hostility toward Chinese immigrants. The notorious dissenting opinion by Justice Harlan in the Supreme Court decision in *Plessy v Ferguson* (1896) also demonstrates this xenophobia: "There is a race so different from our own that we do not permit those belonging to it to become citizens of the United States. Persons belonging to it are, with few exceptions, absolutely excluded from our country. I allude to the Chinese race." In addition to showing a profound anti-Chinese sentiment and the presumption of an absolute difference in lifestyles, Harlan's opinion is curious in the respect that he refers simply to "our own [race]" when, even in 1896 when the case was heard, U.S. society was hardly composed of one distinct ethnic group. The fact that he nevertheless refers to "our own [race]" indicates an ongoing process of deeming and designating who and what was "properly American" versus that which remained foreign.

The suspicions against Lee, and the actions taken against him, rest entirely upon this uncertainty and tension within American society about the status of Chinese people. Not only was Lee singled out for scrutiny because of his ethnicity, as Vrooman conclusively demonstrated, but throughout the entire investigation and prosecution his ethnicity was consistently used as the lynchpin for his treatment. When members of the FBI and the U.S. Attorney's Office sought an unreasonably broad and vindictive search warrant for Lee's home, they stated that he was suspected because he was "overseas ethnic Chinese." And when they were attempting to persuade Judge Parker to deny a pretrial release of Lee, FBI Special Agent Messemer testified that Mandarin Chinese is a duplicitous language that inherently lends itself to espionage and that Lee's behavior was "nefarious."[10] Following similar misguided notions, the government would successfully seek a court order banning Lee from speaking Mandarin with his family during their severely restricted visits each week, despite the fact that this was their usual language of communication. It is inconceivable that a current court would make a parallel ruling concerning, for instance, the speaking of Spanish or German; yet it is all too imaginable that such a prohibition would be made concerning the speaking of Arabic in this latest round of national security and ethnic paranoia.

Given that casting Lee as an untrustworthy "stranger" was the crux of the government case, the racism inherent in this attitude must be taken to task. A great deal of abusive leeway was afforded the FBI and the Department of Justice as a result of their invocations of paranoia and bigotry against Chinese Americans. Their presentations of Lee as nefarious, deceptive, and inscrutable played upon some of the oldest and most problematic of discriminatory attitudes concerning the Yellow Peril and the devious and brilliant Chinese criminal. Since in the end the furor was based upon no evidence whatsoever, it was *only* these racist attitudes that sustained the accusations against Lee and the draconian treatment he was subjected to. The blend of fear about national security and anxiety about Chinese "strangers" proved a successful enough recipe to allow the Justice Department to incarcerate Lee before his trial for nine months in solitary confinement, during which time they engaged in a number of thinly veiled acts of torture. In addition to prohibiting him from speaking Mandarin with his family and limiting family visits to one hour a week (during which FBI agents were always present), they kept him indoors in a cell with no windows for more than a month, kept his cell lighted and supervised by a guard at all times to deny his privacy, kept him shackled at the wrists and ankles during all movements and exercise periods, and denied him clothing and bedding of adequate warmth during the winter.[11]

Of course the conduct and allegations of the government during the affair were shocking and reprehensible, but almost more troubling is the way that much of the racism that sustained the case survived its official unraveling and has persisted until now, even among ostensibly critical treatments of the case. The *New York Times*, bearing a major responsibility for the affair due to its factually inaccurate and inflammatory articles of March 1999, was moved to issue a kind of apology when it became clear that it was implicated in a major embarrassment. While this "apology" did indicate some wrongdoing on the part of the paper, it held onto a troubling and racist portrayal of Lee as still suspicious in his actions and person, as if to allege that the paper's claims were not so off-base after all, since clearly there were many things mysterious and unaccounted for about Lee. It is precisely this notion of the impenetrable mystery of the East that underlies anti-Asian racism and buttresses the "permanent foreigner" status accorded to Asian Americans. Thus the *Times* never moved very far from the presumption that motivated the entire prosecution. In effect, it continued to allege that Lee was guilty.

One of the first books to appear on the matter, written by journalists Dan Stober and Ian Hoffman, is saddled by the same presumption of Lee's lingering "mystery" and contains so many factual inaccuracies that its interpretation of the case is tenuous at best.[12] For instance, as Lee pointed out to me when we were discussing the book in February 2002, the authors reversed the names of his mother and father and misstated the famous wartime Santa Fe address for then-secret Los Alamos ("P.O. Box 1663") as "P.O. Box 1337." These and many other inconsistencies seem to better qualify the book as fiction than as history.

Lacking a thorough understanding or research grounding about either the national security bureaucracy or the community and laboratory of Los Alamos, the book lapses into the style of a Cold War spy novel and tale of intrigue. It is also severely constrained by the ethos of journalistic objectivity. In their goal to "cover both sides of the story" the authors do criticize the government's excesses in the case, but they also perpetuate the government's suspicion of Lee, without questioning the sources and dimensions of this suspicion. This effort to cast blame on both Lee and the government results in an overview of the case that fails to analyze many of its most important dimensions. In addition, the authors repeat a number of false claims made by the government, both during the prosecution and in committee reviews of alleged Chinese espionage, which were conclusively laid to rest during the denouement of the case. In their persistent portrayal of Lee as a middle-rate scientist whose actions lacked reason, they fail to call into question the way in which Lee was figured as a suspicious "stranger" by the government and the media.

(Of course, as journalists they themselves contributed to this portrayal during the case.) And perhaps most damaging of all, the authors never interviewed Lee, thus further silencing and obscuring him. Indeed, given that one of the government's goals in keeping Lee in solitary confinement was to prevent him from appearing in public as a real person, a true American, and a family member, this decision by Stober and Hoffman readily contributed to Lee's public erasure.

The racism of the case has also remained relatively uncriticized in the area of academic responses to the affair. Although a certain tone of moral outrage has since been adopted regarding the treatment of Lee and the way in which the prosecution was conducted, the racism at the core of the case remains unexamined, much as it does in the *Times* response and in the Stober and Hoffman account. While criticism of the government is dished out, the *presumption of Lee's suspicion* is often still tenaciously posited.[13] That even those who are setting out to criticize the case are unable to see this as a fundamental issue is indicative of the persistent strength of claims made under the heading of national security and of the continuing anxiety in the United States concerning the loyalty and belonging of Asian Americans. At a minimum, an analysis of the Wen Ho Lee Affair *must* scrutinize the presentation and treatment of Lee himself as an example of the most pernicious anti-Asian racism within the context of a United States anxiety-ridden about its ethnic constitution.

PRODUCTION OF ENEMIES BY THE NATIONAL SECURITY STATE

The Wen Ho Lee Affair illustrates clearly the process by which the U.S. National Security State not only responds to perceived external threats to the country but also defines and creates enemies "credible" enough to justify continued development of weapons and intelligence operations. Further, the U.S. military and intelligence infrastructure is involved in a dialectical process by which it does not merely "defend" and respond but also undertakes actions that antagonize or frighten other societies, thus increasing mistrust and military antagonism between states.

The history of the Cold War, for example, cannot be told purely and simply as a tale of the democratic United States responding to threats from the totalitarian Soviet Union. While of course threatening moves were made by the Eastern Bloc—for instance, in the blockade of Berlin—it is also the case that a number of actions and policies undertaken by the United States and other Western powers caused fear and anxiety in Moscow. During World War II, for instance, Britain and the United States kept the Manhattan Project secret from the Soviets even while they were fighting as allies against the Nazis. And at Potsdam, Churchill and Truman sought to intimidate Stalin by references to their powerful new secret weapon. Scholars in

international relations and diplomatic history now agree that the use of atomic
bombs in Japan was motivated, in part, by power projections that would threaten
the Soviet Union.[14] Clearly, these moves could not have inspired either confidence
or security in Moscow; if anything, they gave the USSR a strong impetus to develop its own nuclear weapons, beginning with its first atomic bomb test in 1949.

The history of the Chinese nuclear program has some similar contours.
Though often presented by U.S. administrations and diplomatic historians as an
offensive move by China to project its own imperialist power, the development of
the Chinese atomic bomb was likely motivated by other factors. Mao was quite explicit in saying that China was directly pressured to develop the bomb due to its
fear of a nuclear-armed United States that had continued to engage in power pro-
jection in Asia. The fact that the use of nuclear weapons was openly discussed in
the United States during the Korean War, and that a number of politicians and
generals called for the atomic bombing of China, clearly indicates that the United
States inspired little trust and security in Asia. Nonetheless, the Chinese nuclear
program, which in scope and character has never been even remotely capable of
challenging the U.S. arsenal, is frequently viewed with fear and mistrust in the
West. It is important that we learn from our own fear that, indeed, other nations
fear our policies and actions as well. The Wen Ho Lee Affair was a significant factor in this regard, given that it represented a bold attempt by certain officials in the
U.S. weapons establishment (Paul Robinson, among others) to misrepresent China
as a major threat holding the same degree of nuclear superpower status as the Soviet Union once had. Recall the early unsubstantiated claims by the *New York
Times* that China had stolen sophisticated designs from U.S. laboratories, allowing
it to close the technical and engineering gap between its own nuclear program and
that of the United States in one fell swoop. In a decade of uncertainty for the U.S.
weapons program defined by the implosion of the major strategic rival of the Soviet Union and the end of nuclear testing, serious doubts were expressed concerning the continuation of U.S. nuclear research. Against this background, the exag-
gerated claims about China provided a ready-made justification for continued
nuclear development, now that China was deemed able to take the Soviet Union's
place. Recall, too, that the W-88 warhead was central to the Wen Ho Lee controversy. This is a crucial factor, given that the W-88 is small and compact, yet powerful. Its size allows for more than one warhead to be placed on each ballistic missile, a technical achievement known as MIRVing (for Multiple Independent
Reentry Vehicles), which multiplies force power and which it was thought that
China had not yet reached. Hence China's acquisition of such information might
have resulted in its increased level of threat to the United States.

Yet, as we have seen, the claims about Chinese nuclear espionage and development were inflated and unsubstantiated. Thus the true story is not about the U.S.
defense infrastructure's response to an external threat; quite the contrary, it is about
this formidable bureaucracy's efforts to ensure its survival and legitimate its existence through the demonstration of pernicious external threats. Awareness of pre-

cisely this kind of reflexivity in international relations is key if we are to develop a more accurate and less unipolar-hegemonic view of world affairs—a view that can extend beyond the arrogant presumption of the United States as the main actor in world affairs and acknowledge it as just one actor among many others around the globe. In fact, this is a major problem for the U.S. empire, and it exists as deeply in contemporary political science and international relations studies in the United States as it does in the actions undertaken by the CIA and the Central Forces Command (indeed, the link between "academic disciplines" and military-intelligence organizations is not to be underestimated). A globalization that would take the form of an authentic new internationalism concerned with just relations between the peoples of different regions and different nations must criticize and move beyond this problem of empire and nationalism.

Particularly important for political economy and international relations in the United States is to develop a concept of reflexivity in world affairs according to which actions undertaken by states are read not only as simple responses to provocations from another nation but also in terms of the way in which these actions contribute to a sense of fear or insecurity in other societies. In this connection, consider the foolhardy development of the anti-ballistic missile (ABM) system by the United States. Although this program is consistently justified in U.S. public discourse by reference to supposed threats from the outside, such as North Korea, a much more immediate and material consequence of the development of this system has been the antagonizing of Russia and China. Indeed, although this technology is something of a technical pipe dream, the fear it has generated in these countries is sufficient to have undercut their strategic deterrent against the United States. It is in this sense that both nations have denounced the ABM as a destabilizing "first-strike weapon" that raises the possibility of a U.S. preemptive strike. This is also why the "star wars" missile defense clearly violates the ABM treaty and the reasoning behind it. Particularly frightening is the fact that the current U.S. arrogance over the ABM clearly signals the government's abandonment of its old deterrence logic, flawed as it was, in favor of a drive toward overwhelming U.S. military superiority coupled with the delusional dream of an invulnerable United States.[15]

The outrageous claims leveled against Wen Ho Lee had much more to do with the generation of credible enemies by the National Security State than with an actual threat from the People's Republic of China, and, by extension, they were aimed at guaranteeing the continued operation of the vast defense bureaucracy in the United States. In his pivotal text *Economy and Society*, the German sociologist and political economist Max Weber carried out a number of studies in which he examined the way that bureaucracies and organizations operate. One of his main conclusions was that bureaucracies seek, above all, to maintain themselves and to augment their functions. Rarely, he said, do we encounter organizations that voluntarily disband or relinquish responsibilities with which they have been specially charged. The U.S. National Security State in general, and the nuclear weapons infrastructure in particular, are examples of such bureaucracies. The CIA, responsible for keeping tabs on the military readiness of the Soviet Union during the Cold War, routinely overestimated the force strength of the Soviets—with the effect of increasing the importance of, and funding for, the CIA. Long tales of infighting between the different branches of the U.S. military, and of their opposing one another over responsibility for various tasks, indicate that these bureaucracies, too, function in the way that Weber described. In particular, the Air Force and the Navy each demanded a major share in the U.S. strategic nuclear posture, with the result that the Navy developed a number of ballistic missile submarines, such as the Poseidon and the Trident missile ships, and the Air Force gained responsibility for land-based missiles in silos and for strategic bombers like the B-52, the B-1, and the B-2. And not wanting to be left out, the Army and the Marines pushed for the development and deployment of "battlefield" or "tactical" nuclear arms that would fall under their command and be usable by field artillery. At present, there are demands from the Air Force, the Navy, and the Marines for their own advanced fighter jets, despite the fact that U.S. air power is already markedly stronger than that of any other nation.

The nuclear weapons design and development infrastructure of the United States functions in much the same way. As a vast bureaucracy with many sites of research, development, and production across the country, it has long resisted any paring down of its operations and sought to provide the necessary justifications for its continued operations. Even though the "end of the Cold War" was oft-cited as a circumstance that decreased the threat and changed the global strategic picture, various components of the nuclear community opposed any significant alterations in their activities. For instance, even as Clinton was negotiating the Comprehensive Test Ban Treaty and seeking to sign on, bomb designers and testers from Los Alamos, Livermore, and the Nevada Test Site were presenting a number of reasons, ranging from stockpile readiness and reliability to public safety, that they claimed necessitated continued testing of nuclear weapons. Of course, these cries were coming directly from those whose jobs and institutional purpose relied upon the process of contriving "experiments" that would then have to be brought to the desert in Nevada to be carried out. Similar arguments had been heard in 1963 when U.S. nuclear testing was shifted to underground testing from prior atmospheric testing in the Pacific and in Nevada in the wake of the Limited Test Ban Treaty. At the time, scientists claimed that, with underground testing, they would be unable either to develop new weapons or to vouch for the reliability and safety of existing weapons. In 1974, when the Threshold Test Ban Treaty was introduced along with limits on the power of weapons that could be tested (150 kilotons), testers again raised arguments about their ability to develop new weapons and certify the safety of old ones. In the 1960s and 1970s, as in the 1990s, the institutional survival of the weapons bureaucracy was much more at stake than any actual external threat. Wen Ho Lee became the figure through which a concerted ploy was created to provide ironclad reasons for the maintenance and augmentation of nuclear research within the Department of Energy.

In a state where the national security infrastructure is busily involved in producing and demonstrating new enemies in order to legitimize itself, the unfortunate fate of Wen Ho Lee also demonstrates the pairing that exists between foreign and domestic politics. Conventional reckonings of the U.S. political spectrum treat domestic affairs and foreign affairs as if they are separate and largely distinct, but this is an analytic distinction of convenience that, upon closer inspection, bears very little weight. For one thing, it relies upon an unrealistic picture of the nation-state as an independent and isolated unit, when in fact any nation-state is in contact with myriad flows and pressures that influence its situation. Through Lee's fate, as well as a great number of other historical examples, we see that the designation and production of enemies by the National Security State immediately affects the way in which different portions of the domestic U.S. population are viewed and treated.[16] In a paranoid situation involving overblown fears about China, Wen Ho and other Chinese Americans working in U.S. defense became suspects of treason and espionage, and Chinese Americans throughout the U.S. technoscientific community reported greater levels of harassment and suspicion. The discourse about China's threat had the effect of casting all Chinese Americans in the "stranger" status discussed by Simmel. And in an equally sad testament to the xenophobic nationalism of U.S. society, a number of Indian American scientists reported that they, too, came to be seen with greater suspicion or disdain during the Wen Ho Lee Affair. This loathsome U.S. panic over ethnicity and security ultimately led Ling-chi Wang of U.C. Berkeley to initiate a boycott among Asian Americans against taking new jobs in U.S. Department of Energy laboratories. As Wang and other supporters reasoned, this action not only spared those who might have applied for work from the same nefarious mistreatment visited upon Lee but also highlighted the significant role played by Asian Americans in the U.S. defense infrastructure. In fact, since this boycott came into effect, the Los Alamos National Laboratory (LANL) has received no applications from Asian Americans or citizens of Asian nations for their prestigious postdoctoral programs in physics and engineering.[17]

NOTES

1. See, for example, Sidney Lens, *Permanent War* (New York: Schocken, 1987), and Stanley Aronowitz, *The Death and Rebirth of American Radicalism* (New York: Routledge, 1996).

2. Patrick J. Buchanan, *The Death of the West: How Dying Populations and Immigrant Invasions Imperil Our Country and Civilization* (New York: Dunne, 2002). Ironically, I saw Buchanan's book displayed side-by-side with Wen Ho Lee's *My Country Versus Me* in the Dallas–Ft. Worth airport during my recent trip to New Mexico to visit Lee.

3. French Historian Michel Foucault described his approach as one involving the writing of various histories (e.g., about criminology, madness, sexuality, and modern clinical medicine) that would specifically bear on the contemporary state of affairs and help to inform current political struggles. He called this approach "writing the history of the present."

4. Los Alamos and Department of Energy Operational Security and Counterintelligence briefings in the 1990s.

5. Michel Foucault, *Surveiller et punir* (Paris: Gallimard, 1975).

6. Bail hearing in the Federal Court of Albuquerque, New Mexico, December 29, 1999.

7. *Albuquerque Journal* (December 1999) and interviews with Sandia and Los Alamos personnel.

8. Robert Vrooman, in a sworn statement to the Federal Court of New Mexico, in *U.S. v Wen Ho Lee*, 2000.

9. Charles E. Washington, in a sworn statement to the Federal Court of New Mexico, in *U.S. v Wen Ho Lee*, 2000.

10. Bail hearing in the Federal Court of Albuquerque, New Mexico, December 29, 1999.

11. Wen Ho Lee, with Helen Zia, *My Country Versus Me: The First-Hand Account of the Los Alamos Scientist Who Was Falsely Accused of Being a Spy* (New York: Hyperion, 2001); personal communication with Wen Ho Lee.

12. Dan Stober and Ian Hoffman, *A Convenient Spy: Wen Ho Lee and the Politics of Nuclear Espionage* (New York: Simon and Schuster, 2001).

13. In March 2002, during a conference at Columbia University on *Racial (Trans)formations,* discussions of the case were mired in hypothetical claims that Lee was perhaps guilty of espionage after all. The fact that the same suspicion was the basis of the government's case indicates that such claims are neither novel nor radical. Even activist intellectuals critical of the media have stopped short of dismissing the racist air of mystery attributed to Lee.

14. See Gar Alperovitz's *Atomic Diplomacy: Hiroshima and Potsdam—The Use of the Atomic Bomb and the American Confrontation with Soviet Power* (New York: Simon and Schuster, 1965) and *The Decision to Use the Atomic Bomb* (New York: Knopf, 1995).

15. In January 2002, I gave a presentation in Paris, under the auspices of the Institute for European Studies at Université de Paris, on the "Myth of the Invulnerability of the U.S. Homeland" in which I paid heed to precisely these strange dynamics. Against all existential expectations, U.S. policy has long acted as if it were possible to guarantee an absolute security of the territory of the United States. Clearly an index of empire, this curious reflex ignores the fact that the very means intended to provide such security (i.e., the "nuclear umbrella," the North American Air Defense Command, etc.) are what create the danger itself. The story of Wen Ho Lee fits into this dynamic directly, inasmuch as he was portrayed as someone who had created a major vulnerability at the very heart of the U.S. defense infrastructure. Further, Congress allocated $11 billion to ABM research in April 1999—within a month after the Lee case broke—and much of the associated rhetoric was about Lee and about China (*Congressional Record* 3–4/1999).

16. The fate of interned Japanese Americans during World War II has already been mentioned in this regard. Similarly, Muslim Americans, Arab Americans, and anyone else who might fit the label of "terrorist" remain under intense and unreasonable scrutiny today. At the time of this writing, thousands are still being detained by the INS on flimsy or nonexistent pretenses said to be related to terrorism.

17. Interviews with LANL personnel on the impact of the boycott, Summer 2001 and February 2002.

3

Making Us Less Free

War on Terrorism or War on Liberty?

MICHAEL RATNER

INTRODUCTION

I am writing this a little more than six months after the September 11 attacks re-arranged the world's legal and political landscape for all of us. In this brief, hyper-politicized period of time, basic legal protections embedded in the U.S. Constitution and in international law have been swept aside by the Bush administration's "War on Terrorism." Legal constraints on arbitrary executive and government power have been tossed away. Courts, which once stood as a safeguard of individual rights, have largely surrendered to new "anti-terrorist" measures. The very laws of war, fashioned over hundreds of years, have been subverted. Human rights, struggled for and embodied in documents such as the Magna Carta, the French Declaration of the Rights of Man and of the Citizen, the Bill of Rights of the Constitution of the United States, and the International Covenant on Civil and Political Rights, are in jeopardy. We have entered a dark period.

It has been more than six months since I witnessed, from just a few blocks away, the terrible devastation at the World Trade Center. The heart-wrenching human suffering of that day is still vivid to me, as it is to everyone in New York. Like everyone else who saw or was affected by the attacks, I yearn to live again in safety: I want those who attacked us arrested and punished, and the network that plotted to harm us eliminated. But my concern for safety at home is mixed with concern over what appears to be broad popular support for the new anti-terrorism measures—even those that curtail freedom and constitutional rights.

After all, it's hard to see how building a Fortress America can possibly prevent another terrorist attack. The United States has 7,500 miles of border with Canada and Mexico and thousands of miles of coastline, most of it not patrolled. There are more than 10,000 air flights a day in the United States. Eleven million trucks and over 2 million rail cars cross into the United States each year, as do millions of noncitizen visitors. Terrorists intent on harm can easily slip into the country. Of course, good law enforcement has a role in protecting people; but all the laws in the world are not enough to really make the United States safe.

If the U.S. government truly wants its people to be safer and wants terrorist threats to diminish, it must make fundamental changes in its foreign policies. Without going into these questions in detail, the terrible events of April 2002 in Israel and Palestine should demonstrate the folly of repressive "anti-terrorist" measures as a way to ensure peace. The United States' actions in the Middle East, particularly its unqualified support for Israel, its embargo of Iraq, its bombing of Afghanistan, and its actions in Saudi Arabia, continue to anger people throughout the region, and to fertilize the ground where terrorists of the future will take root.

But there is very little room left in the United States for those who question the new initiatives, or who challenge U.S. foreign policies. Since September 11, such criticism has been painted as the equivalent of support for those who attacked the United States. As John Ashcroft, the attorney general of the United States, testified at a congressional committee in December 2001, "to those who scare peace-loving people with phantoms of lost liberty, my message is this: your tactics only aid terrorists."[1] He went on to say that criticism of the administration "gives ammunition to America's enemies and pause to America's friends."[2] Similarly, White House spokesman Ari Fleisher warned "all Americans . . . to watch what they say [and] watch what they do."[3]

However, I believe it is more essential than ever to speak up. Without basic alterations in U.S. policies, there is little hope of ending the draconian curtailment of liberties in the United States. The struggles involved in regaining lost liberty and creating a more just world abroad are really one struggle—and that is not just rhetoric. We and our children will not be safer and freer until the world is as well.

In the current climate, it will obviously not be easy to substantially change the course the United States and its allies have embarked upon. Yet the U.S. administration has been forced to modify some of its more draconian proposals, such as its original refusal to apply any part of the Geneva Conventions to combatants captured in Afghanistan. It has been pressured into taking steps to make trials before military tribunals fairer. And, following a great uproar in the press, it has apparently closed the disinformation and propaganda office it had established at the Pentagon.

These changes in policy have come, in some cases, from dissent within the United States and, in others, even from pragmatic voices within the U.S. armed forces. But outcry from the countries of Europe, some of which still take the rule of law seriously, has greatly helped press these modifications upon the United States.

There have also been a number of lawsuits filed—some successful, most with appeals still pending—to improve the treatment of immigrants in the United States and of captured combatants. On March 26, 2002, a judge in New Jersey gave civil rights organizations access to the records of those detained in the United States after September 11, saying that secret arrests are "odious to a democracy." On April 4, 2002, a federal judge in Michigan ordered public access to immigration hearings that had been closed in the wake of September 11, saying that government secrecy "only breeds suspicion." In a decision on March 13, 2002, the Inter-American Human Rights Commission of the Organization of American States urged the United States to immediately provide court or tribunal hearings for those detained at Guantanamo Bay, Cuba. And on April 30, 2002, a federal judge, addressing the case of one of the post–September 11 detainees in the United States, ruled that the government had no right to jail innocent people to ensure their testimony before a grand jury. The judge found that even in the aftermath of September 11, the innocent could not be imprisoned: "A proper respect for the laws that Congress does enact—as well as the inalienable right to liberty—prohibits this court from rewriting the law, no matter how exigent the circumstances."[4] Clearly, these cases show that some judges are still courageous enough to uphold fundamental rights against a government bent on their elimination.

In the following sections, I will discuss some of the overall themes of the post–September 11 period and analyze in detail some of the new "anti-terror" laws and restrictions in the United States. I hope that voices around the world will respond to these issues so that justice can truly be served.

OVERVIEW: PERMANENT WAR ABROAD

The U.S. government's immediate reaction to September 11 was to make war abroad. On September 14, 2001, in its resolution entitled "Authorization for Use of United States Military Force," Congress gave the president unbridled power to go to war. He was authorized to attack any nation, organization, or person involved directly or indirectly in the September 11 attacks. The resolution did not name any particular nation, organization, or person but, instead, left the designation of guilty parties to the president alone. Congress basically gave the president a blank check to make war upon whomever he wants anywhere in the world, even inside the United States.

Under the language of the resolution the president does not need to prove a link to the attacks of September 11 in order to wage war against another country or group. To declare war on Iraq, for example, he could justify his actions merely by claiming that someone allegedly from Al Qaeda had allegedly met with an Iraqi official. With such broad powers, it is hard to see any check on the president's single-handed ability to declare and wage war.

This war has been conceptualized as a permanent war abroad. It is a war that the president has repeatedly stated will take many years; it is a war without end. Vice President Cheney said that the United States may take military action against "forty to fifty countries" and that the war could last half a century or more.[5]

Within six months of September 11, active U.S. forces had involved themselves not only in Afghanistan and Pakistan but also in Colombia, the Philippines, and potentially, Somalia and the Sudan. Future countries targeted included the countries named by President Bush as the "axis of evil": Iraq, Iran, and North Korea.

A permanent war abroad means permanent anger directed against the United States by countries and people who will be devastated by U.S. military actions. Hate will increase, not lessen; and the terrible consequences of that hate will be used, in turn, as justification for more restrictions on civil liberties in the United States.

PERMANENT WAR AT HOME

After September 11 the United States also launched a permanent war on terror at home, by rapidly building a fortified surveillance and National Security State. Attorney General John Ashcroft, a religious fundamentalist with an antediluvian record on civil rights, saw September 11 as an opportunity to lift restrictions that had been placed on the nation's spy agencies in the 1970s and to grant law enforcement agencies the additional powers they have been wanting for years.

Among the most pernicious tendencies at work in Ashcroft's new order are the pervasive censorship of information, the silencing of dissent, and widespread ethnic and religious profiling.

Overall, the new anti-terrorist laws represent a tremendous expansion of executive power. The president can now make war against anyone without additional congressional authority, can wiretap attorneys and their clients without a court order, can jail noncitizens permanently on the word of the attorney general (even if they have committed no crimes), and can set up military tribunals that, in turn, can mete out the death penalty without appeal. The country's system of checks and balances, made up of the courts, Congress, and the executive, and, purportedly, the pride of the U.S. constitutional system, is in jeopardy.

The new laws and restrictions also mean fundamental changes in the way the United States, historically a nation of immigrants, treats the 20 million noncitizens residing in the country. Since September 11, enforcement of the new laws against noncitizens, mostly those from the Middle East, has included incommunicado detentions, the questioning of thousands by FBI agents, and widespread racial, ethnic, and religious profiling. The government's campaign against noncitizens, particularly Muslims, has at times flowered into explicit religious bigotry, as expressed in this remarkable quote from Attorney General Ashcroft: "Islam is a religion in which God requires you to send your son to die for him. Christianity is a faith in which God sends his son to die for you."[6]

In general, the war at home is marked by an unprecedented strengthening of the U.S. intelligence and law enforcement apparatus, an erosion of the U.S. system of checks and balances, and a new xenophobia and anti-immigrant sentiment. These tendencies are deeply troubling.

In the next sections I will discuss in more detail some aspects of the war on terrorism. Some include challenges to international justice, such as indefinite detention of battlefield detainees outside the standards of the Geneva Convention, the establishment of military tribunals to try suspected terrorists, and the possible use of torture to obtain information. Others include domestic initiatives such as the creation of a special new cabinet office of Homeland Security, massive arrests and interrogation of immigrants, the passage of legislation granting intelligence and law enforcement agencies much broader powers to intrude into the private lives of Americans, the wiretapping of attorney-client conversations, and the FBI's new license to spy on domestic, religious, and political groups.

Overall, I fear that the entire situation, when coupled with the ideology of the Republicans currently in control of the executive branch of the government, portends the worst both for international human rights and for constitutional rights at home.

THE NEW LEGAL LANDSCAPE

The U.S. government has established a wide-ranging series of measures in its efforts to eradicate terrorism. Below, I will look more closely at some of the key measures and analyze their implications.

The President's Military Order: Detainees and Tribunals

On November 13, 2001, President Bush, as commander-in-chief, signed a military order establishing military commissions or tribunals to try suspected terrorists.[7] In addition to authorizing military tribunals, the same military order of November 13 requires the secretary of defense to detain anyone whom the president has reason to believe is an international terrorist, a member of Al Qaeda, or an individual who is harboring such persons. There is no requirement that detained individuals ever be brought to trial. Detention without any charges and without any court review can last an entire lifetime.

Subsequent to the issuance of the military order, U.S. and Northern Alliance forces in Afghanistan captured thousands of prisoners. On or about January 11, 2002, the U.S. military began transporting prisoners captured in Afghanistan to Camp X-Ray at the U.S. Naval Station in Guantanamo Bay, Cuba. As of April 2002, U.S. authorities had detained 300 male prisoners representing 33 nationalities at the Guantanamo compound, and that number was expected to grow. These prisoners are the ones who may be indefinitely detained or tried by military tribunals to face the death penalty.[8] Remarkably, Secretary Rumsfeld has stated that he reserves the right to continue detaining prisoners even if the tribunals acquit them.

There have been allegations of ill treatment of some prisoners in transit and at

Guantanamo, including reports that they were shackled, hooded, and sedated during the twenty-five-hour flight from Afghanistan, that their beards and heads were forcibly shaved, and that upon arrival at Guantanamo they were housed in small cells that failed to protect against the elements.[9] While such treatment is never acceptable, more serious is the fact that these prisoners exist in a legal limbo, their identities secret and the charges against them unknown.

It is the official position of the U.S. government that none of these detainees are prisoners of war (POWs). Instead, officials have repeatedly described them as "unlawful combatants." This determination was made without the convening of a competent tribunal, despite the requirements of Article 5 of the Third Geneva Convention, which mandates such a tribunal "should any doubt arise" as to a combatant's status. In its most recent statement on the status of those detained at Guantanamo, the U.S. government announced that although it would apply the Geneva Conventions to those prisoners it decided were from the Taliban, it would not extend them to prisoners it believed were members of Al Qaeda.[10] However, in no case were any of the detained to be considered POWs. The United States has repeatedly refused the entreaties of the international community to treat all detainees according to the procedures established under the Geneva Conventions.[11]

The U.S. government's treatment of the Guantanamo detainees violates virtually every human rights norm concerning preventive detention. It has denied the detainees access to counsel, consular representatives, and family members; failed to notify them of the charges they are facing; refused to allow for judicial review of the detentions; and expressed its intent to hold the detainees indefinitely.[12] It continues to do so despite an important ruling from the Inter-American Human Rights Commission that it immediately give the detainees some form of judicial process. In this ruling the commission requested that the United States take the urgent measures necessary to have the legal status of the detainees at Guantanamo Bay determined by a competent tribunal.

The military order also provides for special commissions to try the captives now being held. Under this order, noncitizens (whether from the United States or elsewhere) who are accused of aiding international terrorism can be tried before one of these commissions at the discretion of the president. The commissions are not standard courts-martial, which provide far more protections for the accused.

The executive order was accompanied by Attorney General Ashcroft's explicit statement that terrorists do not deserve constitutional protections. (By "terrorists," Ashcroft means accused or suspected individuals, not those proved in a court to have committed terrorist acts.)

There was a broad outcry against the unfairness of such tribunals, both in the United States and Europe, and even from conservatives. This outcry was probably a factor in the government's decision to have the so-called 20th hijacker, Moussaoui, tried in a regular federal court in the United States. It certainly contributed to the reasons for modifying the order in March 2002.

The provisions of the military order that established these commissions call for the secretary of defense to appoint the judges, most likely military officers, who will decide questions of both law and fact. Unlike federal judges who are appointed for life, these officers will have little independence and every reason to decide in favor of the prosecution. Normal rules of evidence, which provide some assurance of reliability, will not apply. Hearsay and even evidence obtained from torture will apparently be admissible.

Under the original order, unanimity among the judges was not required, even to impose the death penalty. That was modified in March 2002, to require a unanimous verdict for a death sentence, but not for the finding of guilt for a crime carrying a potential of a death sentence. The original order did not give suspects a choice of counsel; that too has been modified, but only to the extent that a suspect can pay an attorney and that the attorney passes security clearances from the U.S. government. Initially, the only appeal from a conviction was to the president or the secretary of defense; the modified order allows an appeal to a three-person military review panel that then gives a "recommendation" to the secretary of defense or the president as to the disposition of the case. However, it's important to note that there is still no provision for review by a civilian court, and that the final decision remains in the hands of the president or secretary of defense.

Incredibly, the entire process, including execution, can be carried out in secret, although the modified order specifies that the proceedings will be open unless the presiding officer determines otherwise. In other words, proceedings can still be closed in the interests of "national security" and other similar reasons. The trials can be held anywhere the secretary of defense decides. (A trial might occur on an aircraft carrier, for example, with no press allowed, and the body of the executed disposed of at sea.)

Although military tribunals were used during and immediately subsequent to World War II, their use since that time does not comply with important international treaties. The International Covenant on Civil and Political Rights as well as the American Declaration of the Rights and Duties of Man require that persons be tried before courts previously established in accordance with preexisting laws. Clearly, the tribunals are not such courts.

In addition, the Third Geneva Convention of 1949 requires that prisoners of war be tried under the same procedures that U.S. soldiers would be tried for similar crimes. U.S. soldiers are tried by courts-martial or civilian courts and not by military tribunal.

Surprisingly, a number of prestigious law professors have accepted and even argued in favor of these tribunals, saying that secrecy is necessary for security.[13] The primary argument is that it might be necessary to disclose classified information in order to obtain convictions. But, in fact, procedures for safely handling classified information in federal courts have been successful, as in the trial of those convicted in the 1993 bombing of the World Trade Center. Those 1993 trials demonstrate that trials of suspected terrorists do not require special military tribunals but can safely be held in federal courts.

Trials before military commissions will not be trusted either in the Muslim world or in Europe. The military commissions will be viewed as what they are: "kangaroo courts." It would be much better to demonstrate to the world that the guilty have been apprehended and fairly convicted in front of impartial and regularly constituted courts.

An even better solution would be for the United States to go to the United Nations and have the United Nations establish a special court for the trials, staffed by judges from the United States, Muslim countries, and other countries with civil law systems.

The Office of Homeland Security

On September 20, 2001, President Bush announced the creation of the Homeland Security Office, charged with gathering intelligence, coordinating anti-terrorism efforts, and taking precautions to prevent and respond to terrorism. It is not yet known how this office will function, but it will most likely try to centralize the powers of existing U.S. intelligence and law enforcement agencies—a difficult if not impossible job—and coordinate the work of some forty bickering agencies.

Those concerned with its establishment are worried that the Office of Homeland Security will become a super spy agency and, as its very name implies, that it will encourage the military to play a hitherto unprecedented role in domestic law enforcement. The recent appointment of a U.S. Army general who will be in charge of "defense of the homeland" and the proposed repeal of a federal statute that prohibits the military from playing a domestic law enforcement role are clear signals of what can be expected in the future.

FBI Arrests and Investigations

Arrests of Noncitizens. The FBI has always done more than chase criminals; like the Central Intelligence Agency it has long considered itself the protector of U.S. ideology. Those who have opposed government policies—whether civil rights workers, anti–Vietnam War protesters, opponents of the covert Reagan-era wars, or cultural dissidents—have repeatedly been surveilled and had their legal activities disrupted by the FBI.

In the immediate aftermath of the September 11 attacks, Attorney General John Ashcroft focused FBI efforts on noncitizens, whether permanent residents, students, temporary workers, or tourists. Normally, an alien can be held for only forty-eight hours prior to the filing of charges. Ashcroft's new regulation allows arrested aliens to be held without any charges for a "reasonable time," presumably months or longer.

After September 11, the FBI began massive detentions and investigations of individuals suspected of terrorist connections, almost all of them noncitizens of Middle Eastern descent; over 1,300 were arrested. In some cases, people were arrested merely for being from a country such as Pakistan and having an expired student visa. Many were held for weeks and months without access to lawyers or knowledge of the charges against them; as of this writing, many are still in detention. None, as yet, are proven to have a connection with the September 11 attacks; as many as half remain in jail despite having been cleared.[14]

Stories of mistreatment of such detainees are not uncommon. Apparently, some of those arrested are not willing to talk to the FBI, although they have been offered shorter jail sentences, jobs, money, and new identities. Astonishingly, the FBI and the Department of Justice are discussing methods to force them to talk, which include "using drugs or pressure tactics such as those employed by the Israeli interrogators."[15] The accurate term to describe these tactics is torture.

There is resistance to this even from law enforcement officials. One former FBI chief of counterterrorism said in an October 2001 interview: "Torture goes against every grain in my body. Chances are you are going to get the wrong person and risk damage or killing them."[16] As torture is illegal in the United States and under international law, U.S. officials risk lawsuits by using such practices. For this reason, they have suggested having another country do their dirty work; they want to extradite the suspects to allied countries where security services regularly threaten family members and/or use torture. It would be difficult to imagine a more ominous signal of the repressive period we are facing.

In fact, with regard to a number of alleged Taliban or Al Qaeda members captured or arrested outside the United States, the U.S. government has secretly sent them to other countries and not brought them to the United States or to Guantanamo. They have been taken to Egypt or Jordan where they can be tortured, in some cases with the involvement of the CIA.

Investigations of Middle Eastern Men and of Dissenters. In late November 2001, Attorney General Ashcroft announced that the FBI or other law enforcement personnel would interview more than 5,000 men, mostly from the Middle East, who were in the United States on temporary visas. None of these men were suspected of any crime. The interviews were supposedly voluntary. A number of civil liberties organizations and Muslim and Arab American groups objected that the investigations amounted to racial profiling and that interviews of immigrants who might be subject to deportation could hardly be called voluntary. Several law enforcement officials, including a former head of the FBI, objected as well, saying that such questioning would harm the relationship of police departments with minority communities, that the practice was illegal under some state laws, and that it was a clumsy and ineffective way to go about an investigation. A few local police departments refused to cooperate.

Although Ashcroft claimed the questioning was harmless, the proposed questions themselves made this assertion doubtful. The initial questions concerned the noncitizen's status; if there was even the hint of a technical immigration violation, the person could well find himself in jail and deported. Information was requested regarding all of the friends and family members of the questioned person; in other words, the FBI wanted complete address books. Once the FBI had such information, it would open files and investigations on each of those named, even though no one was suspected of a crime. The FBI was also instructed to make informants of the persons it questioned, and to have them continue to report on and monitor the people they were in contact with. Oliver "Buck" Revel, a former FBI assistant executive director, has criticized this practice as "not effective" and as "really gut[ting] the values of our society, which you cannot allow the terrorists to do."[17]

In March 2002, Ashcroft announced that the Justice Department was launching a new investigation of 3,000 more noncitizens, mostly young Arab men—this despite the fact that just over half of the initial group of 5,000 could even be found for the interviews and that little, if any, information was obtained. The American-Arab Anti-Discrimination Committee (ADC) was sharply critical of this new effort, saying that it was an "ineffective method of law enforcement and constituted an unacceptable form of racial profiling."[18]

The FBI is also currently investigating political dissident groups it claims are linked to terrorism—among them pacifist groups such as the U.S. chapter of Women in Black, which holds peaceful vigils to protest violence in Israel and the Palestinian Territories. The FBI has threatened to force members of Women in Black to either talk about their group or go to jail. As one of the group's members said, "If the FBI cannot or will not distinguish between groups who collude in hatred and terrorism, and peace activists who struggle in the full light of day against all forms of terrorism, we are in serious trouble."[19]

Unfortunately, the FBI does not make that distinction. We are facing not only the roundup of thousands on flimsy suspicions but also an all-out investigation of dissent in the United States.

Renewed FBI Spying on Religious and Political Groups.   According to a front-page *New York Times* story in December 2001, Attorney General John Ashcroft was considering a plan that would authorize the FBI to spy upon and disrupt political groups.[20] This spying and disruption would take place even without evidence that a group was involved in anything illegal. A person or group could become a target solely for having expressed views different from those of the government or taking a position in support of, for example, Palestinian rights.

Ashcroft would authorize this plan by lifting FBI guidelines that were put into place in the 1970s following disclosure of abuses committed by the agency, including spying upon and efforts to disrupt the activities of such nonviolent leaders as Dr. Martin Luther King. These earlier actions were carried out under a program called Cointelpro, which stands for "Counterintelligence Program." As of this writing, three months after the first stories appeared about Ashcroft's interest in resurrecting Cointelpro, it remains unclear what elements of the plan have been approved.

Violation of the Attorney-Client Relationship

Wiretapping of Attorney-Client Communications.   At the heart of the effective assistance of counsel is the right of a criminal defendant to a lawyer with whom he or she can communicate candidly and freely without fear that the government is overhearing confidential communications. This right is fundamental to the adversary system of justice in the United States. When the government overhears these conversations, a defendant's right to a defense is compromised.

On October 30, 2001, with the stroke of a pen, Attorney General Ashcroft eliminated the attorney-client privilege and said that he will wiretap privileged communications when he thinks there is "reasonable suspicion to believe" that a detainee "may use communications with attorneys or their agents to further facilitate an act or acts of violence or terrorism."[21] Ashcroft said at the time that approximately 100 such suspects and their attorneys might be subject to the order. He claimed the legal authority to act without court order—in other words, without the approval and finding by a neutral magistrate that attorney-client communications are facilitating criminal conduct. This is utter lawlessness by our country's top law enforcement officer and is flatly unconstitutional.

The Wiretapping and Indictment of a Lawyer: The Lynne Stewart Case.   On April 9, 2002, Ashcroft flew to New York to announce the indictment of a well-known defense attorney, Lynne Stewart. Stewart had represented Sheik Omar Abdel Rahman in his 1995 trial for conspiracy to bomb the World Trade Center, for which he had been convicted and sentenced to life plus sixty-five years. She had continued to represent him in prison.

Stewart was arrested by the FBI and freed the same day on a $500,000 bond. Also on that day, the FBI raided her office, removed the hard drives from her computers, and took many of her legal files. Several of Stewart's clients are facing trials in federal courts; now the FBI and the Justice Department have possession of those confidential legal files. The damage that can be done to the constitutional rights of her clients is incalculable.

The indictment, for which Stewart faces forty years in prison, primarily accuses her of having given material support to a terrorist organization. It charges that she "facilitated and concealed communications" between the sheik and members of an Egyptian terrorist organization, the Islamic Group. The essence of the claim is that on an occasion when Stewart visited her client in prison, the Arabic translator who accompanied her spoke to the sheik regarding messages that the sheik wanted transmitted to the terrorist group. In other words, the translator allegedly did not just translate for Stewart but had his own agenda with the sheik. It is claimed that Stewart permitted and even facilitated those conversations. Apparently, though, these alleged communications resulted in no terrorist incidents.

It seems highly improbable that Ashcroft will have sufficient evidence to support these charges against Stewart. As she does not speak or understand Arabic, she could not have known the content of the conversations that allegedly occurred between the translator and the sheik. If she was unaware of the supposed illegal nature of the conversations, it is difficult to see how she could be accused of giving material aid to a terrorist organization.

The alleged conversations occurred prior to Ashcroft's tenure, when Janet Reno was the attorney general. The claimed "evidence" was gathered through a wiretap obtained by former Attorney General Reno that has been in effect for almost two years. This wiretap was not authorized by a warrant, nor did it meet the "probable cause" standard of the Fourth Amendment that is normally required in criminal investigations. Rather, a special secret court, the Foreign Intelligence Surveillance Court, authorized the wiretap without any showing of "probable cause." Such a wiretap raises serious legal questions, particularly as attorney-client conversations were monitored.

Ashcroft is now using this indictment of Stewart to justify his claim that there is a need to wiretap attorney-client conversations in terrorism cases. In addition, he claims the authority to do so without any court approval, even that of the Foreign Intelligence Surveillance Court. There is no reason for this bypassing of the Constitution; courts are the appropriate place to approve, or disapprove, any such requests for wiretapping. Hopefully, the court test of and rejection of this new reach for power will come swiftly and decisively.

It is difficult to divorce Stewart's indictment from the politics of John Ashcroft. It seems more than likely that the indictment was contrived, and that one of its main purposes was the intimidation of those who believe all persons, even those accused of terrorism, are entitled to constitutional protections—most importantly, the right to a lawyer. Because of Ashcroft's action, it will be increasingly difficult to find defense lawyers willing to take these unpopular cases.

The New Anti-Terrorist Legislation

On October 26, 2001, Congress passed and President Bush signed sweeping new anti-terrorist legislation, the USA Patriot Act (Uniting and Strengthening America by Providing Appropriate Tools Required to Intercept and Obstruct Terrorism), aimed at both aliens and citizens. The legislation met more opposition than one might expect in these difficult times. A National Coalition to Protect Political Freedom, comprising over 120 groups ranging from the right to the left, opposed the worst aspects of the proposed new law. They succeeded in making minor modifications, but the most troubling provisions remain. These are described below.

"Rights" of Aliens.   Prior to this legislation, anti-terrorist laws passed in the wake of the 1996 bombing of the federal building in Oklahoma had already given the government wide powers to arrest, detain, and deport aliens based upon secret evidence—evidence that neither the aliens nor their attorneys could view or re-

fute.[22] The new legislation makes it even worse for aliens. First, the law permits "mandatory detention" of aliens certified by the attorney general as "suspected terrorists." These could include aliens involved in barroom brawls, or aliens who have provided humanitarian assistance to organizations disfavored by the United States. Once certified in this way, an alien could be imprisoned indefinitely with no real opportunity for court challenge. Until now, such "preventive detention" was believed to be flatly unconstitutional.

Secondly, current law permits deportation of aliens who support terrorist activity; the proposed law would make aliens deportable for almost any association with a "terrorist organization." Although this change seems plausible on the surface, it represents a dangerous erosion of the constitutionally protected rights of association. "Terrorist organization" is a broad and open-ended term that, depending on the political climate or the inclinations of the attorney general, could include liberation groups such as the Irish Republican Army, the African National Congress, or even NGOs that have never engaged in any destruction of property, such as Greenpeace. An alien who gives only medical or humanitarian aid to similar groups, or simply supports their political message in a material way, could also be jailed indefinitely.

More Powers to the FBI and CIA.   A key element in the USA Patriot Act is the wide expansion of wiretapping. In the United States wiretapping is permitted, but generally only when there is probable cause to believe a crime has been committed and a judge has signed a special wiretapping order that specifies limited time periods, the number of telephones being wiretapped, and the type of conversations that can be overheard.

In 1978, an exception was made to these strict requirements, permitting wiretapping to be carried out to gather intelligence information about foreign governments and foreign terrorist organizations.[23] A secret court, the Foreign Intelligence Surveillance Court, was established that could approve such wiretaps without requiring the government to show evidence of criminal conduct. In this way, the constitutional protections necessary when investigating crimes could be bypassed.

The secret court has been little more than a rubber stamp for wiretapping requests by the spy agencies. It has authorized over 13,000 wiretaps in its twenty-two-year existence (about 1,000 during 2001) and apparently has never denied a request for a wiretap. Under the new law, the same secret court will have the power to authorize wiretaps and secret searches of homes in criminal cases—not just to gather foreign intelligence. The FBI will be able to wiretap individuals or organizations without meeting the stringent requirements of the U.S. Constitution, which requires a court order based upon probable cause that a person is planning or has committed a crime. The new law will authorize the secret court to permit roving wiretaps of any phones, computers, or cell phones that might possibly be used by a suspect. Widespread reading of e-mail messages will also be allowed, even before the recipients open them. Thousands of conversations will be listened to or read that have nothing to do with any suspect or any crime.

The new legislation permits many other expansions of investigative and prosecutorial power, including wider use of undercover agents to infiltrate organizations, longer jail sentences and lifetime supervision for people who have served their sentences, a longer list of crimes that can receive the death penalty, and longer statutes of limitations for prosecuting crimes. Another provision of the new bill makes it a crime for a person to fail to notify the FBI if he or she has "reasonable grounds to believe" that someone is about to commit a terrorist offense. The language of this provision is so vague that anyone—however innocent, with any connection to anyone even suspected of being a terrorist—can be prosecuted.

The New Crime of Domestic Terrorism.   The USA Patriot Act creates a number of new crimes. One of the most threatening to dissent and to those who oppose government policies is the crime of "domestic terrorism." It is loosely defined as acts that are dangerous to human life, violate criminal law, and "appear to be intended to intimidate or coerce a civilian population" or to "influence the policy of a government by intimidation of coercion." Under this definition, a protest demonstration that blocked a street and prevented an ambulance from getting by could be deemed domestic terrorism. Likewise, the demonstrations in Seattle against the World Trade Organization in 2000 could have fit within the definition.

This was an unnecessary addition to the criminal code; there are already plenty of laws making such civil disobedience criminal without labeling protest as "terrorist" in order to impose severe prison sentences.

CONCLUSION

Overall, the severe curtailment of legal rights, disregard for established law, and new repressive legislation represent one of the most sweeping assaults on liberties in the last fifty years. It is unlikely to make us more secure; it is certain to make us less free. It is common for governments to reach for draconian law enforcement solutions in times of war or national crisis. It has happened often in the United States and elsewhere.

We should learn from historical example. Times of hysteria, of war, and of instability are not the times to rush to enact new laws that curtail our freedoms and grant more authority to the government and its intelligence and law enforcement agencies.

The U.S. government has conceptualized the war against terrorism as a permanent war, a war without boundaries. Terrorism is frightening to all of us, but it's equally chilling to think that in the name of anti-terrorism our government is willing to permanently suspend constitutional freedoms.

NOTES

1. Quoted in Neil A. Lewis, "Ashcroft Defends Antiterror Plan; Says Criticism May Aid U.S. Foes," *New York Times* (December 7, 2001), p. A1.

2. Ibid.

3. "Say What You Will," editorial in *The Oregonian* (October 2, 2001), p. B10.

4. First Opinion and Order at 59 in *U.S.A. v Osama Awadallah*, 01 Cr. 1026 (SAS), decided April 30, 2002.

5. John Pilger, "The Colder War" (January 31, 2001), available online at www.counterpunch.org/pilgercold.html.

6. American Arab Anti-Discrimination Committee, Action Alert, "Protest Ashcroft's Anti-Islamic Statements" (February 11, 2002).

7. "Detention, Treatment, and Trial of Certain Non-Citizens in the War Against Terrorism" (November 13, 2001), available online at http://www.whitehouse.gov/news/releases/2001/11/20011113–27.html.

8. See, for example, Richard Sisk, "Airport Gun Battle Firefight Erupts as Prisoners Are Flown to Cuba," *New York Daily News* (January 11, 2002), p. 27.

9. See, for example, Amnesty International, USA, "AI Calls on the USA to End Legal Limbo of Guantanamo Prisoners," AI Index: AMR 51/009/2002, issued 15/01/2002, available online at http://web.amnesty.org/ai.nsf/Index/AMR510092002.

10. White House Press Release, available online at http://www.whitehouse.gov/news/releases/2002/02/20020207–13.html.

11. On February 8, the day after announcement of the United States's position, Darcy Christen, a spokesperson for the International Committee of the Red Cross (ICRC), said of the detainees: "They were captured in combat [and] we consider them prisoners of war." See Richard Waddington, "Guantanamo Inmates Are POWs Despite Bush View—ICRC," *Reuters* (February 9, 2002).

12. These detentions are currently under challenge in U.S. courts, and the author of the present chapter is one of the attorneys involved in the cases. The court papers are available online at: www.campxray.net.

13. See, for example, the remarks of Yale Professor Ruth Wedgewood during a debate on NPR's *Justice Talking* (featured show: "Military Tribunals," January 14, 2002), available online at http://www.justicetalking.org/getshow.asp?showid=195.

14. Homeland Security Director Tom Ridge said that there was no evidence yet that any of the more than 1,000 people detained was a terrorist. See "U.S. Draws Up List of Over 5,000 Men It Wants Interviewed in Terrorism Probe," *Wall Street Journal* (November 14, 2001), p. A6.

15. Walter Pincus, "Silence of 4 Terror Probe Suspects Poses Dilemma," *Washington Post* (October 21, 2001), p. A6.

16. Ibid.

17. Quoted in Jim McGee, "Ex-FBI Officials Criticize Tactics On Terrorism," *Washington Post* (November 28, 2001), p. A1.

18. "ADC Reiterates Objections to Government Investigations Based on Racial Profiles" (March 20, 2002), available online at www.adc.org/press/2002/20March2002.html.

19. Report by Ronnie Gilbert, "FBI Investigation of Women in Black" (October 4, 2001), available online at www.labournet.net/world/0110/wmnblk1.html.

20. David Johnston and Don Van Natta, Jr., "Ashcroft Seeking to Free F.B.I. to Spy on Groups," *New York Times* (December 1, 2001), p. A1.

21. National Security, "Prevention of Terrorist Acts of Violence," 28 Code of Federal Regulations, Parts 500 and 501.

22. This 1996 legislation was aimed at aliens, although U.S. citizens living in the United States carried out the bombing of the federal building.

23. Foreign Intelligence Surveillance Act (1978).

4

Fear, American Style

Civil Liberty After 9/11

COREY ROBIN

In early November 2001, while traveling to Los Angeles for an academic conference, I happened to take the shuttle train from Penn Station in New York City, where I live, to Newark Airport. It was about 3:30 on a weekday afternoon, and the train was crowded with commuters. After I found my seat, I noticed a man two rows in front of me, wearing a turban, sitting alone. For the next ten minutes, crowds of people streamed into the car. When the train finally pulled out of the station, every seat was taken—except for the one next to the man with the turban. At the Newark stop, he got up to go, and for the first time, I saw his face. He had a full beard and was sporting dark, almost aviator-style glasses. He was wearing gray dress pants, a plaid jacket, a sweater vest, and a tie. Smack in the middle of his left jacket lapel was a large button with letters curving around the top, spelling out "I am an American Sikh." Underneath the caption flew an American flag, and underneath the flag, "God Bless America."

Though such sights were common enough in the immediate aftermath of 9/11, what struck me about the incident was not what it said about ethnic relations in the United States but what it said about free speech. Here was a man conscripted, perhaps even coerced, into making a political statement (whether he believed in America or not, it's fairly certain he would not have affirmed his patriotism had he not been afraid of becoming yet another victim of targeted harassment or violence)[1] without the state holding a gun to his head, or threatening him with imprisonment, fines, or exile. In the United States, civil libertarians have long opposed state coercion and force as means of compelling or restricting speech. But when it comes to more nebulous forms of social pressure and coercion, they have less to say.[2] I can't know for sure, but I suspect that the button worn by the man on the train was designed to ward off people in the street and not the FBI or the INS. And despite what John Stuart Mill claimed in *On Liberty*—that "society can

and does execute its own mandates," that "its means of tyrannizing are not restricted to acts which it may do by the hands of its political functionaries," that
"social tyranny" is often "more formidable than many kinds of political oppression"[3]—civil libertarians are still usually more concerned about the FBI and the
INS than they are about quiet, everyday forms of intimidation that don't involve
the state.

I do not mean to suggest that civil libertarians are wrong to focus on state coercion. Nor am I arguing that this incident on the train or other similar incidents
occur in isolation from actions taken by the state. Whatever President Bush may
have declared, post-9/11, about the virtues of tolerance and multiculturalism, we
cannot understand the popular outbursts in this country—loud and subtle, violent
and nonviolent, overt and covert—against Arabs, Muslims, and South Asians in
the absence of 9/11 and the ensuing round-up and questioning of immigrants of
Middle Eastern and South Asian descent.

What I am arguing, and what I would like to show in this chapter, is that when
it comes to violations of civil liberties, particularly freedom of speech, there has been
a division of labor in the United States between the state and civil society. Rather
than a repressive state acting alone to curtail speech, institutions, organizations, and
individuals outside the state sector have often done the work of repression that the
American state is forbidden to do, or have supplemented the work of repression that
the American state is forbidden to do but does anyway. In other words, *pace* Mill
and contemporary civil libertarians, we must understand the repressive acts of the
state and civil society not as an either/or but as a joint venture. Each sector—public and private—has a role to play. There is no orchestrated or informal conspiracy
to make the state and civil society play these parts; it is just that given the constitutional limitations on state action, those who would silence dissent are often com-
pelled to find other instruments of coercion. And thus far, civil libertarians have not
done enough to deny these instruments to the forces of repression.

In addition, as I will show, what has been most effective in silencing dissent is
not so much particular acts of repression by the state or civil society—whether indefinite detentions or vigilante assaults, vague and over-broad laws like the USA
Patriot Act or social ostracism—but the *fear* that those acts arouse in targeted and
nontargeted populations. In other words, while particular acts may silence particular individuals, what makes those acts truly lethal is their effect on the other men
and women who associate or are likely to associate with those targeted individuals.
Like civil society vis-à-vis the state, fear does the work—or enhances the work—of
repression, ensuring that specific incidents have a resonance and power extending
far beyond the incidents themselves.

I call these twin features of repression in the United States—the division of
labor between the state and civil society, and the fear that enhances or substitutes
for repression—"Fear, American Style." And, as I will show, the effects of "Fear,
American Style" are most visible today within communities of immigrants and citizens from the Middle East and South Asia, and in the workplace.

FROM MOROCCO TO MALAYSIA

By now, the facts of the federal government's domestic response to 9/11, insofar as it affects civil liberties within Middle Eastern and South Asian communities, is well known. Since 9/11, the government has rounded up over 1,200 immigrants, virtually all of them, as far as we know, men linked by birth or descent to any one of the countries lying between Morocco and Malaysia. According to the most recent press reports, not a single one of these men has been charged with a terrorism-related offense, much less membership in Al Qaeda or participation in the 9/11 attacks; indeed, most of these men were eventually released.[4] In November 2001, the Justice Department announced plans to interview 5,000 men—all of Middle Eastern descent or Muslim faith, all between the ages of eighteen and thirty-three. And then, in mid-March, the Justice Department announced that it planned to interview 3,000 additional men—this despite the fact that the Justice Department had just been forced to publicly admit that it was able to locate and interview fewer than half of the original pool of 5,000 and that, of those, only twenty were arrested, none on terrorism-related charges.[5] In addition, in late October, Congress passed and President Bush signed the USA Patriot Act, a 342-page piece of legislation that, among other provisions, broadens the definition of terrorism, expands the government's surveillance powers, imposes ideological immigration tests, and enhances the government's already considerable powers to detain and deport immigrants.[6]

As draconian as these measures are, however, they do not come close, in terms of numbers, either to the detention of Japanese Americans and Japanese immigrants during World War II or to the Red Scare following World War I, when the government rounded up some 10,000 men and women and deported about 600.[7] That the U.S. government has not resorted to such broad measures of coercion, at least not thus far, is testimony to the efforts of civil libertarians throughout the 20th century to curtail the powers of the state.

Despite this progress, the domestic response of the Bush administration provides little cause for celebration, for the comparatively low numbers of the current moment conceal the darker, more ironic truth of civil liberties in 20th-century America. As civil libertarians have managed to place some restraints upon a repressive state, the twin factors of fear and civil society have served as increasingly effective substitutes or supplements to state coercion. And this is no accident: Fear and civil society are not subject to the restrictions of the First, Fourth, Fifth, Sixth, Seventh, and Eighth Amendments. Fear is an individual passion, a response of persons to threatened or possible harm, and civil society is that arena of common life lying outside the state, at least in theory. Given that the Bill of Rights governs neither fear nor civil society, it stands to reason that both factors would play a more important role today than they might have in the past, when the state was given a freer hand.

McCarthy-era repression confirms the truth of this claim. Though McCarthyism was a time of intense repression, a careful scrutiny of how and where that repression took place reveals just how important civil society and fear were to the suppression of dissent. During the McCarthy era, approximately two hundred men and women spent time either in jail or in an INS detention center because of their views, usually for no more than one or two years, and few individuals were deported. By contrast, one to two of every five American employees at the time were subject to some kind of political investigation or loyalty test, and thousands lost their jobs because of their political beliefs and associations.[8] And though we remember McCarthyism as a time of rampant lawlessness, the fact is that most of the state's actions—its laws, its prosecutions and indictments, its trials and convictions—were carefully calibrated, targeting members of the Communist Party and its front groups. But even with all the checks and balances, even with all the legal exactitude and liberal nicety, fear enveloped broad swaths of the left, creating an atmosphere that stifled progressive dissent and restricted political activity—a fact that did not go unnoticed by the U.S. Supreme Court. Justice Felix Frankfurter, who fully supported the decision to prosecute the leadership of the Communist Party, understood perfectly well that due process was no protection against the spread of fear and, indeed, that fear would augment the repressive power of state action. As he wrote in his concurring opinion in *Dennis v United States*,

> Suppressing advocates of overthrow inevitably will also silence critics who do not advocate overthrow but fear that their criticism may be so construed. No matter how clear we may be that the defendants now before us are preparing to overthrow the Government at the propitious moment, it is self-delusion to think that we can punish them for their advocacy without adding to the risks run by loyal citizens who honestly believe in some of the reforms these defendants advance. It is a sobering fact that in sustaining the conviction before us we can hardly escape restriction on the interchange of ideas.[9]

In the face of loyalty investigations conducted in accordance with many of the canons of due process, hundreds of thousands, perhaps millions, of Americans—anyone leaning slightly to the left—were intimidated into silence. They simply did not want to attract the attention of the government. Political retreat seemed the proper, the safest, course of action. With the government and private employers administering tests asking men and women whether there was too much inequality of wealth, whether the blood supply of the Red Cross ought to be desegregated, or the poll tax eliminated[10]—and with affirmative answers to these questions eliciting government or employer suspicion of communist leanings[11]—the natural response of men and women was to either reply in the negative or refuse to take a position altogether. All it took was a few, fairly minimal government actions—plus the tremendous fear such action aroused, and the cooperation of civil society—to engineer a comprehensive political retreat.

Though the contemporary evidence is spotty, there is much to suggest that beneath today's headlines of state action, there lurks a subterranean economy of fear. A close reading of press reports about the domestic front of the war on terrorism indicates how even the most minimal actions by the state can arouse fear—and how civil society helps extend that fear. As one Palestinian man put it in November 2001, having lived in the United States for eleven years: "I'm scared to death. I don't want to stay in this country." Or, in the words of a man who claimed he was so desperate to return to Lebanon that he was willing to forgo a $15,000 deposit he had put on a home prior to September 11, "When it comes to safety, you don't care about money." According to these and other residents in the United States, the fear of repression has grown so great that many within the Middle Eastern community are planning to return to their home countries. Even some of those who are now citizens claim, in the words of one Jordanian American woman, "We planned to live here forever. But now I think we go back home, too."[12]

In a direct reprise of the McCarthy era, individuals within vulnerable immigrant communities have found that politically controversial—and even noncontroversial—statements or actions attract the attention of the authorities, leading other individuals to avoid making such statements or engaging in such actions. Take the case of Mohammad Yaseen Haider, a young Pakistani student at the University of Oklahoma, who in November 2001 found himself locked up in an INS detention center. Haider, president of the university's Pakistan Student Association, was being held on immigration charges but, in a classic case of slightly less than six degrees of separation, was thought to have some information about Zacarias Moussaoui, the suspected 20th 9/11 hijacker. Haider had once lived next door to two University of Oklahoma students, one of whom had once lived with Moussaoui. Despite the fact that Haider was connected to Moussaoui only by the most circuitous links of geography, the authorities held Haider for questioning. But what was truly chilling, from a civil libertarian point of view, was how Haider came to the attention of the authorities in the first place. It was not that his former neighbors provided his name to the FBI. Nor was he on any list of suspects. Rather, it was that Haider had complained to local police and university officials about an incident of racial harassment immediately following September 11. According to Haider, on September 16, three men had shouted racial epithets and assaulted him in the parking lot of a convenience store. His complaint caught the attention of FBI agents who thereupon requested copies of the complaint, connected the dots, and had Haider placed in an INS detention center.[13] For anyone in the Pakistani or immigrant communities, the moral of the story was clear: Be careful not to complain to the authorities, particularly about ethnic or other politically sensitive matters; it might land you in jail. Even though government officials surely did not intend to send such a message, their actions very likely had this effect.[14]

Immigrants who voice strong opinions on questions of foreign policy or politics have also attracted unwanted attention to themselves—often through collaboration between private citizens and FBI agents. In one case, a Bangladeshi Muslim taxicab driver in New York got into an argument with a passenger about Middle

Eastern politics and American foreign policy. Afterward, apparently having found
the strong political talk of the cab driver suspicious, the passenger called the authorities, who discovered that the driver's immigration documents were not fully in
order. According to Mamnunul Haq, an organizer with the New York Taxi Workers Alliance, the driver has since disappeared, and his friends assume that he is now
being held in an INS detention center.[15] In another case, two FBI agents visited
Ramzi Zakharia, a Palestinian living in Jersey City, after, they claimed, they discovered that he had posted "subversive comments" about U.S. foreign policy on a
web site.[16] Statements deemed critical, subversive, or unpatriotic have consistently
brought particular individuals to the attention of the FBI or the INS. And no matter how minimal the state's actions are in response—or whether the state ultimately
prosecutes these individuals—the fact that politically suspect speech occasions government attention can only lead men and women to be much more careful about
what they do and say.[17]

Even the much-heralded noncoercive "interviews" conducted by the government can arouse fear in this manner. While civil libertarians debate whether the interviews are truly voluntary, virtually no one has pointed out that even the most
noncoercive discussions between the government and vulnerable populations will
have the negative side-effect of discouraging political dissent and argument. In
published guidelines issued by the Justice Department, field agents conducting the
interviews were instructed to "ask the individual if he noticed anybody who reacted
in a surprising or inappropriate way to the news of the Sept. 11 attacks." Agents
were also told to "ask him how he felt when he heard the news."[18] What constituted an "inappropriate" response was not spelled out, but presumably it included
anything from hailing the collapse of the World Trade Center to insufficiently condemning Osama bin Laden to criticizing Israel or claiming that it was high time for
Americans to review their foreign policy. The upshot of such questions, claimed
several individuals, was either withdrawal from the Arab American community,
particularly on campuses, or abject fear. As one Palestinian man in Los Angeles put
it, after being contacted by the FBI for questioning: "I'm left with this feeling of
not knowing what they want from me. If I'm being watched, if they'll come to my
house and tell my daughters that the F.B.I. wants to talk to me. You stay in a very
emotional state, not knowing what's going on."[19]

Lest the notion of fear aroused by minimal government action sound hyper-
bolic, consider the experience of the Muslim community in San Diego, one of the
largest in the country. In December 2001, Mohadar Mohamed Abdoulah, a
Yemeni resident in San Diego, was granted $500,000 bail after being detained for
two months as a material witness and for having lied on his asylum application.
Initially, the local community rallied to Abdoulah's cause, pledging, according to
his lawyers, $400,000 for his bail fund with promises to raise more. But then it was
announced that each person who contributed to Abdoulah's bail fund would have
to provide his or her name to the government and perhaps appear before the judge.
"When people were told they'd have to go to court and answer questions from the

judge," said Abdoulah's lawyer, "they chilled out." "One day," added the lawyer, "it's all about solidarity and standing tall. Then they run. This community isn't split. This is about abject fear." A colleague of Abdoulah's observed, "Even people who do know him well and support him are worried because they don't want to be stigmatized. . . . They have families and houses and things. They don't want all that sabotaged because they are associated with this."[20]

The repressive roles of fear and civil society were brought home to me in November 2001 while I was addressing a largely Pakistani audience at a community center in Brooklyn, not far from where I live. I had been asked to speak about civil liberties post-9/11, and with me on the panel was a young law professor of Middle Eastern descent. After explaining the policies of the Bush administration, the professor informed the audience that they should be careful about everything they did or said, everything they signed, every organization to which they gave money. He recommended that each person hire an attorney with whom he or she could consult before undertaking political activities. While this professor was obviously trying to be helpful, his well-taken advice was inadvertently a counsel of fear and repression. His essential message to the audience was that the safest course of action was to do and say nothing—which, given the current climate, is no doubt true, but nevertheless is not conducive to robust dissent or debate. To the extent that men and women followed his advice, this incident suggests that repression depends not just on the state but also on the thousands of well-meaning, influential individuals throughout civil society who urge caution and restraint upon their listeners and followers.

FEAR AT WORK

Of all the works on American political culture, probably none is more read—or cited—than Alexis de Tocqueville's *Democracy in America*. And with good reason. With his searing portrait of social conformity and informal coercion, Tocqueville managed to identify one of the key innovations of American democracy: the tendency of the state to subcontract repression to civil society, which he called the tyranny of the majority. But while many students know Tocqueville's account of the tyranny of the majority, few are aware of the exchange between him and a Baltimore physician during his travels in America in the early 1830s—an exchange that attests to the politically repressive role of work in the United States. When Tocqueville asked his interlocutor why there were so few atheists among "the enlightened classes," he was told that avowed nonbelievers would find their careers ruined.[21] Tocqueville never did much with this information. But as we examine the current state of civil liberties, we need to be mindful of just how coercive an institution the workplace can be—not just in terms of the tremendous power that employers wield over employees in matters peculiar to the workplace, but in matters pertaining to their political beliefs and actions as well.[22]

Since 9/11, the most high-profile case of the suppression of political dissent has been that of ABC television host Bill Maher. After making disparaging comments about the cowardice of American troops relative to that of the 9/11 hijackers, Maher, host of *Politically Incorrect*, was forced to make a televised statement renouncing his heresy. Though his subsequent commentary about the war on terrorism was generally supportive, his show was ultimately canceled. While Maher's experience was held up as an example of intolerance and wartime hysteria, no one pointed out the obvious connection in this case between the workplace and repression. The pressure for Maher to recant came from advertising sponsors and local affiliates, who explained to ABC network heads that they would no longer sponsor or broadcast *Politically Incorrect* if Maher did not retract his statements, a message that Maher's employers then conveyed to their star employee. It was a classic case, familiar to any historian of the McCarthy-era blacklist, of television's iron triangle—the repressive links among corporate sponsors, network executives, and show producers—at work.[23] What makes such repression possible is the economic power employers have over their employees, even over employees like Maher who have considerable resources and power of their own.

For a time, the Maher inquisition was the flashpoint of a burgeoning national discussion about the suppression of political dissent,[24] but that discussion subsided long before anyone asked the logical question raised by the case: If someone of Maher's stature could so easily be put down by his employers through threats of economic sanctions, how would everyday workers fare, politically, in their workplaces? Millions of men and women go to work everyday, and though it's not a well-known fact, the overwhelming majority of them have no legal right to free speech on the job. While employers are legally forbidden to hire, fire, or discipline men and women on the basis of race, sex, religion, age, and national origin, they can, with full legal impunity, discipline, fire, or refuse to hire men and women on the basis of their political beliefs, statements, and activities. Without the protection of a union contract—a privilege currently enjoyed by less than 15 percent of the working population—men and women have no legally enforceable right of free speech on the job.[25] It is for that reason that the workplace has historically been a critical instrument for the suppression of dissent. And though the evidence of contemporary workplace repression has thus far been sparse (given the secrecy of what happens behind the proverbial factory gates, how could the evidence be anything but?), I suspect that the workplace may again become an important weapon in the suppression of dissent.

In this regard, two kinds of workplaces merit particularly close scrutiny: the media and academia. Twin pillars of the culture industry, the media and the university play a critical role in shaping public and elite opinion, and thus are the front lines in the state's battle to formulate a sense of cohesive purpose and national identity, particularly during wartime. As Thomas Hobbes wrote more than four centuries ago, "The core of rebellion . . . are the Universities; which nevertheless are not to be cast away, but to be better disciplined: that is to say, that the politics there taught be made to be (as true politics should be) such as are fit to make men know, that it is their duty to obey all laws whatsoever that shall by the authority of the King be enacted."[26] Or, as McCarthyite blacklisters, explaining the importance of radio, put it on the eve of the Korean War:

IN AN EMERGENCY (at any given time)
IT WOULD REQUIRE ONLY THREE PERSONS (subversives)
   one engineer in master control at a radio network
   one director in a radio studio
   one VOICE before a microphone
TO REACH 90 MILLION AMERICAN PEOPLE
with a message.[27]

Though many academics, journalists, and intellectuals understand the cultural power of their own institutions—indeed, complaining about and monitoring the political bias of the culture industries has become a cottage industry in its own right—they have not paid sufficient attention to the workplace coercion that enables these institutions to shape public opinion. Universities, newspapers, publishing houses, television networks, and movie studios may be enterprises that trade in ideas or prize creativity, but they are also coercive institutions of discipline, hierarchy, and authority. Journalists, professors, and screenwriters are the employees of editors, publishers, deans, and producers, and like all employers, editors and the like are willing to threaten sanctions to make sure that their employees propound correct doctrine. To understand how and why the culture industries—particularly the media—are today playing such an uncritical role in American political culture, we have to be mindful of the very real threats that dissenting writers, academics, and intellectuals face in the workplace—and the fear that those threats arouse among everyone else.

It's hardly news that since 9/11 the American media have been peddling almost unquestioning support for the U.S. war on terrorism. In October 2001, National Security Advisor Condoleezza Rice met with network heads from ABC, CBS, NBC, Fox, and CNN, instructing them in the proper protocol for airing the videotaped statements of Osama bin Laden, with which many complied. In late October, CNN chair Walter Isaacson announced that CNN staffers should pair any scene of civilian destruction in Afghanistan with reminders of the devastation of 9/11 and the cruelty of the Taliban. It "seems perverse," he said, "to focus too much on the casualties or hardship in Afghanistan." Fox anchor Brit Hume declared, "Civilian casualties are historically, by definition, a part of war, really. Should they be as big news as they've been?" NPR's Mara Liasson echoed Hume's remarks: "Look, war is about killing people. Civilian casualties are unavoidable." And finally, in November 2001, Fairness and Accuracy In Reporting (FAIR) issued a detailed study documenting the decidedly pro-U.S. and militaristic line emanating from the op-ed pages of the two most prestigious papers in the United States.

As Hume declared, "Look, neutrality as a general principle is an appropriate concept for journalists who are covering institutions of some comparable quality. This is a conflict between the United States and murdering barbarians."[28]

While some of this bias can be attributed to the media's residual horror over the attacks of 9/11 as well as to heartfelt jingoism, some of it is a response to pressure from without and above, which is then translated to staffers below. As was true during the McCarthy era, conservatives in government and civil society have managed to orchestrate pressure campaigns on media executives who then order their employees to proffer the proper line. After ABC News president David Westin told Columbia University journalism students that objectivity required him not to take a stand on the question of whether the Pentagon was a legitimate target for enemy attacks, conservative activists, including Rush Limbaugh, demanded that he issue an apology, which he immediately did. According to the *New York Times*, ABC executives acknowledged "that they were eager to stop an onslaught of negative public attention." Or, as Erik Sorenson, president of MSNBC, put it, "Any misstep and you can get into trouble with these guys and have the Patriotism police hunt you down." Even CNN's Isaacson, who is ideologically sympathetic to government strictures, has admitted that he and other executives are wary of provoking national public opinion. "In this environment it feels slightly different," he said. "If you get on the wrong side of public opinion, you are going to get into trouble."[29]

While top media execs have openly confessed that fear—their fear, that is, of powerful constituencies and political elites—dictates their coverage, there has been far less reporting on how that fear is then translated down to employees and staffers. This is, of course, no surprise, since large corporations—including the media—are notoriously unwilling to air their dirty laundry in public. Nevertheless, one little-noticed report in 2001 may provide a window on the coercive employment mechanisms that help reproduce media bias. On October 31 of that year, Ray Glenn, chief copy editor of the *Panama City News Herald* in Florida, issued a memo to newspaper staffers that read in part:

> Per Hal's [executive editor Hal Foster] order, DO NOT USE photos on Page 1A showing civilian casualties. Our sister paper in Fort Walton Beach has done so and received hundreds and hundreds of threatening e-mails and the like. Also per Hal's order, DO NOT USE wire stories which lead with civilian casualties from the U.S. war on Afghanistan. They should be mentioned further down in the story. If the story needs rewriting to play down the civilian casualties, DO IT. The only exception is if the U.S. hits an orphanage, school or similar facility and kills scores or hundreds of children.[30]

And then, as if the editor had not made the imperative for censorship sufficiently clear, he concluded the memo with the following: "Failure to follow any of these or other standing rules could put your job in jeopardy."[31] Thus, hovering over each writer's and editor's decisions about editorial content is the possibility of being fired or demoted—and, again, without a union, there is nothing any writer or editor can do to protest that.

It's impossible to know whether the case of the *Panama City News Herald* is typical or not, whether it is particular to small-town newspapers or applies to major national newspapers as well. Within weeks of 9/11, there were two reports of journalists at newspapers in Texas and Oregon being fired for dissenting statements they made or wrote, but since then, there have been virtually no additional reports.[32] This could be because people in the media have genuinely come to be convinced of the virtue of the war on terrorism and therefore do not voice dissenting sentiments, or it could be because the early cases of firing and threats were enough to scare them off from making any controversial comments. These explanations are not mutually exclusive: Inner conviction—or at least inner doubt about the legitimacy of opposing the government—and fear often work hand in hand. But we should not be too quick to dismiss the possibility that most men and women who work in the media have simply internalized the dominant codes of legitimate discussion in order to avoid censure or sanction. For even an established journalist like Michael Kinsley has confessed that

> John Ashcroft can relax because people have been listening to their Inner Ashcroft. I know this for a fact because I'm one of them. As a writer and editor, I have been censoring myself and others quite a bit since September 11. By "censoring" I mean deciding not to write or publish things for reasons other than my own judgment of their merits. What reasons? Sometimes it has been a sincere feeling that an ordinarily appropriate remark is inappropriate at this extraordinary moment. Sometimes it is genuine respect for readers who might feel that way even if I don't. But sometimes it is simple cowardice.[33]

If journalists of Kinsley's stature are afraid to dissent, it seems unlikely that lowly newsroom staffers who face the threat—whether overt or covert—of firing on a daily basis would not be as well.

As for academia, one story out of UCLA best captures, I think, the real dilemmas facing university employees. For while senior professors enjoy the protections of tenure,[34] junior and adjunct faculty (increasingly the majority of instructional staff at institutions of higher education) and university staff (that often-forgotten sector of the university workforce, which includes librarians, secretaries, electricians, janitors, laboratory technicians, and the like) enjoy none of those protections. And it is these groups, naturally, that are most vulnerable to sanctions and threats. On September 14, 2001, for example, UCLA suspended library assistant Jonnie Hargis for a week without pay after he sent out an e-mail denouncing American foreign policy, particularly U.S. support for Israel and the bombing of Iraq. Hargis had been responding to a colleague's e-mail praising U.S. foreign policy. UCLA charged Hargis with "contribut[ing] to a hostile and threatening environment," but the university did not file similar charges against the sender of the

original e-mail. Luckily, Hargis had a union and was able to file and win a grievance against the university.[35] But, as is true of so much of the American workplace,
most university employees do not enjoy the protections of unions—or tenure.
Given the centrality of political discussion on academic campuses, it stands to reason that many university employees will find themselves facing disciplinary charges
similar to those Hargis faced—and will conclude that silence is the better course to
follow.[36]

WHOSE SECURITY? WHOSE FREEDOM?

Since 9/11, one of the most commonly heard refrains is that we need to strike a
new balance between the demands of security and of freedom. Throughout the
20th century, we are told, Americans were relatively safe from foreign attack, but
now the illusion of total security has come to an end, and so must our hard-won
freedoms. I'd like to close by suggesting that this notion is misleading and does not
seriously address the problems and challenges that civil liberties in America are currently facing. For when politicians and pundits, security experts and civil libertarians, speak of the need for a new balance to be struck, they look at the state's measures—the USA Patriot Act, the detentions, and the like—without looking at their
impact on targeted populations. Freedom, in other words, is measured by the specific details of state policies, not by their consequences. Most discussants do not
take into account how the government's measures have generated a fear of dissent
within vulnerable communities, nor do they consider the role of repression in the
private sector. By confining themselves to a debate about the formalities of new
laws, discussants fail to see just how extensive the climate of fear and the impact of
repression truly are and can be. And this failure leaves civil libertarians floundering
when asked why any American should care about civil liberties given that the administration has freed many of the detainees, has hardly used the USA Patriot Act
thus far, has liberalized the rules of the military tribunals, and so on.[37] Thus, without taking into account at least some of the evidence presented in the present chapter, the discussion regarding new balances between freedom and security will remain hopelessly out of touch with reality.

But there are two other reasons to be suspicious of this algebra of freedom and
security. First, when pundits and politicians talk about new balances, they use the
words *we* and *our*: *We* need to strike a new balance between *our* freedom and *our*
security. *We* need to give up some of *our* liberty for the sake of *our* security. But the
pundits don't really mean *we* and *our*. After all, white Americans like myself are not
going to give up any freedom. I am not going to have to sit in an INS jail for
months on end or submit to interviews with the FBI, be a subject of racial profiling, or face deportation. What the pundits and politicians really mean is that the
costs of *my* freedom and *my* security—and that of the white majority—will be

born by people who are Middle Eastern and South Asian, or, as one reporter who studied post-9/11 racial profiling at the Los Angeles Airport discovered, by the usual suspects in America: black and brown people.[38]

If we are going to have a serious discussion about security and freedom in this country, we need to start with a different set of questions. Who is going to bear the cost for *all* of our freedoms and *all* of our security? How can we ensure that those costs are borne equally—by citizens and residents, by the native-born and immigrants, by Middle Easterners and midwesterners? If this means longer lines at airports so that everyone's bags and effects are thoroughly searched—and Middle Easterners are not profiled—so be it. If it means a national ID card, so be it.[39] The bottom line is that whatever we do to promote security, it must be the product not of an abstract discussion about freedom versus protection but of a concrete discussion regarding the equitable distribution of costs and benefits.

Second, it's high time that civil libertarians challenged the false *political* dichotomy of freedom versus security. For too long, civil libertarians and people on the left have accepted the notion that *we* care about rights and principles, while *they*—the Right, the statists, the Demopublicans—care about security. We care about expression, they care about protection. We care about freedom, they care about order. The problem with this dichotomy is that it relegates danger and security, protection and safety, to the status of nonpolitical goods. It assumes that danger is pretty much what Oliver Wendell Holmes thought it was when he invoked in *Schenck v United States* that famous metaphor of a man falsely shouting fire in a crowded theater: Danger, in other words, becomes an obvious, non-negotiable, indubitable threat to the well-being of an entire community, which allows no time for argument, deliberation, or discussion.

But danger in politics is not the equivalent of falsely shouting fire in a crowded theater. Danger—and, more important, how we respond to danger—is and should be something we argue about, something we aggressively debate. Is the war on terrorism really making us safer? Not if we take into account the genuine anger it seems to be arousing in the Muslim world. Are military tribunals and the death penalty conducive to bringing terrorists to justice in the United States? Not if we consider those European countries that refuse to extradite to the United States suspects who might be facing execution. Are round-ups, detentions, and racial profiling bringing us security? Not if we take note of the Arab immigrants who are fleeing the United States, going back to their homes in the Middle East where they will present this country in a less-than-flattering light. And if the Bush administration is truly committed to the security of all Americans, why did it stall for months on any serious investigation of the failure of U.S. intelligence agencies prior to 9/11? Why is it that when it comes to rollbacks of constitutional guarantees, there is no time to be wasted, but when it comes to marshaling information so that we can improve our intelligence policies, we can wait another day?

Domestic and national security, it turns out, are as political as Social Security. Like all political questions, security requires argument and debate—and that means more freedom, more dissent, not less. Those of us who are civil libertarians have to make the case that we need freedom today more than ever—not because it outweighs security but precisely because it offers the only real path to security. We need freedom and robust debate in order to press the case that the Bush administration's policies will make us less secure, less safe—that in the end, Bush's policies will harm us, not protect us. And to make that case effectively, we need more freedom, not less.

In the past, civil libertarians and liberals have been notoriously reluctant to argue that rights and liberties are valuable or worthy for any reason beyond the individual voices that rights and liberties protect. Rights, in the civil liberties paradigm, protect individuals; when rights are betrayed, it is individuals who are harmed. Society, in this view, is affected by such infringements only insofar as its principles of fairness and justice are compromised; society itself—its well-being, its security, its interests—is not substantively threatened by such infringements.

If civil libertarians are going to make an effective case to the public about the danger of the Bush administration's policies, they must abandon this way of thinking about rights and liberties. As this chapter has demonstrated, infringements on rights don't just affect particular individuals; they have a chilling effect on political discussion throughout society. Violations of rights harm society by narrowing the political spectrum, by limiting what can be said. And this narrowing of discussion is harmful not because diversity or dissent is good in the abstract but because the views that are being exiled or marginalized are critical to our collective security and advancement. If they are going to be politically effective, civil libertarians must make the case that civil liberties ought to be upheld for the sake of living and for the sake of living well.

NOTES

1. On November 20, 2001, the American-Arab Anti-Discrimination Committee issued a report titled "The Condition of Arab Americans Post 9/11," which cited 520 hate crimes, including 6 murders, directed against Arab Americans, "or those perceived to be such," and "several hundred cases of employment discrimination . . . including numerous terminations." While some subsequent press reports have called these numbers into question, other press reports have brought to light even more extensive, and more subtle, forms of discrimination and harassment, particularly in the workplace. But regardless of the truth of these reports, there is no doubt that talk of harassment pervaded the political atmosphere of post–9/11 America, making for a climate of fear among vulnerable populations. See American-Arab Anti-Discrimination Committee, "The Condition of Arab Americans Post 9/11" (11/20/01), available online at http://www.adc.org/adc/index.php?id=99; "Sept. 11 Backlash Murders and the State of Hate," *Washington Post* (January 20, 2002), p. A3; and Mary Beth Sheridan, "Backlash Changes Form, Not Function," *Washington Post* (March 4, 2002), p. B1.

2. Indeed, almost all of the commentary about the state of civil liberties, post–9/11,

has focused on state coercion rather than social coercion. For two representative examples, see Ronald Dworkin, "The Threat to Patriotism," *New York Review of Books* (February 28, 2002), pp. 44–49; and Bruce Ackerman, "Don't Panic," *London Review of Books* (February 7, 2002).

3. John Stuart Mill, *On Liberty*, ed. Stefan Collini (New York: Cambridge University Press, 1989), p. 8.

4. Peter Ford, "Legal War on Terror Lacks Weapons," *Christian Science Monitor* (March 27, 2002); Tamar Lewin, "Accusations Against 93 Vary Widely," *New York Times* (November 28, 2001), p. B6; David Firestone and Christopher Drew, "Al Qaeda Link Seen in Only a Handful of 1,200 Detainees," *New York Times* (November 29, 2001), p. A1.

5. Philip Shenon, "Justice Dept. Wants to Query More Foreigners," *New York Times* (March 21, 2002), p. A19.

6. For an excellent analysis of the act, see Nancy Chang, *Silencing Political Dissent: How Post–September 11 Antiterrorism Measures Threaten Our Civil Liberties* (Boston: Seven Stories Press, 2002).

7. William Preston, Jr., *Aliens and Dissenters: Federal Suppression of Radicals, 1903–1933* (New York: Harper and Row, 1963), p. 221; Robert K. Murray, *Red Scare: A Study in National Hysteria, 1919–1920* (New York: McGraw-Hill, 1955), p. 251; Robert Justin Goldstein, *Political Repression in Modern America: From 1870 to the Present* (Cambridge, Mass.: Schenkman Publishing, 1978), pp. 156, 160.

8. Ellen W. Schrecker, *Many Are the Crimes: McCarthyism in America* (Boston: Little, Brown, 1998), pp. 361, 532; Ralph S. Brown, Jr., *Loyalty and Security: Employment Tests in the United States* (New Haven: Yale University Press, 1958), p. 181; Griffin Fariello, *Red Scare: Memories of the American Inquisition* (New York: Avon Books, 1995), p. 43.

9. *Dennis et al. v United States* (341 U.S. 494).

10. Nora Sayre, *Running Time: Films of the Cold War* (New York: Dial Press, 1982), p. 11; Schrecker, *Many Are the Crimes*, p. 282.

11. As the chair of one loyalty board put it, "Of course, the fact that a person believes in racial equality doesn't *prove* that he's a Communist, but it certainly makes you look twice, doesn't it. You can't get away from the fact that racial equality is part of the Communist line." Quoted in Schrecker, *Many Are the Crimes*, p. 282.

12. Greg Winter, "Some Mideast Immigrants, Shaken, Ponder Leaving U.S.," *New York Times* (November 23, 2001), p. B1.

13. Jo Thomas, "Hearing for Pakistani Student," *New York Times* (November 15, 2001), p. B6.

14. Not long after Haider's story was reported by the *New York Times*, the Oklahoma press revealed that Haider was himself no boy scout and might well have been, among other things, a pathological liar. In October, Haider allegedly tried to induce a woman he met in an Internet chat room to spend the night with him. When she refused, he allegedly e-mailed her the following two messages: "I HATE YOU SLUT WOMAN I WANT YOU OUT OF MY LIFE" and "I WILL SEND YOU ANTHRAX IN THE MAIL AND BIN LADEN WILL HUNT YOU DOWN MUHAHAHAHAHAH." On October 18, Haider contacted the local FBI, claiming that someone had hacked into his computer and sent these messages. After being detained by the government on November 8 for immigration violations (the government had been watching Haider ever since mid-September, when he filed his hate crimes complaint), Haider allegedly confessed to the FBI that he did in fact send the e-mail messages and had lied to the government after he heard Attorney General John Ashcroft announce that the Justice Department would prosecute anyone perpetrating anthrax scares or hoaxes. On December 13, the INS ordered Haider deported for violating the terms of his visa by working off-cam-

pus, but one week later, he was indicted for lying to the FBI. Subsequent revelations indicated that Haider also had been accused of stalking and indecent exposure, and in January 2002, his accusations of being harassed after 9/11 were publicly called into question. As of April 2002, Haider was still on trial for lying to the FBI. None of these allegations and revelations about Haider, however, challenge my basic point that the government's actions discourage immigrants from raising politically sensitive complaints. See Randy Ellis, "Pakistani Student Indicted on Lie About Anthrax Threat," *Daily Oklahoman* (December 21, 2001); Nolan Clay and Randy Ellis, "OU Student Admitted Lying About Anthrax, Officer Says," *Daily Oklahoman* (January 3, 2002); Ryan Chittum, "U. Oklahoma Student Readmitted After Threat of Lawsuit," *Oklahoma Daily* (January 17, 2002); Randy Ellis, "Judge Rules Pakistani's Confession Not Coerced," *Daily Oklahoman* (March 13, 2002).

15. Chisun Lee, "Manhunt Puts Middle Easterners at Mercy of Ordinary Americans," *Village Voice* (January 29, 2002), p. 45.

16. Ironically, the statement from Zakharia that convinced the FBI that he was not dangerous was his admission that he was gay and Muslim. "If the Taliban knew about me," Zakharia said, "I'd be on their top 10 list." Being the target of Islamic repression, in other words, saved him from being a target of American repression. See Robert F. Worth, "Gay Muslims Face a Growing Challenge Reconciling Their Two Identities," *New York Times* (January 13, 2002), p. 30.

17. Of course, members of immigrant communities are not the only ones who have been subject to this kind of surveillance and harassment. There have also been many reports of American citizens making comments critical of the United States, only to find themselves subsequently questioned by the FBI or local police authorities. Again, regardless of what happens to these individuals, the message is the same: Wherever one goes, the government has eyes and ears. See Nat Hentoff, "J. Edgar Hoover Lives!" *Village Voice* (February 19, 2002), p. 37; Nat Hentoff, "Eyeing What You Read," *Village Voice* (February 26, 2002), p. 25; Nat Hentoff, "Big John Wants Your Reading List," *Village Voice* (March 5, 2002), p. 27; Matthew Rothschild, "Red Squad Hits Denver," *The Progressive* (March 14, 2002); Ann Davis, Maureen Tkacik, and Andrea Petersen, "Nation of Tipsters Answers FBI's Call," *Wall Street Journal* (November 21, 2001); Matthew Rothschild, "An Olympic Experience," *The Progressive* (March 27, 2002); David Rosenbaum, "Competing Principles Leave Some Professionals Debating Responsibility to Government," *New York Times* (November 23, 2001), p. B7; Matthew Rothschild, "Don't Criticize Bush at Your Gym," *The Progressive* (December 19, 2001); Matthew Rothschild, "If You Don't Want American Flag Stamps, Watch Out!" *The Progressive* (December 8, 2001).

18. Jodi Wilgoren, "Michigan 'Invites' Men from Mideast to Be Interviewed," *New York Times* (November 27, 2001), p. A1.

19. Danny Hakim, "Inquiries Put Mideast Men in Spotlight," *New York Times* (November 16, 2001), p. B10; Greg Winter, "F.B.I. Visits Provoke Waves of Worry in Middle Eastern Men," *New York Times* (November 16, 2001), p. B1.

20. James Sterngold, "Muslims in San Diego Waver on Bail Pledge," *New York Times* (December 9, 2001), p. B6.

21. George Wilson Pierson, *Tocqueville in America* (Baltimore: Johns Hopkins Press, 1938/1996), p. 500.

22. For two recent—and rather harrowing—accounts of workplace coercion, see Barbara Ehrenreich, *Nickel and Dimed: On (Not) Getting By in Boom-Time America* (New York: Metropolitan Books, 2001); and Jill Andresky Fraser, *White-Collar Sweatshop: The Deterioration of Work and Its Rewards in Corporate America* (New York: Norton, 2001). Also see my review essay, "Denied the Fruits of Their Labors," *Dissent* (Fall 2001), pp. 131–135.

23. John Cogley, *Report on Blacklisting II: Radio—Television* (Fund for the Republic, 1956).

24. See Leslie Bennetts, "One Nation, One Mind?" *Vanity Fair* (December 2001), pp. 176–182.

25. Wayne N. Outten, Robert J. Rabin, and Lisa R. Lipman, *The Rights of Employees and Union Members*, 2nd ed. (Carbondale: Southern Illinois University Press, 1994), p. 20.

26. Thomas Hobbes, *Behemoth* (Chicago: University of Chicago Press, 1990), p. 58.

27. Cogley, *Report on Blacklisting II*, p. 15.

28. Jim Rutenberg and Bill Carter, "Network Coverage a Target of Fire from Conservatives," *New York Times* (November 7, 2001), p. B2; "Networks Accept Government 'Guidance,'" FAIR Media Advisory (October 12, 2001); "CNN Says Focus on Civilian Casualties Would Be 'Perverse,'" FAIR Media Advisory (November 1, 2001); "Op-Ed Echo Chamber: Little Space for Dissent to the Military Line," FAIR Media Advisory (November 2, 2001); "Fox: Civilian Casualties Not News," FAIR Media Advisory (November 8, 2001); Project for Excellence in Journalism, "Return to Normalcy?" (January 28, 2002), available online at http://www.journalism.org/publ_research/normalcy3.html.

29. Rutenberg and Carter, "Network Coverage a Target of Fire from Conservatives," p. B2; Alessandra Stanley, "Opponents of War Are Scarce on Television," *New York Times* (November 9, 2001), p. B4.

30. The memo's full text is available online at http://www.poynter.org/medianews/memos.htm.

31. Available online at http://www.poynter.org/medianews/memos.htm.

32. See National Coalition Against Censorship, "Free Expression After September 11th," available online at http://www.ncac.org/issues/freex911.html.

33. Michael Kinsley, "Listening to Our Inner Ashcroft," *Washington Post* (January 4, 2002), p. A27.

34. However, in the well-publicized case of Sami Al-Arian, a tenured University of South Florida engineering professor who is a refugee from Palestine, tenure has not guaranteed immunity from firing; Al-Arian's union is currently appealing the decision. It should also be noted that senior professors, like senior journalists such as Kinsley, are often afraid to dissent because they fear the loss of professional prestige or the loss of research funding and special privileges from university deans and so forth. See Eric Boehlert, "The Prime-Time Smearing of Sami Al-Arian," *Salon* (January 19, 2002); Jonathan Kaufman, "University of South Florida Decides to Fire Tenured Professor Linked to Terror Group," *Wall Street Journal* (December 20, 2001), p. A18; and American Federation of Teachers, "Union Takes on Academic Freedom in Florida," *On Campus* (March 2002), p. 3.

35. "College Staff Find Chilling Free Speech Climate," AP Wire Service (October 15, 2001); David Glenn, "The War on Campus," *The Nation* (December 3, 2001).

36. Emily Eakin, "On the Lookout for Patriotic Incorrectness," *New York Times* (November 24, 2001), p. A15. For cases of repression within secondary schools, see National Coalition Against Censorship, "Free Expression After September 11th," available online at http://www.ncac.org/issues/freex911.html.

37. As *The New Yorker*'s Jeffrey Toobin reports, "In recent months, debate over the civil-liberties aspect of the anti-terrorism policy has become somewhat muted. 'What concerns me most is that the new law is so broad and indiscriminate,' Ronald Dworkin, a professor of law at New York University, said. 'It gives them a discretion to charge people with crimes that I think they shouldn't have.' But even critics like Dworkin recognize that the Administration has not yet used its new authority in untoward ways. 'The motive seems to be to draw it as widely as we can and then decide down the road how broadly we are going to use it,' he said. 'They're saying, "Trust us," but the time to worry

about it is not later but now.'" See Jeffrey Toobin, "Ashcroft's Ascent," *The New Yorker* (April 15, 2002), p. 61.

38. Ben Ehrenreich, "Boarding Games," *LA Weekly* (February 22, 2002), p. 24.

39. It should be pointed out, of course, that neither of these proposed measures truly addresses the two main issues underlying the security dilemma in the United States: First, the United States needs to drastically revise its foreign and defense policies in order to minimize the amount of hatred it stirs up in much of the world; and, second, 9/11 was the result not of expansive civil liberties and freedoms but of the massive failure of the U.S. intelligence community to respond to real warning signs. Since 9/11, there has been no credible evidence presented, to my knowledge, demonstrating that the hijackers were able to profit from generous freedoms, but there has been significant evidence attesting to the negative effects of incompetent, turf-obsessed bureaucrats.

5

The Globalization of Violence in the 21st Century

Israel, Palestine, and the War on Terror

HEATHER GAUTNEY

French Press "Isn't it cowardly to use your women's baskets to carry bombs that have killed so many innocent people?"
M'Hidi "And you? Is it less cowardly to drop your napalm on defenseless villages, killing thousands more? With planes, it would have been easier for us. Let us have your bombers and you can have our women's baskets."

PONTECORVO'S *THE BATTLE OF ALGIERS*

INTRODUCTION

Violence is the substance of the 21st-century world order, an order marked by its close proximity to pure war. In the second half of the 20th century, war remained somewhat limited to the Cold War battlefields of the Third World; the machinery of war and the proliferation of weapons of mass destruction were deterrent by nature, as the specter of holistic destruction loomed in the fore. The expanse of a disciplinary mode of social organization and the domestication of all species toward world order sought to reconcile the dialectic of assault and defense into the smooth function and peaceful coexistence characteristic of pure war: Quick-handed intervention and preemptive policing continues to allow for violation without a human face. More recently, however, war has shown itself to be less territorially bound and less "humanist." The speed through which war operated in the Gulf and initially in Afghanistan is being matched by a chaotic stream of fits and starts as paramilitary installations scan the globe for Al Qaeda, Israeli Defense

Forces (IDF) plunder villages and refugee camps in the West Bank, and civil war continues to erupt in Afghanistan. Like diplomacy, quick-handed military solutions—the air assault and precision weaponry—appear inadequate to deal with such conflict.

The attack on the World Trade Center and the subsequent War on Terror demonstrate a crisis of world order and its desire to contain reckless violence (cruelty, "the specifically human aspect of war"[1]). The post–Cold War battlefields extended to the insulated ground of the United States with a disastrous human toll, which appears to have stimulated a steady unraveling of world order via localized events throughout the globe. The Palestinian Intifada; the turmoil in Argentina, Venezuela, and Kashmir; and the increasing threat of "terrorism" have posed a series of intermittent and diffuse interruptions at various points within the system in a generalized disruption of the legitimacy of the United States as the sole superpower. The repeated deployment of despotic regimes around the world to police U.S. investments—from Hussein to bin Laden—has blown back[2] with effects that remain, especially now, uncertain. These challenges to U.S. supremacy may foreshadow events to come. The Bush administration has promised a prolonged War on Terror, including police actions in Iraq and other "terrorist-harboring" countries, that is likely to introduce a more generalized insecurity into the already unsteady currents of globalization.

POWER, LEGITIMACY, AND GLOBAL VIOLENCE

In "On Violence," Hannah Arendt distinguishes between justification and legitimacy in terms of power and the use of violence. For Arendt, violence is always instrumental; it is always a means to an end. Power, on the other hand, is an end in itself. Power rests on legitimacy, which appeals to the past, while violence and its justification, situated within a means-end schema, is directed toward the future. For her, "[v]iolence can be justifiable, but it never will be legitimate"; it can never lead to power, and it only "appears where power is in jeopardy" (Arendt, 1972, 151). Arendt's concept of legitimacy rests on the liberal notion of power as based on the consent of the people, who, although they sacrifice their autonomy, retain the right to challenge the authority of the state when it fails to serve their interests. However, power relations—the politics—of the contemporary world order tend to operate through a continuum of violence, the common substance through which various modes of power manifest. Gilles Deleuze articulates the tendency of world order toward pure violence vis-à-vis Clausewitz: Whereas war may once have been a continuation of politics by other means, the relation now operates in reverse. In the new world order, the "war machine" takes peace, security, and order as its object, and seeks to flatten opposition and alternatives into its one-dimensional order: "The world became a smooth space again . . . over which reigned a single war machine, even when it opposed its own parts. Wars had become part of peace. More than that, the States no longer appropriated the war machine; they reconstituted a war machine of which they themselves were only the parts" (Deleuze, 1987, 467).

Deleuze's rendition is associated with Virilio's concept of "pure war," marked by "the exponential development of military science and technique, which obviously aim not toward the multiplication of violent exchanges, but toward their disappearance—*a kind of absolute colonization*" (Virilio, 1990, 32; original emphasis). Virilio details the character of this arrangement, including how the war machine "finds its new object in the absolute peace of terror or deterrence"; terrifies, by warrant of the sinister character of its peace; and operates against an "unspecified enemy" (Deleuze, 1987, 467). Pure war is a post-human, technocratic order that

> is neither peace nor war; nor is it, as was believed, "absolute" or "total" war. Rather it is the military procedure itself, in its ordinary durability. The balance of terror, the nuclear coalition, peaceful co-existence—in short, the dissolution of the state of war and the military's infiltration into the movements of daily life—reproduce the metamorphosis of the hunter: from direct confrontation of the wild animal; to progressive control over the movements of certain species; then with the help of the dog, to guarding semi-wild flocks; and finally, to reproduction, breeding. Domestication is the logical outcome of prey. Atrocities, blows, wounds and bloodshed, in the final account, run counter to the unlimited use of violence. (Virilio, 1990, 35)

The "metamorphosis of the hunter" is a total transformation of the social body toward an end of politics, or a politics that acts "as a continuation of war by other means." The fundamentalist project—the holy war—is a form of such apolitical "justice," similar in its post-humanist tendency to the nuclear theocracy of pure war: an end of life by way of tragedy or spirituality.

Although the apolitical violence of pure war has not completely taken hold, it certainly informs the violence of the contemporary world order that operates through technics of surveillance and intervention combined with fundamentalist, imperial ethico-politics. Michael Hardt and Antonio Negri (2000, 9, 18) articulate the mechanisms through which Empire enacts its "absolute peace of terror or deterrence" via a system of imperial "justice": Bush's Afghanistan, Sharon's Palestine, and Berlusconi's Genoa are just a few examples of its force. Empire relies on a "new inscription of authority and a new design of the production of norms and legal instruments of coercion" that are based on the integration of a universal ethics of order or "peace" and the ability to apply force *effectively*. Empire's violence justifies itself on the basis of an order that transcends the interests of states, and poses itself as the "humanitarian" protectorate of the species. Paul Virilio (2000, 52) has aptly exposed the "degenerate humanism" of Empire's ethico-political complex, fused into the war machinery itself: the one-hit-wonder air assault aimed at reducing military casualties while multiplying those of civilians, and nonlethal weapons (biological, chemical, etc.) with unknown, lasting effects.

Despite its successes in social engineering and military technoscience, Empire's constitution is a network of only fleeting alliances, a far cry from the "absolute colonization" it so desires. In the Middle East, Empire's regional alliances are routinely formed on the basis of economic interest and protectionism, aimed at stabilizing and sustaining a capitalist system largely fueled by oil. The U.S.-Israeli and U.S.-Saudi alliances are bases from which massive military installations and supplementary comprador regimes ebb and flow in the service of Empire. Much of the conflict in the region is a result of class antagonisms that are often smoothed over by way of force, rendering masses of civilians—many of which compose a permanent, nomadic underclass of exploited labor—both the subjects and objects of warfare. Low-level conflict, civil war, and the opportunistic deployment of U.S.-sponsored despotic regimes have been long-time tactics of Empire-building in the Middle East: Palestinian resistance has been used to justify Israeli land acquisition; Operation Desert Storm diminished the superfluous and, in some cases, nationalist (pan-Arab) labor force and solidified U.S. military presence in the Gulf;[3] and in Afghanistan, the conflict between the Northern Alliance and the U.S.-trained Taliban as well as the War on Terror have provided the United States with an inroad to the otherwise remote Unocal pipeline.

The role of force in setting the global distribution of power creates an appearance of a world order increasingly directed toward pure violence, in which consent—materialized in elections, in consumptive habits, in a general lack of involvement—emerges as a hollow confirmation of the force of Empire. It is tacit consent as opposed to participation: an anti-democratic politics of order. The overwhelming presence of violence around the globe—from the threat of world destruction to police brutality to the technical supervision of everyday life—has not obliterated the power of the people as a legitimate force; however, it has seriously jeopardized the role of consent (and dissent) as a *necessary* constituent of legitimate power. Granted, Bush, Sharon, and Berlusconi were all voted into office (although Bush's electoral victory was highly questionable), yet their power, and that of their right- (and left-) wing colleagues, is inextricably linked to their ability to apply force effectively and to provide a semblance of security: from threats of terrorism, intensified immigration, economic devastation, dilution of national culture, and so on.

The ongoing Israeli-Palestinian conflict spotlights weaknesses in the U.S. program of Empire-building and its faltering attempt to enact world order through the use of unilateral, unabashed force in tandem with manifold ethico-political components. Although this conflict, in its current form, represents a mere disturbance in Empire's vast network of deployments—a micro-conflict—it is a notable one: It implicates not only the anti-politics of the War on Terror, which has been overappropriated as a war on opposition, but also the political ecology of Empire's version of globalization, which gentrifies territories at the behest of capital, while marginalizing and despoiling others, leaving entire enclaves of people denationalized.[4]

THE CASE OF ISRAEL AND PALESTINE

The U.S.-Israeli alliance was fashioned in the interests of oil—a necessary component in the smooth functioning of Empire. The ethico-politics of this alliance involves a fusion of ethno-nationalist values and geostrategy as the foundation for its legitimacy. Israel's socio-politics is first and foremost predicated on its program to establish and secure a pure Jewish state, a privilege of birthright (Genesis 17:8), of reparation (the Holocaust), and of divine right ("Palestine, a country without a people"). The U.S. agenda to establish an oil protectorate in the region coupled with Israel's ethno-nationalist objectives, seated within a predominantly Arab-populated territory, have led to a massive military buildup that serves both nations' geopolitical interests.

Historically, the Palestinian people have posed a threat to this program: The establishment of a Palestinian state—and the possibility of a Right of Return—has been positioned in opposition to Israel itself,[5] the fundamentalist Israel that requires a Jewish majority for its vitality. This threat carries with it a degree of weight because it challenges the legitimacy of Israel as a sovereign state. Israel has been publicly criticized for its apartheid-like social system by Bishop Desmond Tutu, by its former attorney general Michael Ben-Yair,[6] and, recently (in 2001), at the highly controversial World Conference Against Racism in Durban. The U.S.-Israeli alliance has also been criticized by the international community: in 1974, when Arafat appeared before the UN General Assembly for the first time, despite objections from the United States and Israel; in 1988, when the General Assembly held a special session in Geneva for Arafat (after the United States had, illegally, denied him a visa to the meeting in New York); and lately (and more indirectly) in Kofi Annan's address to the UN Security Council on April 4, 2002, in which he openly condemned the Israeli aggression and urged the United States to intervene. Despite objections from legitimate international bodies, Israel's ethno-nationalist objectives and the United States' diplomatic hegemony, undergirded by the combined military might of these countries, have translated into a progressive erasure of Palestinian existence. The terrorist-card, an old trick of "diplomacy," is matched by another old trick on which Ellison, DuBois, and Fanon have written extensively: the invisibility factor. (Also see Fisk, 1997, 321.)

Israel utilizes the invisibility factor when manufacturing its equations of right, of diplomacy, and when constructing the political ecology of the landscape itself. Milton Fisk has identified the logic and internal mechanisms through which the Palestinian people under occupation are rendered "the invisible" within the nexus of the ethno-nationalist framework: "The public is a Jewish public since the state has to be a Jewish state. Those who do not exist as part of the public cannot have their rights violated, at least not in ways that the state is responsible for" (Fisk, 1997, 321). Golda Meir's famous statement—"They did not exist"—echoes not only in the halls of international "justice" and in the closed spaces of diplomacy, but also in print and on television screens, and, of course, in Israel itself.

The Palestinian people have indeed remained largely invisible in the diplomatic events that have shaped their fate (U.S. democracy unveiled). Since the early 20th century, Britain administered the region in favor of the Zionist project. It was not until November 1974, when Yassar Arafat was recognized as "the sole representative of the Palestinian people," that Palestinians were represented at the UN General Assembly, against the wishes of both the United States and Israel. From the first Middle East peace conference in Geneva in December 1973 to the early 1990s, no "Palestinian" delegation has ever been admitted into the diplomatic arena, though representatives have entered as observers or as part of other countries' delegations, such as that of Jordan (Said, 1995, xxxi). Since Oslo in 1993, the Palestinian Liberation Organization (PLO)-turned-Palestinian Authority (PA) has been only intermittently allowed entry, contingent upon its acceptance of stringent and humiliating conditions set forth by the U.S.-Israeli alliance.

The mainstream U.S. media have also played a major role in maintaining the invisibility of the Palestinian people. With reference to the events of the late 1970s, Edward Said has commented on the historical failure of the U.S. media in this regard:

> In print and on television, Palestinians were dehumanized, turned into vast and frenzied collectives bent on killing innocent Jews for the sheer unregenerate desire of it. The United States vetoed no less than twenty-nine UN Security Council Resolutions censuring Israeli practices which contravened—often with quite unashamed explicitness—many of the norms of international behavior. The U.S. media rarely took note, even though the Israeli press, for instance, was extremely forthcoming on these matters. (Said, 1995, xxvii; see also Said, 2002)

The second Intifada, in progress, has seen a continuation of this trend. Journalists have been barred entry to various "military zones" in Israel; some have been brutalized, shot at, and imprisoned. The International Federation of Journalists has openly accused the Sharon government of violating international law. Israeli deaths are declared in *New York Times* headlines while Palestinian casualties are given only brief mention (FAIR, 2002). My own media analysis has unearthed frightening results. Aside from the continuous banter regarding terrorism and the moral-psychology of the suicide bombers on news channels such as CNN and MSNBC, the history of the region has been grossly mis- and underrepresented. One CNN reporter commented that "these people" do not ever use the "Gandhian" sort of resistance but, rather, "always move straight to violence." The history of the Intifada, the mass demonstrations and general strikes *against occupation*, the conspicuous lack of military infrastructure—all rendered invisible in a ten-second news clip viewed by millions of people.

The Palestinians have also been rendered invisible in their own land. They constitute the largest refugee population in the world; their land has literally been seized from underneath them, and continued attacks by the Israeli military in its program to "cleanse" the land mean that millions have been forcibly expunged from the region. Successive Israeli regimes have made use of massacres, forced mass expulsions, and torture—both physical and psychological—in the name of "defense" or "security" but, in actuality, with the intent to implement compulsory "transfer" and the "clearing" of "Palestine, a country without a people."[7] The intent to cleanse Israel of the Palestinian "problem" was present at Ben-Gurion's entrance into the 1948 war ("During the assault we must be ready to strike a decisive blow; that is, either to destroy the town or expel its inhabitants so our people can replace them") and later realized in July 1948, when 60,000 Palestinians were expelled by force from the villages of Lydda and Ramle. The mass exile from Lydda was accomplished by means of psychological torture and military pressure—many Palestinians were expelled at gunpoint in accordance with the orders of then-Lieutenant-Colonel Yitzhak Rabin: "(13.30 hours on 12 July) The inhabitants of Lydda must be expelled without attention to age." According to Arab chroniclers and an Israeli witness, hundreds of children died in the exodus from Lydda: The "refugee column" began "with [jettisoned] utensils and furniture, and, in the end, bodies of men, women and children" (Masalha, 2001, 43–46). Deir Yassin in 1948, Kibya in 1953, and Sabra and Shatila in 1982 witnessed a similar mode of violence, aimed at the liquidation, exile, or submission of the Palestinian people. Despite the PLO's stated willingness to negotiate, Israel invaded Lebanon in 1982, forcing hordes of Lebanese to the north and destroying entire Palestinian compounds. After the Americans under Reagan arranged for the evacuation of nearly 12,000 Palestinians from Lebanon in late August, Israeli forces continued the assault. Tomis Kapitan's account of Sabra and Shatila is worth repeating:

> On September 12, Lebanon's new president, Bashir Gemayel, agreed to Israel's request that Phalangist forces . . . eliminate the 2,000 "terrorists" that Israelis claimed were still in Beruit's refugee camps. On September 14, Gemayel was killed in a powerful explosion, and a day later the IDF moved into West Beirut in violation of the evacuation agreement, sealing off the Sabra and Shatilla refugee camps with tanks. Sharon authorized entry of the Lebanese militia on September 16 and for the next thirty-six hours, aided by Israeli flares at night, the militiamen raped, mutilated, and massacred civilians. The International Committee of the Red Cross gave a figure of 2,400 killed or unaccounted for . . . , but some bodies had been buried before evacuating and sources among both Phalangists and Palestinians claimed at least 3,000 people had perished. . . . Among the dead, none could be identified as members of the PLO military unit. (Kapitan, 1997, 31)

The political ecology of the territory has been organized and reorganized according to the invisibility factor. Land and population reengineering is often directly linked to war and aggression, which has historically translated into more

land for Israel—and more misery and less territory for Palestinians. In 1949, after
the first Arab-Israeli War, Israel was given 77 percent of the territory, including
West Jerusalem, while Jordan occupied East Jerusalem and the West Bank, and
Egypt, the Gaza Strip. 750,000 Palestinians were displaced in this process. During
the second Arab-Israeli War in 1967, Israel regained control over the entire territory as well as the Sinai Peninsula and the Golan Heights. In November 1967, UN
Resolution 242 required that these territories be returned to the pre-1967 borders,
but this outcome was never implemented. The 1993 Oslo Accords produced a Declaration of Principles (DoP), signed by Arafat and Rabin, that transferred the administration of the Occupied Territories (Gaza and the West Bank) to the Palestinian Authority, but ultimate control remained in Israel's hands. Oslo effectively
denied the Palestinians' rights to self-determination and an independent, sovereign
state and failed to resolve the Right of Return issue for Palestinian refugees. The
DoP did not explicitly prohibit the expansion of Israeli settlements, and border
and settlement issues were tabled for further negotiation, to be finalized in 1996.

The post-Oslo construction of Israeli settlements ensued, and the settler population in the West Bank and Gaza doubled, from 109,784 in 1992 to 213,672 in
2001; as of February 2002, there were 400,000 Israelis living in occupied territory
(including East Jerusalem and the Golan Heights). Some 206,000 Israeli settlers
and 2 million Palestinians live in the West Bank. The settlements and other Israeli-
acquired land in the West Bank constitute 59 percent of the area, most of which
accesses the main aquifer beneath the West Bank. The Gaza Strip, about seven
miles wide and twenty miles long, houses 1.1 million Palestinians as well as 7,000
settlers, who control 20 percent of the land ("Settlement Facts," 2002).

Israeli settlements form an upper-middle-class oasis of green grass, shopping
malls, and swimming pools amidst open desert and enclaves of Palestinian refugee
camps, villages, and towns with limited access to water. Settlements are for Jews
only: They have separate courts, separate economic and health systems (as well as
other social institutions), and separate roads. Israel controls, via checkpoints, the
roads in and among Palestinian-inhabited areas, and the roads themselves are configured in such a way that the average Palestinian may spend half a day just getting
to school or work. Palestinian cars are not permitted in the West Bank, and Palestinians must enter on donkeys or on foot or risk being shot. Israelis, on the other
hand, move freely, and have a network of bypass roads that connect directly to Israel
and to each other (Wallis, 2001). The Clinton-Barak proposal, a belated resolution
to the pending issues of Oslo—which were not resolved in Oslo II (1995), Wye
River (1998), or Wye River II (1999)—focused on consolidating the 200 scattered
West Bank Palestinian areas into three zones, all under Israeli control and all separate from one another, in what Noam Chomsky and others have described as a Ban-
tustan proposal (Chomsky, 2002). The issue remains unresolved as the "peace
process" has been delayed in the wake of the second Intifada and another major Israeli assault, which has already demolished large portions of the meager infrastructure in the Occupied Territories, perhaps in anticipation of new settlements.

In his famous work on the Algerian liberation movement, Franz Fanon (1963) said, "In all armed struggles, there exists what we might call the point of no return. Almost always it is marked off by a huge and all-inclusive repression which engulfs all sectors of the colonized people" (p. 90). The second Palestinian Intifada is one such point. In the absence of any means through which to express dissent, failed diplomacy and an impotent PLO leadership, land and water confiscation and mass exile, taxation without representation and lack of civil rights, scant social and economic development, daily humiliation, untenable living conditions, and an historical memory of Deir Yasin, Sabra and Shatila, and now Jenin, the Palestinian resistance, like that of other popular uprisings, has made use of mass protest to resist occupation, sometimes employing violence in the struggle to reclaim existence. Problematically, this Intifada has largely been characterized as "terrorist," and the "War on Terror" has largely obscured its legitimacy as a revolutionary movement waged against an illegal and oppressive occupation.

THE SECOND INTIFADA AND THE WAR ON TERROR

Amidst the spectacle of the War on Terror, the problem of what constitutes "terrorism" has been the centerpiece of much public debate among diplomats, state officials, and political analysts. Within the realm of contemporary political violence and international conflict resolution, there is an apparent contradiction between what is understood as a legitimate use and means of force versus the "illegitimacy" of that which is termed "terrorism." The propositions being put forth by the U.S. administration and its supporters are being waged within a narrow, moralistic framework, in the search for a universal ethic of violence from which all modes of resistance are understood as "terrorist." Many of these distinctions have created a great deal of confusion, and are obviously self-serving and hypocritical: While the United States claims to abhor terrorism in all its forms, it asserts that the practice of torture and intensification of surveillance for the purpose of preventing terrorism is legitimate. This is not a new phenomenon: To serve its interests, the United States has long trained and funded well-known tyrannical regimes, including the Taliban, the mujahadeen, and the contras.[8]

The history of the Israeli-Palestinian conflict is fraught with contradictions and dreadfully cavalier uses of the term "terrorism."[9] Despite the Israeli government's continued disregard for international mandates regarding human rights, insurrections by the Palestinian people and their few allies have repeatedly been crushed in the name of increasing security and fighting terrorism. This was the official line when Menachem Begin's Likud Party came to power in 1977 (Said, 1995, xxvi), and it has been resurrected in the current (second) Intifada: Suicide bombers and religious and secular "extremists" have become "the sole legitimate representative of the Palestinian people"; UN emergency relief workers have been deemed "spies"; and large portions of Palestinian civilians have been targeted, and their infrastructure and livelihood demolished, on the grounds that they are "could-be" terrorists:

> [T]here are reports of 300 dead and countless injured. 548 Palestinian men now living in Romani have been dumped by Israeli soldiers at a nearby Salem checkpoint after having been arrested or escaping from Jenin. 160 were dumped naked outside of Syba. . . . A young Palestinian man was forced from his home in Jenin, and used as a human shield by Israeli soldiers. His back and neck are burned by cigarettes. . . . A Palestinian UNRWA (United Nations Relief and Works Agency) employee was detained at a checkpoint for three days without food, and only Israeli soldiers' urine to drink. The right side of his face paralyzed due to severe beating. The Israeli interrogators, described as torturers, told the imprisoned man that all UNRWA employees are spies for Hezbollah. ("Statement from 13 Internationals," 2002)

Amidst the deluge of commentary in the aftermath of the World Trade Center attack, Michael Walzer, editor of *Dissent*, attempted to pinpoint "the political roots of terror." In his piece entitled "Five Questions About Terrorism," Walzer asserts that any defense of what is being called "terrorism" (a highly debatable term, he admits) is part of a "culture of excuse and apology":

> [T]error, we are told, is the weapon of the weak, that last resort of subject nations. In fact, terror is commonly the first resort of militants who believe from the beginning that the Enemy should be killed and who are neither interested in nor capable of organizing their own people for any other kind of politics: the FLN and PLO resorted to terror from the beginning; there was no long series of attempts to find alternatives. And as we have seen, there is at least one alternative—nonviolent mass mobilization—that has proven itself a far more effective "weapon of the weak." (Walzer, 2002)

Although he erroneously characterizes the FLN[10] as a rogue organization, Walzer is quite correct in saying that political frailty does not sufficiently explain the use of violence as a mode of resistance (in his terms, "terrorist" modes of resistance). However, one's historical context and the alternatives available to them within it undoubtedly inform the choices they make. Walzer's view of "nonviolent mass mobilization" as a more effective "weapon" than violent means of resistance echoes that of the many pacifists, anti-war activists, and human rights proponents who understandably decry violence in all its forms. Proponents of nonviolent resistance often cite the success of Gandhi in liberating the Indian people from British colonial rule to demonstrate its value, yet Gandhi's *satyagraha* was possible only within a specific historical context. India was already on the verge of liberation, and it should come as no surprise that today she is heavily armed (to say the least). Others point to the American civil rights movement as an example of successful nonviolent resistance, but it remains a point of debate whether Martin Luther King would have received the same reception without the threat of the Black Panthers and the Nation of Islam in the background.

The problem with the pacifist position is that it relies on an ethic of nonviolence as a governing principle for democratic social action—an ethic that assumes a common value system and a semblance of equality among those involved in a given conflict. Some pacifists may argue that it is precisely the lack of equality and the ultimate helplessness of the oppressed materialized in nonviolent action that spotlights the aggression of the oppressor. But this position assumes a certain degree of empathy that is at odds with the current world climate and especially the Palestinian context. Despite the fact that the Intifada has elicited sympathy around the globe, neighboring Arab states have done little in recent years, other than sending money and weapons, to aid them in their resistance. In fact, many Arab states have been downright abusive toward the Palestinian people, especially refugees, who typically serve as a permanent underclass and indentured labor supply in the Middle East.[11] It was only after hundreds if not thousands of Palestinians perished in the second Intifada (a number that remains unknown but is surely increasing as I write this) that the members of the European Union began to discuss the possibility of imposing economic sanctions on Israel (they have taken no such action to date). Only a handful of anti-capitalist globalization activists (acting as human shields for the Palestinians) and relief organizations provide direct support. Furthermore, the seriously lagging diplomatic processes focused on the conflict have turned a blind eye and a cold shoulder to the immediacy of the situation: Within the span of U.S. Secretary of State Colin Powell's April 2002 diplomatic mission— which included stops in Morocco, Cairo, and Madrid prior to his arrival in Israel—dozens of Palestinians and Israelis perished. In addition, the UN fact-finding mission to investigate the Israeli assault on the Jenin refugee camp was canceled in May 2002 due to Israeli opposition, thereby not only absolving Israel of its ongoing accountability to the international community but also representing a withdrawal of UN support—and protection—for the Palestinians.

Today's "just war" theorists identify terrorism with its effects on innocent civilian populations and, on that basis, almost uniformly decry it as unethical (Statman, 1997, 134). Yet to label an act of aggression "terrorist" on such grounds would necessarily involve the indictment of all states involved in modern combat. Within the cycle of violence that is world order, civilians are the *subjects* of modern warfare: "[V]isiting terror against civilian populations in order to invert public indignation against their own governments, rather than the putative aggressor, is becoming an acceptable aspect of warfare" (Aronowitz, 2000, 225). Civilians were the subjects of the Gulf and Kosovan Wars, and they are undoubtedly subjects of the War on Terror, as evidenced by Israel's feeble attempt to turn the people (as if they hadn't already turned) against Arafat ("if only he would condemn the suicide bombers"); by Al Qaeda's *jihad* ("I ask the American people to force their government to give up anti-Muslim policies. The American people had risen against their government's war in Vietnam. They must do the same today"[12]); and by the militants of the second Intifada ("We have to convince the Israelis that whatever else Sharon brings them, it won't be their security"[13]). Civilians are also the *objects* of modern warfare: An estimated 3,700 were killed in Afghanistan as a direct result of U.S. bombings, and refugees, such as those in the Maslakh camp thirty miles west of Herat City, number in the tens of thousands (McKinlay, 2002); U.S. bombs in Iraq killed tens of thousands of civilians, a number that continues to increase exponentially as a result of U.S. sanctions (Herold, 2002); and, in light of the ongoing tensions between India and Pakistan, the Pentagon has warned that a full-scale nuclear exchange between them could kill up to 12 million people immediately and injure up to 7 million—a necessarily civilian war, built into the machinery of war itself (Shanker, 2002).

Walzer's analysis of terrorism reinforces the ahistorical and self-serving position of the War on Terror. Whereas revolutionary violence may once have occupied the space between the dichotomy of violence as a mode of international conflict resolution (war) and violence used in the administration of criminal justice within and among states (policing), the conflation of revolutionary violence with terrorism tends to confuse random and extremist acts with those employed in the service of a legitimate political project. It also collapses the two traditional categories of *jus ad bellum* (the right to make war) and *jus in bello* (law in war) into one, rendering states with modern implements of war at their disposal as guardians of "justice."

Contrary to popular accounts of the Intifada, nonviolent methods of resistance have been employed throughout the years, including daily demonstrations, commercial strikes, boycotts, nonpayment of taxes, barricades, and the setting up of underground schools (after they were closed as punishment during the first Intifada). However, Israel's progressive disclosure on Palestinian land has undercut the Palestinians' potential for traditional venues of warfare: The IDF has bulldozed entire villages, leaving combatants and noncombatants alike buried beneath the rubble. Furthermore, the "sole legitimate representative of the Palestinian people"—the PLO headed by Yasser Arafat—has not only repeatedly failed to provide the basics of social development in the Occupied Territories but, worse, has brazenly sold out Palestinian interests and hijacked their movement to self-determination, most obviously with the 1993 Oslo Accords (Said, 2001, 5). Hence the Palestinian resistance is necessarily an atypical defense or, in Virilio's terms, a "popular assault" (1990, 56). Without diplomatic leadership, without a national territory from which to wage resistance, and in light of the failure of traditional modes of nonviolent resistance to produce results, the Intifada necessarily employs sporadic forms of combat. Similar to M'Hidi's poignant response to the French press, F-16s would be an easier means with which to wage a war of liberation—certainly preferable to the rocks, homemade rifles, and Molotov cocktails that have traditionally composed the Palestinian arsenal.

A May 2002 article in the *Wall Street Journal*, written by Middle East expert Ahmed Rashid and reviewed on mainstream television stations throughout the world, warned of the detrimental effects of the War on Terror on Central Asian countries such as Kyrgyzstan, Kazakhstan, Uzbekistan, and Tajikistan. Rashid asserted that "Central Asian governments have used the threat of Islamic fundamentalism as a pretext for increased crackdowns on dissent, calculating—correctly, so far—that Washington would register only mild criticism" (Rashid, 2002). Such impositions of "security" as an excuse for state terrorism and the criminalization of dissent are peppered throughout world history, manifest not only in the war crimes committed by despotic governments but also in the call for a "state of emergency" or "militarized zones" in Seattle, Genoa, Göteburg, and Quebec City. The USA Patriot Act and the reactionary war on opposition ("You are either with us or against us"[14]) have revitalized a globalized McCarthyism in which civil disobedience, violent protest, and other means of criticizing the state have been institutionally merged under the rubric of criminal activity. This phenomenon not only ignores the history of mass movements around the world but also formalizes an overall disclosure on political dissent, thereby undermining the public's capacity to challenge the legitimacy of the state: democracy sold out for order.

Beyond the morality of tactics and "justice in war," the aggressive foreclosure on dissent coupled with the violence of capital's new enclosures—from IMF-fiscal takeovers to the brash acquisition of territory via forced settlement to the post-interventional deployment of puppet despots—are likely to lead to new forms of resistance and new fundamentalisms as well as to intensified police action and surveillance at the will of Empire's security. The growing incidence of suicide bombings—the World Trade Center, the Intifada, the Tamil Tigers in Sri Lanka—is a case in point. Suicide bombers are becoming an emblem of modern conflict. They are the epitome of *biopower* and the embodiment of civilian warfare—the subjects and objects (aggressors and victims) of a desperate form of war that leaves no space and no body untouched. They are the seemingly logical outcome of the globalization of violence and its tendency toward an end of politics[15]: a nomadic resistance that wages war on the multimedia cyber-territory of television, radio, and Internet (see Virilio, 1990, 56–58). Yet by warrant of the life to which they lay claim, they remain relegated to the status of "criminal against humanity" without any real interrogation into the character of their death or the conditions that give rise to such modes of assault and resistance—such as the anomie about which Emile Durkheim wrote in *Suicide* a little more than a century ago.

CONCLUSION

Violence in the 21st century is marked by a growing frequency of seemingly random and "extremist" events, continuous infiltrations of new and "unspecified enemies," and rabid fundamentalisms, boundless and sundry. The events of the last few years, from the Palestinian Intifada to the bombing of the World Trade Center to the "13 million strong" in Italy,[16] continue to shake Empire at its core. Against the claims of the War on Terror, violence—the primary interlocutor of Empire's "peace"—gives birth to multiple fields of power: There is a distinct violence of powerlessness as well as a violence of domination, and both are part of the system that underlies world order. At its personal best, Empire attempts to diffuse reckless violence and impose a deceptively benevolent, unilateral order: a viral force that maneuvers below the skin and opportunistically colonizes the social body by way of technical mastery.

In its current formulation, Empire is failing to enact its version of global stability, unable to contain its own "accidents."[17] The World Trade Center attack and the suicide bombers are the likely result of a modern warfare in which imperial force is met by an atypical, elusive tactics characteristic of desperation. The folding of all forms of dissent under the rubric of "terrorism" is part and parcel of a paradigm of domination that operates in the service of order—an order of smooth complicity, rooted in fear and manufactured scarcity (the sinister character of this peace). As the War on Terror continues to ransack the globe, narrowing spaces of resistance and foreclosing alternatives, rigorous interrogations of Empire's irresolvable contradictions and corruptive[18] sensibilities must be undertaken and critical resistance must endure.

In the shadows of pure war, the violence of powerlessness and liberation are necessarily revolutionary: The violence of freedom can never be as terrorist as the violence of pure war, which is nothing less than absolute negation. However, although the sometimes reckless violence of revolution and resistance is a more authentic show of political power (consent/dissent) than the forced or tacit consent characteristic of contemporary world politics, it is indeed the project of revolution to establish spaces of resistance and legitimate bases of power that transgress the violence of world order, perhaps to the between-space of the violence of autonomy and liberation, but most certainly beyond, to the province of freedom.

The Enlightenment turns on itself again and again. I say this with optimism. Although the project of science encompasses the domination of human over human, reason retains a promise of emancipation—of learning and compassion—despite the conjecture that we have entered the End of History. In the service of freedom and against the hollowing program of Empire (which presents itself as a given, natural arbiter), it is essential that the history and political programs of modern conflict be understood and reasoned, and freed from the tautology of violence that plagues the new world order.

NOTES

1. See Bataille (1986): "War was different in kind from animal violence and it developed a cruelty animals are incapable of, especially in that the fight, frequently followed by a massacre of the enemy, was as often as not a prelude to the torture of the prisoners. This cruelty is the specifically human aspect of war. . . . Violence, not cruel itself, is essentially something organized in the transgression of taboos. Cruelty is one of its forms; it is not nec-

essarily erotic but it may veer towards other forms of violence organized by transgression. . . . Organized war with its efficient military operations based on discipline, which when all is said and done excludes the mass of the combatants from the pleasure of transgressing the limits, has been caught up in a mechanism foreign to the impulsions which set it off in the first place. . . . Primitive war itself can hardly be defended: from the outset it bore the seeds of modern warfare, but the organized form we are familiar with today, that has traveled such a long way from the original organized transgression of the taboo, is the only one that would leave humanity unsatisfied!" (pp. 78–80).

2. Originally, *blowback* was used to refer to the cloud of radioactive gas that blew back over atomic bomb test sites. This term has been appropriated by the CIA to refer to individuals or groups who received training from the United States and later turned against it. (See 9–11peace.org, 2001–2002.)

3. Prior to the Gulf War, and throughout the 1970s and 1980s, the Ba'ath Party's state model was not in sync with the IMF paradigm that dominated much of the Middle East. In *Midnight Oil: Work, Energy, War, 1973–1992*, the Midnight Notes Collective (1992) writes: "One motivation for the war was the desire to destroy the basis of working class power in Iraq and fundamentally alter the relationship between capital and labor. Before the war, many Iraqi workers had a kind of informal and tacit social contract with the Iraqi government. But the US achieved what the Ba'ath Party was unable to do alone: annul the social contract and render the workers free to starve and the state and private capital free to accumulate" (p. 48).

4. See "Form-of-Life" and "Beyond Human Rights" by Giorgio Agamben in *Radical Thought in Italy: A Potential Politics*, edited by Paolo Virno and Michael Hardt (University of the Minnesota Press, 1996).

5. To date, Israeli Prime Minister Ariel Sharon has not agreed to adopt the Saudi peace plan and return to the pre-1967 border, which has been accepted by the United States and the European Union. Sharon stated that such a move would be "the destruction of the state of Israel" (see Fisk, 2002). Further, in May 2002, against Sharon and the stated program of the United States, the Likud Party voted in favor of a resolution to never allow an independent Palestinian state (see Erlanger, 2002).

6. Archbishop Desmond Tutu visited the region in 1989 and likened it to South Africa (Ashmore, 1997, 131–132). Also see Bishop Tutu and Ian Urbina's statement in the July 15, 2002, issue of *The Nation*. For Ben-Yair's statement, see the issue of *Ha'aretz* dated March 3, 2002. In addition, the UN General Assembly's Resolution 3379, drafted in 1975, described Zionism as a form of racism; this resolution was rescinded in 1991, partly due to pressure from the United States (Kapitan, 1997, 27).

7. "In its initial stage, Zionism was conceived by its pioneers as a movement wholly depending on mechanical factors: there is a country which happens to be called Palestine, a country without a people, and on the other hand, there exists the Jewish people, and it has no country. What else is necessary, then, to fit the gem into the ring, to unite this people with this country?" This statement was made by Chaim Weizmann, president of the World Zionist Congress and first president of the state of Israel in 1914; here, "a country without a people" refers to Palestine under Arab control, which many of the first Zionists viewed as uncultivated and uncivilized (Masalha, 2001, 37–38).

8. The list goes on: Somoza in Nicaragua, Batista in Cuba, the Shah in Iran (etc.).

9. Although from the mid-19th century on the Palestinians were understood as the "terrorists" of the region, former Israeli prime ministers Menachem Begin and Yitzhak Shamir were implicated in war crimes and terrorist activities. For example, in 1946, Begin headed the Irgun Zvai Leumi, which was known to be responsible for Deir Yassin as well as the 1946 underground attack on the King David Hotel in Jerusalem, the headquarters of

the British administration (Feron, 1992). In addition, Ariel Sharon was found by an Israeli commission of inquiry to be "indirectly responsible" for the 1982 massacre in Sabra and Shatila, after which he was forced to resign from his post as defense minister (Kapitan, 1997, 31).

10. Walzer's characterization of the Front de Libération (National Liberation Front, or FLN) is incongruous with Fanon's account, which asserts that the FLN had the mass support of the people: "French colonialism must know these things. It can no longer hide from the fact that the Algerian government can mobilize any Algerian at any time. Even the winners in the elections, forcibly registered on the administration's electoral lists, would resign if ordered by the National Liberation Front" (Fanon, 1965, 31).

11. See Said, 2002; Said, 1995, xlii; Midnight Notes Collective, 1992, 48.

12. Statement by Osama bin Laden, quoted in *Mir*, 2001.

13. Statement by Jamal Abu Samhandanah, Popular Resistance Committee (PRC) leader, quoted in Usher, 2002.

14. Statement by George W. Bush in his late September 2001 national address, with reference to the newly inaugurated War on Terror.

15. For a more detailed discussion on the relationship between biopolitics and an "end of politics" in the contemporary world order, see Giorgio Agamben in *Homo Sacer* and the various works of Paul Virilio already cited herein.

16. On April 16, 2002, 13 million Italian workers engaged in a general strike to protest Berlusconi's attempt to reform labor laws that would make it easier to fire workers in Italy, where most people have lifetime job security (Henneberger, 2002).

17. *Accidents* is used here in the sense elucidated by Virilio, whose contention, considered post–September 11, appears as omen: "We are forced to expand the question of technology not only to the substance produced, but also to the accident produced. . . . In classic Aristotelian philosophy, substance is necessary and the accident is relative and contingent. At the moment, there's an inversion: the accident is becoming necessary and substance relative and contingent. Every technology produces, provokes, programs a specific accident. . . . The invention of the boat was the invention of shipwrecks. . . . The invention of the highways was the invention of three hundred cars colliding in five minutes . . . the invention of the airplane was the invention of the plane crash" (Virilio and Lotringer, 1983, 32).

18. See Hardt and Negri's (2000) concept of "corruption": "It is no mystery how we recognize corruption and how we identify the powerful emptiness of the mist of indifference that imperial power extends across the world. . . . Corruption is easily perceived because it appears immediately as a form of violence, as an insult . . . when in practices of imperial government the threat of terror becomes a weapon to resolve unlimited or regional conflicts and an apparatus for imperial development. Imperial command, in this case, is disguised and can alternatively appear as corruption or destruction, almost as if to reveal the profound call that the former makes for the latter and the latter for the former. The two dance together over the abyss, over the imperial lack of being" (pp. 390–391). Also see Hardt and Negri, 2002, 201–202.

WORKS CITED

Agamben, Giorgio. 1996. "Form-of-Life" and "Beyond Human Rights." In *Radical Thought in Italy: A Potential Politics (Theory Out of Bounds, Vol 7)*. Paolo Virno and Michael Hardt (eds.) University of Minnesota Press.

Agamben, Giorgio, Daniel Heller-Roazen (translator). 1998. *Homo Sacer: Sovereign Power and Bare Life*. California: Stanford University Press.

Arendt, Hannah. 1972. "On Violence." *Crisis of the Republic*. San Diego: Harcourt, Brace & Company.

Aronowitz, Stanley. 2000. "Essay on Violence," in *Smoke and Mirrors: The Hidden Context of Violence in Schools and Society*, ed. Stephanie Urso Spina. New York: Rowman & Littlefield.

Ashmore, Robert B. 1997. "State Terrorism and Its Sponsors," in *Philosophical Perspectives on the Israeli-Palestinian Conflict*, ed. Tomis Kapitan. New York: M. E. Sharpe.

Bataille, Georges. 1986. *Erotism: Death and Sensuality*, trans. Mary Dalwood. San Francisco: City Lights Books.

Ben-Yair, Michael. 2002. "The War's Seventh Day." *Ha'aretz*, March 3. Available online at the American Committee on Jerusalem website: http://www.acj.org/Daily%20News/March02/march_4.htm#4.

Chomsky, Noam. 2002. "Interview with Chomsky: In-Depth Discussion on Israel/Palestine." *ZNet* (*Z Magazine* online), April 2, http://www.zmag.org/content/Mideast/chomsky_palestine_april2.cfm.

Deleuze, Gilles, and Félix Guattari. 1987. *A Thousand Plateaus: Capitalism and Schizophrenia*, trans. Brian Massumi. Minneapolis: University of Minnesota Press.

DuBois, W.E.B. 1995. *The Souls of Black Folk*, with a new Introduction by Randall Kenan. New York: Penguin.

Durkheim, Emile. 1997. *Suicide: A Study in Sociology*, trans. J. A. Spaulding and G. Simpson. Reissue edition. New York: Free Press.

Ellison, Ralph. 1995. *Invisible Man*, 2nd Vintage International Edition. New York: Random House.

Erlanger, Steven. 2002. "Mideast Turmoil: The Overview; Rebutting Sharon, Party Repudiates Palestinian State." *New York Times*, May 13.

Fairness and Accuracy In Reporting (FAIR). 2002. "Palestinian Deaths Aren't Headline Material at the *New York Times*," April 12. Available online at www.fair.org/activism/nyt-israel-headlines.html.

Fanon, Franz. 1965. *A Dying Colonialism*. New York: Grove Press.

————. 1963. *The Wretched of the Earth*, trans. Constance Farrington. New York: Grove Press.

Feron, James. 1992. "Menachem Begin, Guerilla Leader Who Became a Peacemaker." *New York Times*, March 10.

Fisk, Milton. 1997. "Zionism, Liberalism, and the State," in *Philosophical Perspectives on the Israeli-Palestinian Conflict*, ed. Tomis Kapitan. New York: M. E. Sharpe.

Fisk, Robert. 2002. "View from Beirut." *The Nation*, April 22.

Hardt, Michael, and Antonio Negri. 2000. *Empire*. Cambridge, Mass.: Harvard University Press.

Henneberger, Melinda. 2002. "Millions of Italians Take to the Streets in a General Strike." *New York Times*, April 17.

Herold, Marc W. 2002. http://pubpages.unh.edu/~mwherold/Afghanistan.doc. Press release available at www.globalexchange.org.

Kapitan, Tomis, ed. 1997. *Philosophical Perspectives on the Israeli-Palestinian Conflict*. New York: M. E. Sharpe.

Masalha, Nur. 2001. "The Historical Roots of the Palestinian Refugee Question," in *Palestinian Refugees: The Right of Return*, ed. Naseer Aruri. London: Pluto Press.

McKinlay, Doug. 2002. "Refugees Left in the Cold at 'Slaughterhouse' Camp: 100 Afghans Perish Daily as Strained Aid Network Collapses Under Flood of New Arrivals." *The Guardian*, January 3.

Midnight Notes Collective. 1992. *Midnight Oil: Work, Energy, War, 1973–1992*. Brooklyn: Autonomedia.

Mir, Hamir. 2001. "Interview with Osama bin Laden." *Dawn* (Kabul), November 9. Available online at http://DAWN.com.

9-11peace.org. 2001–2002. "Blowback." Issue 5: The CIA and Afghanistan. Available online at www.9-11peace.org/bulletin5.php3.

Pontecorvo, Gillo. 1967. *The Battle of Algiers* (movie), Stella Productions Inc., produced by Antonio Musu, story and screenplay by Franco Solinas and Gillo Pontecorvo. Igor Film (Rome) and Casbah Films (Algiers).

Rashid, Ahmed. 2002. "To Boost Military Campaign, U.S. Blinks at Repression in Central Asia." *Wall Street Journal*, May 13.

Said, Edward W. 2002. "What Price Oslo?" *Al-Ahram Weekly Online*, March 24–20, note 577, http://www.ahram.org.eg/weekly/2002/577/op2.htm.

_____. 2001. "Introduction: The Right of Return at Last," in *Palestinian Refugees: The Right of Return*, ed. Naseer Aruri. London: Pluto Press.

_____. 1995. *The Politics of Dispossession: The Struggle for Palestinian Self-Determination, 1969–1994*. New York: Vintage Books.

"Settlement Facts." 2002. Foundation for Middle East Peace. *Israeli Settlements in the Occupied Territories: A Guide: A Special Report of the Foundation for Middle East Peace*, March.

Shanker, Thom. 2002. "12 Million Could Die at Once in an India-Pakistan Nuclear War." *New York Times*, May 26.

"Statement from 13 Internationals." 2002. Statement obtained from IMC-Palestine, available online at http://jerusalem.indymedia.org. See also the NYC Direct Action Network (DAN) listserv from activists reporting from Palestine on April 10.

Statman, Daniel. 1997. "*Jus in Bello* and the Intifada," in *Philosophical Perspectives on the Israeli-Palestinian Conflict*, ed. Tomis Kapitan. New York: M. E. Sharpe.

Tutu, Desmond, and Ian Urbina. 2002. "Against Israeli Apartheid." *The Nation*, July 15.

USA Patriot Act. 2001. H.R. 3162, S.1510, Public Law 107-56. October 26.

Usher, Graham. 2002. "Palestine Militias Rising." *The Nation*. April 29.

Virilio, Paul. 2000. *Strategy of Deception*, trans. Chris Turner. London: Verso.

_____. 1990. *Popular Defense & Ecological Struggles*, trans. Mark Polizzotti. New York: Semiotext(e) Foreign Agent Series.

Virilio, Paul, and Sylvere Lotringer. 1983. *Pure War*, trans. Mark Polizotti. New York: Semiotext.

Wallis, Jim. 2001. "Inside Israeli Apartheid: An Interview with James Kuttab." *Sojourners Magazine*, September–October.

Walzer, Michael. 2002. "Five Questions About Terrorism." *Dissent Magazine*, Vol. 49, No. 1 (Winter).

6

Beyond Good and Evil

A Contribution to the Analysis of
the War Against Terrorism

BRUNO GULLÌ

*in relation to human affairs, not to laugh, not to cry, not to become indig-
nant, but to understand*

BARUCH DE SPINOZA

In order to achieve a balanced and meaningful analysis of the tragic events of September 11, we must avoid preconstructed ideological positions and facile rhetorical discourse. Contributing to a political analysis of these events is today perhaps
the most delicate task we can take on in the process of attempting to understand
the events themselves. In fact, as the days go by and the blackmail logic mounts,
we become increasingly aware that at stake is nothing more nor less than the future
of the whole world, the destiny of humanity.

It should be evident to anyone with a minimum of political common sense
and historical memory that the events of September 11—though unbelievable and
unthinkable, or thinkable only from a science-fiction perspective—are nothing but
a moment within a logic of violence that has ensnared the entire world. If this language sounds cold and scientific, it is only because I am trying to see whether it's
still possible to make good use of reason and truth—that is, whether a form of universal humanism is still viable. In fact, I am convinced that humanity has, at this
point, two main options: Either we think critically and in a more enlightened, secular,[1] and healthy way, or we succumb to that strange mixture of irrational, superstitious, and Manichean moods that welcomes Nostradamus's prophecies as much
as any pseudo-explanation of these recent events based on a simple logic of good
and evil. Paradoxically, popular superstition (the acceptance of a destiny of worldly

evil) and official promises of victorious revenge (a crusade to extirpate and expunge evil) go hand in hand. Both rest on the assumption that *there is* evil, but also that this evil is external to the system of goodness with which superstition and revenge are identified, an excrescence that finds no rational (historical) justification. Thus, both share in the same theodicy—that is, in the holy justification and defense of this identity vis-à-vis a cancerous force that threatens to destroy it. Gog and Magog, figures of the Antichrist, come to mind, for the geography and the rhetoric are really the same.

Let us then use the above-noted statement as a pointer: *that the events of September 11 are nothing but a moment within a logic of violence that has ensnared the entire world.* If there is anything we could give to the victims of September 11, as well as to the numberless and often easily forgotten victims of this entire logic of violence, if there is any way we could contribute to a dissolution of this logic and a restoration of the true concept of peace, it would be a lucid analysis of this turning point in world history and perhaps a hint as to what a new synthesis, freed from Manichean elements, could be. This is not a time to take sides in a game that has already been established and whose outcome is only going to multiply universal suffering and pain. It is certainly not a time for thoughtless action. Rather, this is a time to denounce all ignorance and all lies; it is a time for that form of action that thinking itself is; it is a time for critical discussion, understanding, and education.

The logic of violence I am talking about does not have its roots in what goes by the name of terrorism. Rather, the opposite is the case: "Terrorism" has its roots in this logic of violence. And this is not simply because Osama bin Laden is a (partial) product of the CIA; other, more fundamental reasons are involved. By referring to the CIA, I have already disclosed my belief that the United States is an element within the motor of this logic of violence. Indeed, this is an undeniable fact. The United States, for all its rhetoric of freedom, has been the cause of much ruin and suffering all over the world. We shall return to this point later, but for now let us look briefly at the history of the past century.

Probably no one would deny that the history of the 20th century was essentially determined by the struggle of the "free" world against communism—in other words, that this struggle, made up of cold and not so cold wars, can be used as a baseline for understanding the main events of the whole century, from the struggle for independence in the colonial world and the formation of new nation-states to the ideological reshaping of the old world. Even World War II, in which the powerful Red Army played a fundamental role in determining the victory of the allies, turned soon from being a war against the countries of the axis to being a war against the expansion of communism.[2] Almost all of the subsequent wars involving the United States were fought on the same grounds. Even the war against communism was fought domestically in the United States and other countries of the so-called "free" and "democratic" world against a background of repressive measures that bordered on, if they didn't actually become, a systematic and systemic regime of terror. This long war against communism was not, or at least was not always, a war against the Soviet Union. Rather, it was a war against the communist idea of a different and better world, freed from all forms of oppression (from private property to superstitious beliefs). That the communist aspiration was later *hijacked* into the construction of another form of terror, totalitarianism, says nothing about that aspiration itself—but it says a lot about the hijackers. We will consider the question of the meaning of totalitarianism below. For now, let us only note the central argument under discussion: *that the twentieth century's war against communism was in reality nothing but a moment in the war the "free" world has been waging against freedom itself—that is, against universal freedom.*

Besides Russia and a few other countries, where great Marxist thinkers such as Lenin knew exactly what they wanted, the countries that traveled the road toward communist revolution often did so more on strategic and pragmatic grounds than for ideological and philosophical reasons (and this includes the heroic island of Cuba). Very often, countries of the "Third World" that went down the communist path to power did so because the world came to be divided into two main camps: American and Soviet. In order to receive theoretical and material support as they emerged from colonial rule, these countries felt a more natural attraction toward the Soviet Union than toward Western imperialism (notwithstanding the Soviet Union's own tendency toward brands of imperialism). This is not to underestimate the attraction some countries (or more precisely, some movements within those countries) felt toward Marxist philosophy as such, for that was the most sophisticated and powerful theory of revolution in existence. Yet, all the revolutionary struggles within the "Third World" had liberation from the colonial yoke and constitution of a national dignity as their immediate priorities; theirs were anti-colonial struggles for self-determination, and some were not at all communist in character. Indeed, some were cautious and stayed distant from communist ideas so as not to unleash the fury of the "free" and "democratic" world (which has always been slow in understanding and accepting the freedom of the others). In fact, the history of these struggles and revolutions well precedes the formation of the Soviet Union, and after 1917, the Soviet Union only became a lighthouse for a process of liberation that would have occurred with or without it. The point I wish to make here is that the road to freedom may take different forms: anti-colonial and nationalist, communist, or a combination of the two. This is what history has shown in the last couple of centuries. Yet, the "free" and "democratic" world has, for some reason, always opposed these forms of liberation and, in general, has justified this opposition on the basis of a sacred duty to defend democracy and freedom.

Thus, to give just one example, many Americans have either forgotten or don't know that the United States' systematic and shameful efforts to break communist rule in Cuba have nothing to do with such values as democracy and freedom. (The Cubans themselves know very well what these values are.) The Cuban Revolution, in fact, began not with the attack on the Moncada barracks on July 26, 1953, but long before that with the first and second wars of independence. Also easily forgotten is the fact that the great Jose Martí, the father and martyr of free Cuba, and perhaps the most perfect example of the Gramscian intellectual of a new type, in his last, unfinished letter wrote: "It is my duty—inasmuch as I realize it and have the spirit to fulfill it—to prevent, by the independence of Cuba, the United States from spreading over the West Indies and falling, with the added weight, upon other lands of our America. All I have done up to now, and shall do hereafter, is to that end. . . . I have lived inside the monster and know its insides."[3] But no, the "free" world, with the United States as its front-runner, has always had difficulty understanding a concept of freedom at variance with the narrow, particularistic one it presents. Thus, from imperialist opposition to anti-colonial struggles for the self-determination of peoples, from the successful attempt to "contain the spread of communism" to the present struggles against "terrorism," the "free" world, with the United States in the lead, has constructed a logic of violence that is now returning like a boomerang to its own shores.

It is shocking to see the extent to which this new war against terrorism resembles the past war against communism. But the stakes are higher now, of course, for terrorism—as an absolute aberration of the use of freedom and power—poses a real threat to freedom itself. In the social and political movements that even generically shared in the communist worldview and philosophy of liberation and freedom, there were (as there still are in the new forms of these movements)[4] a universal principle of hope and an attention to human dignity that are completely missing from the holy war being constructed today. Yet, these movements were fought and often crushed with the same determination one finds in the current war against terrorism.

I am saying that the "free" world (i.e., the "West") has in the past employed all its might for the destruction of ideas and movements of liberation, only to push humanity to the verge of an abyss. The gap the "free" world has not only refused to bridge but has actually either created or deepened—the gap between North and South, wealth and poverty, life and death, a gap epitomized by the situation in Palestine—is now making manifest the void within its structure of legitimization. The "free" world has lost its mandate, notwithstanding its pathetic attempts to mask the truth and recompose a vision that is already blurred and will soon fade. However, the effort to maintain the status quo will not succeed without an intensification of regimes of terror. The events of September 11 were horrific, but they were also—in Edward Said's apt phrase—a "spectacular horror." The spectacle of wholesale death, of this relatively "clean" and technologically monitored massacre, the spectacle of the two fire-breathing birds and the two falling towers, of the fire itself that bridged the gap between truth and spectacle while opening a new gap within people's consciousness (between belief and disbelief)—this spectacle, whether seen on TV or from a rooftop, will justify and legitimize a more intense regimentation of the society of control in which we already live; and perhaps worse, we will freely choose our own incarceration—to be controlled "inside" for fear of the terror coming from the "outside." In reality, we will exchange one regime of terror for another. The truth is that we can catch all the bin Ladens we want, bring more devastation to the unhappy people of Afghanistan—terror has already triumphed.

The struggle inherited from the history I have too cursorily outlined is a struggle for hegemony. This hegemony is understood as universal and total—though the concept is not often expressed. The fact that the United States has remained the world's only superpower does not bring to completion its ambitious hegemonic project. There are other contenders in the struggle for universal hegemony, and the most conspicuous among them are certain forms of counterpower that base themselves on extreme, perverted Islamic teachings that sometimes end in "terrorism." Yet, the question remains as to why universality and totality are conceived in terms that, if no longer imperialistic, are—as some authors have recently suggested—imperial.[5] In other words, why is it that the concepts of universality and totality, far from bringing about the "secular and earthly plenitude" suggested by Gramsci[6] or the "world that contains many worlds" of the Zapatistas, only breed different varieties of fundamentalisms (Christian, Islamic, Jewish) that bitterly and violently exclude each other?

The United States sees itself as the defender of universal freedom, and in that sense it arrogates a mandate that many popular movements dispute. This is the mandate of universal power. The shift from discourse on freedom to discourse on power is often covered up by a simple/simplistic rhetoric that is nevertheless tacitly and passively accepted by those who represent the people(s) of the world. Thus, the speeches given lately by the president of the United States—speeches filled with veiled or overt threats against actual or potential enemies—become a sort of political and philosophical *vade mecum* for the 21st century.[7]

Let us look closely at some passages from one of these speeches. First of all, it is noteworthy that the president makes no mention of communism, the number-one enemy for almost a century. Yet, it is easy to recognize its "specter" behind the word *totalitarianism*. Speaking of the present-day terrorists, the president says: "They are the heirs of all the murderous ideologies of the 20th century. . . . [T]hey follow in the path of fascism, Nazism and totalitarianism." The fact that there is no mention of communism may be an implicit recognition of the lies that have informed the 20th century's crusade against it. Yet, it is interesting that fascism, Nazism, and totalitarianism are here mentioned separately, as if to suggest that there may be more to the last term than what is naturally included in the first two. This "more" can be nothing other than the concept of communism. It is also interesting to note how in Italy, for instance, the heirs of the fascist movement and regime are today in power with the blessing of the "free" and "democratic" world, and how they have turned Italy into a police state of fascist memory. In addition, as is well known but often and easily forgotten, the United States has often helped these "murderous ideologies" into power. One example may suffice for all: Chile in 1973. So, the rhetoric really works, even though present-day terrorism (which may indeed bear the mark of a murderous ideology) has perhaps nothing to do with fascism and Nazism—certainly nothing to do with totalitarianism, if by that unde-fined word one means communism. Yet, the presidential speech points to a philo-sophical continuity between the terrorists and those previous murderous ideolo-gies, a continuity that revolves around the historically abused concept of the will to power. Accordingly, what defines the terrorists and makes them the heirs of a mur-derous century is their "sacrificing human life to serve their radical visions, [and their] . . . abandoning every value except the will to power."[8]

A few months have passed since I wrote the above. The war against terrorism is certainly not over. That against Afghanistan is over and yet it isn't. The West has been bombing Afghanistan for about four months, and Iraq for more than ten years. The population of Afghanistan, already mired in extreme poverty, is now on the verge of nothingness; one reads reports of still more isolated villages where star-vation and death have become elements of everyday life. In the meantime, the "reclusive Omar"—one-eyed and piratical—is still at large, to say nothing of the devil himself, Osama bin Laden.

The West is offering world history a pathetic representation of itself. With all its might, it is still fighting against an already deeply impoverished country, and this fight seems to have no near end. To complicate an already unstable global sit-uation, India is courting war against Pakistan on the phony basis of the same rhetoric against terrorism, and the nuclear possibilities of both countries do turn their old regional conflict into a matter of global interest. The situation in Palestine isn't any better; rather, it is worse. Aside from denying Arafat the right to go to Bethlehem (a city under his jurisdiction) on Christmas Eve, the Israelis recently razed to the ground a whole neighborhood in Gaza and attacked the Palestinians with missiles. All these situations (and others) are certainly not unrelated. The ar-rogance of Empire to dictate its conditions (at all levels of reality, as we shall see) does give lesser powers the opportunity to gamble on what history itself may con-cede or deny—for, if God is dead, *there is* history.

Now the first prisoners of war (though not called prisoners of war by the United States) are arriving in Cuba. Without really explaining what that means, the American secretary of defense has "characterized" Guantanamo Bay in Cuba as "the least worst place we could have selected." Of course, the United States does not give any weight to the fact that the Cubans are completely unhappy with this choice and may even consider it a form of provocation. In reality, the base at Guan-tanamo Bay, seized in 1898 at the time of the so-called Spanish-American War, is long due back to the legitimate government of Cuba; but the United States feels that this has nothing to do with the principles of democracy and freedom, that the base is really a concrete way to permanently challenge the legitimacy—indeed, the ontological nature—of the Cuban government itself, and of an independent Cuban society. Intuitively, one can discern in this move the obscure and frustrated desire that has obsessed all American presidents since Kennedy: the dream of over-throwing Fidel. In this sense, the recent appointment of Otto J. Reich as assistant secretary of state for Latin American Affairs is fully explained.[9]

Thus the prisoners of war (who, for some reason, are not prisoners of war) arrive in Cuba. Some suffering from tuberculosis, all "wobbly and disoriented," they are being caged in six-by-eight-foot cells with walls of chain-link fence and metal roofs so that control can be constant and thorough—a vulgar version of the Panopticon model discussed by Foucault.[10] A U.S. general called these conditions "humane but not comfortable"—whatever that means. The shallowness of mainstream media lets one immediately see absurdities and contradictions: These prisoners of war are not called "prisoners of war" because to do so would invoke the Geneva Convention; yet the same Convention is invoked when, as a measure "against insults and public curiosity," the Pentagon prohibits journalists to use still or video cameras. So, on the one hand, the prisoners of war who are not prisoners of war are protected by the Geneva Convention; on the other, they aren't. On the one hand, the prisoners of war who are not prisoners of war are still prisoners of war; on the other hand, they are just captives (where *captives* has the meaning of "held *as if*" rather than "held *as*" prisoners of war).[11] This may explain why tropical Cuba is the least worst of places; perhaps there's a nostalgia here for the heyday of the slave trade. These prisoners of war who are not prisoners of war (and yet sometimes they are) show the full extent of American and Western arrogance and abuse of power. Indeed, what gives the United States the right to manipulate the universal medium of language, to manipulate logic, thought, and truth? Political power, military hegemony, can give a country the sheer, brute force to implement all absurd and contradictory notions, but this approach is not sustained by a philosophical and ethical legitimization. Rather, it represents the utmost of authoritarianism, absolutism, and totalitarianism. Even worse, it is a whimsical way of dealing with reality and the world that defies the most fundamental rules of logic and common sense. One is prompted here to think of the Confucian emphasis on the rectification of names.

Indeed, we need a rectification. Names such as *democracy* and *freedom* have completely lost their meaning, or are used in a merely ideological manner; the same is true for names such as *communism*, which is equated with *totalitarianism*. Yet, the prisoners of war who are not prisoners of war offer the clearest example of the disregard and contempt that the powers-that-be have for human intelligence. In reality, such disregard and contempt are symptoms of a social pathology that I call *social idiocy*.[12] The fact that people who are unfit to govern others still do govern can only be interpreted as a sign of the degeneration of the world's societies. Arrogance and ignorance espouse each other in the attempt to revolutionize society from above, where this revolutionizing has the effect of creating a greater degree of leeway for the elites and a thorough control of, and loss of fundamental freedoms for, a huge number of discontented people all over the globe. A clear example of this unity of arrogance and ignorance is seen in Italian official politics, particularly as manifested after the Genoa events in July 2001. There, too, everything seems permissible now, and the sincerity that once sustained critical and enlightened thinking has given way to an asinine, yet dangerous, comedy devoid of all substance and thought. Thus, the Italian prime minister, who at some point in his life must have heard the names of Ibn Sína and Ibn Rushd (to mention just two) but evidently hasn't retained them in memory, declares the historical superiority of Western culture; later, he leads the Italian foreign minister to resign his position by stating that the relationship to other countries is his immediate business—a form of concentration of power that leaves no doubt as to whether one can still characterize Italy as a democracy, yet no mainstream critic would challenge that. In the United States, things are a little different inasmuch as the idea of political correctness has become a social norm, a cultural etiquette, that few in an official position would dare disregard. Yet, abuses against foreigners, particularly those of Arabic or seemingly Arabic provenance, haven't been absent. Even the *New York Times*, which sooner or later prints what it cannot not print, has reported on cases of people detained for months just on the basis of their Arabic names or looks. Many people don't even understand that one can be an Arab and not a Muslim, or a Muslim and not an Arab; that one can have an Arabic look and be from Europe, an Arabic name and be from Chicago or Puerto Rico, or wherever. We hear a lot about patriotism. But this idea is a bit too old, still valid perhaps in countries that have recently known a history of tragic invasions and occupations tearing apart their social and political fabric, but not in the old, comfortable West. There, even during the course of the French Revolution where it originated, the idea of patriotism ultimately produced nothing but the concept of the "Great Nation" and the betrayal of the original, universal ideals of the Revolution itself. But now the people of the world have grown up, and it is only the deliberate will of Empire to ossify the organic course of the world's culture (and I deliberately use the singular) that can keep such an obsolete and empty concept alive. The truth is that reality is split into two parts, in Fanon's sense.[13] On the one hand, there is the global club of the elites (the idle and good-for-nothing rich), which moves freely and expensively and is protected by army and police from Seattle to Genoa, from Davos to New York, with the task of reinterpreting freedom as free trade and democracy as the imposition of an elitist and contemptuous will to power over the world and the people of the world; on the other hand, there is the coming awareness that globalization from below, respectful of local difference, is really a form of secularization of the world's destiny that explodes all obscurantist and fanatical notions associated with the sense of belonging to a faith, a race, an ethnic group, a nation, and so on—a coming awareness that is deliberately and forcefully held in check.

Another dichotomy also comes to mind. On the one hand, we have a world divided into two antagonistic sides: the world of institutions and established power, and the world of popular movements and everyday life. On the other, we have what could be interpreted as an ancient conflict between two civilizations but is in actuality the result of an historical process that brought first European and later Western dominance all over the world. In this sense, even Islamic fundamentalism finds historical explanation, for it entails an almost Machiavellian return to the principles. It is true that there was a moment in history when European military superiority challenged the as yet unchallenged power of Islam, in the political form of the Ottoman empire. Thus, with the Treaty of Carlowitz of 1699, when the Ottoman empire was forced to cede most of Hungary to Austria, Muslims' self-confidence in the victorious power of their divine cause suffered a serious blow. That event marks the beginning of the decline of the Ottoman military might and, in general, the beginning of the end of Islam's political independence. Shortly after that, the Wahabbi movement started in Arabia with the precise intention of re-turning to the principles of the true faith. Yet, even then, the Islamic world cannot be considered a monolithic, homogeneous structure. The same is true of Europe and the West. At the time, Austria was not on better terms with other European countries, and it wouldn't be for at least two centuries; Europe and the West were preparing themselves for fratricidal wars that can scarcely be characterized as "civilized"; nor was the Ottoman empire on good terms with all other Islamic countries (notably, Persia), or the rest of the Islamic countries on good terms with each other. The abuse of historical categories has often the effect of ossifying what needs to be liberated, and of blurring the already unstable and fine line between history and historiography. Indeed, the view that the world is divided into elite and popular strata, rather than into a series of warring civilizations, seems to be a much more accurate representation of reality.

Let us reconsider our prisoners of war in Cuba who are not prisoners of war. How can the form of torture they will undergo be called *humane?* What does this word *humane* even mean? It means nothing, particularly when it is uttered with nothing in mind. And how can their torture be a redress for the victims of September 11? First of all, it must be noted that these prisoners of war who are not prisoners of war may have nothing directly to do with the events of 9/11. Indeed, at the time of this writing, there is no incontrovertible proof that even bin Laden or the now-toppled Afghan government were involved in the attack. It logically follows that the captives in Cuba would be guilty only of having defended their country against foreign aggression. How, then, can they be considered "*unlawful* combatants"? According to which system of laws? In truth, denying that they are prisoners of war is in itself a very serious war crime. But of course, Empire does not care about these logical and ethical subtleties. The prisoners will be left, in cells that are really cages (as Amnesty International has pointed out), at the mercy of mosquitoes in the tropical Cuban nights. They will get neither blankets nor mosquito repellent. This is what is meant by uncomfortable conditions, yet "humane."

Revenge. Torture, slow and constant. Are these aspects of the West's superior culture, its goodness and abhorrence of evil, its civilization? Frankly, from the standpoint of world history, of the logic of violence that informs our world, of the familiarity the world and history have with war, the number of deaths that occurred on September 11 is not even that great. And it is interesting that the site is already turning into a touristic (memorial) place, away from the worldly, "dirty" world of economy and business. Meanwhile, the relatives of some of the victims, already forgetful of their patriotic élan, are complaining that the government money they will get as a recompense is not enough to cover their losses. Of course, it isn't. What amount of money would be? Yet this element of venality is really at odds with the ideality that has sustained the rhetoric of retaliation and war.[14]

But a world that is unable to overcome, even theoretically, the logic of violence and war cannot be surprised that bombs explode in Israel, in Ireland and London, in the Basque region in Spain, and that New York is also finally attacked. All these acts are called acts of terrorism, yet terrorism is not *causa sui*. We are at a point in history when even reasoning about these things has become taboo, for the critic must always be sure to denounce terrorism energetically, lest he or she be seen as defending or justifying terrorism. Yet, this in itself is a form of censorship, a closure of the mind. One can say that there are at least two forms of terrorism: organized and institutional (or state) terrorism. If one denounces organized terrorism, one also has to denounce, even more energetically, institutional terrorism. Wasn't that night in Genoa a night of terror, given all the humiliation and torture that took place? And the police who indiscriminately beat everyone out on the streets, weren't they performing terrorist acts? Such questions may raise controversies or be dismissed as not to the point, as insufficiently serious, as ideological. Yet I think they should be posed, not only to understand the present situation but to understand history as well, thereby informing the present through history.

Think of World War II. The Japanese attack against Pearl Harbor is usually described as a terrorist attack. The American response a few years later, when the war was virtually over—the atomic bombing of Hiroshima and Nagasaki—isn't.[15] Notwithstanding the opposition of the scientists who had worked on producing the atomic bomb and of military men such as General Eisenhower who didn't think the bomb was necessary, the United States decided to bomb Japan. One hundred thousand people died during the two days that Hiroshima and Nagasaki were bombed, and many others died afterward. From the standpoint of world history, even one hundred thousand deaths do not constitute a great number.[16] Millions of people, in just the 20th century alone, have lost their lives through war and violence. But the retaliatory attack against Japan, rationalized by some, simply forgotten by many others, is a useful example when one is trying to understand institutional terror. Few would describe it as a terrorist attack, just as few would call President Truman a terrorist, given all the ethical and legal implications of the term; no one even calls him a murderer for having ordered the deaths of so many people. Some might say that my argument is specious because such events happened in a regime of war. Yet, what is war after all? How can a regime of war be legally and ethically justified? Alternatively, if we formally understand how it can be legally justified, what are the bases for its ethical justification? How can we still insist on looking at war as a possible solution to the world's problems and fail to see it as deepening them?[17] Above all, how can we accept the fact that a regime of war is declared and implemented, or not, according to *one* nation's interest and caprice? Here, of course, we come back to the question of the prisoners of war who are not prisoners of war.

History is mistreated by a handful of arrogant and thoughtless gentlemen. I say that history is mistreated (logic and ethics are abused) because the world is now at a point where the people, not the elites, are ready to take destiny into their hands, change the course of the production of culture, and stop rushing after a useless and dangerous idea of economic growth—one that increasingly deepens the gap between the North and the South of the world and, within both North and South, between those who belong to the global club of money and power and those who are outcast and poor. Yet, history is not these gentlemen's whore. True, this is the age of empire, of Western and American empire—or, rather, the empire of the world's elites, the global empire that, having learned nothing from history, still sits as if unaware of the danger of subterranean fire, still provokes discontent and anger by disseminating misery and ruin all over the world. Yet, as Fernand Braudel once wrote: "History sooner or later takes back her gifts."

NOTES

1. Edward Said also recently made this point. (See "Islam and the West Are Inadequate Banners," *The Guardian*, September 16, 2001.)

2. See, for instance, Gabriel Kolko, *The Politics of War: The World and the United States Foreign Politics 1943–1945* (New York: Pantheon Books, 1968, 1990).

3. Quoted in Philip Foner, *A History of Cuba and Its Relations with the United States*, Vol. 1 (New York: International Publishers, 1963), p. 359.

4. I am referring here to all liberation movements, regardless of whether they understood/understand themselves as communist (Marxist, Leninist, etc.), socialist, anarchist, liberationist, and so on. Many people would not agree with this, but the argument could be made that, as long as they don't share in some right-wing or supremacist ideology, all anti-establishment movements revolve around general principles of communist philosophy.

5. Cf. Michael Hardt and Antonio Negri, *Empire* (Cambridge, Mass.: Harvard University Press, 2000).

6. This is my own rendering of Gramsci's concept of *absolute historicism*. I have explained the reasons for this "translation" elsewhere. Basically, the expression *secular and earthly plenitude* is a more concrete and graspable description of Gramsci's concept of absolute historicism, which is in turn a description of the philosophy of praxis. Gramsci says: "The philosophy of praxis is absolute 'historicism,' the absolute secularization and earthliness of thought, an absolute humanism of history." See Antonio Gramsci, *Selections from the Prison Notebooks* (New York: International Publishers, 1971), p. 465.

7. This was written before the president's recent visit to the Far East (February 2002), whose main purpose seemed to be one of regional destabilization, and before the expression *axis of evil* was added to the rhetorical manual of a new world order. What becomes more and more apparent is that Bush is certainly not the bearer of a Kantian millennium.

8. It is not Nietzsche's concept of the will to power being expressed here but, rather, Reinhold Niebuhr's. With this concept, constructed through a logic of good and evil, Niebuhr provided the ideological substance for the anti-communism of the Truman doctrine. In this connection, see Walter Lafeber, *America, Russia, and the Cold War, 1945–2000* (New York: McGraw-Hill, 2002).

9. Reich arrived in the United States as a fourteen-year-old Cuban refugee. The Center for International Policy describes him as someone who has "protected terrorists and was

involved in the Iran-contra scandal and other efforts to funnel aid to the contras. Part of the anti-Castro Cuban-exile lobby, he is known as an abrasive right-wing ideologue. . . " (http://www.ciponline.org/reich/).

10. See Michael Foucault, *Discipline and Punish: The Birth of the Prison*, trans. Alan Sheridan (New York: Vintage Books, 1977).

11. The news (as of February 7, 2002) that the Geneva Convention does apply to some of the detainees (the Taliban soldiers), but that they will not be considered prisoners of war, only complicates things further.

12. I have explained this concept more fully elsewhere. (See my article "x, X, Gog and Magog: On Poiesis, Praxis, and the Problem of Thinking," *Found Object*, No. 11, Fall 2001–Spring 2002.) Fundamentally, I mean the inability or (more often) the outright un-willingness to look at reality from a vantage point outside one's social interests and cultural constraints.

13. Franz Fanon, *The Wretched of the Earth*, trans. Constance Farrington (New York: Grove Weidenfeld, 1963).

14. Of course, there were those who opposed this rhetoric from the beginning, such as the courageous family who, in an op-ed letter to the *New York Times*, titled "Not in Our Son's Name," asked the president, the nation, and the world to withdraw from the logic of violence and, fundamentally, to *think*. See www.newhumanist.com/rodriguez.html.

15. Many justify the bombing on the grounds that Pearl Harbor had been attacked first. But that *first* is a problem: Then one could justify the Japanese attack on the grounds that the West had attacked and humiliated Japan in the 18th and 19th centuries, and so on. As always, the logic of retaliation takes the path of regression *ad infinitum*—a bad infini-tude, to be sure. How would this logic differ from that of the Mafia? And what is Mafia logic if not the utmost expression of human stupidity, or what we have called social idiocy?

16. Of course, the real issue is not the number of deaths. Yet, this detail becomes im-portant both in historical accounts and in common conversations. It also usually influences military response.

17. I am not suggesting here that all wars are the same. There is certainly a difference between institutional (or state) war and social war. The former strikingly resembles institu-tional (or state) terrorism; the latter is usually a war of liberation or emancipation. Institu-tional wars are legally justified but ethically unjustified and unjustifiable; social wars are legally unjustified, but they are ethically grounded.

7

The Mass Psychology
of Terrorism

ELLEN WILLIS*

I

The symbolism of the Twin Towers has been much remarked on: They are said to have represented the forces of modernity in general and global capitalism in particular. Yet oddly, it has been more or less ignored that the towers were also and quite obviously sexual symbols. What might it mean for men to commit mass murder by smashing symbols of desire—desire that in terms of their religious convictions means impurity, decadence, evil—and at the same time destroy themselves? Can it be that those symbols and the set of realities they represented were at the deepest level a source of intolerable attraction and temptation to these men, one that could be defended against only by means of total obliteration? Was the rage that such an act must entail directed solely against an external enemy, or was it also against the actors' own unfreedom? In short, was the hijackers' plunge a spectacular dual act of sadomasochism?

When I raised these questions at the conference from which this book arose, the audience responded with nervous tittering. Perhaps people thought I was trying to make some satirical point they didn't get; perhaps they thought I had gone off the deep end. Or maybe they were merely startled by the intrusion of sex into what was supposed to be serious leftist analysis of international politics. In any case, the reaction was not unfamiliar to me. For a brief period in the 1960s and '70s, a portion of the left concerned itself with the psychosexual dimension of politics; but even then such insights were rarely applied to the international arena. By

....

*A portion of this chapter appears in somewhat different form in *The Nation*. (See "Bringing the Holy War Home" in the issue dated December 17, 2001.)

now, in an era of anti-Freudian backlash and pervasive anxiety about changes in our sexual culture, they have been entirely purged from the political conversation.

This absence is, in my view, disastrous. Without understanding the psycho-sexual aspect of political violence and domination—and the cultural questions with which it is intertwined—we cannot make sense of what happened on September 11; indeed, we cannot make sense of the history of the 20th century. I don't propose that we discuss psychosexual politics *instead* of the very real, and certainly crucial, economic and geopolitical issues that have shaped the Middle Eastern and South Asian condition, from oil to the legacy of colonialism and the Cold War to the ascendancy of neoliberalism to the Israeli-Palestinian conflict. Rather, my claim is that the particular kind of crisis Islamic fundamentalism represents erupts when economic and geopolitical issues converge with cultural and psychosexual conflict. Though one member of my restless conference audience accused me of anti-Arab racism for speculating on the hijackers' sexual motivation, I do not view this con-vergence and its consequences as peculiar to the Arab or Islamic world. Indeed, the paradigm of such crises occurred in Europe with Hitler's rise to power. "Ethnic cleansing" in Bosnia—in which Muslims were the victims—is a more recent Euro-pean example, notable for, among other things, the mystified reaction of so many observers: How, in a modern European country and a cosmopolitan city like Sara-jevo could such an outbreak of barbarism occur? Evidently they were unaware that a similar incredulity had followed the Holocaust.

In fact, the necessary condition for such outbreaks is "modernity"—catchall shorthand for the ongoing, worldwide cultural revolution that includes the assaults of capitalism, science and technology, Enlightenment liberalism, and democratic movements in the broad sense against the patriarchal authoritarian form of social organization that in one or another version has dominated human culture for the last 5,000 years or so. This revolution is only about 200 years old. In the United States and Europe, which are supposed to represent its vanguard, it is very much unfinished; and yet it has had an impact virtually everywhere in the world. It is also riven by contradictions: If capitalism and imperialism have propelled it, so have so-cialism, communism, and anti-imperialist movements. To add still another layer of convolutions, both capitalist and anti-capitalist, imperialist and anti-imperialist forces have been counterrevolutionary as well—often upholding or opportunisti-cally allying with patriarchal reaction and, more crucially, substituting their own versions of neo-patriarchal, anti-democratic tyranny for the traditional kind. Yet however contradictory and uneven, the cultural revolution has put freedom, equal-ity, and democracy on the world agenda in an inescapable way; and the cutting edge of this project is a challenge to the structure of sexual life, the family, and male-female relations. Enormous psychological conflict, tension, and anxiety are the inevitable accompaniment of changes in this realm. And under certain circum-stances those emotions get out of control.

Proponents of the "clash of civilizations" thesis are half right. There is such a clash, but not the kind Samuel Huntington has in mind; this is not a question of

East versus West. The struggle of democratic secularism, religious tolerance, individual freedom, and feminism against authoritarian patriarchal religion, culture, and morality is going on all over the world. That includes the Islamic world, where dissidents are regularly jailed, killed, exiled, or merely intimidated and silenced by autocratic governments. In Iran the mullahs still have power, but young people are in open revolt against the Islamic regime. In Pakistan before the Afghan war, the urban middle classes worried that their society would be Talibanized. In Afghanistan the Revolutionary Association of Women of Afghanistan (RAWA) calls for a secular state. There are feminist movements in all these countries as well as in Egypt, Jordan, Turkey, Morocco. At the same time, religious and cultural reactionaries have mobilized to attack secular modernity in liberal democracies from Israel to the postcommunist countries of Eastern Europe to the United States. Jerry Falwell's view of September 11—that the massacre was God's judgment on an America that tolerates abortion, homosexuality, and feminism—mirrors Osama bin Laden's. Moreover, this clash—this culture war, if you will—exists not only within regions and within countries, but also within individuals. Social instability and personal ambivalence are its hallmarks.

When I speak of "patriarchal authoritarian" social organization, I refer to the historic institutions of the father-ruled family and monotheistic religion; to the ideology and morality perpetuated by these institutions, even as the institutions themselves weaken or break down; and to those aspects of all existing societies (such as corporate and state bureaucracies) that still model themselves on patriarchal institutions and replicate patriarchal ideology. The basic impulse of patriarchalism, in this sense, is the drive to dominate nature, a project that requires control over sexuality (nature within us), control of women and children (onto whom the anarchy of nature and sexuality is projected), and social hierarchies that assume people's inability to govern themselves. Desire is equated with unbridled selfishness, aggression, and violence. Morality is equated with self-abnegation, repression of desire, and submission to authority.

A traditional function of the family—now seriously challenged or compromised in many societies—has been to acculturate each new generation into this belief system and moral code by promising (if not always delivering) communal solidarity, economic security, love, and a degree of sexual satisfaction to those who obey its rules, while threatening violators with punishments ranging from physical force and violence to economic, social, or emotional isolation. Children characteristically internalize these promises and threats, identifying with their parents' morality and punishing themselves with guilt or shame for transgressing it. The patriarchal religions have served to reinforce this moral system with their conception of God as the ultimate parent; insofar as they retain social authority or political power, their appeal to the inner force of conscience is backed up by communal and legal sanctions. At the same time, religion has offered a pathway to freedom from the constriction and alienation that patriarchal morality imposes: not only the prospect of immortality as a reward for goodness, but access in the here-and-now to a spiritual realm where the constrictions don't apply, where one can make contact with the infinite and experience ecstasy or glimpse its possibility.

Of course, patriarchal morality and religion also condemn murder and other forms of predatory aggression. Their overriding claim to legitimacy even among unbelievers is their enforcement of such prohibitions, without which no society could survive. But here we run into a curious paradox, for in fact violence is endemic to patriarchal culture—violence that is outlawed and punished; violence that is overtly prohibited but covertly condoned; and violence that is sanctioned by state, familial, or religious authority. For defenders of the system, illicit violence is simply an unfortunate product of human nature, while licit violence is a necessary defense against unprovoked aggression and other kinds of anti-social behavior. Skeptics, however, might ask: Can the high level of violence in patriarchal cultures be attributed to people's chronic, if largely unconscious, rage over the denial of their freedom and pleasure? To what extent is sanctioned or unofficially condoned violence—from war and capital punishment to lynching, wife-beating, and the rape of "bad" women to harsh penalties for "immoral" activities like drug-using and nonmarital sex to the religious or ideological persecution of totalitarian states—in effect a socially approved outlet for expressing that rage, as well as a way of relieving guilt by projecting one's own unacceptable desires onto scapegoats? Might religiously motivated violence, in particular, combine a longing for spiritual transcendence with guilt transmuted into self-righteous zeal and rage rationalized as service to God?

Most of the time, the ongoing violence of patriarchal cultures is contained and integrated into "normal" social functioning; but periodically it erupts into bloody wars, massacres, sadistic rampages, witch-hunts, the lesser of which make news and the more horrific, history. The 20th century—and now the beginning of the 21st—have been marked by a massive increase in the scale and frequency of such episodes, of which Al Qaeda's holy war is only the latest spectacular example. Not coincidentally, in the same period of history the destabilizing forces of cultural revolution have put traditional patriarchalism on the defensive to an unprecedented degree. This is an age in which mass media, mass migration, economic globalization, and the ubiquity of modern technology have vastly increased the points of provocative contact between modernity and its antagonists. Opponents of the cultural revolution have not scrupled to exploit its innovations—from modern mass communications, transportation, and weaponry to elections and civil liberties—while both the avatars of global capitalism and their anti-imperialist opponents have tried to enlist anti-modern movements in their struggles for dominance. As modernizing, liberalizing forces erode the repression that keeps rage unconscious and the social controls that keep violence contained, it becomes ever easier for a match of political grievance to ignite the gas of psychosexual tension, touching off a conflagration. Eventually, the fire is put out, for the time being. The gas remains.

II

In the 1920s Germany was a modern capitalist state with a liberal democracy that was, however, a fragile veneer over an authoritarian, sexually repressive culture; the patriarchal family ruled, subordinating women and youth—though the latter, stirred by new permissive currents, were growing restless. The Germans had no shortage of political grievances: a humiliating defeat in World War I, an economy crippled by unemployment and hyperinflation. The left offered an analysis of why the calamity of the war had happened and attempted to rally workers to fight for their concrete economic and political interests. Hitler instead offered a virulent backlash against Enlightenment values, centering on a racial myth *cum* paranoid fantasy: Aryan Germany had been "stabbed in the back" by the racially inferior Jews—the preeminent symbol of international capitalists, communists, cosmopolitans, sexual libertines, homosexuals, emancipated women, "race mixers," all the contaminating, alien influences of modernity. The majority of Germans, workers as well as the lower middle class, opted for Hitler's fantasy.

Right-wing industrialists supported Hitler because of his anti-communism, in the mistaken belief that they could control him; the Western powers abetted his rise in the hope that he would fight the Soviet Union (a strategy that set up a dramatic case of "blowback"). But Nazism was not a creature of the capitalist, imperialist right; it was a mass movement, of the kind that, ironically, was fostered by the very liberal democracy it despised. As radical psychoanalyst Wilhelm Reich put it in his classic work *The Mass Psychology of Fascism*, what defines a fascist movement is its "mixture of rebellious emotions and reactionary social ideas."[1] Political abjectness and economic ruin could explain why Germans wanted to rebel, but not why their rebellion took the form of support for totalitarian, genocidal sadism, or why they were so resistant to democratic and socialist appeals to rational self-interest.

It was in response to this conundrum that Reich and other psychoanalytically minded radicals, including the Marxist social theorists of the Frankfurt School, challenged the conventional economistic wisdom of the European left to argue that unconscious psychosexual conflict had played a central role in the triumph of Nazism. In the view of this Freudian left, the liberalism of Weimar had stirred up repressed longings for freedom—and rage at its suppression—that people whose characters had been formed by patriarchalism could not admit. While their anger was encouraged and legitimized by real political complaints, their underlying fear of freedom prevented them from contemplating real revolution.

For the mass of Germans, then, Hitler offered a solution to this impasse: He represented the authoritarian father who commanded submission—only in this case submission entailed the license, indeed the obligation, to vent rebellious rage by supporting and participating in persecution and mass murder. For young people caught between subservience to the family and guilt-ridden desires for freedom and sexual pleasure, this prospect had particular appeal: In the name of patriotic

duty they could at once discharge and deny their unconscious hatred of the patri-
arch by directing that hatred toward the perceived enemies of the fatherland. At the
same time, their repressed sexuality could find distorted expression in the sadistic
pleasures of actual or vicarious cruelty, in the surrender to a charismatic leader, and
in the quasi-religious ecstasy of mass rallies.

If this hypothesis of unconscious conflict allows us to make sense of the
spectacle of an entire nation succumbing to a manifestly irrational ideology, it
also sheds some light on the ubiquitous claim by Germans, Western governments, and Poles living in close proximity to Auschwitz that they didn't know the
Holocaust was going on. I suspect that most *didn't* know, that such knowledge
was blocked from consciousness along with a widespread emotional complicity
in anti-Semitism. Indeed, the most disturbing implication of the Freudian left
analysis is that Nazism was not a phenomenon peculiar to post–World War I
Germany but, rather, had fulfilled a potential inherent in patriarchal culture,
even in "advanced" societies—a potential that might be activated anywhere by
destabilizing political events.

After World War II, the enormity of the Nazi catastrophe could no longer be
denied, and so for a time blatant racism and anti-Semitism were socially unacceptable. Liberal Western governments preached tolerance while capital, chastened by
the crisis it had barely survived and by the looming presence of the Soviet Union,
cooperated with government and labor in curbing its most predatory features, fostering mass prosperity and with it social stability. The USSR and the communist
dictatorships of Eastern Europe simply suppressed the culture war, imposing a
modern secular regime (albeit without freedom or democracy) by fiat.[2] Meanwhile,
moralists spoke of the Holocaust as an evil beyond comprehension, a confirmation
of original sin, proof of the need for religion and the futility of utopian projects.
The culture that had produced the Nazis was not confronted; its overtly pathological aspects were merely re-repressed.

This détente did not last long. The 1960s and '70s brought a resumption of
culture war in the United States and Western Europe, as a revolt from the left on
behalf of racial equality, personal and sexual freedom, feminism, and gay liberation
was soon followed by a backlash of religious and secular conservatives aimed at
restoring traditional morality, social discipline, and white male dominance. In the
'70s, American business reneged on its compact with labor and the welfare state,
launching an era of renewed class warfare: While many factors contributed to this
development, including the OPEC oil cartel, America's impending loss of the Vietnam War, and the rise of the transnational corporation, surely part of the story was
that corporate investment in high wages and social welfare could no longer buy a
compliant middle class—on the contrary, economic security had produced a generation with a subversive sense of entitlement.

The '60s revolt in the West was in turn a crucial influence on the democratic
revolutions of Eastern Europe; yet the reality of the postcommunist era would turn
out to be far darker than the euphoric expectations of 1989. With the collapse of

communism, global capitalist triumphalism went into high gear. Neoliberal "shock therapy" and the abolition of communist social benefits devastated Eastern Europe's standard of living at the same time that fascists, nationalist fanatics, and religious reactionaries who had been silenced by communist regimes were once again free to operate. In Yugoslavia the combination proved lethal.

Not long after Francis Fukuyama declared "the end of history,"[3] the war in Bosnia would show that, if anything, history was taking up where it had left off in 1945. Yugoslavia was a poor country that had lived fairly well by borrowing from the West; but in the new era, Western banks were calling in its debt and Western governments were turning their back. It was also a country that was superficially modern and profoundly patriarchal, with a traditionalist, sexually repressed population. For a communist-apparatchik-turned-nationalist-demagogue like Slobodan Milosevic, or a fascist like Franjo Tudjman, these circumstances offered ample opportunity to mobilize people's rebellious emotions behind reactionary social ideas. The result was an insane genocidal war in which people turned their rage against neighbors who shared their language and culture—neighbors they had lived with, worked with, married without making ethnic distinctions. And again the world declined to look this irrationalism in the face or examine its roots, preferring to blame evil individuals and "ancient ethnic hatreds."

To examine Islamic fundamentalism through the lens of the last century's history is to discern a familiar pattern: psychopathology brought to the surface by the promise and threat of modernity and aggravated by political oppression. As with fascism, the rise of Islamic totalitarianism has partly to do with its populist appeal to class resentments and to feelings of political subordination and humiliation, but is at bottom a violent defensive reaction against the temptations of freedom. Islamic militants demonize the United States not simply because of its foreign policy—as so many American leftists would like to believe, despite the explicit pronouncements of the Islamists themselves—but because it exports and symbolizes cultural revolution.

In the wake of 9/11 it has often been noted that militant Islamism filled a vacuum created by the failures of secular leftist movements in the Middle East to improve the condition of the people or do away with corrupt regimes, from Egypt to Saudi Arabia, that collaborate with the West's neocolonial policies. And of course those failures are in no small part the result of relentless American opposition to leftism of any sort (in contrast to our support for Islamist fanatics we have deemed to be on our side, from the Saudi rulers to the Afghan mujahadeen). Yet none of this can really explain why so many people should be attracted to a movement that has no agenda for solving their real economic and political problems but, rather, serves up the fantasy that the answer is murder-suicide in pursuit of a holy war against infidels and the imposition of a draconian religious police state. The appeal of this fantasy cannot be understood without reference to the patriarchalism that governs the sexual and domestic lives of most people in the Islamic world. Osama bin Laden and his gang are themselves products of an ultra-patriarchal theocracy

hardly less tyrannical than the Taliban's; if the catalyst for their rebellion was opposition to the Saudi regime, their ideology clearly derives from their upbringing
within it.

Another clue to the psychopathology that drives the Islamist movement is its
increasingly hysterical Jew-hatred, which has borrowed liberally from both Nazi
and medieval Christian polemics. True to its characteristic evasions, the left has
tended to dismiss Islamist anti-Semitism as a mere epiphenomenon of justified
anger at Israel, which would presumably go away if justice were done. But is it not
worth examining the strange mental processes that transmute a political grievance
against Israel into a widespread delusion that the Jews masterminded the World
Trade Center massacre? And what do we make of the execution of an American
journalist who, before being beheaded, is forced to intone, "I am a Jew, my mother
is a Jew, my father is a Jew"?

In any case, the war between Israel and the Arab and Islamic worlds has never
been *only* about conflicting claims to a piece of land, the homelessness of the Palestinians, or the occupation of the West Bank; if it were, it would have been settled
long ago. Rather, Islamist passion for Israel's obliteration has at its core revulsion at
the perceived contamination of the holy land by an infidel nation; worse, a modern democracy; even worse, one populated by that quintessentially alien, blood-
sucking tribe of rootless cosmopolitans, the Jews. Just as the Europeans once
handed their unwelcome Jewish refugee problem to the Arabs, their genocidal anti-
Jewish rhetoric has migrated to the Middle East; but the emotions that give the
rhetoric its power are strictly indigenous. They are unlikely to be assuaged by an
Israeli-Palestinian settlement; they are far more likely to be inflamed.

And if the worst should happen, the world will once again be shocked. We still
don't know—and don't want to know.

III

In America it often happens that the lunatic right, in its feckless way, gets closer to
the heart of the matter than the political mainstream, and so it was with Jerry Falwell's incendiary remark, and Pat Robertson's concurrence, about the cause of
9/11. There was a flurry of indignation in the media, but basically the incident was
dismissed as an isolated moment of wretched excess. Most Americans, from George
W. Bush to Noam Chomsky, resist the idea that the attack was an act of cultural
war, and still fewer are willing to admit its intimate connection with the culture
war at home.

That war has been a centerpiece of American politics for thirty years or
more, shaping our debates and our policies on everything from abortion, censorship, and crime to race, education, and social welfare, to the impeachment of Bill
Clinton and the 2000 election (with those ubiquitous maps of "blue" liberal
coasts versus "red" heartland). Nor, at this moment, does the government know

whether foreign or domestic terrorists were responsible for the anthrax offensive. Yet we shrink from seeing the relationship between our own cultural conflicts and the logic of *jihad*. We are especially eager to absolve religion of any responsibility for the violence committed in its name: For that ubiquitous post-9/11 cliché, "This has nothing to do with Islam," read "Anti-abortion terrorism has nothing to do with Christianity." Post-Enlightenment, post-Reformation, post-feminist, post-sexual-revolution, liberal democratic nation though we are, the legacy of patriarchalism still weighs on us: Our social policies on sex and the family are confused and inconsistent, our psyches more conservative than the actual conditions of our lives. We are deeply anxious and ambivalent about cultural issues, and one way we deal with this is to deny their importance, even sometimes their existence.

For the most part Americans speak of culture and politics as if they were two separate realms. Conservatives accuse the left of politicizing culture and see their own cultural-political offensive against the social movements of the '60s as an effort to restore to culture its rightful autonomy. Centrists deplore the culture war as an artifact of "extremists on both sides" and continually pronounce it dead. The economic-justice left regards cultural politics as a distraction from its efforts to win support for a populist economic program. Multiculturalists pursue the political goal of equality and respect for minority and non-Western cultures, but are reluctant to make political judgments about cultural practices: Feminist universalists have been regularly attacked for "imposing Western values" by criticizing genital mutilation and other forms of female subjection in the Third World.

The artificial separation of politics and culture is nowhere more pronounced than in the discourse of foreign policy and international affairs. For the American government, economic, geopolitical, and military considerations determine our allies and our enemies. Democracy (almost always defined narrowly in terms of a freely elected government, rather than as a way of life) and human rights (only recently construed as including even the most elementary of women's rights) are invoked by policy makers mainly to justify alliances or antagonisms that already exist. While the Cold War inspired much genuine passion on behalf of freedom and the open society, there's no denying that its fundamental motive was the specter of an alternative to capitalism spreading across the globe and encouraging egalitarian heresies at home. The one cultural issue that seems genuinely to affect our relationship with foreign states is our mania for restricting the international drug supply (except when we ourselves are arming drug cartels for some strategic purpose). The left, meanwhile, criticizes the aims of American foreign policy; yet despite intensified concern with human rights in recent years, most leftists still share the government's assumptions about what kinds of issues are important: the neoliberal economic agenda and struggles over resources like oil, the maintenance of friendly client states versus national self-determination, and so on. And like the United States, leftists have often displayed a double standard on human rights, tending to gloss over the abuses of populist or anti-imperialist regimes.

Given these tropisms, it's unsurprising that the absence of religious and personal freedom, the brutal suppression of dissent, and the extreme oppression of women in Islamic theocracies have never been serious subjects of foreign policy debates. Long before the Taliban, many feminists were upset by U.S. support for the mujahadeen; yet this never became a public issue. Even now the Bush administration, for all its self-congratulatory noises about Afghan women's liberation, refuses to lead or even allow an international peace-keeping force in Afghanistan that could stop fundamentalist warlords from regaining power.

Back in the 1950s, in pursuit of its Cold War aims in Iran, the United States overthrew an elected secular government it judged too left-wing and installed the tyrannical and deeply unpopular Shah, then dumped him in the face of Khomeini's 1979 revolution. Except for feminists, the American left, with few exceptions, supported the revolution and brushed off worries about the Ayatollah, though he had made no secret of his theocratic aims: The important thing was to get rid of the Shah—other issues could be dealt with later. Ten years later, on the occasion of the *fatwa* against Salman Rushdie, the Bush I administration appeared far more interested in appeasing Islamic governments and demonstrators offended by Rushdie's heretical book than in condemning Khomeini's death sentence, while an unnerving number of liberals and leftists accused Rushdie and his defenders of cultural imperialism and insensitivity to Muslim sensibilities. Throughout, both defenders and detractors of our alliance with "moderate" Saudi Arabia have ignored Saudi women's slave-like situation, regarding it as "their culture" and none of our business, except when it raises questions about how Americans stationed in the Gulf are expected to behave. It's as if, in discussing South Africa, apartheid had never been mentioned.

There are many things to be learned from the shock of September 11; surely one of the more important is that culture is not only a political matter but a matter of life and death. It follows that a serious long-range strategy against Islamic fundamentalist terrorism must entail open and emphatic opposition to theocracy, to authoritarian religious movements (including messianic Jewish fundamentalists in Israel and the West Bank), and to the subjugation of women. The corollary is moral and material support for the efforts of liberals, modernizers, democratic secularists, and feminists to press for reforms in Middle Eastern and South Asian societies. Yet to define the enemy as fundamentalism—rather than "evil" anti-American fundamentalists, as opposed to the "friendly" kind—is also to make a statement about American cultural politics. Obviously nothing of the sort can be expected from George W. Bush and John Ashcroft, but our problem is not only leaders who are fundamentalist Christians. More important is the tendency of the left and the center to appease the right and downplay the culture war rather than make an uncompromising defense of freedom, feminism, and the separation of church and state. It remains to be seen whether fear of terrorism will trump the fear of facing our own psychosexual contradictions.

Notes

1. Wilhelm Reich, *The Mass Psychology of Fascism*, first English ed., trans. Theodore P. Wolfe (New York: Orgone Institute Press, 1946).

2. While this chapter focuses on fascism and religious fundamentalism, a comprehensive discussion of the mass psychology of terrorism would also have to address communist totalitarianism, including such episodes as the Stalin terror, the Chinese Cultural Revolution, and the mass killing in Cambodia. Communism has its own distinctive psychopolitical dynamics, whose most striking feature is the Orwellian disconnect between professed values—freedom, justice, peace, etc.—and actual behavior.

3. Francis Fukuyama, "The End of History?" *The National Interest*, Summer 1989.

PART II

Globalization, the State, and the Political Economy

8

Globalization and Democracy

MICHAEL HARDT AND ANTONIO NEGRI*

"And [Jesus] asked him, What is thy name? And he answered, saying, My name is Legion: for we are many" [et interrogabat eum quod tibi nomen est et dicit ei Legio nomen mihi est quia multi sumus].

MARK 5:9

The dominant modern notion of democracy has been intimately tied to the nation-state. To investigate the contemporary status of democracy, then, we should look first at the changing powers and role of the nation-state. Many theorists claim, and many others contest, that the diverse phenomena commonly grouped under the term "globalization" have eroded or even negated the powers of nation-states.[1] Too often, however, this is posed as an either/or proposition: either nation-states are still important or there is a new global order. Both, in fact, are true. The era of globalization has not brought the end of the nation-state—nation-states still fulfill extremely important functions in the establishment and regulation of economic, political, and cultural norms—but nation-states have indeed been displaced from the position of sovereign authority. A focus on the concept and practices of sovereignty helps to clarify this discussion.

We propose the concept of Empire to name our contemporary global arrangement. Empire refers above all to a new form of sovereignty that has succeeded the sovereignty of the nation-state, an unlimited form of sovereignty that knows no boundaries or, rather, knows only flexible, mobile boundaries. We borrow the concept of Empire from the ancient Roman figure in which Empire is seen to supersede the alternation of the three classical forms of government—monarchy, aris-

....

*This chapter is a reprint. It was first published in "Democracy Unrealized: Document11_Platform1," edited by Okwui Enwezor et al. (Ostfildern-Ruit, Germany: Hatje Cantz, 2002), pp. 323–336.

tocracy, and democracy—by combining them in a single sovereign rule. Our contemporary Empire is indeed monarchical, and this is most apparent in times of military conflict when we can see the extent to which the Pentagon, with its atomic weapons and superior military technology, effectively rules the world. The supranational economic institutions, such as the WTO, the World Bank, and the IMF, also at times exercise a monarchical rule over global affairs. Our Empire, however, is also aristocratic, that is, ruled by a limited group of a elite actors. The power of nation-states is central here because the few dominant nation-states manage to govern global economic and cultural flows through a kind of aristocratic rule. This aristocracy of nations is revealed clearly, for example, when the G8 nations meet or when the UN security council exercises its authority. The major transnational corporations too in concert and in conflict constitute a form of aristocracy. Finally Empire is also democratic in the sense that it claims to represent the global people, although, as we will argue below, this claim to representation is largely illusory. The entire group of nation-states, the dominant and the subordinated ones together, fulfill the primary role here to the extent that they are assumed in some way to represent their peoples. The UN general assembly is perhaps the most prominent symbol of this democracy of nations. When we recognize that nation-states do not in fact adequately represent their peoples, however, we can have recourse to nongovernmental organizations (NGOs) as the democratic or representative institutions. The functioning of the various different kinds of NGOs as democratic or representative mechanisms is a very complex and important question, which we should not pretend to treat adequately here. In short, Empire is a single sovereign subject that comprehends within its logic all three of these classical forms or levels of rule, the monarchic, the aristocratic, and the democratic. Empire, in other words, is a distinctive form of sovereignty for its ability to include and manage difference within its constitution.

From this perspective we can see that the functions and authority of nation-states have not disappeared. It is probably more accurate to say that the primary functions of nation-states—the regulation of currencies, economic flows, population migrations, legal norms, cultural values, and so forth—have maintained their importance but been transformed through the contemporary processes of globalization. The radical qualitative shift should be recognized rather in terms of sovereignty. Nation-states can no longer claim the role of sovereign or ultimate authority as they could in the modern era. Empire now stands above the nation-states as the final authority and indeed presents a new form of sovereignty.

We should point out that this is a major historical shift only from the perspective of the dominant nation-states. The subordinate nations were never really sovereign. The entry into modernity for many nation-states was the entry into relations of economic and political subordination that undercut any sovereignty to which the nation might pretend. This shift in the form of sovereignty—from the modern sovereignty located in the nation-state to our postmodern imperial sovereignty—nonetheless affects us all. Even where national sovereignty was never a reality, the passage to Empire has transformed our forms of thought and the range of our political possibilities. In the light of Empire we have to reconsider and reconceive all the key concepts of political philosophy.

DEMOCRACY UNREALIZED, DEMOCRACY UNREALIZABLE

This brings us back, first and foremost, to the concept of democracy. The dominant modern notion of democracy was, as we claimed at the outset, based on representational institutions and structures within the bounded national space and dependent on national sovereignty.[2] What was represented in the democratic national institutions was the people and hence modern national sovereignty tended to take the form of popular sovereignty. The claim that the nation was sovereign, in other words, tended to become identical to the claim that the people was sovereign. But what or who is the people? The people is not a natural or empirical entity; one cannot arrive at the identity of the people by summing up or even averaging the entire population. The people rather is a *representation* that creates of the population a unity. Three elements are centrally important here. First of all, the people is one, as Hobbes and the entire modern tradition often repeated. The people can be sovereign only as an identity, a unity. Second, the key to the construction of the people is representation. The empirical multiplicity of the population is made an identity through mechanisms of representation—and here we should include both the political and the aesthetic connotations of the term representation. Finally, these mechanisms of representation are based on a notion and a condition of measure—and by measure here we mean not so much a quantifiable condition but rather a bounded one. A bounded or measured multiplicity can be represented as a unity, but the immeasurable, the boundless, cannot be represented. This is one sense in which the notion of the people is intimately tied to the bounded national space. In short, the people is not an immediate nor an eternal identity, but rather the result of a complex process that is proper to a specific social formation and historical period.

We can simplify this complex situation for a moment and consider only the institutional, political mechanisms of representation, of which the electoral process was at least ideologically the most important. The notion of "one person, one vote," for example, was one of the ideals toward which the various modern schema of popular representation and sovereignty tended. There is no need for us to argue here that these schema of popular representation have always been imperfect and in fact largely illusory. There have long been important critiques of the mechanisms of popular representation in modern democratic societies. It is perhaps an exaggeration to characterize elections as an opportunity to choose which member of the ruling class will misrepresent the people for the next two, four, or six years, but there is certainly some truth in it too and low voter turnout is undoubtedly a symptom of the crisis of popular representation through electoral institutions. We think that today, however, popular representation is undermined in a more basic and fundamental way.

In the passage to Empire national space loses its definition, national boundaries (although still important) are relativized, and even national imaginaries are destabilized. As national sovereignty is displaced by the authority of the new supranational power, Empire, political reality loses its measure. In this situation the impossibility of representing the people becomes increasingly clear and thus the concept of the people itself tends to evaporate.

From an institutional, political perspective, imperial sovereignty conflicts with and even negates any conception of popular sovereignty. Consider, for example, the functioning of the supranational economic institutions, such as the World Bank, the IMF, and the WTO. To a large extent the conditionality required by these institutions takes out of the hands of nation-states decisions over economic and social policy. The subordinate nation-states most visibly but also the dominate ones are subject to the rule of these institutions.[3] It is clear that these supranational economic institutions do not and cannot represent the people, except in the most distant and abstract sense—in the sense, for example, that some nation-states, which in some way represent their peoples, designate representatives to the institutions. If one looks for representation in such institutions, there will always inevitably remain a "democratic deficit." It is no accident, in our view, in other words, that these institutions are so isolated from popular representation. They function precisely to the extent that they are excluded from mechanisms of popular representation.

Some of the best liberal Euroamerican theorists of globalization do in fact argue that we need to reform the global system and re-enforce the mechanisms of democratic political rule, but even they do not imagine that such supranational institutions could ever become representative in any popular sense. One of the fundamental obstacles is the problem of determining what or who is the people in such a conception. One would presumably have to develop a notion of the global people that extends beyond any national or ethnic conception to unite the entirety of humanity, a challenge well outside the scope of all of this liberal theorizing.

What then does constitute democratic reform in the views of the various leading liberal reformers such as Robert Keohane, Joseph Stiglitz, David Held, Richard Falk, and Ulrick Beck? It is striking in fact how widespread is the use of the term democracy in this literature and how universally accepted it is as goal. One major component of democratic reform is simply greater transparency—Glasnost and Perestroika, perhaps we should understand this as a Gorbachov project for the age of globalization. Transparency itself, however, is not democracy and does not constitute representation. A more substantive notion, which is omnipresent in the literature, is "accountability" (which is often paired with the notion "governance"). The concept of accountability could refer to mechanisms of popular representation, but it does not in these discourses. One has to ask "accountable to whom?" and then we find that the reformers do not propose making global institutions accountable to a global (or even a national) people—the people, precisely, is missing. Rather the reform would involve making the global institutions accountable to other institutions and especially to a community of experts. If the IMF were more transparent and accountable to economic experts, for example, there would be safeguards against its implementing disastrous policies, such as those dictated by the IMF in Southeast Asia in the late 1990s. What is central and most interesting about the use of the terms "accountability" and "governance" in these discussions, however, is that these terms straddle so comfortably the political and the economic realms. Accountability and governance have long been central concepts in the theoretical vocabulary of capitalist corporations.[4] The notions of accountability and governance seem to be directed most clearly at assuring economic efficiency and stability, not at constructing any popular or representational form of democratic control. Finally, although the term "democracy" is omnipresent in the literature, no global version of democracy in its modern liberal form—that is, as popular representation—is even on the agenda. It seems, in fact, that the greatest conceptual obstacle that prevents these theorists from imagining a global representative schema is precisely the notion of the people. Who is the global people? It seems impossible today to grasp the people as a political subject and moreover to represent it institutionally.[5]

We have thought it important to dwell so long on the question of the democratic reform of these institutions not only to take seriously the arguments of the reformist theorists but also and more importantly because this discourse can be found so widely among various factions of the protest movements against the WTO, the World Bank, and the IMF. Groups call for greater inclusion and representation in the decision-making process of the institutions themselves, demanding, for example, trade union representation or NGO representation or the like. Such demands may have some positive results, but they ultimately face insurmountable obstacles. Our argument casts all this on a much more general plane. If we conceive democracy in terms of a sovereign authority that is representative of the people, then democracy in the imperial age is not only unrealized but actually unrealizable.

DEMOCRACY OF THE MULTITUDE

We thus have to explore new forms of democracy, forms that are non-representative or differently representative, to discover a democracy that is adequate to our own times. We have already argued that the modern notion of democracy is intimately tied to national sovereignty and a fixed national space, that the modern notion, in short, is founded on measure. Now we should turn our attention back to explore further the other element in the equation, the people. The people, as we said earlier, is a product of representation. In modern political theory, the people is most strongly configured as the product of the founding contractual act of bourgeois society, as all the modern liberal theorists explain, from Hobbes to Rawls.

The contract makes of the population a united social body. This contractual act, however, is nonexistent, mystificatory, and outdated. The contract is nonexistent in the sense that no anthropological or historical fact allows us to assume its reality; rather, the contract negates any memory of its foundation, and this is certainly part of its violence, its fundamental denial of difference. The contract is mystificatory, secondly, in the sense that the people it constructs is presented as equal when the subjects that form it are in fact unequal; the concepts of justice and legitimacy that ground it serve only the strongest who exercise a force of domination and exploitation on the rest of the population. This concept of a people formed through the contract is outdated, finally, because it looks to a society forged by capital: Contractualism, people, and capitalism function in fact to make of the plurality a unity, to make of differences an homologous totality, to make of the wealth of all the singular lives of the population the poverty of some and the power of others. But this no longer works: It used to work as long as labor, needs, and desires were so miserable that they received the command of capital as a welcome comfort and a source of security when faced with the risks of the construction of value, the liberation of the imagination, and the organization of society. Today, however, the terms have changed. It is rather our monstrous intelligence and our cooperative power that are put in play: We are a multitude of powerful subjects, a multitude of intelligent monsters.

We thus need to shift our conceptual focus from the people to the multitude. The multitude cannot be grasped in the terms of contractualism—and in general in the terms of transcendental philosophy. In the most general sense, the multitude defies representation because it is a multiplicity, unbounded and immeasurable. The people is represented as a unity but the multitude is not representable because it is monstrous in the face of the teleological and transcendental rationalisms of modernity. In contrast to the concept of the people, the concept of the multitude is a singular multiplicity, a concrete universal. The people constituted a social body but the multitude does not—the multitude is the flesh of life. If on one side we contrast the multitude with the people, on the other side we should contrast it with the masses or the mob. The masses and the mob are most often used to name an irrational and passive social force, dangerous and violent precisely because so easily manipulated. The multitude, in contrast, is an active social agent—a multiplicity that acts. The multitude is not a unity, as is the people, but in contrast to the masses and the mob we can see that it is organized. It is an active, self-organizing agent. One great advantage of the concept of the multitude is that it displaces all the modern arguments based on the fear of the masses and even those about the tyranny of the majority, which have so often served as a kind of blackmail to force us to accept and even call for our own domination.

From the perspective of power, however, what can be done with the multitude? In effect, there is nothing to do with it, because the nexus among the unity of the subject (people), the form of its composition (contract among individuals), and the mode of government (monarchy, aristocracy, and democracy, separate or combined) has been blown apart. The radical modification of the mode of production through the hegemony of immaterial labor-power and cooperative living labor—this onto-logical, productive, biopolitical revolution—has overturned the parameters of "good government" and destroyed the modern idea of a community that functions for cap-italist accumulation, as capitalism imagined it from the beginning.

Allow us a brief parenthesis. Between the fifteenth and sixteenth centuries, when modernity appeared in the form of a revolution, the revolutionaries imagined themselves as monsters. Gargantua and Pantagruel can serve as emblems for all the giants and extreme figures of freedom and invention that have come down to us through the ages and proposed the gigantic task of becoming more free. Today we need new giants and new monsters that bring together nature and history, labor and politics, art and invention to demonstrate the new power that the birth of "general intellect," the hegemony of immaterial labor, the new passions of the ab-stract activity of the multitude provide to humanity. We need a new Rabelais or, re-ally, several.

Spinoza and Marx spoke of the democracy of the multitude or, rather, a form of democracy that no longer has anything to do with the democracy that along with monarchy and aristocracy comprises the classical forms of government. The democracy that Spinoza advocates is what he calls an *absolute* democracy—absolute in the sense of being unbounded and immeasurable. The conceptions of social contracts and bounded social bodies are thus completely cast aside. When we say that absolute democracy is outside of the theory (and the mystificatory practice) of the classical forms of government we mean also, obviously, that any attempt to re-alize democracy through the reform of the imperial institutions will be vain and useless. We mean, furthermore, that the only path to realize a democracy of the multitude is the path of revolution. What does it mean, however, to call for a rev-olutionary democracy adequate to the imperial world? Up to this point we have simply focused on what it is not. It is no longer something that depends on the concept of nation (on the contrary, it is increasingly defined by the struggle against the nation). We have also seen that it is something that does not correspond to the concept of the people and in fact is opposed to any attempt to present as unitary what is different. We need at this point to look to other concepts to help us un-derstand a democracy of the multitude. The concept of counterpower seems fun-damental to us when we deal with these new contents of the absolute democracy of the multitude.

MODERN COUNTERPOWER AND
THE PARADOXES OF MODERN INSURRECTION

The concept of counterpower consists primarily of three elements: resistance, in-surrection, and constituent power. It is important to recognize, however, that like the dominant concept of democracy also the dominant concept of counterpower was defined in modernity by the national space and national sovereignty. The effect was that during the modern era—at least since the French Revolution and throughout the long phase of socialist and communist agitation—the three elements of the concept of counterpower (resistance, insurrection, and constituent power) tended to be viewed as external to one another, and thus functioned as different strategies or at least different historical moments of revolutionary strategy. Once the elements were thus divided the entire concept of counterpower tended to be reduced to one of its elements, the concept of insurrection or, really, civil war. Lenin's political thought is exemplary in this regard. For Lenin counterpower—that is, in his terms, the dualism of power that consisted of the rise of a proletarian power against the bourgeoisie—could only exist for a very brief period, precisely in the period of insurrection. Resistance, which for Lenin principally took the form of syndicalist wage struggles, had an important political role but it was fundamentally separate from the revolutionary process. Constituent power too tended to disappear in Lenin's vision because every advance of constituent power immediately became an element of the new State, that is, transformed into a new constituted power. What remained of the revolutionary concept of counterpower for Lenin was thus primarily the great force of insurrection or, really, civil war against the dictatorship of the bourgeoisie.

Once we recognize how the modern notion of counterpower was reduced to insurrection, we should look more closely at the conditions and fortunes of modern insurrection. Paradoxically and tragically, even when the modern communist insurrection managed to win, it really lost because it was immediately imprisoned in an alternation between national and international war. Finally it becomes clear that national insurrection was really an illusion.

The Parisian Communards set the model in 1871 for all modern communist insurrection. Their example taught that the winning strategy was to transform international war into civil war—national, inter-class war. International war was the condition of possibility for launching insurrection. The Prussians at the gates of Paris not only toppled the Second Empire of Louis Bonaparte, but also made possible the overthrow of Thiers and the Republic. Paris armed is revolution armed! Forty years later the Bolsheviks too needed the inter-European war, that is, World War I, as the condition of insurrection. And once again the Germans, the national enemy, acted as condition of possibility. The Bolsheviks too transformed international war into civil war.

The tragedy of modern insurrection, however, is that national civil war is immediately and ineluctably transformed back into international war—or, really, a defensive war against the united international bourgeoisie. A properly national, civil war is really not possible insofar as a national victory only gives rise to a new and permanent international war. Therefore exactly the same condition that makes possible the national communist insurrection—that is, international war—is what imprisons the victorious insurrection or, rather, distorts it into a permanent military regime. The Parisian Communards were caught in this double bind. Marx saw clearly the mistakes of the Commune but did not show that the other options open to them would have equally been mistakes. The choice was either give all power to the Central Committee and march on the bourgeois army at Versailles—that is, become a military regime—or be defeated and massacred. It would not have ended with a victory at Versailles, either. The Prussian and the English ruling classes would not have allowed that. The victory of the Commune would have been the beginning of an unending international war. The Soviet victory only confirmed that double bind. The military victory in Russia, the complete defeat of the national bourgeoisie, only opened an international war (hot and then cold) that lasted for over seventy years.

Insurrection during the Cold War operated under the same structure, but only refined the model, reducing international war to its essential form. The Cold War fixed the conditions of modern insurrection into a permanent state. On one hand, there was a permanent state of international war that was already coded in class terms. The representational structure of the two opposing powers forced its coding on all new movements. The alternative was also determining in material terms since an insurrectionary movement could solicit the aid of one of the superpowers or play them off against one another. The formula for national insurrection was ready-made. But also ready-made and ineluctable were the limits of national insurrection. No movement could escape the great Cold War alternative. Even insurrectionary movements that did not conceive of themselves primary in class terms—anti-colonial movements in Asia and Africa, anti-dictatorial movements in Latin America, black power movements in the U.S.—were inevitably forced to be represented on one side of the great struggle. National insurrection during the Cold War was ultimately illusory. The victorious insurrection and the revolutionary nation was finally only a pawn in the great Cold War chess game.

The contemporary relevance that emerges from this brief history of modern insurrection centers around two facts or, really, one fact with two faces. On one side today, with the decline of national sovereignty and the passage to Empire, gone are the conditions that allowed modern insurrection to be thought and at times to be practiced. Today it thus seems almost impossible even to think insurrection. On the other side, however, what is gone is also exactly the condition that kept modern insurrection imprisoned, in the interminable play between national and international wars. Today, therefore, when considering the question of insurrection we are faced with both a great difficulty and an enormous possibility. Let us move back, however, to the more general consideration of counterpower.

A COUNTERPOWER OF MONSTROUS FLESH

With the contemporary decline of the sovereignty of the nation-state, it is possible once again to explore the concept of counterpower in its full form and return to its conceptual foundation. Today the relationship among resistance, insurrection, and constituent power has the possibility to be an absolutely continuous relationship and in each of these moments there is the possibility of the expression of the power of invention. In other words, each of the three moments—resistance, insurrection, and constituent power—can be internal to one another, forming a common means of political expression. The context in which—and against which—this counter-power acts is no longer the limited sovereignty of the nation-state but the unlimited sovereignty of Empire, and thus counterpower too must be reconceived in an unlimited or unbounded way.

Here we are faced with a new imposing and exciting theoretical and political problematic. In our present imperial context we need to rethink the concepts of resistance, insurrection, and constituent power—and rethink too their internal connections, that is, their unity in the concept and practice of counterpower. When we look across the field of contemporary theoretical production we can see that we do already have some tools to work with on this terrain. Certainly, Michel Foucault's development of the concept of resistance along with all the work that has followed on his, the anthropologist James Scott's notion of the weapons of the weak, and all the other work that has emerged on micropolitical resistance should be a foundation for any investigation into this problematic. The great limitation of all this work, however, is that it never manages to discover the internal connection that resistance can have with insurrection and constituent power. Resistance can be a powerful political weapon, in other words, but isolated, individual acts of resistance can never succeed in transforming the structures of power.[6] Today, however, the other two components of counterpower remain completely undeveloped. An insurrection is a collective gesture of revolt, but what are the terms for insurrection today and how can it be put into practice? It should be clear that we can no longer translate insurrection immediately into civil war, as was so common in the modern era, if by "civil" we mean a war within the national space. Insurrection is indeed still a war of the dominated against the rulers within a single society, but that society is now tends to be an unlimited global society, imperial society as a whole. How is such an insurrection against Empire be put into practice? Who can enact it? Where is the internal connection between the micropolitics of resistance and imperial insurrection? And how can we today conceive of constituent power, that is, the common invention of a new social and political constitution? Finally, we need to think of resistance, insurrection, and constituent power as one indivisible process, the three forged together into a full counterpower and ultimately a new alternative social formation. These are enormous questions and we are only at the very first stages of addressing them.

Rather than confronting them directly it seems better to us to shift registers and take a different view on the entire problematic. We have to find some way to shake off the shackles of reasonableness, to break out of the common forms of thinking about democracy and society, to create more imaginative and inventive perspectives. Let us begin by looking at the most basic foundation of counterpower where its three elements—resistance, insurrection, and constituent power—most intimately correspond. The primary material of counterpower is the flesh, the common living substance in which the corporeal and the intellectual coincide and are indistinguishable. "The flesh is not matter, is not mind, is not substance," Maurice Merleau-Ponty writes. "To designate it, we should need the old term 'element,' in the sense it was used to speak of water, air, earth, and fire, that is, in the sense of a *general thing* . . . a sort of incarnate principle that brings a style of being wherever there is a fragment of being. The flesh is in this sense an 'element' of Being."[7] The flesh is pure potentiality, the unformed stuff of life, an element of being. One should be careful, however, not to confuse the flesh with any notion of naked life, which conceives of a living form stripped of all its qualities, a negative limit of life.[8] The flesh is oriented in the other direction, toward the fullness of life. We do not remain flesh, flesh is but an element of being; we continually make of our flesh a form of life.

In the development of forms of life, we discover ourselves as a multitude of bodies and at the same time we recognize that every body is itself a multitude—of molecules, desires, forms of life, inventions. Within each of us resides a legion of demons or, perhaps, of angels—this is the basic foundation, the degree zero of the multitude. What acts on the flesh and gives it form are the powers of invention, those powers that work through singularities to weave together hybridizations of space and metamorphoses of nature—the powers, in short, that modify the modes and forms of existence.

In this context it is clear that the three elements of counterpower (resistance, insurrection, and constituent power) spring forth *together* from every singularity and from every movement of bodies that constitute the multitude. Acts of resistance, collective gestures of revolt, and the common invention of a new social and political constitution pass together through innumerable micropolitical circuits— and thus in the flesh of the multitude is inscribed a new power, a counterpower, a living thing that is against Empire. Here are born the new barbarians, monsters, and beautiful giants that continually emerge from *within* the interstices of imperial power and *against* imperial power itself. The power of invention is monstrous because it is excessive. Every true act of invention, every act, that is, that does not simply reproduce the norm, is monstrous. Counterpower is an excessive, overflowing force, and one day it will be unbounded and immeasurable. This tension between the overflowing and the unbounded is where the monstrous characteristics of the flesh and counterpower take on a heightened importance. As we are waiting for a full epiphany of the (resistant, revolting, and constituent) monsters, there grows a recognition that the imperial system, that is, the contemporary form of repression of the will to power of the multitude, is at this point on the ropes, at the margins, precarious, continually plagued by crisis. (Here is where the weak philosophies of the margin, difference, and nakedness appear as the mystifying figures and the unhappy consciousness of imperial hegemony.)

Against this, the power of invention (or, really, counterpower) makes common bodies out of the flesh. These bodies share nothing with the huge animals that Hobbes and the other theorists of the modern state imagined when they made of the Leviathan the sacred instrument, the pitbull of the appropriative bourgeoisie. The multitude we are dealing with today is instead a multiplicity of bodies, each of which is crisscrossed by intellectual and material powers of reason and affect; they are cyborg bodies that move freely without regard to the old boundaries that separated the human from the machinic. These multiple bodies of the multitude enact a continuous invention of new forms of life, new languages, new intellectual and ethical powers. The bodies of the multitude are monstrous, irrecuperable in the capitalist logic that tries continually to control it in the organization of Empire. The bodies of the multitude, finally, are queer bodies that are insusceptible to the forces of discipline and normalization but sensitive only to their own powers of invention.

When we point to the powers of invention as the key to a formation of counterpower in the age of Empire, we do not mean to refer to some exclusive population of artists or philosophers. In the political economy of Empire the power of invention has become the general and common condition of production. This is what we mean when we claim that immaterial labor and general intellect have come to occupy a dominant position in the capitalist economy.

If, as we have argued, the dominant form of democracy that modernity and European history has bequeathed us—popular, representational democracy—is not only unrealized but actually unrealizable, then one should not view our proposition of an alternative democracy of the multitude as a utopian dream. The unrealizability of the old notion of democracy should rather force us to move forward. This also means that we are entirely within and completely against imperial domination, and there is no dialectical path possible. The only invention that now remains for us is the invention of a new democracy, an absolute democracy, unbounded, immeasurable. A democracy of powerful multitudes, not only of equal individuals but of powers equally open to cooperation, to communication, to creation. Here there are no programmes to propose—and who would dare still today to do such a thing after the twentieth century has ended? All the modern protagonists—the priests, the journalists, the preachers, the politicians—may still be of use to imperial power, but not to us. The philosophical and artistic elements in all of us, the practices of working on the flesh and dealing with its irreducible multiplicities, the powers of unbounded invention—these are the leading characteristics of the multitude. Beyond our unrealized democracy, there is a desire for a common life that needs to be realized. We can perhaps, mingling together the flesh and the intellect of the multitude, generate a new youth of humanity through an enormous enterprise of love.

Notes

1. The most detailed and influential argument that globalization has not undermined the powers of nation-states and that globalization is in this sense a myth is presented by Paul

Hirst and Grahame Thompson, *Globalization in Question: The International Economy and the Possibilities of Governance*, 2nd ed. (Cambridge, Eng.: Polity, 1999).

2. This is the fundamental argument of David Held, *Democracy and the Global Order* (Stanford: Stanford University Press, 1995).

3. Many authors characterize and lament this shift in decision making from national to supranational institutions as the increasing domination of the economic over the political (with the assumption that the nation-state is the only context in which to conduct politics). Several of these authors invoke the work of Karl Polanyi in the argument to re-embed economic markets within social markets. See, for example, James Mittleman, *The Globalization Syndrome* (Princeton: Princeton University Press, 2000), and John Gray, *False Dawn* (New York: The New Press, 1998). In our view it is a mistake to separate the economic and the political in this way and to insist on the autonomy of the political. The supranational economic institutions are also themselves political institutions. The fundamental difference is that these institutions do not allow for (even the pretense of) popular representation.

4. We are indebted to Craig Borowiak for his analyses of the concept of accountability in the contemporary globalization discussion.

5. From this perspective, the project for the construction of a political Europe can appear to some as the solution to the puzzle of democracy in the age of globalization. The hypothesis is that the continent can substitute for the nation and revive the mechanisms of representational democracy. This seems to us, however, a false solution. Even if one could represent institutionally the European people as a coherent subject, a political Europe is not capable of claiming sovereign authority. Regional powers, like nation-states, are merely elements that function within the ultimate sovereignty of Empire.

6. From our perspective Félix Guattari, especially in his work with Deleuze, is the one who has gone furthest to push the notion of resistance toward a conception of molecular revolution.

7. Maurice Merleau-Ponty, *The Visible and the Invisible*, ed. Claude Lefort, trans. Alphonso Lingus (Evanston, Ill.: Northwestern University Press: 1968), p. 139. Consider also Antonin Artaud's conception of the flesh: "There are intellectual cries, cries born of the *subtlety* of the marrow. That is what I mean by Flesh. I do not separate my thought from my life. With each vibration of my tongue I retrace all the pathways of my thought in my flesh." Antonin Artaud, "Situation of the Flesh," in *Selected Writings*, trans. Helen Weaver (Berkeley: University of California Press: 1988), p. 110.

8. See Giorgio Agamben, *Homo Sacer*, trans. Daniel Heller-Roazen (Stanford: Stanford University Press, 1998).

9

Over, Under, Sideways, Down

Globalization, Spatial Metaphors,
and the Question of State Power

PETER BRATSIS

The vast majority of contemporary commentaries regarding the state and political power argue that, within the context of globalization, the state becomes increasingly powerless. Typically, such arguments follow the logic that political power now resides "above" and "beyond" the state, that the state becomes increasingly "hollow," and that power now occupies a reterritorialized national political space that subverts state autonomy and short-circuits national politics. This chapter is a brief attempt to make sense of such claims and identify some of the assumptions hidden within them. Its main argument is that all such characterizations of the state in the global era reflect an overly legalistic understanding of what the state is and rely on imprecise spatial metaphors in their attempt to identify the loci and circuits of contemporary political power. As a conclusion, some implications of these critiques of the globalization literature for political strategy and activism will also be discussed.

In what sense are the spatial claims of the globalization literature metaphorical? Obviously, not all statements regarding spatial movements and positions are metaphorical. If we say that something is under a rock, above the floor, and so forth, the meaning is quite literal. The physical spaces of nature and our built environment, however, are quite different from the space of the state. We see that migrating birds, hurricanes, and acid rain have no regard for the space of the state. No matter how we draw and redraw political boundaries, it makes no difference for these phenomena of nature. The space of the state has meaning only for humans. It is a symbolic and epistemic space, a social fact.[1]

Given this, what is it that is "above" the state? Under what conditions do statements asserting that power now resides "above" the state make sense? Certainly, laws establish for us a fundamental inside-outside distinction for contemporary politics. Legal treaties and declarations establish the territorial scope and limits of political sovereignty. Thus, contemporary arguments regarding the decline of the state and its sovereignty focus on the steady erosion of significance of these territorial boundaries through such legal and formal arrangements as NAFTA, the European Union, the United Nations, the IMF, and so on. The weak version of such arguments (e.g., Strange, 1996; Shaw, 2000) claims that we are now increasingly faced with a supranational state, a super-state that is inclusive of numerous formally sovereign national states. The strong version of such arguments (e.g., Hardt and Negri, 2000) claims that we are faced with a shift away from territoriality and the state form itself, that we have entered a new political logic of "Empire," and that the inside-outside logic of the state has itself been superseded. In both cases, the "above" and "beyond" where political power now resides is in relation to the formal territorial limits of the national state.

But is this legal outside a real outside? Can we take legal distinctions and declarations at face value? As Göran Therborn (1976) has argued, social science begins at a very specific point in historical time. It is not simply concurrent with the Enlightenment; social science as we know it (with the partial exception of economics) arrived much later than physics, mathematics, and chemistry. Social science emerged in the wake of the bourgeois revolutions at the end of the 18th century and the beginning of the 19th, when law established the formal equality of all citizens. Laws declared all citizens equal, and social science (particularly sociology) emerged in order to evaluate this claim, to ask if reality corresponded to this assertion. Previously, law provided a shortcut for political understanding. Questions regarding the loci and distribution of political power could be answered simply by looking to the laws; from this vantage point the power positions of slaves, serfs, landowners, and feudal lords were obvious. Following the bourgeois revolutions, however, political analysis could no longer rely on the study of laws; by then, a disconnect had been established between legal declarations and real political conditions.

Today, we see a regression back to pre-scientific social thinking. Political power is beyond the state; how do we know it, where is this "beyond," all we have to do is look to the laws. International law has established the distinction, the laws tell us what is outside, the laws tell us how the national state has lost agency to international or post-national institutions, the laws tell us that the state is an actor and that any loss of the ability of the state to act and make decisions is concurrent with a loss of autonomy. In short, the contemporary understanding of politics proceeds as if the last two hundred years of social scientific thinking never occurred, with no critical distance between us and laws and appearances.

Using these legal distinctions of insides and outsides, we tend to treat the space of the state as if it were akin to the spaces of nature and architecture. We rely on our spatial experiences in everyday life and assert that the spaces of politics and the state are like the spaces we experience in our daily existence. We rely upon metaphors. To say that these understandings are metaphorical is to say that they are imprecise and pre-scientific; they are pre-theories of contemporary politics.[2] Rather than ensuing from rigorous analysis and causal explanation, they are reflective of our experiences of globalization and descriptive of the ways globalization appears and presents itself. Such pre-theories are not necessarily bad, in that they can be useful for pushing analytical questioning in new directions and are themselves the outcomes of our curiosity and desire to understand and explain contemporary political transformations. Nonetheless, they are naive and misleading understandings.

The legalism/formalism prevalent in these claims regarding the decline of the state results in misunderstandings about the state and political power. It leads us to accept a historicist conception of the state as a unitary actor, much like the realist position in international relations theory, and to assume that sovereignty is about the ability of the state to make autonomous decisions. But just because the state is an autonomous actor for international law does not mean that we should take it as such. We all know that throughout the world, from Mexico and Algeria to the Koreas and Japan, there have always been strict limitations and "outside" controls regarding what can be done. Even the most "powerful" of states—the United States, France, the former Soviet Union, and so forth—have been "limited" as well. The scenario is not one in which the state acts as a metaphorical person, "choosing" this policy or that; rather, the social struggles and distributions of power within each society function to determine laws and policies. Although these struggles may occur within an institutionally bounded terrain and have differing chances of success given the form and selectivities of the institutions involved, it would be misleading and simple-minded to say that, for example, the United States once chose to be protectionist and isolationist and now chooses to be the opposite.[3] If we assume, contrary to the legalistic understanding of the state, that politics is shaped by and concurrent with social struggles, the proper question can never be one concerning the "autonomy" of the state. Always and everywhere the state will lack autonomy since it is nothing more that a condensation of the struggles and conflicts of social groups and classes. Similarly, a common emphasis of those who argue that the state is declining in importance and those who argue that it is not (i.e., Weiss, 1998) is the state's capacity to pass laws and regulate society; again, sovereignty is presented as the ability to make autonomous decisions. However, the real power or powerlessness of the state is not visible through the lack or presence of decisions and regulations. The lack of regulations is simply another mode of the presence of regulations.[4] We cannot refer to the state as if it were a thinking, calculating agent that would really have preferred to do this or that but has lost the capacity for autonomous decision making to transnational institutions and actors.

The metaphor of political power that resides "above" the nation-state thus alludes to a fictional and nonexistent space, a space beyond the state that is nowhere to be found. We are never really "outside the state," even though we may be outside or inside a particular state. The inside-outside distinction does, however, tell us something about modern politics and the spatial organization of contemporary society. In keeping with the initial observation that the space of the state exists as a social fact, as a symbolic and epistemic category, how do we conceptualize the inside-outside distinction in our minds? The substantive corollary to this legal/formal distinction of insides and outsides is the national political community. The real inside is that which is within our society *qua* political community. The nationalization of individuals is the process that makes legal political boundaries compelling and legitimate. When we agree that we are Canadians, or Irish, or Cypriots, or Israelis, national political boundaries are accepted and internalized as a constitutive element of our social world. A real subversion and going "beyond" the space of the state would thus imply a crisis of national identification whereby national identities are subverted by the globalizing process and the inside-outside dialectic of the state becomes less and less accepted and relevant for politics. Do we see this happening? I think that it is safe to say that, if anything, national identification has grown stronger in the recent past. Post–September 11th America is in the midst of a resurgence of nationalism; this reality is obvious to anyone who walks the streets of New York City, let alone those in Des Moines or Tulsa. The intensity with which Americans articulate the naturalness and obviousness of national interests and the political community is acute. Even presumably leftist, progressive publications such as *The Nation* and *Dissent* echo the patriotic nationalist spirit.[5] Similarly, post-Soviet Eastern Europe has been a home to a great number of nationalist projects. Nationalist fervor, as a great many self-proclaimed experts on the region assure us, is an innate property of these relatively backward peoples. In contrast to the "civic" nationalism of the developed multicultural West, the "ethnic" nationalism of the East has reappeared now that communist repression has been lifted and the reality of the societies in this region is visible to all. (Of course, this "civic"/"ethnic" distinction is as good a sign as any of the semantic games played by modern political analysis in order to justify the nationalism and chauvinism of the West while presenting those of the East as pathological.)

Even the globalization literature itself (as the discussion so far illustrates) is unable to generate knowledge that breaks from the category of the state, given that many of its claims are based on the existence and centrality of spatial forms and allusions that the state creates for itself. Analysis as well as political practices constantly assure us that only by way of the categories of the nation-state can we understand and exist in the modern world. The spatial metaphors of "over" and "above" necessarily refer to the territoriality of the nation-state. Even the European Union is constantly rearticulating the primacy of the nation-form: The new Euro coins each have images on one side that are particular to the various participating states. European regulations themselves find their limit in the cultural specificity of each national community. The political ideology of European integration has functioned so well up to now because everyone knows we are not supposed to take it too seriously. No one really suspects that Greeks will be prosecuted, or even chastised, for eating, against EU regulations, the intestines of goats and lambs. It would be a sign of disconnection from political realities for any EU bureaucrat to insist on an equal application of EU regulations for all member-states, to take literally and seriously the claim that all member-states are truly and equally "European." Imagine the fiasco that would ensue if, for example, taxes on alcohol were reduced in Sweden or taxes on cigarettes were raised in Italy in order to conform to European standards.

It becomes increasingly clear that, when contrasted to the ancient conception of space, the territoriality of the nation-state is inherent and necessary to its functioning as a capitalist state. The ancient Western conception of political space is totally lacking in the inside-outside spatial dimension that has been discussed so far. As Nicos Poulantzas argues in *State, Power, Socialism:*

> The space of Western Antiquity is a space with a *centre:* the *polis* (which itself has a center: the *agora*). But it has no frontiers in the modern sense of the term. It is concentric, but, having no real outside, it is also open. This centre (the *polis* and *agora*) is inscribed in a space whose essential characteristics are homogeneity and symmetry, not differentiation and hierarchy. Moreover, this geometric orientation is reproduced in the political organization of the city and the 'isonomy' relationship among its citizens. . . . In this space (which is the one represented by Euclid and the Pythagoreans) people do not change their position, they simply move around. They always go to the same place, because each point in space is an exact repetition of the previous point; when they found colonies, it is only to form replicas of Athens or Rome. (Poulantzas, 1978, 101)

Ancient Greek society had hierarchies, but they were not organized in spatial terms. Granted, women, slaves, merchants, and other noncitizens occupied a lower political position than citizens, but their status was inscribed onto their bodies. Anywhere they went, at whatever point in this concentric space they found themselves, they were always at the same point. Similarly, the political community itself was not spatially determined. The *polis* was nothing else than the citizens; it had nothing to do with territory. As Thucydides put it, *"Andres gar polis"* (the *polis* is the men). Likewise, the constitutions that Aristotle wrote about had nothing to do with the laws that governed particular territorial entities: The proper translation of his analysis of Athenian law is *The Constitution of the Athenians*, not *The Constitution of Athens,* inasmuch as Aristotle wrote on how the Athenians constituted themselves. The self-creation of the Athenians was the *polis.* When the citizens were at war, Athens was on the move. All the decisions, all the deliberations, were made by the citizens, for only they were the *polis* (see Castoriadis, 1991).

There is a great distance between the homogenous space of the ancient world and the homogenous moment of space in the modern capitalist world. In modern societies our space is segmented and fractured. The social hierarchies of capitalism correspond to the spatial-technical division of labor in capitalist production. One's place in the social hierarchy is largely a function of one's literal place within the production process. Whether the assembly line, the kitchen, or the retail store, there is a definitive serial, parceled, and cellular organization of space that is necessary for capitalist exploitation. The spatial matrix of class division and hierarchy of today differs from that of pre-modern class societies in that individuals now change class position by traversing the distance between these segmentations. This was made explicit by *The Jeffersons*, a popular American sitcom of the 1970s: Changing class position literally involves a "moving on up." The segmented space of capitalism, within which we exist on a daily basis, is homogenized in two ways. First, there is the imaginary homogenization that takes place at the level of national fantasy—namely, the popular fiction and belief that we are one people, that despite our radically different positions within the social hierarchy and our varying interests, we really do share interests and a nonantagonistic existence in modern society as a people. Second, there is the homogenization that takes place through the capitalist labor process tending toward worldwide application, the result of what Marx termed the "law of the tendency for the rate of profit to decline." As capitalism spreads around the globe, all societies come to share the same fractured, cellular space of capitalism. In this sense, the international movements of capital can occur only by way of its transnationalization. Capital can spread only through the dominance of the state form in all societies; there is no longer an "outside" of the state form.

Unlike previous modes of production, capitalism, with its segmented spaces and its separation of the worker from the means of production, relies upon the institutions of the state (in the broad sense) in order to secure the reproduction of social relations (cf. Althusser, 1971). No longer do the economic spaces reproduce themselves in a simple way, as had been the case with slaves and feudal societies. The mediation of the antagonisms and divisions endemic to capitalism, the production of a political community that views itself as a territorially bounded entity unified through some mystical connection to the fatherland, and the organization and regulation of the cultural and economic spaces of modernity all rely upon and presuppose the political form of the state. The territoriality of the state is thus not some free-floating phenomenon that can change according to political whims. The spatial organization of the capitalist production process as well as the requisites of economic regulation and political legitimization it engenders function to make the spatial form of the state necessary and endemic to modern capitalist societies.

These brief schematic observations on globalization and the state are not intended merely as methodological, conceptual considerations. The shift away from the metaphorical understanding of contemporary political power is very much connected to the question of political strategies and "anti-globalization" resistance. The conceptual position advocated so far implies a rejection of three strategic positions common to much of the literature on globalization. First, we see that, despite claims to the contrary, globalization is not producing a postnational political subject freed from the fetters of territoriality. The old political problem of how to build an internationalist political movement in a nationalized world remains; the problems of Marx, Rosa Luxemberg, and Gramsci remain. After all, as we already know from Luxemberg, Gramsci, and others, the revolutionary subject does not automatically arise from the economic workings of society. The people, or, to use Hardt and Negri's term, the multitude, is as fractured and segmented as the spaces it occupies. Nationhood attempts to unify them and neuter their political potential through national identification. Of course, such efforts can never totally succeed; there is always an excess that can never be fully appropriated. This still segmented and fractured excess enters the political realm as resistance and political opposition. But it is a dispersed and incoherent resistance. It is identity politics and the politics of interests—in other words, multiculturalism. It is an apolitical politics in which there is no challenge to the homogenizing and totalizing categories and visions of the state-form. Politics proper, as practiced in the Athenian *polis* and as Marx and the Marxists envisioned for the proletariat, is always a referent to universality, to the surpassing of the particularity of identity and interests.[6] For example, because as a *polis* we consciously strive for the "good," for the advancement of our collective existence, we always and everywhere keep at bay, as much as possible, the vulgar interests of particularity. For Machiavelli, let us recall, the Roman Republic became corrupted when individual economic well-being replaced universal good as the motivation for politics. With the proletariat as well, through the particularity of their struggle, universal advancement is produced: the end of patriarchy, the end of alienation, the end of all sources of human domination.

Today, whether we look to labor unions, the struggles of immigrants and ethnic minorities, or the struggles of ecological groups, we see a tendency to stay bounded by particularity, to never rise to the level of politics. In order to counter the bourgeois hegemony we have to be able to claim universality. Some current movements do attempt this. The more enlightened and radical elements of the feminist movement say to us that in order to fully understand and overcome subjection we have to understand and overcome the deepest and most privileged form of social subjection: gender. Elements of the ecological movement tell us that we must forget the abstract universals of the fatherland and the free market, that our real universal is a common coexistence in space, that we truly coexist with one another not as national subjects but as community members sharing the same natural space. In this context, anarchism and communism also deserve special mention inasmuch as they lay claim to the universal and tell us to forget all the narrow substantive political claims; true freedom, they maintain, can be attained only when the hierarchical form and organization of all domination are done away with by instituting true democracy, by eradicating the state-form and all divisions between leaders and those who are led.

Second, this last point brings us to the question of organization and coordination. What is a democratic organization? How can we organize all the fractured cellular pockets of resistance into a coherent and democratic opposition to capitalism and the state? How can all the particular moments of struggle and demands be institutionally focused and articulated? This question is necessitated precisely because of the fragmented spaces and positions from which political resistance arises, and it remains the key political and strategic question for today's revolutionary political movements. For example, in relation to what is usually termed the "anti-globaliza-tion" movement, we commonly hear it observed in today's media that no clear mes-sage or political goal is discernible precisely because of the multiplicity of voices and political goals this movement includes. How does one preserve the autonomy of the individual voices within such a movement and at the same time maintain some de-gree of coordination and strategic control? The contemporary anarchist strategy of "affinity groups" addresses this question, emphasizing the democratic nature of orga-nization before any particular substantive claim. The means of the struggle are con-current with its ends. The long-term functionality of affinity groups toward strategic coordination and social democratization remains to be seen, but the question of co-ordination and organization clearly remains key for substantive social change.

Third and last, the observation that the space of the state is a symbolic and epistemic space implies that the proper resistance to the state must be fundamen-tally pedagogical. A counter-hegemonic project as envisioned by Gramsci is neces-sary to counter the symbolic existence of the state in our minds. Attempts to change existing social relations must not only contain opposition to this or that el-ement of global capitalism but must also be productive by engendering new ways of thinking and categorizing that will displace the thinking and categorizing en-gendered by the state-form. Protests in the streets may be necessary, but they are not sufficient for bringing about social transformations. The struggles over curric-ula, concepts, and theories are still of the utmost strategic importance. The actual character and content of such a counter-hegemonic project are yet to be realized, but the necessity of the project persists.

In short, once we abandon the metaphorical formulations prevalent in most of the contemporary efforts to come to terms with globalization and the question of political power, a number of strategic questions that would otherwise be dismissed regain their importance. If globalization is not doing away with territoriality and nationality, then we must still contend with the strategic problems that they pose. If the spaces of capitalism and of the state remain fragmented and cellular, then we must still contend with the question of organizing and coordinating all those at-tempts at resistance that remain bound and separated by such fragmented spaces. If the space of the state is primarily a symbolic and epistemic space, then we must still produce concepts and ways of thinking that liberate us from the state-form and allow for the creation of new, democratic realities. The advancement of politi-cal analysis and strategy requires that we move away from commonsense notions of the state and globalization and engage in rigorous social scientific examinations of existing reality.

NOTES

1. See Durkheim (1982) for the standard definition of what a social fact is and Bratsis (2002) for a more detailed examination of the state as a social fact.
2. See Bachelard (1987) on the incongruity of metaphors and scientific thinking.

3. On the question of the selectivity of state institutions, see Offe (1973), Poulantzas (1978), and Jessop (1990).

4. This argument had been made by many, from Gramsci (1971, 160) to Katznelson (1986).

5. This is illustrated by the patriotic position, exposed by both publications, that the September 11 attacks have no connection to American foreign policies or capitalist inequalities and their tendency toward the George Bush argument that such attacks were manifestations of "evil" or, at least, of "bad" men, cultures, and ideologies. Notably, Christopher Hitchens (2001) argues that attempts to explain September 11 are simply rationalizations of terrorism and anti-American violence; and Mitchell Cohen (2002), coeditor of *Dissent*, argues that the linking of terrorism to questions of globalization, corporate power, and class struggles is an atrocity and that those who attempt such a linking are opportunistic, simple-minded intellectuals who deserve no credibility: "One almost expects them to explain that bin Laden's crew attacked the World Trade Center because Thomas Jefferson owned slaves (sold to him, undoubtedly, by Zionists)."

6. On the question of universality and the contemporary political context, see Butler, Laclau, and Žižek (2000).

WORKS CITED

Althusser, Louis. 1971. "Ideology and Ideological State Apparatuses," in *Lenin and Philosophy and Other Essays*. New York: Monthly Review Press.

Bachelard, Gaston. 1987. *The Psychoanalysis of Fire*. London: Quartet Books.

Bratsis, Peter. 2002. "Unthinking the State: Reification, Ideology, and the State as a Social Fact," in *Paradigm Lost: State Theory Reconsidered*, ed. Stanley Aronowitz and Peter Bratsis. Minneapolis: University of Minnesota Press.

Butler, Judith, Ernesto Laclau, and Slavoj Žižek. 2000. *Contingency, Hegemony, Universality*. New York: Verso Books.

Castoriadis, Cornelius. 1991. "The Greek *Polis* and the Creation of Democracy," in *Philosophy, Politics, Autonomy*. New York: Oxford University Press.

Cohen, Mitchell. 2002. "Editor's Page." *Dissent*, Vol. 49, No. 1.

Durkheim, Emile. 1982. *The Rules of Sociological Method*. New York: Free Press.

Gramsci, Antonio. 1971. *Selections from the Prison Notebooks*. New York: International Publishers.

Hardt, Michael, and Antonio Negri. 2000. *Empire*. Cambridge, Mass.: Harvard University Press.

Hitchens, Christopher. 2001. "Against Rationalization." *The Nation*, October 8.

Jessop, Bob. 1990. *State Theory*. University Park: Pennsylvania State University Press.

Katznelson, Ira. 1986. "Rethinking the Silences of Social and Economic Policy." *Political Science Quarterly*, Vol. 101, No. 2, pp. 307–325.

Offe, Claus. 1973. "Structural Problems of the Capitalist State," in *German Political Studies*, ed. K. von Beyme. London: Russell Sage.

Poulantzas, Nicos. 1978. *State, Power, Socialism*. London: Verso Books.

Shaw, Martin. 2000. *The Theory of the Global State*. Cambridge, Eng.: Cambridge University Press.

Strange, Susan. 1996. *The Retreat of the State*. Cambridge, Eng.: Cambridge University Press.

Therborn, Göran. 1976. *Science, Class and Society*. London: Verso Books.

Weiss, Linda. 1998. *The Myth of the Powerless State*. Ithaca, N.Y.: Cornell University Press.

10

The Anti-Capitalist Movement After Genoa and New York

ALEX CALLINICOS*

The year 2001 was a watershed for the movement against corporate globalization. It was defined by two dates. One, of course, was September 11 and its aftermath. The attacks on New York and Washington and the subsequent "war on terrorism" launched by the United States represented the biggest challenge so far for a movement that previously had known nothing but success and growth. The other key date indeed marked the climax the movement had then reached—July 21, when 300,000 people in Genoa defied the violence of the Italian state, which the day before had claimed the life of a young protester, Carlo Giuliani, and demonstrated against the Group of Eight summit taking place in the city.

It is striking that both events raise the same issues for the movement against corporate globalization. So let me explain why, in the rest of this chapter, I call this movement the anti-capitalist movement. The name more usually applied to it—the anti-globalization movement—is plainly an absurd appellation for a movement that revels precisely in its international character and that has been able to mobilize highly effectively across national borders on all five continents. Leading figures in the movement have rightly distanced themselves from this name. Naomi Klein writes: "It is not useful to use the language of anti-globalization."[1] At the first World Social Forum at Porto Alegre in January 2001, Susan George said: "We are 'pro-globalization' for we are in favour of sharing friendship, culture, cooking, solidarity, wealth and resources."[2] And at the second World Social Forum in February 2002, the social movements adopted a statement that made their real target ab-

---

*This chapter is based on talks given at the Globalization and Resistance Conference, CUNY Graduate Center, New York, November 16–17, 2001, and the second World Social Forum, Porto Alegre, January 31–February 5, 2002. The issues it raises are further explored in a forthcoming book, *An Anti-Capitalist Manifesto* (Cambridge: Polity, 2003).

solutely explicit: "We are building a large alliance from our struggles and resistance against a system based on sexism, racism and violence, which privileges the interests of capital and patriarchy over the needs and aspirations of people."[3]

It is this sense of the interconnection of different issues through the systemic logic of capitalism that defines the anti-capitalist movement by contrast with earlier campaigns that concerned themselves with more specific (though hugely important) issues such as nuclear weapons, apartheid, and even the environment. Even as unsympathetic an observer as James Harding, writing a survey of the movement for the *Financial Times* that started the very day of the attacks on New York and Washington, rejected the anti-globalization label:

> Instead, this is counter-capitalism. The new wave of political activism has coalesced around the simple idea that capitalism has gone too far. It is as much a mood as a movement, something counter-cultural. It is driven by the suspicion that the companies, forced by stock markets to strive for ever greater profits, are pillaging the environment and failing to enrich the poor as they promised. And it is fuelled by the fear that democracy has become powerless to stop them, as politicians are thought to be in the pockets of companies and international political institutions are slaves to a corporate agenda.[4]

"Anti-capitalism" seems a simpler label, and one that has been embraced by many activists, at least since the protests in the City of London on June 14, 1999, which were among the harbingers of the Seattle demonstrations later that year. The unifying sense that there is something wrong with capitalism as a system coexists with differing analyses, strategies, and visions of the alternative. There is, in particular, a large divide between those who seek a more controlled and humane version of capitalism—tying down Gulliver, as Jeremy Brecher puts it—and those who seek to replace it altogether. But, when all the necessary qualifications have been made, the fact remains that the global triumph of liberal capitalism in 1989 that Francis Fukuyama celebrated as the End of History provoked, within a decade, a new rebellion against the system itself.

GENOA AND SEPTEMBER 11

The key issue that I want to consider in this chapter is the significance of Genoa and September 11 for the anti-capitalist movement. There are important connections between the two events. To begin with, there is the attempt made by opponents of the anti-capitalist movement to smear it by association with the terrorists responsible for the atrocities in New York and Washington. For example, John Lloyd, a journalist closely associated with Tony Blair's New Labour government, writes: "The only political grouping now using the tactics developed by the global [anti-capitalist] movements—sporadic use of violence and oppositionism through uncontrollable and unpredictable networks—is Bin Laden's al-Qa'ida."[5] This kind of comparison should be treated with the contempt it deserves. There is a world of difference between a secret organization that regards the mass killing of office workers, airline staff, and firefighters as a legitimate tactic and a movement that works publicly and democratically to mobilize mass action against the closed and unaccountable processes through which the world economy is run by the leading capitalist states, the multinational corporations, and the international institutions that they control between them.[6]

But in a deeper and more interesting respect, both Genoa and September 11 raise the same issues—for example, that of the role of violence in both sustaining and challenging the existing global distribution of power. The attacks mounted on the protesters by the Italian *carabinieri* both during the demonstrations on July 20–21, 2001, and as a result of the police raid on the Indymedia centre immediately afterward starkly exposed how the organized violence of the state can be deployed to defend corporate control of the world. But there are also other forms of systemic violence that cause mass deaths as a result of the impersonal workings of economic mechanisms reinforced by the policies of the leading capitalist powers— for example, the 10 to 12 million children who die each year from malnutrition or disease. The significance of different kinds of violence became an issue after September 11—for example, in the debate between Christopher Hitchens and Noam Chomsky over whether the attacks on New York and Washington represented a greater crime than, say, the deaths caused by the Clinton administration's destruction of Sudan's main source of medicines in August 1998.[7]

Genoa and September 11 also highlighted the issue of the moral legitimacy and political efficacy of violence that purports to be directed against the system. Of course, the atrocities in New York and Washington were strongly condemned by all sections of the anti-capitalist movement. But within the movement, ever since Seattle, there has been a debate over the tactics of the anarchist Black Bloc, whose members have consistently used protests organized by others to trash shops, banks, and cars or, less frequently, to attack the police. The scale of the police violence at Genoa, mainly directed at peaceful protesters, along with the considerable evidence of collaboration between the *carabinieri* and the Black Bloc, unleashed a storm of criticism against these tactics. Whether intentionally or not, the Black Bloc's violence—usually petty and sometimes downright childish (How did burning ATMs used by ordinary workers and cheap cars probably parked there by protesters along the Genoa waterfront in any way undermine global capitalism?)—certainly played into the police's hands by legitimizing a violent response.

Whatever the precise role played by *agents provocateurs*, successive anti-capitalist protests seemed to be caught on a rising escalator of violent confrontation; the police shootings of three protesters at the European Union (EU) summit in Gothenburg (Göteborg) during June 2001 were rapidly followed by the killing of Carlo Giuliani amid an orgy of official brutality at Genoa. The reaction of one wing of the movement was expressed by Susan George:

My own dilemma, one surely experienced by numerous comrades, is that I am responsible for a major anti-neo-liberal globalization association (i.e., vice-president of ATTAC France—30,000 local members, 200-plus local committees). I cannot now encourage our members to put life and limb on the line, to participate in demos where we have the police trapping people and shooting live ammunition on the one hand, and on the other the Black Bloc, completely infiltrated by police and fascists, running wild and apparently unable or unwilling to police its own ranks.[8]

A contrasting view was offered by the American activist Starhawk:

I was at Genoa. Because of what I experienced there, including the moments of real terror and horror, I am more convinced than ever that we need to stay on the streets. We need to continue mounting large actions, contesting summits, working on the global scale. Our large-scale actions have been extraordinarily effective. I've heard despairing counsels that the protests have not affected the debates in the G8 or the WTO or the IMF/World Bank. In fact they have—they have significantly changed the agendas and the propaganda issuing forth. In any case, the actual policies of these institutions will be the last thing to change. But for most of us on the streets, changing the debate within these institutions is not our purpose. Our purpose is to undercut their legitimacy, to point a spotlight at their programmes and policies, and to raise the social costs of their existence until they become insupportable.[9]

This debate was cut short by 11 September, which had the immediate effect of pushing the movement off the streets, at least in the United States. The protests scheduled for the IMF/World Bank annual general meeting in Washington on September 28–30, 2001, were called off even before the meeting itself was canceled. Subsequent demonstrations in the United States and Canada against the war in Afghanistan and the World Trade Organization summit in Doha in November 2001 were comparatively small and muted. The *Financial Times* comforted its anxious readers with this reflection: "One of the less remarked consequences of the U.S. terrorist attacks has been to halt in its tracks the mass movement against globalization."[10] James Harding, concluding his survey (which was truncated after September 11), painted a similarly downbeat picture of the movement:

It has been robbed of its momentum. Counter-capitalism was not just a movement, it was a mood. Its main platform—the street—is not as open as it was. Its message, always complicated, is now much more loaded. Its audience—politicians, the press and the public—are seriously distracted. And its funding base, already tiny, threatens to shrivel as charitable foundations and philanthropists see their fortunes shrink with the stock market.[11]

Walden Bello, one of the most eloquent and forceful representatives of the anti-capitalist movement, acknowledged the negative impact of the attacks on New York and Washington: "In classical drama, September 11 was what you called a deus ex machina—an external force or event that swings a destiny that in the balance is in favour of one of the protagonists. The Al Qa'ida New York mission was the best possible gift to the U.S. and global establishment."[12] The disarray into which the anti-capitalist movement was thrown as a result of September 11 helped to create a space in which the leading capitalist powers, imbued with a greater sense of urgency thanks to the American economic slowdown and the terrorist attacks, could achieve in Doha what they had failed to get under way in Seattle two years previously—namely, a new round of negotiations on international trade liberalization. The tone for the summit was set by U.S. Trade Representative Robert Zoelick, who said that free trade "promotes the values at the heart of this protracted struggle." The rhetoric of the "war against terrorism" succeeded where all the wiles of the Clinton administration had failed.

WAR, IMPERIALISM, AND THE STATE

So is the most important connection between September 11 and Genoa that one trumped the other, that the "war on terrorism" killed off the anti-capitalist movement? The picture is in fact much more complex than this question suggests. In large parts of Europe, the anti-capitalist movement emerged as the driving force in the opposition to the Anglo-American war against Afghanistan. The largest anti-war mobilizations took place in Italy, where the Genoa movement—particularly the enormous demonstration on July 21, 2001—had helped to stimulate a massive radicalization. After more than twenty years of bitter defeat and disarray, the Italian left began to revive. Social forums modeled on the Genoa Social Forum spread like wildfire around the country. The radicalization embraced sections of the official workers' movement. Both Rifondazione Comunista and the metalworkers' federation (FIOM) participated in and firmly identified themselves with the Genoa protests. The Genoa movement fed effortlessly into opposition to the war. An unprecedented 300,000 people took part in the annual Peace March from Assisi to Perugia on October 14, 2001. Then, on November 10, 140,000 demonstrated in Rome against the war, overwhelming the 30,000 who took part in the pro-war "USA Day" rally organized by the right-wing government of Silvio Berlusconi.

It was striking that elsewhere in Europe the anti-war movement was particularly robust where there had been strong mobilizations for Genoa. In Britain, for example, it is only a slight exaggeration to say that the war in Afghanistan transformed what had previously been an anti-capitalist mood into a movement. Before September 11, anti-capitalist ideas were circulating widely; thus Naomi Klein's *No Logo* enjoyed an astonishing success in Britain. Globalise Resistance, founded in February 2001, was able to provide a broad framework for anti-capitalist activists and to organize a sizable and militant British contingent to Genoa. There was, however, no real *movement* to match ATTAC in France or the dense network of coalitions and activist groups in North America. Nevertheless, the U.S. response to September 11, strongly supported by the Blair government, led to the formation of the Stop the War Coalition. Two huge anti-war demonstrations in London on October 13 and November 18, 2001, mobilized respectively 50,000 and 100,000 people. As Andy Beckett acknowledged in the pro-war liberal daily *The Guardian*,

> The significance both of both demonstrations was clear by then [18 November]: far more people than expected were prepared to actively oppose a war that, according to the government and most conventional wisdom, was so morally straightforward as to require little debate. And this anti-war coalition looked remarkably like the alliance that had been opposing globalization prior to September 11.[13]

Against this background one might consider the impact of September 11 on the anti-capitalist movement in light of a metaphor used by Toni Negri: "It is like water descending a mountain: one can try to stop it, but if in the first instance it goes round the obstacle, it will always cut through a new course for itself. We are in a situation of this kind, we are in a situation where there is a blockage that we must get round before resuming our course."[14] (There were, of course, other, more negative experiences, above all in the United States, which I discuss below.) Another way of looking at it would be to say that the impact of September 11 has been to bring into sharper focus a problem that had already emerged as part of the learning process experienced by the anti-capitalist movement since Seattle.

This is the problem of the state, implicit in the issue of violence discussed above. Leading intellectuals associated with the anti-capitalist movement have tended to celebrate its dispersed, fragmented structure as a strategic virtue that allows it to outflank the centralized power of its opponents. Famously comparing the movement to a swarm, Naomi Klein approvingly quoted Maude Barlow of the Council of Canadians: "We are up against a boulder. We can't remove it so we try to go underneath it, to go around it and over it."[15] But what happens if the boulder—in the shape of the capitalist state—doesn't meekly stand there and allow its opponents to walk round it? What if it goes out to get them? The confusion that this can create is evident in the following reflections on Genoa by Luca Casarini, one of the leaders of the *tute bianche* (white overalls) movement famous for the imaginative and nonviolent street tactics they developed in the late 1990s. In a notorious incident at Genoa on July 20, 2001, the *tute bianche*–led contingent based at the Carlini stadium was ambushed by massed forces of heavily armed *carabinieri*. Interviewed shortly afterward, Casarini said:

> The police charged violently. We fought back and I stand by our response as a political fact. Nonetheless, for us to also take up militaristic tactics would be

crazy and political suicide. At Genoa there were all the forces of order, the army, the secret services of the eight most powerful—both economically and militarily—nations on the planet. Our movement can't measure up with that type of military power. We would be crushed within three months. . . . Two, three years ago we thought at length about how to act in a conflict without it becoming destructive. Our technique was different: we stated publicly what we wanted to do, letting it be known that if the police attacked us, we would defend ourselves only with shields and padding. It was our rule because it was essential that we create conflict and consensus about the objectives that we set up for ourselves. In Genoa we expected that more or less the same thing as usual would happen. They deceived us. . . . The police forces used firearms, even though they had assured us that they would not. The right to demonstrate that [Italian Foreign Minister Renato] Ruggiero agreed was an inalienable right was run over under the wheels of the police armoured cars.[16]

Genoa highlighted the role of organized state violence in defense of capitalist property relations. The war in Afghanistan then underlined the external dimension of state violence, as the enormous military strength of the Pentagon was deployed to reassert U.S. global hegemony. The latter also drew attention to the relative complexity of the system against which the anti-capitalist movement was campaigning. For many activists and writers, the main target was provided by the multinational corporations and the destructive influence they exerted through both the policies of the G-7 governments and the activities of the international financial institutions. Now, however, anti-capitalists were reminded that global capitalism embraces geopolitics as well as economics. The Marxist theory of imperialism has sought systematically to connect the economic competition between capitals with the geopolitical rivalries among states. The intellectual rediscovery of this tradition that was encouraged by the appearance of an avowedly heterodox contribution, Michael Hardt and Toni Negri's *Empire*, was therefore timely.[17]

So the world since September 11 has provided the anti-capitalist movement with an opportunity to develop a deeper political understanding. The movement already understood that the problem is systemic; now it has to see that this system embraces imperialism as well as capitalism. Some leading figures already understood this very clearly. For Walden Bello, for example, neo-liberal globalization was comprehensible only in the context of U.S. imperialism's drive to maintain its hegemony.[18] It was hardly surprising that Noam Chomsky, the single greatest critic of American foreign policy since the 1960s, became a key reference point after September 11.[19] But others found the going much more difficult. After all, this was the first major war that the anti-capitalist movement had had to confront since it exploded onto the scene at Seattle. It had, in particular, to deal with the fact that the Afghan war was the latest in a succession of wars in which the U.S. and its allies fought regimes that were, in themselves, thoroughly reactionary. Those involved in opposing the earlier wars in the Gulf and the Balkans had argued that, detestable though Saddam Hussein and Slobodan Milosevic were, this neither justified the Western resort to force nor altered the fact that Washington had chosen to fight these regimes, with which it had until recently enjoyed fairly cordial relations, for geopolitical rather than humanitarian reasons.[20]

The confusion to which failing to draw the necessary distinctions can lead is indicated by the following remarks by Susan George:

> We must at all costs avoid the "clash of civilizations" à la Samuel Huntington. This is the scenario Bin Laden and his fellow fascist fundamentalists most devoutly desire, believing as they do that indiscriminate American action will radicalize millions of Moslems and lead to full-scale holy war against the hated West. Egyptian President Hosni Mubarak has described Bin Laden as "a megalomaniac who wants to take power over the world". We must hand him no opportunities.[21]

Of course, a clash of civilizations would be an appalling horror, but avoidance of it will not be helped if critics of capitalism apply to radical Islamism misleading clichés derived from the dominant ideological discourses. At the Globalization and Resistance conference in New York in November 2001 that inspired the present collection, George defended her description of Al Qaeda as fascist by arguing that they had a "doctrine of blood and soil," an extraordinary assertion. The Muslim concept of the *ummah*—the community of the faithful—is precisely a transnational one, something that the Al Qaeda network has strictly observed (whatever respects in which its interpretations of Muslim doctrine may differ from those of others), incorporating as it does activists from many different national backgrounds. Moreover, citing Mubarak as an authority on the evils of Islamist terrorism shows a remarkable lack of judgment, given that his regime has waged a savage dirty war against the Islamists that has drastically restricted the civil liberties of all Egyptians (and, arguably, helped to drive alienated young men into bin Laden's arms) at the same time as it has pursued neo-liberal policies involving, for example, the restoration of the landowners expropriated by Nasr and the Free Officers Movement a generation ago.[22]

The anti-capitalist movement in the United States certainly faced a much more urgent problem than the dangers of intellectual confusion just illustrated. September 11 and its aftermath underlined one mistake frequently committed by both champions and critics of globalization.[23] The nation-state has not, after all, been reduced to impotence by the greater global economic integration of the past generation. Not simply did the U.S. attack on Afghanistan dramatize the military capabilities that some states at least can command, but the geopolitical maneuverings generated by the efforts of different regional powers such as Russia, China, India, Pakistan, and Iran to realign themselves with respect to the American "war on terrorism" underlined that states remain crucial political actors. Finally, the outpourings of American patriotism that followed the attacks on New York and Washington highlighted the capacity of even the state at the center of the current wave of corporate globalization to draw on ideological representations that address individuals as bearers of a specific and exclusive national identity rather than as consumers in a homogenized world market. Nationalist discourses continue to exercise their sway, not merely, as many commentators argued after 1989, in relatively peripheral regions such as the Balkans or the former Soviet Union, but at the very heart of global capitalism.[24]

The problem that September 11 poses for the anti-capitalist movement in the United States is more than the pressure that surges of nationalism generally place on dissenters. Perhaps the greatest achievement of Seattle as a political mobilization was the Teamster-Turtle alliance—a coming together of, on the one hand, activists whose starting point was provided by issues such as the environment and Third World debt and, on the other hand, some of the key sections of organized labor in the United States, traditionally a working-class movement that is hardly famed for its willingness to back radical political causes.[25] This new alliance wasn't a feature of subsequent mobilizations in the United States, though there were major labor contingents at the protests at the Free Trade of the Americas summit in Quebec City in April 2001 and at Genoa a few months later. In any case, September 11 threatened to shatter it altogether: The aftermath of the destruction of the World Trade Center was characterized by a distinctive sense of proletarian injury and pride generated both by the massacre of office workers, janitors, and firefighters and by the heroism and sheer persistence shown particularly by blue-collar public employees in the subsequent efforts at rescue.

So, whereas in Italy and Britain the impact of September 11 and the war in Afghanistan was to sustain or even to accelerate the preexisting process of radicalization, anti-imperialism thus serving to reinforce anti-capitalism, in the United States these developments threatened to isolate activists from the larger working-class community on which they had begun to exercise an influence. There can be no easy, short-term answer to this problem, but two lessons of history—specifically of past anti-war movements—are most helpful. The first is the importance of activists keeping their nerve—of sustaining their criticisms and continuing to initiate protests—in a political environment that is, after all, far less threatening to dissenters than it was, for example, in most belligerent states during the First World War. The second is the importance of time. Opposition to America's war in Vietnam built up gradually, from the cause of exceptionally small and despised minorities to one of the greatest mass movements of the 20th century. If the Bush administration does pursue a global "war on terrorism," the series of bloody entanglements in alliance with corrupt and repressive regimes to which this policy may well lead will generate growing opposition. The strength of the anti-war movement in some European countries is in part a consequence of a learning process—of the cumulative experience of the succession of wars waged by its allies since 1991. It is easy to see why this process was for many Americans short-circuited by September 11, but it does not follow that this state of affairs will continue indefinitely.[26]

The collapse of the "New Economy" into the fourth major world recession of the past thirty years will also create opportunities for the anti-capitalist movement to rebuild its audience in the ranks of organized labor. U.S. military victory in Afghanistan was rapidly followed by two recessionary consequences that offered vivid reminders of the reasons why the movement had emerged in the first place—the spectacular collapse of yet another neo-liberal showcase, Argentina, this time amid a massive popular rebellion, and the bankruptcy of the huge energy trading company Enron, its rise and fall a classic case of American-style crony capitalism that dragged in such accomplices as investment banks, the accountants at Arthur Anderson, the Bush administration, and the Blair government. According to Walden Bello, "[t]hese towering twin disasters threaten to push the global elite back to the crisis of legitimacy that was shaking its hegemony world-wide prior to September 11."27

Two events at the beginning of February 2002 that have become regular features of the activist's diary offer evidence of the vitality of the anti-capitalist movement. The corporate jamboree of the World Economic Forum, moved from Davos to New York in the hope of escaping protests, proved to be a muted affair; the demonstrators came anyway, about 20,000 of them, mainly youngsters from New York City and environs—the most important North American mobilization since September 11. Meanwhile, the rival World Social Forum (WSF) attracted between 65,000 and 80,000 to Porto Alegre, three to four times the number who had attended the first WSF a year earlier. The event, combining celebration, protest, and debate in an atmosphere of increasing radicalization, prompted even the *Financial Times* to acknowledge that "the strong turnout showed the movement had regained some of the momentum it lost after the terrorist attacks in the U.S. last September."28

PROBLEMS OF STRATEGY

September 11 did not kill off the movement against capitalist globalization. What it has done is bring into sharper focus issues that were already emerging. As we have seen, the most important of these concerns the state. This is a problem that does not simply pose itself negatively—the state as an obstacle to change and as the main source of organized violence both domestically and globally. More positively, can the nation-state (or indeed other forms of "governance" at the regional or global level) serve as an instrument of democratic transformation? Since its inception the anti-capitalist movement has skated over the question of how precisely it intends to change the existing system and what it will put in its place. The consequence has been, on the whole, a productive ambiguity that has allowed the movement to be as inclusive as possible, embracing a wide variety of political approaches and forms of organizing. But it is not an ambiguity that can be maintained indefinitely without causing growing political costs.

Already one powerful wing of the movement is articulating a strategy that bears a strong resemblance to that offered by classical reformism within the international socialist movement. This strategy is most strongly defended by ATTAC France. Indeed, there is a sense in which the strategy is implicit in ATTAC's central demand, for the Tobin Tax on international financial speculation. Necessarily such a tax would have to be imposed by the state—or, rather, by a number of states acting in concert.[29] The tax's original devisor, James Tobin, made it clear that his main objectives were both "to throw some sand in the well-greased wheels" of the international financial markets and to "restore to national economies and governments some fraction of the short-run autonomy they enjoyed before currency convertibility became so easy."[30]

The logic of the Tobin Tax is thus to restore a degree of economic power to the nation-state. It is not surprising, therefore, that leading figures in ATTAC France, such as Bernard Cassen, are close to the veteran left nationalist politician Jean-Pierre Chevènement, champion of *souverainisme*—the restoration of national sovereignty. A comparable objective is advocated by Bello, who argues that the Bretton Woods system that governed international finance after the Second World War was "a relatively pluralistic global system, where hegemonic power was still far from institutionalised in a set of all-encompassing and powerful multilateral institutions," thanks to which "the Latin American countries and many Asian countries were able to achieve a modicum of industrial development in the period from 1950–70."[31] As Susan George makes amply clear, this strategy seeks not to get rid of capitalism but to make it more humane, more democratic, and more nationally regulated than its current version:

> I regret that I must confess that I no longer know what "overthrowing capitalism" means at the beginning of the 21st century. Perhaps we are going to witness what the philosopher Paul Virilio has called "the global accident." If it happens, it will certainly be accompanied by immense human suffering. If all the financial markets and all the stock exchanges collapsed at the same time, millions of people would find themselves back on the dole, bank failures would massively exceed the capacity of governments to prevent catastrophes, insecurity and crime would become the norm and we would be plunged into the Hobbesian hell of the war of all against all. Call me a "reformist" if you like, but I don't want such a future any more than the neo-liberal future.[32]

Such broad strategic choices have practical political implications, particularly given that some national governments—in Europe at any rate—have begun to respond to the anti-capitalist movement. The confrontation at Genoa brought divided reactions from the social-democratic parties that largely dominated the European Union. Predictably enough, the Blair government in Britain was unremitting in its hostility to the protesters. Indeed, the *Financial Times* reported shortly after the summit "Mr Blair has told friends that while the events of Genoa were 'unacceptable,' they might actually prove 'helpful' to those fighting for the cause of free trade and economic liberalization."[33] Blair's plans to launch an ideological assault on the anti-capitalist movement were in the event diverted into his drive after September 11 to act as a worldwide ambassador for the Bush administration and its "War Against Terrorism," but his government continued to be one of the most uncritical Western defenders of the Washington consensus.

The response to Genoa of French Prime Minister Lionel Jospin was very different. He said: "France denounces the violence by a tiny minority under the pretext of highlighting the evils of globalization; but it is delighted to see the emergence of a citizens' movement at the planetary level which wants a majority of men and women to share the potential benefits of globalization between rich and poor countries."[34] Jospin's fellow social democrat, German Chancellor Gerhard Schröder, had adopted the slogan *die neue Mitte* (the new center) and toyed with Blair's Third Way, but in September 2001 he called for a debate on the "weak spots" in the international financial markets and on "how we can react to these relatively autonomous speculative financial flows."[35] The French and German governments followed this up by establishing a high-level working group on controlling international financial markets—a move that the *Financial Times* described as "a further feather in the cap of the anti-globalization protesters."[36]

The courtship between the Jospin government and the anti-capitalist movement was not cut short by September 11. A series of meetings took place between ATTAC leaders and members of the prime minister's staff, and in November 2001 the French National Assembly passed an amendment supporting the Tobin Tax. The following January the second World Social Forum (WSF) in Porto Alegre attracted a flood of French politicians including six of Jospin's ministers and Chevènement, along with two other candidates for the French presidency. The French left-liberal daily *Le Monde* devoted an eight-page supplement to the WSF, in which it celebrated "The Planetary Success of the Children of Seattle."[37] Henri Weber, a former revolutionary of the 1968 generation now close to Finance Minister Laurent Fabius, leader of the right wing of the French Socialist Party, called the WSF "a historic social movement, whose articulation with the governing left is fundamental."[38]

Undoubtedly this official attention reflected the impact of the anti-capitalist movement. Nevertheless, the social democratic courtship needs to be treated with suspicion. Despite the care with which Jospin sought to cultivate a left-wing image, his "plural left" government pursued neo-liberal policies with considerably greater success than its conservative predecessor. As Philip H. Gordon of the Brookings Institution points out, "Jospin, as the head of a Socialist-Communist-Green coalition supposedly sympathetic to a statist economy, has actually privatized FFr 240bn worth (€36.4bn, £22.5bn) of state enterprises, more than the past six French governments combined."[39] It is easy to understand why both Jospin and Schröder should have sought to draw closer to a movement that had demonstrated its capacity to mobilize mass support in the lead-up to hotly contested elections in both

France and Germany. Jospin's defeat in the April 2002 presidential contest will, if anything, intensify efforts by some Socialist Party politicians to gain radical credibility this way. The danger for the movement, however, is that in the process it will find that its teeth have been drawn.

After all, there are two ways in which the established order can respond to a movement demanding change—repression and incorporation. The first was on display at Genoa and also reflected in the assault on civil liberties mounted especially by the American and British governments after September 11. But it would be a mistake to believe that the resort to repression excludes pursuit of the alternative response. Thus Vittorio Agnoletto of the Italian Social Forum movement has argued that Genoa marked a shift by the neo-liberal system to reliance solely on violence.[40] But the explosion of popular resistance in Italy itself after Genoa indicates that the present balance of social forces rules out a purely repressive response to the anti-capitalist movement. Blair and Berlusconi may represent the wing of the European ruling classes that wants a tough pro-American neo-liberal stance. But there are other elements, particularly powerful in France, that are pursuing a strategy of incorporation, and not without success.

Thus in France after September 11 there was a striking divergence from the pattern noted elsewhere. As we have seen, in Italy and Britain anti-capitalism and anti-imperialism proved mutually supporting. In France, on the whole, this was not the case. Overt opposition to the war in Afghanistan was limited: The demonstrations were small, and efforts to rally left intellectuals against the war were hampered by deep internal divergences. This was surprising when one considers the explosion of social movements after the mass public-sector strikes of November–December 1995 and the development of ATTAC, in whose leadership were figures with a long history of opposing U.S. foreign policy.[41] No doubt the fact that the major parties of the French left were actually in government and supporting the war acted as an inhibiting factor, but the influence that this government could exert on the extra-parliamentary left, particularly ATTAC, is also worth considering. ATTAC France opposed the war, but it seems to have made little effort to mobilize its considerable support base (an estimated 27,000 members at the end of 2001) against it.[42]

Behind this stance of formal opposition to the war but failure to build the kind of anti-war movement that developed elsewhere in Europe may have lain a kind of schizophrenia that has been seen before in the history of the anti-capitalist left. On the one hand, there is "normality"—the course of capitalist development with its attendant injustices and dysfunctions. On the other hand, there are "abnormal" events—wars and other catastrophes. The task of anti-capitalists is to focus their attention on normality, on the system that it is their task to transform. As for the abnormal events, anti-capitalists may have to take a stance with respect to them, but they are not their main concern.

The difficulty with this kind of division is that, in modern capitalism, the abnormal becomes normal. Sudden, unexpected, and catastrophic events are, pre-

cisely, to be expected. The terrorist atrocities on September 11 were not predictable in their awful detail, but that American foreign policy, against the background of growing global inequality, would produce such disasters was entirely
predictable.[43] As Walter Benjamin eloquently argued, capitalism does not progress
smoothly and continuously, but through sudden, jerky phase-transitions; any
strategy by its opponents that fails to take this into account is doomed to failure.[44]
To put the same point more concretely, the capitalist world economy is closely in-
terwoven with the international state system: Economic competition and geopolitical rivalries are inseparable. An effective movement against capitalism has to be
one that can respond to the military face of globalization as well as to its economic
manifestations.

Bello acknowledged the importance of drawing connections: "If there is a clear
silver lining in the post-September 11 situation, it is that three movements that
had formerly gone their own independent ways—the peace movement, the human
rights movement, and the anti-corporate globalization movement—now find it
critical to collaborate."[45] But the need is for more than the convergence of distinct
movements, desirable though that undoubtedly is. We have to develop a deep, historically informed, and nonformulaic understanding that the same logic that is at
work in the processes of economic competition among firms also drives the geopolitical rivalries between states.[46] It is the sense of being up against a system that has
been decisive in giving the anti-capitalist movement its generalizing *élan* in the first
place. Now we need a better grasp of what this system involves. Here the Marxist
tradition has much to offer. Its totalizing impulse and insistence on how an immense variety of social phenomena are shaped by the imperative logic of capital accumulation made classical Marxism a target for attack during the heyday of postmodernism in the 1980s and 1990s. Exactly these qualities are what constitute its
greatest political value today.

But the deeper the insight we get into capitalism's functioning as a system, the
harder it is to imagine any partial solution to the problems that it generates. The
latest debacle of neo-liberalism in Argentina could undoubtedly help to generate
support for a national-Keynesian alternative to the Washington consensus. The
Peronist president Eduardo Duhalde, installed in office after three predecessors had
been driven out by the rising of December 2001, implied as much when he was
elected. These hints rapidly dissipated as the Duhalde administration flung itself
into the arms of the IMF and acceded to its demands for exactly the same budgetary austerity that had produced economic slump and popular rebellion in the
first place. This slide back into neo-liberal orthodoxy did not arise simply from the
cowardice and venality of the Argentine political establishment. The international
economic pressures to which any deviant national government can now be subjected are undeniably vast. To that extent, the theorists of globalization are right.
The tactics currently being canvassed by critics of the Washington consensus are
therefore international; consider, for example, the formation by southern states of
a debtors' cartel that would have the collective power to impose a moratorium on

debt repayments or even a joint default on northern governments and banks.[47] A pause to reflect on what implementing this demand would involve politically, given the way in which neo-liberalism has been hard-wired into the core leadership of most Third World states over the last two decades, rapidly reveals that an enormous upheaval would be required, based on mass mobilizations that would dwarf even the protests of the past few years.

It is impossible to predict what would emerge from the clash between such a mass movement and a capitalist system that, as we have seen, is also imperialism, heavily armed against domestic and external enemies. But it would seem both unadventurous and dangerous to restrict the horizons of those seeking change to a more humane and nationally diverse version of capitalism. Dangerous, because regarding the nation-state, alone or in alliance with others, as an instrument of democratic transformation can blind the movement to the reality revealed in Genoa—the state as concentrated violence, mobilized not to facilitate but to block the pressures for change. Unadventurous, because refusing to consider the possibility of alternatives to capitalism fails to take seriously one of the movement's most powerful slogans: "Another World is Possible!"

Another *world*—that is, a world based on different social logic, run according to different priorities from those that prevail today. It is easy enough to specify what the desiderata of such an alternative social logic would be—social justice, economic efficiency, environmental sustainability, and democracy—but much harder to spell out how a reproducible social system embodying these requirements could be built. And then there is the question of how to achieve it. Both these questions—What is the alternative to capitalism? What strategy can get us there?—can be answered in many different ways. One thing the anti-capitalist movement is going to have to learn is how to argue through the differences that exist and will probably develop around such issues without undermining the very powerful sense of unity that has been one of the movement's most attractive qualities. The ideal of unity in diversity to which we all subscribe is likely to be much more harshly tested in the tougher times inaugurated by September 11 than it was previously.

The anti-capitalist movement is a new movement: Wherever we place its exact origin, it has existed only a few years; it also employs, as its advocates ceaselessly remind us, innovative methods of organizing. But, new movement though it is, it increasingly faces some old problems—problems, that is, that have beset every movement that has sought to challenge capitalism over the past two centuries. The dilemma of reform or revolution, the problem of the state, the menace of imperialism and war, the questions of what to replace the present system with, and how—all these and other challenges cannot be wished away or evaded by the poetic metaphors favored by prominent figures associated with the movement. On how they are addressed depend the prospects for the best chance to achieve real social transformation in a generation. A heavy responsibility rests on the shoulders of the activists and intellectuals who have rallied to the call of Seattle and Genoa and Porto Alegre.

NOTES

1. N. Klein, "Reclaiming the Commons," *New Left Review*, Vol. 2, No. 9 (2001), p. 87.

2. S. George, "Que faire à present?" January 15, 2001.

3. "Porto Alegre II: Call of the Social Movements," February 4, 2002.

4. J. Harding, "Globalization's Children Strike Back," *Financial Times*, September 11, 2001.

5. J. Lloyd, *The Protest Ethic* (London: Demos, 2001), p. 67.

6. The Marxist tradition in particular has a long-standing critique of terrorism. See, for example, L. D. Trotsky, *Against Individual Terrorism* (New York: Pathfinder, 1974).

7. The Chomsky-Hitchens debate is available online at www.thenation.com. For further discussion of these issues, see A. Callinicos, "Plumbing the Depths: Marxism and the Holocaust," *Yale Journal of Criticism*, Vol. 14 (2001), and "Theory, History, and Commitment: An Interview with Alex Callinicos," *Imprints*, Vol. 6, No. 1 (2002).

8. S. George, contribution to "After Genoa—What Next?" *Socialist Review*, September 2001, p. 13. The Association for the Taxation of Financial Transactions for the Aid of Citizens (ATTAC) campaigns for the regulation of financial markets, in the first instance through the introduction of the Tobin Tax on international financial transactions. Founded in France, it now has affiliates in a total of forty countries.

9. Starhawk, contribution to "After Genoa—What Next?" *Socialist Review*, September 2001, p. 11.

10. *Financial Times*, October 6, 2001.

11. J. Harding, "Clamour Against Capitalism Stilled," *Financial Times*, 10 October 2001.

12. W. Bello, "The American Way of War," December 2001, available online at www.focusweb.org.

13. A. Beckett, "Did the Left Lose the War?" *The Guardian*, January 17, 2002.

14. "Ruptures dans l'Empire, puissance de l'exode: Entretien avec Toni Negri par Giuseppe Cecco et Maurizio Lazzarato" (October 27, 2001), forthcoming in *Multitudes*.

15. N. Klein, "The Vision Thing," *The Nation*, July 10 2000, p. 4; available online at www.thenation.com.

16. *Il Manifesto*, August 3, 2001.

17. For a critical appraisal of *Empire*, see A. Callinicos, "Toni Negri in Perspective," *International Socialism*, Series 2, No. 92 (2001). And for further discussion of the theory of imperialism, see A. Callinicos et al., *Marxism and the New Imperialism* (London: Bookmarks, 1994); and A. Callinicos, "Marxism and Global Governance," forthcoming in D. Held and A. McGrew, *Governing Globalization* (Cambridge: Polity, 2002).

18. W. Bello et al., *Dark Victory*, 2nd ed. (London: Pluto, 1999).

19. See N. Chomsky, *9–11* (New York: Seven Stories Press, 2001).

20. On the Balkan War of 1999, see N. Chomsky, *The New Military Humanism* (London: Pluto, 1999), and T. Ali, ed., *Masters of the Universe?* (London: Bookmarks, 2000).

21. S. George, "Clusters of Crisis and a Planetary Contract," *Sand in the Wheels*, November 21, 2001, available online at www.attac.org.

22. For a more balanced assessment of contemporary Islamist movements, see C. Harman, *The Prophet and the Proletariat*, rev. ed. (London: Bookmarks, 2002).

23. See, for example, a relatively moderate critic: N. Hertz, *The Silent Takeover* (London: Heinemann, 2001).

24. See the perceptive analysis by Michael Mann in "Globalization and September 11," *New Left Review*, Series 2, No. 12 (2001). It has, of course, been frequently noted that contemporary globalization is culturally ambiguous between genuine multiculturalism and

Americanization, but the reaffirmations of American national identity after September 11 were much more about exclusion than inclusion. The face that the United States currently turns to the rest of world is an invitation, not to join a polychromatic throng at McDonalds, but to acknowledge the power of what George W. Bush calls "the Good Country" and decide whether we wish to be its (obedient) friend or its enemy.

25. On the problems and opportunities of building alliances between trade unionists and anti-capitalist activists, see K. Moody, "Unions," in E. Bircham and J. Charlton, eds., *Anti-Capitalism: A Guide to the Movements* (London: Bookmarks, 2001).

26. Compare Chomsky's remarkably upbeat assessment of the current state of the American left: "It's certainly much better than it's been in the past. . . . It was much worse in the 60s. . . . Back in those days, in the early '60s, I remember very well attempts to raise the mildest criticisms of the [Vietnam] war at that time. You couldn't get four people in an auditorium to listen to you. In Boston, which is a pretty liberal city, we couldn't have a public demonstration against the war until about 1966 without it being physically attacked by people and protected by the police. It's incomparably better." See "The Salon Interview with Noam Chomsky," January 2002, available online at www.freedomofpress.tripod.com.

27. W. Bello, "The Twin Debacles of Globalization," January 2002, available online at www.focusweb.org.

28. *Financial Times*, February 5, 2000.

29. For a detailed discussion of the Tobin Tax and its implementation, see, for example, M. ul Haq et al., eds., *The Tobin Tax* (New York: Oxford University Press, 1996), and H. Patomäki, *Democratizing Globalization* (London: Zed, 2001).

30. J. Tobin, "A Proposal for Monetary Reform" (1978), Appendix 2 in Patomäki, *Democratizing Globalization,* pp. 239, 240.

31. W. Bello, "Reforming the WTO Is the Wrong Agenda," in K. Danaher and R. Burbach, eds., *Globalize This!* (Monroe, Maine: Common Courage Press, 2000), p. 117.

32. George, "Que faire à présent?"

33. *Financial Times*, August 2, 2001.

34. Ibid., July 24, 2001.

35. Ibid., September 5, 2001.

36. Ibid., September 7, 2001.

37. "L'Autre Monde de Porto Alegre," *Le Monde,* January 27, 2002.

38. *Le Monde*, February 5, 2002.

39. P. H. Gordon, "Liberté! Fraternité! Anxiety!" *Financial Times*, January 19, 2002. (Note that *bn* stands for "billion.")

40. Agnoletto made this argument in several speeches at the second World Social Forum, Porto Alegre, January 31–February 5, 2002.

41. See J. Wolfreys, "Class Struggles in France," *International Socialism*, Series 20, No. 84 (1999).

42. See "Contre le terrorisme, la justice et non pas la guerre!" statement of the ATTAC movements of Europe, November 10, 2001, available online at www.attac.org. It is interesting that, according to Pierre Bourdieu's friend, the housing activist Annie Pourre, despite the involvement of some of his collaborators in ATTAC "Bourdieu regarded it as too reformist, too close to the authorities." See C. Losson and V. Filippis, "Penseur 'anti,' militant en marge," *Libération*, January 25, 2002.

43. See Chalmers Johnson's remarkable, prophetic book, *Blowback* (New York: Metropolitan Books, 2000).

44. W. Benjamin, "Theses on the Philosophy of History," in *Illuminations* (London: Jonathan Cape, 1970). In contemporary radical writing this sense of imminent catastrophe is very well evoked by Mike Davis; see, for example, his *Ecology of Fear* (New York: Metropolitan Books, 1999).

45. Bello, "American Way of War."

46. That this understanding is nonformulaic is a point worth stressing. Thus, for instance, during the war in Afghanistan the Internet buzzed with articles seeking to explain the U.S. attack in terms of the interest shown by American oil companies in Afghanistan as a potential pipeline route for Central Asia's vast energy reserves. This kind of reductionist explanation confused the main reason why U.S. policy makers have directed increasing attention on Central Asia over the past half-decade with the Bush administration's motive in attacking Afghanistan. This issue was not economic but political, inasmuch as it was concerned primarily with the reassertion of American global hegemony after the humiliation of September 11. Getting better access to Central Asian oil and gas is a welcome potential byproduct of this operation rather than its prime objective. For more analysis, see J. Rees, "Imperialism: Globalization, the State, and War," *International Socialism*, Series 2, No. 93 (2001).

47. See, for example, A. McEwan, "Economic Debacle in Argentina: The IMF Strikes Again," *Sand in the Wheels*, January 16, 2002, available online at www.attac.org; and J. Brecher et al., "Two, Three, Many Argentinas?" January 2002, available online at www.villageorpillage.org.

11

Race to the Bottom?

WILLIAM K. TABB

Globalization, understood as a "race to the bottom," is perhaps the dominant approach to the question of international trade on the left, but it is an inadequate and, in important ways, misleadingly confining framework in some of its accompanying formulations. Even as it remains essentially useful to understanding what is going on, its simple story needs qualification and supplementing.

I understand that to many, especially unionized industrial workers in the core countries, globalization is indeed seen as a "race to the bottom" in which transnational corporations close plants at home and open others abroad where labor costs are lower. To retain jobs, workers are told they must grant concessions within what is a negative-sum game; but no matter what concessions are made, the employers say there is another group of workers willing to settle for less, thus initiating a new round of demands for concessions. Even the threat of runaway relocation can frighten workers. There is awareness that conditions are far worse in the so-called developing countries such as China, where twelve-hour days, seven days a week, are the norm and government prevents the working class from organizing, independent trade unions from forming, and complaints from being freely voiced. The plausibility of such threats has strengthened the power of capital over labor.

Seeing trade as a "race to the bottom" is not the whole story, if for no other reason than that for the most oppressed workers, as bad as things may be, the new industrial employment represents a step up. They would not be better off without the opportunity to work for transnational corporations. At the same time, they deserve far better treatment and compensation than they typically receive. Both aspects of their relation to capital are essential to the nature of their position, and to the position of workers generally. This is not to excuse their exploitation or the growing inequalities between rich and poor countries, and between the rich and poor within individual countries, that characterize contemporary globalization. It is to point to the basic character of existing capitalism, the contemporary world system in which billions of people live on less than a dollar a day, subsisting in a state of malnourishment, without access to clean water, and in perpetual want. But transnational capital does not always or even generally go to where people are willing to work for the lowest pay. At the bottom, malnourishment, political instability, and lack of infrastructure would make for low productivity even if the desperate worked for next to nothing.

The "race to the bottom" framework may describe the experience of workers in the core countries who compete for jobs with lower-wage laborers in less developed economies. However, the race for profit is somewhat more complicated. Most trade does not represent a race to the bottom. 80 percent of all foreign direct investment goes from advanced economies to other advanced economies. The factories and service jobs that go to the less developed economies go to very few of them, and these are generally not the ones with the rock-bottom wages. It is not the case that trade is always bad any more than taking down barriers to trade is always good. There are divisions of labor that make sense. There are social controls over trade and investment that would address the injustices caused by so-called free trade. However, these would need to go well beyond the sort of reforms that make it into mainstream discussions. A different logic of globalization would be needed, and this in turn would be resisted by capital. Any effort to control corporate greed and the social costs it imposes is characterized as illegitimate so as to deflect attention from who gains and who loses.

Within the labor movement there has been a rethinking of the simple version of the race to the bottom and the nationalist-protectionist demands that have usually followed from it. This rethinking results from the realization that American workers gain from growing employment in export industries, that there are gains from trade that can be substantial, and that the politics of demanding fair trade over free trade is a better framing of the issue. The next step, the hard one for the U.S. labor movement to take, is to recognize that the problem is one of class power, involving the coercion of weaker countries by more powerful ones, the coercion of workers by employers, and the uneven distribution of the gains from trade based on coercive exercise of economic, political, and military power. Those in subordinate positions in unequal exchange suffer from the social relations of the contemporary world system. Trade itself is coerced. The social relations of production and in production are coerced exchange.

Fear of competition from potential labor market competitors who could lower their living standards has led organized workers to fight against immigration and to demand protectionist measures against imports from low-wage countries—a strategy that is divisive as well as ineffective. The Sweeney leadership of the AFL-CIO has rejected this approach and called for organizing immigrant labor and fighting for the rights of the undocumented, knowing that such solidarity is in the interest of all workers. Whereas the Meany-Kirkland Cold Warriors saw their task as fighting communist influence in the world's trade unions, thus dividing labor and weakening struggles against corporate exploiters everywhere their splitting tactics were employed, the new AFL-CIO leadership has to some extent distanced itself from being the tool of the State Department and the CIA. A full transition to a true international solidarity has not been achieved, but pressure from the rank and file and other progressive activists in the post–Cold War period makes further movement toward more effective solidarity possible within a context of broader political consciousness than that previously found at the top of the U.S. labor federation.

When John Sweeney was invited to address the movers and shakers who convened in Davos in 2000, he asked rhetorically, "What is the fundamental test of globalization?" His answer was this: "It's not whether markets are more or less open. That mistakes the means for the end. The end is human development. The fundamental question is whether globalization is helping to lift the poor from poverty; whether it is empowering the many, not just the few; whether its blessings are shared widely; whether it works for working people." The call is for new global rules—criteria that the public demonstrations in Seattle and elsewhere must meet through, as Sweeney says, "workers North and South marching together. And the many different voices made one clear statement: the current course cannot be sustained; fundamental reform is needed." Sweeney went on to talk about sustainable development, food safety, democratic participation, debt forgiveness, and other issues that were foregrounded by the diverse movements. In addition, statements by Sweeney, Kofi Annan, and others contained the implicit warning that the grassroots critique of global injustice went further and was contributing to the growth of a new anti-capitalist movement. Unless real reforms are forthcoming, the movement will become more radical in its analysis and aspirations.

A radicalizing process is indeed under way. It is increasingly clear to many more people not only that there has been a dramatic growth of inequality but also that the world economy is growing too slowly to generate employment and payment sufficient to alleviate poverty. The world has experienced redistributional growth, expansion in some areas accompanied by stagnation and worse in others, a global process of uneven development. It is clear that almost everywhere there is increased job and income insecurity and that capital has gained in comparison to labor as a result of redistributed wealth and power. The pattern of corporate globalization has imposed severe ecological costs as well; great harm has been done to the environment, and far worse is threatened in the future. It has also restructured public decision making as corporations have been increasingly freed from social control through deregulation, privatization, and other neoliberal measures. There has been great cost in terms of states' willingness and ability to provide needed public goods. Competition for jobs and investment has resulted in lower taxes on capital as well as poorer services and higher taxes for workers. The more mobile factor of production, capital, has increased its already structurally greater bargaining power. The social relations of capitalism more basically support the corporations against their workers' efforts to appeal to "their" government for help.

Trade brings the workers of the world into a single labor market as never before. Repressive regimes that deny labor rights and other democratic freedoms not only oppress their own citizens but restrict the prospects of others. Free trade in such a context puts pressure on workers who have been able to win benefits and bargaining rights in their own societies. It is for such reasons that Americans opposed permanent most-favored-nation status for China. Well over a hundred million dollars in lobbying, political donations, advertising, and other activities was required to ensure that Congress voted the way transnational capital wanted on this issue. The Clinton administration staffed a 150-person China War Room to work with the corporate lobbyists, making sure that political favors and money got to the right people to win the votes needed. Reports of hundreds of thousands of dollars being offered in exchange for votes and dire punishment if Congress people failed to come on board made the rounds in Washington. The class politics over China policy was clear.

China raises "race to the bottom" issues for American workers who, unable to stop greater trade with China, are being pushed to a class solidarity position of supporting unionization and democratization in China and other low-wage countries. Chinese industrial workers, mostly rural migrants who have no tradition of union membership, and certainly do not enjoy the iron rice bowl security of state-sector employment, are clearly residents of the industrial world that Marx described so well. They work twelve hours a day, seven days a week, and would be fired if they complained. National laws that require a forty-four-hour basic work week, a local minimum wage in the factory zones, and overtime pay beyond forty-four hours are not honored. Local officials collaborate. Although China is a party to the International Convention on Social, Economic, and Cultural Rights, which calls for free trade unions, China's unions are organs of the state. They are there to help workers adjust to their oppressive conditions, not change them. Independent unionization efforts are crushed. Activists are given harsh prison sentences. Insisting that basic labor rights be enforced as solidarity groups demand would help the self-organization of Chinese workers and have an impact on the political system.

It is not just in manufacturing that low-wage Asian countries have excelled. India, for example, has become a center for back-office and other business services used by airlines for their frequent-flier record keeping, by banks for credit card operations, and by insurance companies that use Indian call centers to interface with customers. In addition, Amazon.com has cut jobs in Seattle and added positions in India. Such relocation lowers costs for these companies by 40 to 50 percent. Transcribing medical records from doctor dictation is a multibillion-dollar business in India. Outsourced knowledge services include software programming. Indian lawyers do research for American and British firms. Indian engineers design construction projects. Indian scientists carry on basic research and development for Western firms. Indian animators subcontract for Hollywood. And so on. India itself remains poor, of course, and a relatively small part of its population is employed in such venues; but the growth rate is impressive. Given its reservoir of English-speaking, well-educated people, foreign firms are able to employ highly skilled and motivated people at a fraction of what similar talent would cost at home.

These workers become a growing market for exports from the United States and elsewhere. However, adjustment is not instantaneous or automatic in the job-losing countries. Displaced workers in the West may not be easily reemployed at comparable jobs and wages. Transnationals demand tax incentives to refrain from moving jobs, and government revenues fall. Labor policies adjust to the harsher climate. Yet, the "race to the bottom" does not stress either the lack of benefits from such developments experienced by the vast majority of Indians or the need to support the unions that represent, or seek to represent, Indians and other workers.

The cases of China and India, though important, should not obscure the fact that, to an overwhelming extent, rich countries invest in other rich countries. Seventy percent of private capital flows goes to only ten countries. The United States and the United Kingdom lead the list of inward investment; China and Brazil are on the list as well. Looking at just the foreign direct investment to developing countries, we find that the five most important hosts receive over half of all such inflows. China alone receives over a quarter of all foreign direct investment; Brazil, Mexico, Argentina, and Malaysia together receive 22 percent. Most poor countries cannot attract even minimal foreign investment. A number of factors are involved here. First, there is a working out of the law of one price in which better-paid workers facing competition from low-wage workers now in the same global labor force are pressed to make concessions, work for less, and lose their jobs. This is the "race to the bottom" aspect of trade. Second, there is a concentration on investment primarily in the advanced countries as corporations jockey for greater market power at the expense of weaker rivals. Third, there is a process of uneven development whereby many countries do not attract foreign investment and poverty and inequality grow on a global scale. The politics of the 21st century will increasingly reflect the effects of the concentration and centralization of capital among fewer and fewer giant transnationals. Throughout the second half of the 1990s, foreign direct investment, growing at over 30 percent a year (primarily targeted, as noted, to other rich countries), was almost always earmarked for mergers and acquisitions. The United Nations World Investment Report 2000 shows that 100 percent of inward foreign direct investment to developed countries went to mergers and acquisitions as big transnationals got bigger and extended their global penetration. In developing countries the figure was closer to 40 percent overall, though higher in Latin America (60 percent) and lower in developing Asia (20 percent). Such regional differences reflected the quality of local subcontractors in Asia. Rather than owning factories in developing countries, transnationals prefer to buy from subcontractors who take the business risks and discipline local labor more effectively. This relationship between transnationals and independent producers is of course dominated by the transnationals themselves.

What is called international trade is more realistically seen as transborder transfer of goods and services within individual large corporations that organize production and distribution on a global basis. Fewer, larger firms dominate the world economy as megamergers work to create an oligopolistic structure, a competition among the few with national companies swallowed up or placed in a con-tracting relationship that is subordinate to these giants. Trade liberalization reduces the ability of national governments should they wish to govern independent of cor-porate influence. Globalization is both engendered by and fosters a free-market ideology that is hostile to government efforts to improve quality of life through public provision of goods and services to the majority of citizens, because it forces them to cater to the demands of transnational corporations and compete for for-eign investment.

Transnationals are aware not only that they have become much more visible as they have grown into global giants but also that public resentment has increased. Indeed, a backlash occurs when the public is informed of these corporations' cor-rupt labor and environmental practices, lack of business ethics, and irresponsibility toward the societies in which they operate. Corporate citizenship has come into vogue as a result of consumer boycotts and other protest activities, followed by company codes of conduct with high-sounding ethical commitments and stepped-up public relations efforts. After the demonstrations at the World Trade Organiza-tion's Seattle meetings, increased use has been made of corporate security advisers who gather intelligence on anti-corporate groups and offer companies advice on dealing with such groups. Their assistance involves infiltrating such organizations at a corporation's request. Corporate charitable contributions have grown—espe-cially for the many companies with image problems, such as Microsoft and Shell. "Community betterment" is now a prominent value in corporate mission state-ments. And companies' advertising budgets now reflect the understanding that as-sociations with non-profit-making bodies and their social causes can be the decid-ing factor for consumers choosing products that show "they care."

Of course, doing good is not what corporations are centrally about. They are about doing well. They will be only as ethical as they must appear to be to make more money. For most of them the calculation is a narrow cost-benefit analysis that has nothing to do with ethics but everything to do with appearing to be ethical. In their core operations they encourage selfishness and materialism. As employers they treat people as means to their ends and force upon the larger society a definition of freedom, as in free trade, under which every consumer is free to choose, to buy, to pursue personal satisfaction through material possessions, and to do whatever is necessary to obtain the money for these possessions—even if this means stepping on or over one's fellows. Corporations have no loyalties to country, community, or people other than what is forced upon them by those for whom solidarity and community are real values. They do not believe in real democracy because partici-pation by ordinary people in the struggle for social justice comes at the expense of their priorities, which are to accumulate, accumulate, accumulate. We have come to understand (after Enron, Worldcom, and the rest) that pressure to meet and beat quarterly profit targets encourages practices harmful to companies and soci-eties in the not-so-long run. In the expansion phase of the bubble economy it was deemed churlish to demand socially responsible behavior. In the period we have entered, not only the assumptions of neoliberalism but the basis on which large corporations have been run are being questioned.

The dimension of globalization now getting belated attention is the fact that it reflects the ascendancy of an internationally oriented bourgeoisie. In *Canadian Dimension* (July/August 2001), Sam Gindin suggests that if, in the aftermath of Seattle, social justice can no longer be discussed without addressing globalization, globalization can no longer be discussed without addressing the system behind globalization—namely, capitalism. He adds that "[w]here 'globalization' had become a weapon brandished by business, politicians and the media to explain what we couldn't do, placing capitalism itself up for discussion and criticism was part of insisting that the limits we face were socially constructed, and could therefore be challenged, stretched and, one day, overcome."

Anti-globalization, it has been argued, is a misleading characterization of the social justice movement that objects to corporate globalization rather than to international solidarity and the uniting of working people to make a better world in which interdependence is recognized and should be structured as a leveling-up and not a race to the bottom. Anti-capitalism has the virtue of properly characterizing the problem but likewise suffers from a negative formulation that states what people are against but not what they are for. However, saying "no" to injustice and to the structured social relations that re-create and perpetuate inequality is an important starting point. Nonetheless, a positive vision emerges out of challenging injustice and the bottom-line thinking that devalues the collective space of the planet's ecological sustainability, the rights of working people, and the broader arena of the public good. The social justice movement is being pushed to think more systemically.

Behind the WTO are the transnational corporations and international financiers that set its agenda. This scenario drives protesters to address corporate targets, and an anti-corporate consciousness develops. Efforts to force companies to act responsibly hits up against the structural character of capitalism, leading corporations to act in socially irresponsible ways and ensuring that their reform goes only as far as dictated by profit considerations in the light of popular pressure. Competition forces such bottom-line concerns to be uppermost, even if corporate leaders vary in their assessments of how much concession is consistent with profit maximization. The extent to which anti-corporate campaigning and strategy evolve into an anti-capitalist consciousness remains to be seen.

The anti-capitalist convergence has become a significant tendency within what is still called the anti-globalization movement. Capturing this spirit is Richard Smith's photo on the cover of *Against the Current* (March/April 2000), showing protesters carrying a large banner that reads "Think the WTO is Bad? . . . Wait until you hear about Capitalism." It does not tell us how best to talk about capitalism and its ills, something socialists have not been terribly good at, but we are being driven by the realities confronting us to face up to the challenge. As hard as reforming the system is, replacing it is far more difficult. I would conclude with three thoughts. The first concerns the inadequacy of reform. Second, and not contradicting the first point, is that reform is far more likely when the powerful are faced with a strong anti-systemic movement. Challenging capitalism may be the best strategy to achieve reform. Third, it is time for what is called the antiglobalization movement to move from a critique to a proposing of an alternative set of rules. Another world is possible, desirable, and in need of constructing. It is time to be clear on what principles and practices are consistent with the values of international solidarity and social justice. This positive moment for constructing a better alternative has arrived.

12

Time, Poverty, and Global Democracy

WILLIAM DIFAZIO

With the fall of the Soviet Union in 1991, the triumph of capitalist democracy seemed complete. For many scholars and politicians the democratization of the Soviet bloc is part of a process of democratization that began after World War II. Democracies are defined here as nation-states in which leaders are voted into office through contested elections and suffrage exists for the majority of the population. By this definition, the process of democratization is increasing in the world.[1] This is viewed by many as a positive development, of course; but we should remember that this form of democracy is limited. The transition to democracy is never about sharing power and resources in nation-states. It is certainly not the "of the people, for the people, and by the people" mass participatory democracy that has been the goal of Western democracies since ancient Athens. Here, "mass participatory democracy" is understood as an inclusive citizenry comprising all adult members of society in which participation involves not just voting but governance and power sharing as well. Yet, today's scholars and politicians have deemed this type of democracy to be unrealistic and impractical.

In this chapter I argue, on the contrary, that mass participatory democracy is both realistic and practical. Further, I add two conditions for democracy: material equality and the time necessary to participate in processes of governance. There can be no democracy without these.

First, in terms of the condition of inclusiveness, Athenian democracy failed because of the exclusion of women and slaves from citizenship in the *polis*. On inclusiveness and democracy, Aristotle stated: "Tyranny . . . is that form of monarchical rule which is despotically exercised over the political association called the state; oligarchy occurs when the sovereign power is in the hands of those possessed by property, democracy when it is in the hands of those who have no accumulated wealth, who are without means."[2]

Aristotle's concern that affluence and power would lead to the domination of the rich over the poor is very important, but he was also concerned with the unfair power of the many over the few. These are both crucial concerns, but historically the few who are rich have usually been the most powerful in terms of controlling the state and society. The inclusion rule of democracy means that everyone must be included in power sharing and decision making, from the rich to the poor. The problem for the poor and even for the middle class is that the resources they need to be politically involved are limited by their struggle for survival. This is why economic equality and democracy are central to mass participatory democracy.

For the proponents of representative democracy it is possible to have both political equality before the law and economic inequality. I argue that this is a crucial contradiction, the resolution of which is required by participatory democracy. In short, participatory democracy demands both political equality and economic equality.

The second crucial resource for democratic participation is time—a commodity often absent from the lives of both the poor and the middle class. The requirement of time demands a reduction of the working day to a thirty-hour week without a decrease in pay; this would mean that, for ten hours a week, ordinary citizens could participate in democracy. Increased struggle to reduce the length of the working day would help to create a "new democratization" movement linked to the participation of ordinary citizens in governance. Currently, however, with Americans working longer and harder,[3] political participation is much more difficult. With the passage of welfare reform in 1996 and the institution of workfare, which required all able-bodied people receiving benefits to work, all benefits came with time limits, the welfare rolls were greatly reduced, and the number of poor people working low-wage jobs greatly increased. The amount of time that the poor and middle class must spend working makes it increasingly difficult for them to participate in democracy beyond yearly elections.

In all of this the poor are the crucial case in terms of developing a global participatory democracy, because they have the least adequate resources in terms of both time and money. Thus, I begin this chapter by invoking those who are excluded from democracy, both locally and globally, because they are poor. If people are excluded from democracy we have a problem, because democracy must be inclusive. Thus I construct my argument in terms of those who are both locally and globally excluded. Simply put, my contention is that there can be no global democracy unless global poverty is eliminated.

LOCAL PERSPECTIVE

The economic boom of the 1990s bypassed the poor. Indeed, as of this writing in 2002, the lives of the poor are harder. The Personal Responsibility and Work Reconciliation Act of 1996, commonly referred to as welfare reform, has successfully reduced welfare rolls by 7 million recipients or 57 percent,[4] but poverty has barely been affected. The U.S. Census Bureau reported that in the United States, "9.2 percent of families were deemed poor in 2000, a slight improvement from 1989."[5] In New York City, to name just one example of many, the poor continue to suffer: The homeless shelters are full, the soup kitchens and food pantries are over-crowded, and the poor increasingly work at workfare and below-living-wage jobs.[6] With the reduction of welfare rolls, the time limits on those who receive benefits, and severe job losses (in New York City alone, 132,000 jobs were lost in 2001),[7] it has become extremely difficult for people to find jobs that can support themselves and their families. Because of their constant struggle to survive, the poor also find it very difficult to get involved in political action. There are 2.7 million poor people in New York State; in New York City during the 1990s, "the Bronx had the highest percentage of poor people in the state at 31 percent. Brooklyn followed at 25 percent, with Manhattan at 20 percent."[8]

In 2002, as the boom fades, the incomes of poor and middle-class people continue to shrink and the gap between the rich and everyone else increases. This gap is at its widest in New York: "The average income of the top fifth of New York families is 12.8 times greater than that of the bottom fifth. This is the biggest difference of all states and is far worse than the national average ratio of 10 to 1. The average income of the top 5 percent of New York families is 21 times greater than that of the bottom 20 percent."[9] Worse still is the immense problem of hunger in the United States. As the U.S. Department of Agriculture (USDA) reported, "in 1999 ten percent of all U.S. households, representing 19 million adults and 12 million children, were food insecure" as a result of insufficient resources. Of the 10.5 million households that were food insecure, 3.1 million suffered from food insecurity that was so severe that the USDA's very conservative measure classified them as "hungry." Five million adults and 2.7 million children lived in these hungry households.[10]

Welfare reform's success in significantly reducing welfare rolls is not apparent in the welfare-to-work programs that it gave rise to. One-third of welfare "leavers" do not have jobs, and most others experience long spells of unemployment. "One-quarter to one-third of welfare 'leavers' return to welfare within a year of exit. . . . Average wages for unemployed leavers range from about $6,000 to $15,000 per year."[11]

What has been made especially clear by the poverty research conducted during the economic boom of the 1990s is the inadequacy of the U.S. Census Bureau's categorization of the "poverty line." The Bureau's measurement of poverty is unrealistic about how much income is required to allow individuals and families to meet their basic needs. This concern is addressed by the Economic Policy Institute, which, in *Hardships in America: The Real Story of Working Families,* has developed "basic family budgets" based on twice the poverty line for 400 communities in the United States.[12] Specifically, the Institute reports that in 1996 "[n]early 30% of families with incomes below twice the poverty line faced at least one critical hardship such as missing meals, being evicted from their housing, having their utilities disconnected, doubling up on housing, or not having access to needed medical care; and over 72% of such families had at least one serious hardship, such as worries about food, missed rent or mortgage payments, reliance on the emergency room as the main source of medical care, or inadequate child care arrangements."[13]

Hardships in America vividly describes how impossible it is for the poor to take for granted what nonpoor citizens can. They live a life of lacks. That is, they lack food; they lack housing; they lack heat in the winter; they lack new clothes; they lack the time to participate in democracy; and they lack good schools. (The schools that their children attend lack books, paper, auditoriums, and, in some cases, even classrooms.) The concern for the poor expressed by everyone from politicians to advocates is always about what an adequate safety net is and how society can make up for some of these lacks. But the poor also lack power as well as the time and money needed to remedy this lack; in short, they do not have the resources to take part in society. And no one seems to want the poor to participate in the polity.

There really isn't any democracy for the poor in the United States. Democracy here is therefore not truly "of the people, for the people, and by the people." Indeed, the poor—especially those who receive welfare benefits—are ruled over, under permanent surveillance and suspicion, and guilty even when proven innocent. In this country, then, what we have is not mass participatory democracy but capitalist democracy—and the masses, especially the poor and near poor, are greatly feared and excluded from most of the institutions of society. Even the greatest freedom of capitalist democracy, shopping, is rarely available to them. Though American presidents have always linked democracy and capitalism, and though American freedoms are stressed in every speech, capitalism, democracy, and freedom are not for everyone. In fact, the poor are feared because they serve as indicators of the failure of capitalism to provide for all. Thus we cannot seriously talk about democracy in this global capitalist world without also discussing the severe economic inequality that confronts so many. In my opinion, these are the key questions to be asked: Can we have political freedom without economic and social freedom? And can we have political equality without economic and social equality? Economic equality is difficult, indeed, when we consider that justice is contingent on getting the best lawyers—and the best lawyers are the most expensive lawyers. So legal justice is not for everyone, either.

Democracy is about sharing power and decision making and, thus, about taking an active part in governance. In our representative democracy, voting in elections is the basis for citizenship; but even this limited notion of citizenship isn't an active pursuit, given that only half of the electorate takes part in voting. Polling places are suspect and have been questioned during presidential elections.[14] Only elected officials and appointed nonelected officials such as cabinet members take part in governance. The increasing number of nonelected officials who participate in governance is a problem because they are not part of the electoral process. Thus ordinary citizens who vote have less and less power over their government. Inevitably, politicians and nonelected officials represent those who have funded their campaigns—a situation that is likely to continue, despite changes in the law regarding soft money. Indeed, the idea of a democracy where people actually participate as a regular activity seems increasingly farfetched.

Can we imagine a participatory democracy globally when we cannot imagine it locally? Can we imagine a world in which power is shared equally between ordinary citizens and billionaire CEOs of multinational corporations? After all, even Locke and Voltaire had no intention of sharing power with the "rabble." Increasingly, the poor fall through the sizable holes in the safety net; the rabble are excluded not only from democracy but from a welfare state in decline. Nation-states have been hollowed out and are no longer the real bases of power in this increasingly global world. The global corporation has become increasingly important in decisions of governance, and part of the reason the state has been hollowed out is because elected leaders are fearful of alienating the wealthy by making them pay their fair share of taxes. In the United States it seems that there isn't any counterforce to corporate power; corporations increasingly design not only the economy but the polity without any opposition. As Jeffrey Garten states in *The Mind of the C.E.O.*,

> Tearing down barriers is at the heart of [Jack] Welch's strategy for GE, but the idea resonates almost everywhere. It describes what is happening with companies in every industry as hierarchies are flattened, barriers to internal communication are removed and employees become more entrepreneurial. It reflects what is going on among corporations as they join in all kinds of partnerships to expand their range of products and customers. It is a metaphor for what the Internet is doing around the world. It is the essence of the blurring of national borders, the phenomenon we call globalization.[15]

Here the interpenetration of borders is translated into corporate domination. Jack Welch, the boss of GE, a company with a market value of $500 billion, likes democracy as long as it doesn't interfere with his breaking down of borders and his ability to make a profit between every itch and scratch. He flattens hierarchies and organizes horizontally to improve innovation, but there are two important conditions: first, that the CEO remains in control and, second, that profits continue to accumulate. This is the model for both local and global power.

A GLOBAL PERSPECTIVE

The hardships in the United States are real, but it is the richest and the most powerful country in the world. As Branko Milanovic tells us, "The top 10% of the U.S. population has an aggregate income equal to the income of the poorest 43% of people in the world, or differently put, the total income of the richest 25 million Americans is equal to the total income of almost 2 billion poor people."[16]

Still, for all its wealth, free market capitalism hasn't guaranteed a good standard of living for every citizen of the United States. Even after the fall of communism, free markets are having a rough time in Poland, where capitalism has had its greatest success. Poland now suffers from 18 percent unemployment and a deep decline in gross domestic product. Inequality is increasing there, and the Szczecin shipyards workers who became the symbol of Solidarity and the end of communism have now been laid off.[17] Democracy isn't flourishing in Poland; it didn't under communism, and it isn't under capitalism. Democracy cannot flourish where inequality is rampant.

Free markets have not resolved the crisis of millions of refugees from Afghanistan, who are concerned with survival rather than democracy. For them, poverty is so out of control that democracy is a low priority. Throughout the world, over 1 billion people live in extreme poverty. According to the *UN Human Development Report 2001*, "A third of the world's extremely poor—those living on less than a dollar a day—live in countries that are lagging behind or slipping further away from the goal of halving such poverty by 2001."[18] The world becomes increasingly harsh for the less-advanced countries and their people. As noted in *The World Employment Report 2001*, "As of 2001, as much as one-third of the world's workforce of three billion people are unemployed or underemployed. Of these, about 160 million people are openly unemployed, 20 million more than before the outset of the Asian financial crisis in 1997."[19]

Branko Milanovic provides some sobering statistics on the world income distribution: "The richest 1% of people in the world receive as much as the bottom 57%, or in other words, less than 50 million income-richest people receive as much as 2.7 billion poor. . . . 84% of the world population receive 16% of world (unadjusted) dollar income."[20]

The hope for this world, we are told, lies in free markets and upgraded skills. An educated global citizenry could become part of the global computer-aided capitalist democracy of the future. But inequality persists; the advanced countries still earn the lion's share of global income. In the new high-tech information economy, the diffusion of new technology continually favors the advanced countries. For example, in its *World Employment Report 2001*, the International Labor Office (ILO) finds that "nearly 90% of all Internet users are in industrialized countries, with the United States and Canada accounting for 57% of the total. In contrast, Internet users in Africa and the Middle East together account for only 1% of global Internet users. Where ICT [information and communications technology] is most in use, changes in economic relations and behavior are occurring."[21]

A global democracy encompassing the poor and the under- and unemployed seems unlikely at this point in history, given the absence of political, economic, and social equality. In *Choices for the Poor*, a spokesperson for the United Nations reports that "falling incomes and rising poverty are eroding the capacity of poor people to be part of social networks of support, leaving them unable to engage in and maintain social exchange. By cutting people off from vital sources of support, social isolation . . . makes them even more vulnerable to adverse shocks and crisis."[22] Related research demonstrates that reduced social isolation and increased participation in governance will help with "poverty alleviation": "The PSI [Poverty Strategies Initiative] studies confirm the findings of others which show how genuinely participatory governance at the local level can yield benefits in terms of both efficiency and equity, by giving people a sense of ownership, by allocating resources according to people's preferences and by utilizing their skills and knowledge. But the goal of genuine participatory decentralization remains a distant one in most developing countries despite the efforts made during the last half century."[23]

PLURALISM VERSUS PARTICIPATORY DEMOCRACY

"Participation in governance" and the resulting empowerment are not what the West is offering the rest of the world. What is being offered is a representative democracy with roots in the pluralism of the 1950s. Pluralism is another reaction by the ruling elite to the fear of a mass participatory democracy. According to Seymour Martin Lipset, "the distinctive and most valuable element of democracy [is] . . . the formation of a political elite in the competitive struggle for the vote of a mainly passive electorate."[24] Furthermore, "the belief that a very high level of participation is always good for democracy is not valid."[25]

A global pluralist democracy would suffer from the same defects that it had at the national level. *First*, pluralists assume that everyone is starting from the same place in their game of competing interests. But the playing field isn't level; rather, it is governed by asymmetrical power relations in which corporate power is unequal. The pluralists' denial of corporate power seems to reflect their own political position, which favors the current global elite. Pluralists equalize the competition between interest groups. They treat corporate global interests as equal to other groups such as unions and environmentalists, but in fact they are not equal. This denial can be seen in the leftist pluralism of Noberto Bobbio, who is very concerned with the despotism of the state and the "enormous, disproportionate, unjustified inequalities between rich and poor."[26] Still, he sees a democratization process occurring in modern society, not as an increase in direct democracy but as an expansion of democracy beyond the "political sphere (where the individual is regarded as a citizen) to the social sphere (where the individual is regarded as many-faceted) . . . in the extension of the form of ascending power [and] . . . in the arena of civil society in its various manifestations from the school to the workplace."[27]

Civil society in opposition to the state is the site of the "polycratic" organization of modern societies. It consists of multiple centers of power, and it is in this context that Bobbio develops his theory of pluralism. In particular, he emphasizes the crucial dichotomy of state versus civil society; the latter is also the site of pluralism's multiple "oligarchies" that compete for power. One of these centers of power is the economy: "[T]here is pluralism at an economic level, where we have a market economy still partially intact and big businesses are still in competition with each other."[28]

Here even Bobbio, who rails against the inequalities of liberal democracy, is stuck in pluralism's trap—the equalization of asymmetrical power relations. For him, civil society is the sphere of social relations, which includes the self-regulating economic sphere. He fails to see that the economic sphere is not automatic and includes intentional decisions of power. He also fails to see that these centers of power are not equal. Maybe his dichotomous system of state versus civil society is really a tripartite system in which the global corporate sphere is increasingly dominant and the power of the state has been greatly reduced.

For Bobbio, direct democracy is not the solution, because it is monocratic; it's impossible for the masses to be involved in all decisions because of the vastness of the modern world. Bobbio has the disease of pluralists: He suffers from the belief that if ordinary people are empowered they will become corrupt—and nothing is worse than the tyranny of the majority. Thus, "[I]t becomes necessary to resort to representative democracy, the guarantee against the abuse of power."[29] The danger of direct democracy is that it comprises a single interest group, as if everyone were to think alike in a world of multiplicity. For him, only representative democracy can allow for diverse interests and dissent. As he boldly states, "the democracy of a modern state has no alternative but to be a pluralistic democracy."[30]

Bobbio believes in the two dogmas of pluralism: (a) distrust in the ability of the masses to govern themselves and (b) the false equalization of power among competing centers of power. His false dichotomy of the state and civil society as the bases of power in the modern world enables him to deny both the power of global corporations and the abuses of power in representative democracies.

Second, pluralists believe that the history of "rule by the people" demonstrates that it is rule by an incompetent, uneducated rabble who tend to follow dictators. This belief calls to mind Lipset's contention in *Political Man* that the working class is authoritarian, simple, and apathetic.[31] Many pluralists make the claim that the masses are anti-democratic—a claim that reflects Lipset's anti-communism and his belief that the "Communist movement" was seducing the poor and lower classes.[32] The threat of communism was always behind the pluralists' critique of participatory democracy; after the fall of the Soviet Union, they argued that the requirements of global capitalism and foreign affairs make real participation in governance neither practical nor realistic. (In the next section I review this logic in terms of the work of Samuel P. Huntington and F. A. Hayek.)

Third, in interest-group politics, citizens lose a sense of the good of the whole. This is especially true when the interest-group politics aren't competitive or are dominated by the interests of global corporations in their pursuit of more markets for them to dominate. Their particular interests are now defined as the interests of the whole—an ideology that they perpetrate at every turn in the increasingly globally controlled mass media. Free markets, the War Against Terrorism, and the Internet are not solutions to either economic and social inequality or the creation of a global democracy. Currently, even capitalist democracy is only a minority phenomenon. Ultimately capitalist democracy is a façade for capitalist accumulation.

Much of the world understands this. Thus, the week of April 14, 2002, witnessed two examples of citizens' refusal to go along with the new global organization: Millions of people participated in a general strike in Italy, and Venezuelan President Hugo Chavez was forced back into office because the people protested the coup of his administration led by business leaders and the military.

Immanuel Wallerstein has made a key point in this connection. During the development of capitalist democracy, at least in Europe and North America, the "dangerous classes" had to be tamed, and this was accomplished by sharing some of the pie—that is, by creating a welfare state. What welfare capitalism shared was "about one-seventh of a pie: a reasonable standard of living for a minority of the world's population (those famed middle strata). Now this small pie was doubtless a lot more than this one-seventh had had before, but it was far less than an equal share of the pie, and it was almost nothing at all for the other six-sevenths."[33]

In opposition to the pluralists' liberal representative democracy is Barber's call for a strong participatory democracy. For him, the democracy of the pluralists is a "thin democracy." It has survived for a long time but has all the abuses that I have already referred to and at least one more: It denies the possibility of human growth over time.[34] Thus Barber argues that "strong democracy in the participatory mode resolves conflict in the absence of an independent ground through a participatory process of ongoing, proximate self-legislation and creation of a political community capable of transforming dependent private individuals into free citizens and partial and private interests into public goods."[35]

Strong democracy is a developmental approach to a more participatory and inclusive democracy. For the pluralists, representative democracy is the only game in town. Barber tells us that they play a zero-sum game of liberty or power in which there is no middle ground: "Torn from within and divided against itself, liberal democracy sets its means against its ends. Its tools of liberation become instruments of subjugation, while its individualist objectives become the agents of social disorder and anomie."[36] Representative democracy denies the possibility of ordinary people actively participating in government. Barber has two important answers to this claim: First, if ordinary people seem politically apathetic it is because they have little access to power—but that this will change with the advent of strong democracy.[37] Second, strong democracy is a project in which people will learn to pay attention and become politically active, and in which new institutions that nurture political action will be developed. Still, Barber's analysis of strong democracy is flawed in the same way as much current political analysis: It treats as secondary the power of economic forces and their impact on democracy. I contend that there is no possibility of participatory democracy without economic democracy.

In this context consider the Port Huron Statement made in 1962 by the Students for a Democratic Society (SDS)—a statement that goes beyond Barber by acknowledging that economic relations of power are crucial to participatory mass democracy:

As a social system we seek the establishment of a democracy of individual participation governed by two central aims: that individuals share in these social decisions determining the quality and direction of his life; that society be organized to encourage independence in men and provide the media for their common participation.[38]

For the SDS members who produced this document, equality was central to economic democracy: "[T]he economy itself is of such social importance that its major resources and means of production should be open to democratic participation and subject to democratic social regulation."[39]

In the 1960s, the SDS subscribed to participatory democracy and prescribed it for the majority of American citizens. But, after all, the Port Huron Statement was an idealistic, romantic document drafted by college students with little experience in the real world. In this chapter I make the same demands that these students did, but I make them for the world. I contend that despite the current trend toward democratization, there is very little democracy in the world. To the conditions for democracy spelled out in the Port Huron Statement I would like to add another—namely, that democracy requires the time to participate in the decision-making process as well as the time to accumulate the knowledge necessary for governance. One of the pluralists' main charges is that the masses are authoritarian; another is that they are apathetic. What the first charge really means is that the lower classes are uneducated. The guarantee of a first-class liberal arts education that among other things stresses civics and the value of political participation in governance would go a long way toward countering this claim. The charge of apathy is also often a matter of time. In the workaholic world that we live in, where even middle-class people must work longer and harder just to maintain a decent standard of living, it is hard to pay attention to politics, much less to actually get involved. Between work, family responsibilities, everyday chores, and sleep, people just don't have the time for political action.

I believe that what Karl Marx said about the "realm of freedom" is also necessary for direct mass participatory democracy. Marx argued that the realm of freedom requires the reduction of "labor determined by necessity and external expedience."[40] Here, time is tied to inequality—especially the extreme economic, political, and cultural inequality of poverty. The poor and the near-poor constitute the great majority of the world's population, a circumstance that has barely changed over time, even with all the promises of free-market capitalism. (Granted, its promises have never really included the equalization of wealth and power.) At best, free-market capitalism promises an increase in economic opportunity and the possibility of a rising standard of living. But these goals have not been achieved, either. Poor people still have insufficient material resources and spend most of their time exhausted by their struggle for survival. Only a very few can struggle for both survival and democracy simultaneously. It is no accident that representative democracy is preferred, because it solves the problem of time; but it does so in an unequal way. In other words, the great majority of people between the obligation of work and everyday life do not have the time to do more than vote in elections. They barely have the time to pay attention to politics. Representative democracy solves this problem by reducing democracy to the election of leaders who have the time and can represent those who elected them. For the ordinary citizen, then, participation is defined as voting. Power wielded by ordinary citizens is not in the equation of representative democracy. Indeed, since voting seldom happens more than twice a year, even this form of participation in representative democracy is relatively rare. Real participation and power are vested in those who are elected. Ordinary people are aware of the limits of their power, as demonstrated by the low voter-turnout rates in many countries. They are also aware of their lack of time for political participation. Their participation in the polity is limited as a result. It is clear from the following statement by Marx that he well understood the importance of time for democratic participation: "The true realm of freedom, the development of human power as an end in itself, begins beyond it, though it can only flourish with the realm of necessity as its basis. The reduction of the working day is the basic prerequisite."[41]

THE LOGIC OF GLOBAL CAPITALIST DEMOCRACY: HUNTINGTON AND HAYEK

The two major claims for why the United Nations call for more participatory governance for the poor is both unrealistic and impractical is that both the seriousness of world politics and the global economy increasing requires the expertise of scientists, scholars, policy experts, and politicians. The future of the world is at stake and real world citizenry is not possible. In terms of this expertise and global policy the work of Samuel P. Huntington and F. A. Hayek is paramount.

Huntington's *The Clash of Civilizations* contains a powerful statement about the global conflicts that ensued after 9/11, and for many it defines the current global crisis. Though in many ways it seems to describe the world situation, it functions in a conservative way, concealing as much as it reveals. More important, it has become a model for American foreign affairs, especially in such areas as expanding the military budget and maintaining an active military in the post–Cold War world. In *The Clash of Civilizations*, Huntington privileges cultural conflict and masks political and economic conflict. We should remember the source of the phrase "clash of civilizations." It was coined by Huntington in the Summer 1993 issue of *Foreign Affairs,* and in a sense it restates the "end of ideology" position of Daniel Bell,[42] though in a global context. According to both Bell and Huntington, racial and ethnic conflict continues, but class struggle is relegated to the past. For Bell, capitalism has its "cultural contradictions," but from an economic standpoint it has delivered the goods. Thus problems of class, such as poverty, are no longer the crucial problems. Huntington makes a similar case: Since the fall of the Soviet

Union in 1991, the crucial struggles in the world are no longer between communism and capitalism. Ideological conflicts of this type are over; what dominate the globe today are conflicts between civilizations. Of course, the great majority of the world's population is still poor, and one could readily argue that the hopeless, miserable lives of the poor are behind much of the strife in the world. But Huntington doesn't make this argument. Rather, he states that "[i]n this new world the most pervasive, important and dangerous conflicts will not be between social classes rich and poor, or other economically defined groups, but between people belonging to different cultural entities."[43]

The world after the fall of communism is a world of contending civilizations. Huntington argues that seven or eight civilizations structure the politics of the world, with the power of the West still dominant (though in decline). "Global politics," he says, "has become multipolar and multicivilizational."[44] At one level it looks as if Huntington is refuting Francis Fukuyama's restatement of Bell's "end of ideology" thesis as the "end of history." Fukuyama's contention of post–Cold War harmony in a world of victorious market capitalism and liberal democracy seems inconsistent with the notion of a clash of civilizations. But Huntington is not questioning the hegemony of liberal democratic capitalism; rather, he is concerned that the contradictions between civilizations will undermine that hegemony. Thus his "procedural definition" of democracy is important for understanding this new world where capitalism and democracy are always linked and the cultural contradictions between civilizations are a real concern.

Huntington defines *democracy* as "the selection of leaders through competitive elections by the people they govern."[45] He disdains the democracy that ensued during its idealistic and utopian classical phase, when it was concerned with the "will of the people" and "the common good." After all, in the tradition of pluralism, the people never govern but are *to be* governed. For Huntington, Joseph Schumpeter demolished this romantic view of democracy long ago in *Capitalism, Socialism, and Democracy*.[46] Schumpeter stressed competitive elections as central to democracy, and his practical views on democracy have become the standard views. Huntington has added Robert Dahl's two dimensions of democracy to Schumpeter's conceptualization. For Dahl, democracy consists of contestation and participation—and by participation, Dahl means taking part in campaigns and voting. For Huntington, too, this is how citizens participate; but the reference here is not to ordinary people taking part in the governance of their society. As discussed earlier, true democracy is not for everyone. In fact, Schumpeter's procedural definition of democracy is a free-market model in which all voters are in an electoral marketplace where the "best candidate" will successfully compete for votes and win the election. Citizens have "freedom of choice"; they can select the candidate who will govern them. This is an economic model for a supposedly democratic process. Voters can be compared to consumers involved in selecting the "product" of their choice. They do not act like citizens who participate in the polity. In Schumpeter's model, they contest for a political product in elections. This is the very limited notion of democracy that

Schumpeter presents and Huntington argues is the only practical model for representative democracy. Huntington acknowledges the important influence of Western representative democracy on the world and terms it the "third wave" of democratization. And, indeed, many formerly nondemocratic nation-states became democratic, especially between the fall of the Portuguese dictatorship in 1974 and the fall of the Soviet Union in 1989.[47] But Huntington's concerns are really with the maintenance of Western civilization. Central to this goal is the "'American Creed' . . . on which Americans overwhelmingly agree: liberty, democracy, individualism, equality before the law, constitutionalism, private property."[48]

According to Huntington, this American Creed has come under attack by the multiculturalists, posing a threat not only to the United States but to the whole of Western civilization. Here Huntington seems to be reacting to the current wave of immigration to the United States from Asia and South and Central America and its resulting diversity. He even attacked the policies of former president Clinton for his "encouragement of diversity as one of its major goals."[49] For Huntington this diversity is the "Achilles' heel" of liberal capitalism. In his view, it is ultimately this cultural problem that threatens Western hegemony.

In the concluding chapter of *The Clash of Civilizations*, Huntington constructs a World War III scenario between nations over the control and development of oil reserves in the South China Seas.[50] In this scenario, Vietnam as well as "the United States, Europe, Russia and India . . . become engaged in a truly global struggle against China, Japan and most of Islam."[51] According to Huntington, the fear of "the orient" is still very strong. The United States, though the most powerful civilization, is in decline, and China is emerging as a serious threat. Huntington uses this scenario to make a strong argument in favor of the United States' vigilance about its Western identity, which he believes is important to the maintenance of both Western civilization and global capital. This vigilance, however, has a cost: the reduction of the already "thin" democracy in the world. I mention this scenario because it reflects the way in which the constant and seemingly permanent threat of war is used against increasing democratic participation in the world. In the United States, President Bush's War on Terrorism has been constructed as a permanent war that requires eternal vigilance and the sacrifice of civil liberties to guarantee everyone's safety.

Of course, Huntington prefers peace and cooperation to military confrontation. But peace and cooperation depend on what Huntington calls the commonalities rule, whereby "peoples in all civilizations should search for an attempt to expand the values, institutions and practices they have in common with peoples of other civilizations."[52] Huntington believes that we can emphasize the American Creed and institute a "third phase of Euro-American" partnership in NATO that includes a renewed military presence[53] and the continued expansion of liberal, democratic capitalism and still have peaceful cooperation in a multipolar, multicivilizational world. Without such cooperation, he argues, we will end up with sheer chaos and global wars—as in the China scenario.

Yet in all of this analysis, material conditions are glossed over and the six-sevenths of the world's population who live in poverty or near-poverty are ignored. One way to understand the commonalities rule is in terms of how free-market capitalist conditions are imposed by the International Monetary Fund (IMF) and the World Bank on poor countries, from Argentina to Zimbabwe, that are seeking loans in an attempt to get their economies back on track. According to *The Multinational Monitor*, which surveyed twenty-six such countries, these conditions for loans include "[c]ivil service downsizing; privatization of government-owned enterprises, with layoffs required in advance of privatization and frequently following privatization; [p]romotion of labor flexibility—regulatory changes to remove restrictions on the ability of government and private employers to fire or lay off workers; [m]andated wage reductions, minimum wage reductions of containment, and spreading the wage gap between government employees and managers; and [p]ension reforms, including privatization, that cut social security benefits for workers."[54]

Clearly, then, the IMF and the World Bank are imposing capitalist values in their conditions for granting loans. They are making the conditions for global capitalism the conditions of all nation-states. In doing so, they limit the possibilities for democracy. The restrictions on labor organizing and collective bargaining are particularly harmful to the development of participatory democracy. It is often in union organizing that poor working people have their first experience in direct democracy. They make a connection between their political activities in the workplace and the union, on the one hand, and gaining rights and a higher standard of living, on the other. But the loan practices of the IMF and the World Bank restrict these activities in the name of "labor flexibility"; indeed, their wage reductions without collective bargaining restrict the very process of democracy. Yet all of these restrictions make sense in the context of Huntington's "third wave" of democratization.

The world of globalization is one in which prosperity as a result of market capitalism is now taken for granted. This outcome has resulted not from the end of ideology but from its success. At the heart of this success are the economic principles detailed by F. A. Hayek. I argue that these principles are actually values basic to global capitalism, as we have already seen in connection with the IMF and the World Bank. In this context, workers' movements for higher wages are viewed as impediments to a "free economy." With six-sevenths of the world's population left out of even middle-class prosperity, the failure of market capitalism is massive. But the success of free-market ideology is equally massive.

Hayek is singularly responsible for the current emphasis on free-market principles. Central to this development is his stress on the importance of knowledge of a "rational economic order." He argues that collectivism and planning, not just communism (which, for him, is the pure embodiment of these two principles), led the world down the road to totalitarianism. Planning—even when armed with a sophisticated social science methodology—cannot accomplish a rational economic order. The requirements of knowledge are just too great, not only for governments but for science as well. In Hayek's epistemology, humans are just not up to the task. This may seem a strange argument, for he also emphasizes individualism; but what he really means is that individual competition is an economic form of behavior to which all human behavior can be reduced. Yet economic individuals have only a partial and thus insufficient knowledge. Hayek himself refers to "the unavoidable imperfection of man's knowledge and the consequent need for a process by which knowledge is constantly communicated and acquired."[55]

Hayek's economic epistemology is an automatic system that overcomes the problems of government planning and even individual inadequacies. In a world of imperfect knowledge the "marvel" of the price system provides the solution:

> The most significant fact about this system is the economy of knowledge with which it operates, or how little the participants have to know in order to be able to take the right action. In abbreviated form, by a kind of symbol, only the most essential information is passed on and passed on only to those concerned. It is more than a metaphor to describe the price system as a kind of machinery for registering change, or a system of telecommunications which enables individual producers to watch the movements of a few pointers as an engineer might watch the hands of a few dials, in order to adjust their activities to changes of which they may never know more than is reflected in the price movement.[56]

In Hayek's view, the price system provided the automatic machinery for understanding liberal capitalism as a rational economic order. The problem was always too much government intervention, too much economic planning, too many monopolies, and too much egalitarianism. Everything that restricted practical competition, markets, and prices caused problems for a free economy.

A complete analysis of Hayek's work is not possible here, but because his ideas are part of the ideological foundation of current global capitalism and its opposition to participatory democracy, it is important that we look at his position on the rich and the poor.

For Hayek, attempts to remedy poverty through planned redistribution are doomed to failure. Such efforts, in his view, only increase the misery of poor people and those who receive low wages. Thus trade unions struggling for higher wages and full employment only lead to more inequality. If unions resist lower wages, then for some only low-wage jobs will exist, and they will have to be "coerced" to take these jobs that offer lower wages. Those who continue to demand higher wages "must be allowed to remain unemployed. The point that is relevant to us is that if we are determined not to allow unemployment at any price, and are not willing to use coercion, we shall be driven to all sorts of desperate expedients, none of which can bring any lasting relief and all of which will seriously interfere with the productive use of our resources."[57]

In Hayek's view, economic redistribution to help the poor merely alienates members of other classes and leads society down the "road to serfdom." He also believes that minimum-wage legislation makes workers more expensive and prices them out of the world market. Thus he argues that "[m]inimum-wage legislation, supposedly in his interest, is frequently no more than a means to deprive him of his only chance to better his conditions by overcoming natural disadvantages by working at wages lower than his fellows in other countries."[58] The only opportunity for the poor worker is to continue to work at low wages. That this is not the road out of poverty doesn't seem to bother him. Nor are global capitalists bothered by the failure of this low-wage solution. What does interest them are the rights of the rich. This position can be seen clearly in Hayek's concern with redistribution through progressive income taxation,

> which has now been reached and been used for extreme egalitarian ends. The two consequences of this which seem to be the most serious are . . . that it makes for social immobility by making it practically impossible for the successful man to rise by accumulating a fortune and . . . it has come near to eliminating that most important element in a free society—the man of independent means, a figure whose essential role in maintaining free opinion and generally an atmosphere of independence from government control we only begin to realize as he is disappearing from the stage.[59]

For Hayek, then, democracy is only for those who can afford it. In a surrealistic way, he concurs with Marx regarding "the realm of freedom," given his argument that freedom is relative to independence from necessity but that only the successful can have that independence. According to Hayek, freedom and independence are not for everyone.

Encapsulated in the work of Huntington and Hayek is the logic of the current global world. It is a world where poverty and low-wage workers are not only denied a decent standard of living but also excluded from democracy in terms of both governance and voting. It is a world of serious cultural conflicts but also one in which there is an "end of ideology." Ideology has ended because free-market capitalism has delivered on its promise, or so it is believed. This is so even though governments provide much less protection for the six-sevenths of the world's population who are excluded from prosperity. Hayek provides the rationale for free global markets and for the hollowing-out of nation-states such that they provide fewer and fewer services for their citizens, whereas Huntington provides the rationale for the West's continued control of global capitalism. The world that they have helped to create nurtures neither the poor nor democratic participation. It is a grim world in which the great majorities are excluded and still live at the margins of society.

CONCLUDING QUESTIONS—STILL UNANSWERED

Globalization, in its current transnational corporate form, clearly repudiates certain aspects of the liberal democracies of the West. In particular, it limits, supersedes, and transforms national constitutions, overrides civil liberties, creates miserable working conditions, perpetuates low pay, and pollutes the environment. These liberal democracies, as noted, were already dominated by corporate interests—namely, profit, the accumulation of capital, and the legitimization of both. And as we have seen in the work of Hayek and Huntington, they offered their citizens little active participation in their governments. Such democracies are thus "not for everyone." Though they offered universal suffrage in the twentieth century, this extension of franchise was only formal, as demonstrated by the U.S. presidential election of 2000 in which George W. Bush was elected president by a minority of the electorate.[60] These Western democracies are democratic only in the sense that Raymond Aron described: "[T]here is government for the people; there is no government by the people."[61] According to Aron, the people elect their leaders, and then they are governed. This is better than not having the power to vote; however, as in the contested elections discussed by Schumpeter, citizens vote but do not really get to participate in their actual governance. No citizenship has been minimized, and elections are unequal playing fields where money always has too much power. The candidates for office must solicit the rich and powerful to have even a chance of winning, and then they are bought and sold because they owe the rich and powerful. Political donations always come with strings attached. Thus, Hayek seems to agree with Marx and Engels that capitalist democracy exists at both the national and global levels, "[w]here the only freedom is free trade." Everything else is up for grabs; even our cherished civil liberties are continuously reduced in the interests of corporate or political expediency. It seems as if democracy itself has become an illegal trade barrier. Whether at the national or global level, the key questions for me stay the same. First, in circumstances of social and economic inequality, can there be democracy in the sense of political equality, where citizens really participate in governance? Do middle-class people—much less those living at or barely above subsistence level—have the time and freedom to really participate?

Second, is it in the political process itself that power resides? Or is power vested in some other institution, such as the economy, or in cultural forms such as racial, ethnic, or religious groups? In the West, one can easily argue that power really resides in global corporations, which control markets and see too much democracy as a hindrance to the further expansion of their power and profits. If liberal capitalism is indeed tending toward concentration and centralization, with bigger and bigger monopolies restricting markets, then Hayek's free-market economics is really just smoke and mirrors.

Third, and most difficult, is the question of what a global democracy would look like. Would it feature global pluralism? Would the United Nations govern it? Would it require a reduction in social and economic inequality, and, if so, how would that be achieved? Would there be a social movement for a global living wage? Would guarantees against poverty, hunger, homelessness, illiteracy, and inadequate health care be implemented? Would the working day be reduced so that laborers would have the time to participate in democracy? Would discrimination against racial groups, women, homosexuals, and minority ethnic and religious groups be prevented? Are the current social movements up to these tasks? And would global corporations and nation-states accept these changes?

Global democracy hasn't a chance unless extreme poverty is dealt with. Global corporations would have to share the burden through a global tax on their profits that would be dedicated to assisting the world's extremely poor. Another possibility would be a tax on all global stock transactions to pay the huge costs involved in providing a living wage for workers in the poorest countries. A radical social movement that demands such taxes could make a difference for the world's poor. And when there is at least an approximation of social and economic equality, we can begin to talk of democratic reforms for everyone in the world—in place of democracy at the behest of the West and global corporations.

What specifically would be required to make the world more democratic? Here, Benjamin Barber makes the crucial point that building a mass participatory democracy is a long-term project and not a game of "either/or." The work of multiple social movements would be needed to build institutions that could guarantee a first-class education, provide livable wage jobs for everyone, and enable people to participate in their own governance. Regarding the latter, Barber suggests neighborhood assemblies, telecommunication systems, and civic education as examples of ways in which ordinary people can begin to get involved in self-government.[62]

Finally, as a solution to "the inequalities of time," Juliet B. Schor recommends "mandatory increases in free time."[63] This measure, she says, would enable people to more easily participate in both civic discourse and governance. However, increases in free time must occur without decreases in weekly wages, thus avoiding wage penalties for a reduced working day. Increased free time would encourage the expansion of democracy into more spheres of life and allow ordinary people to collectively make decisions about their lives. Democracy, in turn, would essentially reinforce itself, making political participation as normal as shopping or watching television. Civil rights would be expanded to include guarantees for decent housing, food, health, and education as well as guarantees against the tyranny of the majority over the individual. Free time and material equality are indeed crucial for the development of a mass participatory democracy. As noted in *The Jobless Future*, "in order to realize a program of democratization, we must create a new civil society in which freedom consists in the first place (but only in the first place) in the liberation of time from the external constraints imposed by nature and other persons on the individual."[64]

Alternatively, if the project for mass participatory democracy is not implemented, we will all be left with a "clash of civilizations" and continue to suffer.

NOTES

1. Samuel P. Huntington, *The Third Wave: Democratization in the Late Twentieth Century* (Norman: University of Oklahoma Press, 1991); Anthony Arblaster, *Democracy*, 2nd ed. (Minneapolis: University of Minnesota Press, 1994).

2. Aristotle, *The Politics* (Harmondsworth, Middlesex, Eng.: Penguin Books, 1962), pp. 116–117.

3. Juliet B. Schor, *The Overworked American: The Unexpected Decline of Leisure* (New York: Basic Books, 1991).

4. Robert Pear, "Federal Welfare Rolls Shrink, But Drop Is Smallest Since '94," *New York Times*, May 21, 2002.

5. Peter Kilborn and Lynette Clemetson, "Gains of 90's Did Not Lift All, Census Shows," *New York Times*, June 5, 2002.

6. New York City Coalition Against Hunger, *From Bad to Worse: World Trade Center Attack Further Accelerates NYC Hunger Growth*, Annual New York City Hunger Survey, November 2001.

7. Leslie Eaton, "Worst Job Loss for New York in a Decade: Downturn Preceded 9/11 and Exceeded Estimates," *New York Times*, March 6, 2002.

8. Deepti Hajela, "Number of State's Poor Rose in 1990's," Associated Press, June 2, 2002.

9. Trudi Renwick, *Pulling Apart in New York: An Analysis of Income Trends in New York State* (Latham, N.Y.: Fiscal Policy Institute, April 2002).

10. Quoted in Food Research and Action Center, "State-by-State Rates of Household Hunger and Food Insecurity, 1997–1999," January 2002.

11. National Campaign for Jobs and Income Support, *Leaving Welfare, Left Behind: Employment Status, Income and Well-Being of Former TANF Recipients*, Washington, D.C., October 2001.

12. Heather Boushey, Chauna Brocht, Bethney Gundersen, and Jared Bernstein, *Hardships in America: The Real Story of Working Families* (Washington, D.C.: Economic Policy Institute, 2001), p. 1.

13. Ibid., p. 2.

14. Vincent Bugliosi, *The Betrayal of America: How the Supreme Court Undermined the Constitution and Chose Our President* (New York: Nation Books, 2001).

15. Jeffrey E. Garten, *The Mind of the C.E.O.* (New York: Basic Books, 2001), p. 3.

16. Branko Milanovic, "True World Income Distribution, 1988 and 1993: First Calculation Based on Household Surveys Alone," *The Economic Journal*, Vol. 112 (January 2002), p. 89.

17. See the *New York Times*, June 12, 2002.

18. Quoted in Alan Beattie, "UN Snapshot Captures Failure to Hit Poverty Goals," *Financial Times*, July 11, 2001.

19. "Bridging the Digital Divide: Harnessing ICT for Economic Development, Job Creation and Poverty Eradication," *World of Work: The Magazine of the ILO*, No. 38 (January/February 2001), p. 5.

20. Milanovic, "True World Income Distribution," pp. 88–89.

21. Quoted in "Bridging the Digital Divide," p. 4.

22. United Nations, *Choices for the Poor* (2002), p. 2.

23. Ibid., p. 3.

24. Seymour Martin Lipset, *Political Man* (Garden City, NY: Anchor Books, 1960). Quoted in Arblaster, *Democracy*, p. 50.

25. Ibid., p. 14.

26. Noberto Bobbio, *left & right: The Significance of a Distinction* (Chicago: University of Chicago Press, 1996), p. 83.

27. Noberto Bobbio, *Democracy and Dictatorship: The Nature and Limits of State Power* (Minneapolis: University of Minnesota Press, 1989), p. 156.

28. Norberto Bobbio, *The Future of Democracy: A Defense of the Rules of the Game* (Minneapolis: University of Minnesota Press, 1987), p. 59.

29. Ibid., p. 60.

30. Ibid., p. 59.

31. Lipset, *Political Man*, pp. 108, 121.

32. Ibid., p. 89.

33. Immanuel Wallerstein, *The End of the World as We Know It: Social Science for the Twenty-First Century* (Minneapolis: University of Minnesota Press, 1999), p. 70.

34. Benjamin Barber, *Strong Democracy: Participatory Politics for a New Age* (Berkeley: University of California Press, 1984).

35. Ibid., p. 151.

36. Ibid., p. 14.

37. Ibid., p. 272.

38. Students for a Democratic Society, "The Port Huron Statement," in *The Sixties Papers: Documents of a Rebellious Decade*, ed. Judith Clavir Albert and Stewart Edward Albert (New York: Praeger, 1984), p. 181.

39. Ibid., p. 182.

40. Karl Marx, *Capital: Volume Three* (New York: Vintage Books, 1981), p. 959.

41. Ibid.

42. Daniel Bell, *The End of Ideology* (Glencoe, Ill.: Free Press, 1960).

43. Samuel P. Huntington, *The Clash of Civilizations and the Remaking of the World Order* (New York: Touchstone, 1996), p. 28.

44. Ibid., p. 29.

45. Huntington, *The Third Wave*, p. 6.

46. Schumpeter, *Capitalism, Socialism, and Democracy* (New York: Harper, 1975 [original publication 1942]).

47. Ibid., p. 15.

48. Huntington, *The Clash of Civilizations*, p. 305.

49. Ibid.

50. Ibid., p. 313.

51. Ibid., p. 315.

52. Ibid., p. 320.

53. Ibid., p. 308.

54. In this connection, see the September 2001 issue of *The Multinational Monitor*, pp. 7–8.

55. F. A. Hayek, *Individualism and Economic Order* (Chicago: University of Chicago Press, 1948), p. 91.

56. Ibid., pp. 86–87.

57. F. A. Hayek, *The Road to Serfdom* (Chicago: University of Chicago Press, 1944), pp. 207–208.

58. Ibid., p. 225.

59. Hayek, *Individualism and Economic Order*, p. 118.

60. Bugliosi, *The Betrayal of America*.

61. Raymond Aron, "Social Structure and the Ruling Class," *British Journal of Sociology*, Vol. 1 (1950), p. 9; quoted in Arblaster, *Democracy*, p. 49.

62. Barber, *Strong Democracy*, pp. 261–311.

63. Schor, *The Overworked American*, p. 150.

64. Stanley Aronowitz and William DiFazio, *The Jobless Future: Sci-Tech and the Dogma of Work* (Minneapolis: University of Minnesota Press, 1994), p. 358.

13

Global Capital and Its Opponents

STANLEY ARONOWITZ

A t the height of the Cold War in 1956, having concluded that organized labor had lost its historic opportunity to gain decisive social power, sociologist C. Wright Mills identified three principal institutional orders in the constitution of the power elite: the large corporations, the national political directorate, and the military. Mills's designation of the military as a component of the power elite corresponded to its enhanced, and relatively autonomous, role in creating and sustaining the permanent war economy, a judgment vindicated by Dwight Eisenhower's valedictory warning that there had been formed a "military-industrial complex" that threatened democracy. But the emergence of a powerful military was crucially dependent upon the division of the world into two principal military superpowers after World War II. With the collapse of the Soviet bloc in 1991, the installation of the United States as the only major world military force capable of negotiating enforceable international agreements to sustain the new status quo, and the relative reductions in military spending during the Clinton administration, the power of the military and of the alliances it had cemented with sections of capital were subsumed under civilian political control once more.

Yet since World War II, statecraft as well as economic relations have become global in a new way. The Marshall Plan—by which the United States, investment banks, and industrial corporations made extensive loans to governments and investments in British, German, Japanese, and Italian corporations where, in many instances, they became partners—was among the earliest postwar efforts at economic and political integration. To be sure, these measures were sold on humanitarian and democratic, anti-communist grounds rather than in terms of what they really were: a new realignment of world economic and political power in which the United States occupied the dominant position. The Truman Doctrine, aimed at stopping Soviet expansion, meant in practical terms that the European and Amer-

ican military would now be integrated as well. The third leg of the alliance involved efforts to hammer out common policies between national states concerning
"hot spots" in the developing countries where nationalist revolutions, often led by
communists or nonaligned political movements, threatened the economic and
strategic interests of the anti-communist Western alliance. The stakes were high
because China and India, the two nations with the world's largest populations,
were respectively aligned with or nonaligned but close to the Soviet bloc. Since the
seriously hobbled Western European powers were unable to maintain their own
colonies, these efforts were far less successful than economic and military integration. As France, Netherlands, Belgium, and Portugal faltered, in some cases
through military defeat at the hands of insurgent armies and armed civilian populations, the United States assumed the main military and political burden of coun-
terrevolution in areas such as Africa, the Middle East, and Southeast Asia.

New Globalism

The "old" imperialism was marked by extensive colonization in order to extract
raw materials from these areas and by capital investment associated with the development of extractive industries: mining, oil fields, and agricultural products such
as food and cotton. The main characteristic of the new globalism that emerged
after the struggle for independence of the colonial countries had been won was the
establishment of new, neo-colonial relationships—"neo-colonial" since formal political sovereignty did not translate into economic autarky. Throughout the period
after independence there was a brief time during which India and some African nation-states proclaimed a policy of "nonalignment" with the two great powers. By
the late 1970s, however, most "third world" countries had slowly, but surely, grav-
itated toward one or another of the two great power blocs. For different reasons
China and India—especially after 1956—maintained their own versions of nonalignment. China's foreign policy after 1955, when it severed its ties to the Soviet
Union, was, in turn, isolationist and then, after Mao's death, aggressively sought
Western investment and diplomatic ties; whereas India's foreign policy, during the
reign of the Congress Party (which, led by Gandhi, had sparked the independence
from Britain), entailed a loose favored-nation relationship with the Soviet Union
throughout a good portion of the period before the latter's collapse in 1991. But
even before the demise of the Soviet bloc, Western powers led by the United States
had established a new institutional framework, primarily through the U.S.-domi-
nated World Bank and International Monetary Fund, for restructuring economic
and political relations on the basis of a particular type of global neo-liberalism in
which free trade, unfettered investment, and insistence on transforming the old
dictatorships into liberal democracies became the trio of preconditions for economic development. To these the World Bank added the program of structural adjustment, a euphemism for social austerity. Nations seeking loans from the bank

are now required to drastically scale back government services not directly linked to foreign investment, such as education, health, and transportation.

In Latin America, where most countries had been formally independent before the war, most had been subsumed under the American Empire since the Spanish-American War and in sync with the global pattern whose economies were chiefly oriented toward the extractive industries. Central American economies became dependent upon commodities such as the sugar, fruit, and oil prevalent in Venezuela. Chile was a chief source for the supply of copper and agricultural fertilizers, and its trade relations were primarily conducted with the United States. Mexico, Brazil, and Argentina were partial exceptions to this rule. Although by no means liberal democratic in nature—indeed, after the initial upsurge they had long-term authoritarian governments—each experienced a successful nationalist revolution whose primary aim was to establish a framework for economic as well as political autonomy on the basis of mixed private and public enterprises, albeit with mixed success. However, under the impetus of world economic crisis and domestic political challenges from the left, these three largest states in the region have, under the auspices of U.S.-based bank loans administered by the World Bank and the International Monetary Fund, become clients of the American empire.

On the other hand, Cuba, which had broken from the United States after its 1959 revolution against the U.S. client-government of Batista, was the only country in the Americas able to successfully resist U.S. military and economic domination. But its alliance with the Soviet Union, forged in the aftermath of the Eisenhower and Kennedy administrations' firm refusal to recognize its autonomy within the framework of the American empire, fell victim to the great collapse of its protector. Plagued by a U.S. blockade, by its increasing isolation from the Americas, and by the failure of the Salvadoran, Chilean, and Nicaraguan nationalist and socialist insurgencies to overcome U.S. military and intelligence agencies' subversion of their governments, Cuba has struggled with remarkable fortitude to preserve its independence. But in concert with other prolonged examples of independence from neo-colonial relationships, it has paid the steep price of deferral of democracy and economic well-being. As a result, and in order to generate income to support its deprived population, the government has fostered tourism, developed a cutting-edge pharmaceutical industry, and intensified its sugar production.

While it would be a mistake to overstate the change, there is no doubt that the global integration of production, distribution, and marketing, and of financial and industrial capital, means that economic tremors in one part of the world will sooner or later be felt in another. When a long-term economic slump afflicted most countries of Western Europe in the early 1970s, within a few years the United States was in the throes of its most serious economic downturn since the Depression. And when the weakest of the "big three" automakers, Chrysler, almost collapsed in 1979, it was only when United Automobile Workers (UAW) and the federal government agreed to raise a billion dollars in direct subsidies and wage and work-rule concessions that the company was saved.

The world slump prompted transnational corporations and key nation-states, led by the United States, to create what might be described as a new global state.[1] As we shall see, the constituents of this state are the international economic institutions such as the World Bank and the International Monetary Fund, transnational capital, and, contrary to some who proclaim the demise of the nation-state, the states that harbor the seven largest capitalist economies, especially the United States. Since the war, the imperatives of international relations, including the deployment of large military forces around the world, often in combat situations, have consistently placed limits on what the American state can achieve at home. Most of the domestic programs advocated by labor, liberals, and the black freedom movements in the United States—the world's leading financial as well as military power—were placed on permanent hold and when tested in Congress were, with almost no exceptions, defeated.

The twin programs of neo-liberal economic policies and anti-communist globalization that were forged within the United States during the Cold War era became a model for subsequent moves by the West toward establishing a new world order. Under Democratic as well as Republican administrations the postwar era was marked by policies that concentrated federal spending on fulfilling America's global commitments, particularly before 1990, to defend the "free world" and, subsequently, to foster the program of the global state. This policy was promulgated at a time when the welter of depression-driven and wartime-deferred social needs such as housing and health care became an urgent political priority. Rather than implementing welfare state expansion in the fifteen years immediately following the war, the state actively intervened to assist banks, insurance companies, and the construction industry to build millions of privately owned homes and, through the Federal Highway Program, to facilitate the relocation of industry and huge chunks of the population to the suburbs and exurbs. When the most powerful unions perceived that the political arena was all but foreclosed and negotiated what I term the "private welfare state" through collective bargaining (company paid pensions, health care, and social services), their main business with Congress and the national administration was to press for defense contracts for "their" firms— namely, those with whom they held collective bargaining agreements.

As a political actor, the American labor movement—led by UAW president Walter Reuther, a leading social liberal—became an ally of the dominant power bloc's program of solving social problems such as employment, discrimination, and inequality through policies of economic growth. Following the theories of economist Leon Keyserling, who served in the Roosevelt administration and had been a member of President Truman's Council of Economic Advisors, Reuther advocated policies of job creation rather than confrontation with the white male labor monopolies that excluded blacks and women. He even coined the phrase *reverse discrimination* to characterize left-wing proposals to negotiate special agreements with employers to promote blacks outside the traditional seniority system, which in many industries ensured that blacks, as the last hired, would be the first fired. The fact that federal policies linked to the growth strategy imperiled the environment, were fueled by a commitment to the permanent war economy, and entailed the spread of U.S. influence—primarily by military means, including spying and ideological Cold War, on a world scale—did not detain progressives like Reuther who led the American labor movement.

In fact, there was no more vocal supporter of huge defense expenditures than Reuther, an indefatigable and effective lobbyist on behalf of defense contractors, many of whom negotiated with the UAW and other industrial unions. By the late 1960s Reuther himself became disenchanted by some of the excesses of American foreign policy during the Vietnam War era. But the belated recognition by Reuther and other progressives in the labor movement of the destructive aspects of U.S. commitment to thwart revolution and economic independence in developing countries cannot efface the fact that American labor leaders stood beside the leading fractions of capital and the political directorate in promulgating the domination of American politics and culture by global interests of American corporations.

EMPIRE OR NEW IMPERIALISM

During the 1960s the mass anti–Vietnam War movement explained U.S. involvement in the network of Southeast Asia wars as an illustration of imperialism. Based on the description of the long march by the Vietnamese and their Communist leadership as a prolonged military and political struggle for national independence—first from Holland and then from France, which held the nation as a colony—they interpreted Eisenhower's decision to pick up where the badly battered French military left off in 1954 as an unwarranted abrogation of the right of colonial and dependent nations to self-determination. At the same time, many tried to find economic motives for the escalation begun under the Kennedy administration. Yet while there are always economic factors, the chief reason the United States became embroiled in what became its most colossal military and moral defeat of the Cold War was chiefly strategic and political. Consistent with its Cold War foreign policy, the United States assumed the role of protector of the weak, anti-democratic but anti-communist regime and intervened to thwart the self-determination of the Vietnamese people, especially when they chose to live under communist rule. While it is doubtful that the United States sought to make Vietnam its colony, as with Korea and Central and Latin America, the government followed an historic policy of dominating weaker nations for political and strategic as well as economic advantage.

The United States never held a large number of direct colonies, a fact that prompted many political leaders to declare it the great exception to colonialism. Yet the Monroe Doctrine became for 150 years a rallying cry for American economic and military engagement in Central and South America and, fueled by Cold War considerations, remained a hallmark of American foreign policy until the

1990s. As indicated by the recent struggle of Puerto Ricans to prevent the Navy from maintaining the island of Vieques as a bombing range, the U.S. government retains something of a colonialist mentality. Moreover, contrary to the claims of various American national administrations, we have rarely been at peace. Even the collapse of Eastern European communism and the rapid integration of China into the world market have failed to stem the steady tide of American military intervention into the affairs of weaker, quasi-sovereign nations.

While the rhetoric of anti-communism has, with the notable exceptions of Cuba and North Korea, given way to the rhetoric of human rights as a justification for these involvements, events such as the Gulf War are for many on the left merely examples of the same old imperialist adventures. But according to Antonio Negri and his American collaborator Michael Hardt, the Vietnam War was the last great battle of the old imperialism.[2] In their view we have entered the era of Empire, a "supranational" center consisting of networks of transnational corporations and advanced capitalist nations led by the one remaining superpower, the United States. In this new globalized economic and political system, a genuine world market has been created, national boundaries are becoming increasingly porous, and "imperial authority" is in the process of taking hold.

The new paradigm of Empire "is both system and hierarchy, centralized construction of norms and far-reaching production of legitimacy, spread out over world space."[3] The invocation of human rights is not merely a fig leaf for the imperium; it is part of an effort to create enforceable international law in which the institutions of Empire take precedence over formerly sovereign states; in short, they assume the role of world court as well as policeman. The interests of Empire are also invoked in the economic arena; it may be noted that the American president has largely been refashioned as a high-level trade representative for the transnationals.

While by no means minimizing the fact that the United States stands at the pinnacle of the new system, Hardt and Negri insist that the intensity of its interventions are consistent with the project of creating a system where disputes between nations can be adjudicated by a legitimate international authority and by consensus, upon which world policing may be promulgated to contain them. Even without the institutions in place—most of these initiatives remain ad hoc—they announce the existence of a dominant "system totality" or logic that, however invisible, regulates the new economic and political order that has taken hold almost everywhere. The new paradigm of Empire has gained enormous strength since the collapse of the Soviet Union, but it is not the direct result of Cold War triumph. In my view it emerged organically within the old system as a result of the tremendous power of the postwar labor movements to bid up both money wages and the social wage, the pressure of national liberation movements on the old imperialism, and the gradual delegitimization of the authority of national states and their institutions to maintain internal cultural as well as political discipline.

By the 1960s, having increased its power at the industrial workplace, labor was engaged in what Negri had previously termed "the refusal to work."[4] Even as mass consumption was rising, productivity eroded and profits in some instances actually declined. Nation-states—which since the great 18th- and 19th-century revolutions had been effective in enforcing internalized mass discipline (through education, citizenship for the lower social classes, and imperial ideologies such as racism and patriotism)—were increasingly unable to command popular allegiance as, one after another, their efforts to thwart national liberation movements ran afoul. Things came to a head in 1968 and 1969 when mass strikes, notably in France and Italy, almost toppled sitting governments, and when disruptions and mass demonstrations threatened the stability of the regimes in Mexico and the United States. But the conjunction of economic crisis and the crisis of rule was an occasion for renewal, not breakdown.

The renewal was signaled by President Nixon's early 1970s abrogation of the Bretton Woods agreement, by which the dollar rather than gold became the universal money standard. With U.S. currency weakened by international competition and the rising costs of production and of governance, it was no longer possible to contain world prices by monetary means and preserve the system of internal trade regulation. Now the dollar "floated" along with other currencies. In quick succession the United States removed most major regulatory controls: banks, trucking and other transportation, and most anti-trust restraints. The prices of fuel and many other commodities now floated in the market. While Nixon started the process of ending the stubborn legacy of the New Deal, the so-called Reagan revolution, to which the Clinton administration seems to have been a loyal supplicant, greatly accelerated the changes. The doctrine of Keynesianism, which proclaimed that since capitalism tended toward equilibrium but below a level of full employment governments must intervene directly to stimulate economic growth and employment, was declared dead. The free market and with it the idea that government should, as much as possible, stay out of the economy, except to regulate the supply of money and credit in order to stem inflationary tendencies, became the new religion.

A key element in the new corporate strategy was to reduce wages through curbing the power of organized labor. Battered by the "deterritorialization" of industrial production as corporations removed to plants offshore and to rural Southern areas within the United States and around the globe, and by the relentless anti-labor policies of right-wing governments, organized labor unions in all major industrial countries were in full retreat by the 1980s. In the United States and the United Kingdom, unions proved unable to protect many features that the social wage (welfare state benefits) had won during the 1930s and the early postwar years. In the United States, even as its density shrunk by half, the AFL-CIO became, at least at the electoral level, identical with the Democrats, whose race to the center-right quickened, paradoxically, in proportion to union donations of more funds and workers to its campaigns. While the power of labor in other countries took a longer time to diminish, the 1990s were years of agony for most European workers. Even when labor-backed socialist governments took power in France, Germany, and Italy, welfare-state erosion, the decline of union membership due to heavy losses in the old material goods industries, and the rise of largely nonunion information and communications reduced the power of organized labor unions and, with few exceptions, its will to resist their governments' neo-liberal economic policies.

For some observers, globalization was the major mechanism to solve the crisis. Three key transformations occurred since the 1960s: the shift in the economy from the dominance of industrial production to information; the integration of the world market such that, with global communications, industrial deterritorialization, and accelerated world investment and trade, the lines are now blurred between "inside and outside"; and the decline of the nation-state as the core of political sovereignty and the mediator of economic and political protest. The introduction of new scientifically based technologies led to the creation of entirely new communications and information industries and have largely replaced the old regime of Taylorist and Fordist production. Fordism, which subjected the worker to rationalized tasks by transferring knowledge to the machines—assembly lines and other methods—has largely been replaced with what has been termed Toyotaism or post-Fordism. One characteristic feature of the new production methods is "just in time" production. Through computerized information technologies, management is now able to compress the time between the provision of raw materials to the shop floor and the actual production process.

But the technological revolution has had another effect as well. Information technology signifies the advent of "immaterial" production and with it the emergence of knowledgeable workers who integrate knowledge, skill, and labor—what Robert Reich has designated "symbolic-analytic services," activities that entail "problem-solving" and "brokering" once performed chiefly by managers.[5] The central actor in this new immaterial production no longer stands as a cog in the labor process but is at the center of it. Since these knowledgeable workers are, contrary to popular belief, not immune to the vagaries of exploitation (many of them work on a part-time, contingent, and temporary basis, even in software heartlands), they are among the potential actors in a potentially revived labor movement. Globalism is not primarily a regime of goods production but, with the aid of science, leads to a new paradigm of the relations among humans, their evolutionary partners, and the physical universe. Nature, too, has been integrated into the new system; witness the emergence of industries based on biotechnology that treat life itself as a new field for investment and production. In fact, the transformation of the human gene into an industrial raw material subject to private corporate ownership may signal the last frontier of the global empire.

With many traditional industries such as steel in sharp decline, and the use of nonrenewable energy sources threatened by a growing perception of ecological fragility—as well as the hotly contested thesis that natural oil reserves are being exhausted even as the world's supply is overproduced—bioeconomics and biopolitics now occupy center stage. Naturally the struggle has taken a new turn. Environmentalists have made considerable headway in Europe against insertion of genetically modified organisms into food production, and the struggle against animal, including human, cloning has gained intensity. That the United States remains a bastion of these practices is not surprising, for North America is the heartland of technologically advanced capitalist agriculture. Thirty percent of U.S. exports are food and other farm products. And despite the virtual disappearance of the small "family" farm, corporate farming, in close alliance with biotechnology firms and with leading research universities, is alive and well. In relation to research and development activities, biology has substantially displaced physics as the leading scientific discipline, with respect to its role in both economic growth and military weaponry.

Nation-states, which emerged from the decline of the feudal monarchies and aristocracies and their replacement by liberal democratic systems, have captured the collective imaginations of national liberation movements since the 18th century and, claiming the loyalty of what Hardt and Negri call the "multitude," still perform important tasks for the Empire. Without nation-states, the control of whole populations would be impossible. Yet imperialism has died precisely because nations are no longer the key mediators of international economics and politics. The nation may still ignite fierce loyalties among subordinate peoples, but for Hardt and Negri it is no longer truly independent of the new world order.

In almost none of the present-day "developing" nations are the majority of their populations afforded decent living standards. As of this writing, a third of the world's labor force remain unemployed and underemployed, and millions have migrated in order to make a living. The term *third world* describes the past. Having been subordinated to Empire, these nations no longer express an alternative. But for Hardt and Negri this situation is no occasion for nostalgia. Acknowledging the hardships suffered by victims of war, famine, and unemployment, they see a new proletariat emerging on a world scale out of the enormous exodus of peasants, a proletariat that may become one of the constituents of resistance and power against Empire. The old distinction between industrial production and agriculture has been sundered as hundreds of millions of people are herded into cities in their own countries—and, more to the point, in the advanced societies—to work in the manufacturing sites of the Empire. Those who remain on the land are increasingly subject to capitalist industrial methods; old peasant communes are being converted, literally, to factories in the field.

Although Hardt and Negri's *Empire* sometimes strays from its central theme, it is a bold move away from established doctrine. The authors' insistence that there really is a new world is promulgated with energy and conviction. Especially striking is their renunciation of the tendency of many writers on globalization to focus exclusively on the top, leaving the impression that what happens down below, to ordinary people, follows automatically from what the great powers do. In the final chapters they try to craft a new theory of historical actors, and here they stumble, sometimes badly. The main problem is that they tend to overstate their case. From the incontrovertible observation that the traditional forces of resistance have lost their punch, the authors conclude that there are no more institutional "mediations"; power must be confronted directly. Not so fast.

One of the serious omissions in *Empire*'s analysis is a discussion of the World Trade Organization (WTO), the International Monetary Fund (IMF), and the World Bank, three of the concrete institutions of the repressive world government of Empire. Lacking an institutional perspective—except with respect to law— Hardt and Negri are unable to anticipate how the movement they would bring into being may actually mount effective resistance. Although not obliged to provide a program for a movement, the authors do offer indicators of which social forces may politically take on the colossus. Having argued that the classes of historical capitalism, which relied on the mediating role of the nation-state, and institutions such as trade unions and political parties are no longer reliable forces of combat, they are left with the postmodern equivalent of the 19th-century proletariat, the "insurgent multitude." In the final chapters of the book, incisive prose gives way to hyperbole, and the sharp delineation of historical actors melts into a vague politics of hope. Insisting that "resistance" precedes power, they advocate direct confrontation, "and with adequate consciousness the central repressive operations of Empire," to achieve "global citizenship." At the end, the authors celebrate the "nomadic [communist] revolutionary" as the most likely protagonist of the struggle.

The Seattle demonstrations against the WTO in December 1999, the subsequent anti-IMF and anti–World Bank demonstrations in Washington, Prague, and Quebec, and the protests at the G8 meeting in Genoa in summer 2001 tell a somewhat different story. The 50,000 demonstrators who disrupted the WTO meetings and virtually shut down the city consisted of definite social groups: first, a considerable fraction of the labor movement, including some of its top leaders who were concerned that lower wages and human rights violations would not only undermine their standards but also intensify exploitation in the empire's factories; second, students who had been protesting sweatshop labor for years and were forcing their universities to cease buying from them; and, third, the still numerous, if battered, detachment of environmentalists—together a burgeoning alliance that appears to have continued.

These developments shed a brilliant light on the existence of resistance to Empire, but also on the problem of theories that wax in high abstractions. For it is not clear that, as the authors claim, mediations have exhausted themselves, and for this reason it may be argued that some of the traditional forces of the opposition retain at least a measure of life. While direct confrontation is, in my view, one appropriate strategy of social struggle today, it does not relieve us of the obligation to continue to take the long march through institutions, to test their mettle. After all, "appropriate consciousness" does not appear spontaneously; it emerges when people, nomads or not, discover the limits of the old. And the only way they can understand the nature of the new Empire is to experience the frustrations associated with attempts to achieve reforms within the nation-state, even as the impulse to forge an international labor/environmentalist alliance proceeds.

Perhaps more to the point, Hardt and Negri, together with some observers of the new global order, underestimate the role of the leading nation-states in constituting its institutional infrastructure and completely deny their relative autonomy. What most theorists of Empire do not comprehend is that the nation-state is a constituent of globalization. As the struggle around global warming indicates, even though elements of transnational capital, Japan, and most European powers are willing to entertain significant controls over carbon dioxide emissions (greenhouse gases), the Kyoto Treaty—at best, a compromise that environmentalists term a "first step"—has experienced years of deadlock. In the 2001 Bonn meetings to hammer out an agreement, while ostensibly agreeing with its objectives, the United States and Italy bluntly rejected the treaty and other participants quibbled over provisions that, they believed, might hurt their domestic economies.[6] At the same time, in the meeting of the G8 in Genoa, the seven largest industrialized countries plus Russia failed to conclude major agreements on forgiving third world debt, global warming, and modifying trade agreements to protect workers. One might argue that this was a temporary glitch in the steamroller of Empire. Yet another picture emerges when we more closely examine the composition of the leading institutions that make up Empire. As I show below, nation-states are part of the constituent power of the new global order.

One of the most striking examples of the growth of transnationalism or globalization—mergers between two ostensibly intranational corporations—crossed national boundaries in 2001 and, to some extent, has modified the concept of national sovereignty. We must take seriously the action by the European Union (EU) in opposing the proposed merger of General Electric and Honeywell. In the era of transnationalism it is no longer possible for national states to approve or disapprove such economic alliances without consultation with other power blocs, a message that American politicians have been slow to absorb. That national sovereignty has thereby been partially abrogated, there is no doubt. That such veritable vetoes by foreign powers will exacerbate nationalism is probable. But a novel wrinkle in the evolving story of international economic and political relations is the significance of the EU's contention that corporations based in the United States that produce and distribute complementary products can constitute a global monopoly that threatens the interest of transnational competitors and must be prohibited from taking such action. Will such provocations prompt retaliation of the economic, political, or military sort by the U.S. government in concert with U.S.-based transnationals such as GE? Are we witnessing a new stage of international rivalry? Was the confident assertion of U.S. hegemony over world economic and political affairs premature? It is probably too early to tell, but what is clear is that neither the transparent picture of pluralism nor the verities of the old Marxisms that posited pax corporate Americana are sufficient to understand this new development.

On the contrary. Within the system of liberal democratic capitalism the state's autonomy is a necessary condition of its role in ensuring a measure of inter- and intraclass regulation of sufficient authority to curb acts of creative destruction that threaten the general capitalist interest. As long as the state acts within the bounds of the general systemic interest, its range of decision making may be quite broad and independent of even the most important fractions of the capitalist class. And what that systemic interest actually is may be hotly contested on ideological as well as economic and political grounds, so that there are times when the state acts in a nonrational manner, at least from some perspectives; witness the rejection by Microsoft and its celebrity CEO, Bill Gates, of a district court's finding that it had violated anti-monopoly statutes. Rationality is, after all, subject to partisanship as when, in 2001, a fraction of industrial and finance capital joined to oppose the proposed sharp reduction of the estate tax during the administration of George W. Bush. That this powerful group of leading capitalists lost the legislative battle illustrates that a struggle was under way within the ruling formation over an important domain of politics, tax policy.

A significant indication of the operational autonomy of the American government was Bush's appointment of Paul O'Neill, CEO of the leading aluminum producer, Alcoa, as secretary of treasury. Traditionally the office has been occupied either by a visible figure in the financial services sector, such as Henry Morgenthau during the Roosevelt administration; C. Douglas Dillon, Eisenhower's treasury secretary; and Robert Rubin, Clinton's choice (each of whom were principals in leading Wall Street investment banking firms and became principals in directing America's international economic affairs), or by an economist closely linked to finance capital, such as labor economist George Schultz, who served several Republican administrations, and Lawrence Summers, who succeeded Rubin after serving as his undersecretary for seven years. (Schultz is only one of several labor economists who rose to high office in the political directorate. One may also mention Harvard's John Dunlop and the legal scholar Archibald Cox, both of whom played important roles in taming postwar Labor.) After his tenure in the Clinton administration, Summers went on to become president of Harvard University, not only a leading research institution but for decades the source of a considerable number of key figures at the top of Democratic and, to a lesser extent, Republican administrations.

O'Neill is not only a "dangerous crank" (according to journalist William Greider), given his open hostility to social security and other public goods and his off-the-cuff suggestions that corporate taxes be abolished,[7] but he is also unusual for his main ties to a production sector rather than to financial corporations—connections that may signal that the traditional bipartisan free trade internationalism is being challenged by the Bush administration. In spring 2001, the administration began negotiations with the steel industry and the United Steelworkers, who sought higher tariffs—a protectionist measure scorned by several previous presidents and by finance, which incessantly warns of retaliation by trading partners. In March 2002, in an adroit move to pry an important labor union from its traditional ties to the Democratic Party, much to the delight of the union's leadership, Bush made good by promising to raise steel tariffs by 30 percent. Arguing that his first priority is economic growth, in his first European trip Bush played the nationalist and productivist card by openly defying entreaties from European leaders to sign the Kyoto Treaty, which begins to address the dangers posed by global warming. Moreover, the Bush administration has announced that it would deal with the developing energy crisis in the United States by providing federal assistance to expand the use of nonrenewable fuels such as coal and oil to solve the long-term shortage of electric power, rather than investing in alternative and renewable energy technologies. And enlisting the support of Teamsters Union President James P. Hoffa, Bush has embarked on a policy initiative to drill for oil in part of the Alaska wilderness area. Viewing O'Neill's appointment in the context of a rift between financial and industrial capital and the internationalist and nationalist wings of the conservative hegemony, we get a glimpse of how the invisible becomes visible.

Despite his successful campaign pose as a "compassionate" conservative, a code word for "moderate," Bush has surrounded himself with a nationalist coterie—namely, top officials such as O'Neill; Vice President Dick Cheney, who is acting as perhaps the key operative in this administration; and, especially, Defense's Donald Rumsfeld, who wants to create a defensive missile shield around the United States in violation of established international treaties and has led the war in Afghanistan. Yet at international meetings Bush maintains a strong internationalist (i.e., free trade) line. In the face of powerful anti-globalization demonstrations during the Genoa G8 meeting in summer 2001, Bush took the trouble to denounce the protesters three times by declaring that free trade was the best strategy to help poor countries. This contradiction is more than just a sign of the conflicting rhetorics of an otherwise reactionary administration. Indeed, it is an indication of the limits to national sovereignty in the new Empire.

Needless to say, as the nationalist and right-wing character of this administration comes to the surface, the foreign policy establishment (which has been internationalist for more than a half-century), the leaders of financial corporations, and the members of both political parties who have hewed their line have started to worry that this administration is attempting to shift power decisively by, among other tactics, winning over the beleaguered but still substantial fractions of industrial capital and integrating some ailing industrial unions into a new coalition with the social right. The defection from the Republican Party of Senator James Jeffords, a moderate from Vermont, is only the most visible sign of the erosion, perhaps collapse, of the party's moderate wing. It is socially liberal but fiscally conservative and, above all, internationalist. In Jeffords's case, leaving his party reflects not only Vermont's social liberalism but also the interests of its farm sector, which has been a major supporter of international trade.

Which leaves the right—traditional conservatives who form the constituents of the National Association of Manufacturers and the mainstream farm organizations, hardly a majority—to form the Republican alliance. Obviously, if this program is to succeed Bush—who, in his response to the growing shortage of electrical energy, has already signaled his attraction to a program of internal industrial development in traditional industries such as coal-driven power plants, in an attempt to bring back the Reagan Democrats—it would be forced to make concessions to his new partners in organized labor on trade policy. Such a shift from the bipartisan free trade program of the government could further strain relations between the United States and Western Europe. At the same time, Bush has already incurred the enmity of financial capital and the leaders of the information sector whose interests he seems to hold in low regard, in part because they have shown strong loyalty to the internationalist wing of the Democrats.

Contrary to the emerging conventional wisdom according to which "globalization" signals the end of the sovereignty of national states,[8] the latter play an important part in processes of globalization. The World Bank, the IMF and the WTO—the constituent leadership of which includes the principal states and the main international financial institutions—are charged with regulating the relations between countries in the industrially developed world by reproducing the conditions of domination and dependence.

For example, the World Bank and the IMF played a key role in assisting Boris Yeltsin to consolidate his power after the collapse of the Soviet Union. They provided three major incentives: arranging the extension and partial forgiveness of Soviet debt to Western banks and other financial institutions; sending billions in direct loans and outright grants to effect a smoother transition, including funds to tend Russia's formidable nuclear arsenal; and supplying economic and political consultation to advise the government on privatization of Soviet-era enterprises, labor policy, and development, especially of Russia's awesome oil reserves. Jeffrey Sachs of Harvard University was only the most prominent economist and policy intellectual who was dispatched to work with government planners. In return, the government agreed to vigorously pursue denationalization of many of its basic industries—resulting, most tragically, in the dismantlement of its extraordinary scientific establishment, which has led to the migration of thousands of first-rate scientists to the West and to the forging of familiar "partnerships" with the newly created private industrial sector with foreign capital. These market policies, termed "adjustment," entailed systematic austerity measures: radically altering and otherwise reducing the broad welfare state; disciplining the labor force by lowering its living standards; and renouncing many labor and health protections. This last policy, together with reduced wages and quality of life, has in ten years lowered life expectancy by more than a decade, such that Russians, especially men, can be expected to live, on the average, for less than sixty years—a life span equal to that of people in a struggling third world society.

Under the advice of these international agencies, the new Russia has taken a place in the second tier of European powers; for most of the period until 2000, it received much the same treatment as that given by victorious powers to the defeated. In fact, Russia has assumed considerable portions of accumulated debt and is still required to pay on time. In order to ante up the cash, its people have suffered, as have the populations of many other former communist states. The same is true of populations in Africa and Latin America whose social as well as economic policies remain largely under the control of the World Bank and the IMF. As South

Africa, for example, has discovered, the promise of land reform, along with labor rights, social freedom, and an expanded welfare state, was at the heart of the program of the key movement in the liberation struggle. According to the African National Congress, if the IMF and World Bank disapprove of such programs, the country may be deprived of funds for development. And as Argentina, Brazil, and Mexico have discovered, only if the state agrees to neo-liberal austerity measures can they expect aid.[9]

The governing bodies of the IMF, World Bank, and WTO are composed of the finance ministers of the seven largest industrialized countries, and within these circles the American secretary of the treasury plays a key role in mobilizing finance capital for their activities. As we have seen, the American secretary has been part of the financial institutions upon which these agencies depend. But since their budgets and the funds they are able to disperse are dependent upon banks and other financial institutions and upon the national states that compose their governing bodies, there is always a question of how much autonomy they enjoy, or how much capital they will be able to mobilize. While there is little question that, in their policies as well as their functions, these international agencies embody the neo-liberal orientation of global capitalist interests at any given moment, issues such as which countries they will support, and how, are subject to the politics of nation-states as well as the transnational banks and other financial institutions from which they must receive support.

Following the near collapse of the Argentine economy and its reform government in 2002, there have been indications that the operational efficacy of the World Bank and the IMF are seriously in doubt. Facing runaway inflation amid a huge debt shortly after its assumption of power, the moderate anti-Peronist government faced demands from the Bank that it adhere to the policy of structural adjustment by sharply curbing social programs, maintaining payments on its ballooning debt, and cutting wages and salaries throughout the country. Against its own campaign promises the government bowed to these requests, prompting an intensification of mass layoffs, currency instability, and mass protests. This situation, in turn, prompted the government to resign, leading to a political crisis that was temporarily resolved by a transfer of power back to the Peronistas, but not before several governments fell in short order. Critics shared the view that far from heeding demands to change its policies, the World Bank and the IMF had precipitated the crisis by remaining obdurate.

The U.S. government has played a leading role in these organizations, and the national administrations of both parties have supported their general policies. European states have, in the main, participated as well. On the other hand, the states are constrained, not the least by international economic and political relations that increasingly impinge on their autonomy—a clear indication of the states' dual nature. Collectively they are among the key players in globality and are committed to neo-liberal control over international relations. However, since we have no legal and juridical concept of global citizenship or global regulation, the polity remains, for the time being, confined to the framework of nation-states. This contradiction is played out in the conflict between the policies of fiscal austerity in the United States and Western Europe and the demands of the citizens of those states. In all of these countries since 1990, labor movements have engaged in strikes and other forms of protest against attempts by conservative and social-democratic governments alike to reduce the scope and size of the social wage. While these struggles have been most visible in France and Spain, German and Greek unions have found themselves in conflict with their own labor-supported governments. And, in the United States, production unions have declined, industrial production has been deterritorialized, progressive unions have become more critical of free trade agreements, and the government has been urged to protect some industries from international competition.

Of course, in the United States, Canada, and Western Europe, the neo-liberal global capitalist state has encountered the most resistance from environmentalists, trade unionists, and young proponents of labor rights in what they call the "global sweatshop"—clothing and shoe plants in Southeast Asia and Latin America that force workers to endure nearly intolerable working conditions and extremely low wages. As is well known, no meeting of the IMF, the WTO, the World Bank, or the general policy organization of the seven leading industrialized nations can expect to be free of mass demonstrations by tens of thousands of protesters demanding a voice in determining the policies of these institutions. The alliances of trade unionists, environmentalists, and youth activists, some of whom are anarchists, have become so ubiquitous and effective in challenging the taken-for-granted assumption that capital has the divine right to go anywhere it pleases in the pursuit of profits free of labor regulation and trade unions and environmental protections that the institutions of Empire have resorted to force in order to hold their meetings. They have obliged host nation-states to front a shield of repression to keep the horde at bay.

The decade-long effort to subject the global state to a new, as-yet-unarticulated concept of global citizenship has met with some success—namely, the Kyoto Treaty and pledges by the IMF and World Bank to protect workers' rights in forging new trade agreements, concessions that activists regard with considerable skepticism, and, beginning with the 1996 environment summit in Brazil, promises that the global ruling institutions will consult with nongovernmental organizations on development policies. In fact, the reneging on the agreement by transnational capital and participant nations to involve the NGOs at the Brazil conference was, for many, a kind of parting of the ways from their naïve belief in the ability of "the system" to reform itself. What occurred subsequently in Seattle, Washington, Prague, Quebec, and Genoa was a symptom of the widening cleavage between the exemplars of incipient global citizenship and the Empire. The concrete program of the alliance is still framed in terms of structural reform.

The key reforms of the movements arrayed against global power—democratic participation; relief, if not total forgiveness, for many countries whose economic and social institutions are crumbling under the burden of excessive accumulated debt; and a sharp reversal, rather than modification, of ecologically disastrous development policies—have failed to produce a productive response from the global powers, even though the Green Parties in some countries, notably Germany, Italy, Greece, and Spain, have achieved some electoral victories and are an institutional force for reform. The slow pace of change has led to profound and potentially grave consequences. In 2001 the United Nations issued a report, subsequently supported by one thousand of the world's leading scientists, indicating that within the 21st century global warming will lead to serious crises for world agriculture, create water shortages in large portions of the world, and make some areas, especially in the Southern Hemisphere, unsustainable to life. Less than a year later, many of these scientists declared that global warming was proceeding at a more rapid pace than they had anticipated and that serious eruptions could occur at any time. In March 2002 the collapse of a huge Antarctic glacier into hundreds of smaller icebergs was ascribed to the effects of global warming.

The wide chasm that separates the "anti-globalization" movement from the global state and its components has led a significant fraction of the movement to link its demands with an anti-capitalist ideology, which still lacks a program. But the movement is, in the main, still at the stage of protest and resistance. It has not yet advanced a persuasive and coherent program that addresses the serious consequences of globalization. The search for political alternatives—proposals that would reshape current arrangements toward a democratic, ecologically sound, and egalitarian future—remains to be forged.

NOTES

1. Martin Shaw, *Theory of the Global State* (Cambridge, Eng.: Cambridge University Press, 2000); Sol Yurick, *The Metastate* (Brooklyn, NY: Semiotext, 1985); Michael Hardt and Antonio Negri, *Empire* (Cambridge, Mass.: Harvard University Press, 2000).

2. Hardt and Negri, *Empire.*

3. Ibid.

4. Negri, *The Politics of Subversion* (London: Polity Press, 1990).

5. Robert Reich, *The Work of Nations: Preparing Ourselves for 21st Century Capitalism* (New York: Knopf, 1991).

6. *New York Times*, July 23, 2001.

7. William Greider, "A Dangerous Crank," *The Nation*, July 16, 2001.

8. Indeed, some argue that states are no longer important powers, inasmuch as they are subject to new forces that shift the relative importance of their central functions—namely, repression, domestic economic intervention, and programs such as farm subsidies and social welfare such as veterans' aid and income support for the poor and the aged that are directly related to constituent political power.

9. But as the left-wing Workers Party was poised to win the Brazilian presidency, the IMF suddenly made a $30 billion grant to soften the country's economic crisis.

Part III

The Culture of Globalization and Resistance

14

Globalization Today

JEREMY BRECHER

S ince the beginning of the new millennium, the process of global economic integration that we call "globalization from above" has sped from crisis to
calamity. That has intensified both the need for and the strength of the convergence of social movements that we call "globalization from below."

END OF THE GLOBAL GILDED AGE

The corporations, governments, and elites that promoted globalization from above
promised that it would bring prosperity, democracy, and peace. But globalization
has in fact entered a new, more destructive phase marked by recession, repression,
and militarization. From an era of undemocratic and exploitative rule making we
have entered an era of piracy and plunder.

By 2002, the United States, Europe, Latin America, and most of Asia had entered the first worldwide recession since the 1970s.[1] According to Joseph Stiglitz,
former chief economist at the World Bank, "already we see inklings of the downward spiral that was part of the Great Depression of 1929. . . . Every week brings
new records. . . . [These include] the largest increase in unemployment and decline in manufacturing in two decades . . . [and] the slowest growth in nominal
GDP in any two consecutive years since the 1930s."[2]

Global linkage of this downward spiral is as much an aspect of globalization as
the global currency market or the WTO. European economies, for example, were
widely expected to be little affected by the U.S. downturn, because North America
is not a major market for them—but they were severely hurt by the decline in
Latin American and Asian markets that were in turn being hurt by the U.S. bust.
Globalization, supposedly the solution to the worldwide recession of the 1970s,
has instead become central to the problem.[3]

The collapse of Argentina shows how the promises of globalization from above have been realized. Described by the *Financial Times* as the "IMF's star pupil,"[4] Argentina has suffered four years of recession and seen wages slashed, while unemployment rose to 20 percent and underemployment to 15 percent. In a country with some of the world's richest natural resources, one-third of Argentines are living in poverty. As one IMF-sponsored austerity plan followed another, the people of Argentina finally went into the streets to demand a halt. The result was the fall of four presidents in quick succession and the largest default of sovereign debt in history.

The collapse of Enron shows that the so-called new global economy is largely a fraud, with soaring paper profits based not on real economic activity but on speculative fiction. It reveals the true meaning of privatization, deregulation, neoliberalism, and globalization. Lord Wakeham, who oversaw the privatization of British electricity in the 1980s under Margaret Thatcher, turns out to have been a member of Enron's audit committee. Rodolfo Terragno, Argentina's former minister of public works, said he was pressured to let Enron build a pipeline in Argentina and pay just 15 percent of the international market price for gas. When George Bush was vice president of the United States, Terragno received a mysterious call from Washington. "Mr. Minister, I'm the son of the vice president," he recalls the person saying. "I'm calling you because I know you have a proposal from Enron sitting on your desk. I want to tell you that in my opinion this would be a good thing for your country."[5]

According to Human Rights Watch, "Enron was complicit in human rights abuse in India." Local groups opposed a huge Enron project in Dabhol over concerns about "corruption and the hasty negotiations over the terms of Enron's investment." Farmers complained that "the power plant had unfairly acquired their land and had diverted scarce water for its needs." Local activists raised concerns over environmental damage. Human Rights Watch documented how "police raided a fishing village where many residents opposed the power plant. They arbitrarily beat and arrested dozens of villagers, including Sadhana Bhalekar, the wife of a well-known protester against the plant. They broke down the door and window of Bhalekar's bathroom and dragged her naked out into the street, beating her with batons. . . . Bhalekar was three months pregnant at the time."[6] Nonetheless, the U.S. government lobbied India aggressively for the project and provided Enron nearly $300 million in loan guarantees. (Shortly after coming into office, Vice President Dick Cheney lobbied for the project with Sonia Gandhi, leader of India's main opposition party.[7])

Meanwhile, the promise that a global economy would "lift all boats" has only been fulfilled by a still more devastating race to the bottom. Take, for example, that paragon of export-oriented economic development, the Mexican maquiladora zone. In 2001, nearly 100 maquiladoras shut down and 200,000 maquila workers lost their jobs. The reason is not only the recession in the United States but international competition to lower the price of labor. The average take-home pay for entry-level maquiladora workers is $4 to $5 per day; with payments for transportation, meals, and government fees, a worker costs a company $2 to $3 per hour. But according to the *New York Times*, "the problem is that those figures are far higher than average wages for low-skilled factory workers in El Salvador, where the owners pay an average of $1.59 an hour; the Dominican Republic, where it is about $1.53; Indonesia, about $1.19; and China, about 43 cents."[8]

In many countries, the international race to the bottom promotes an internal race to the bottom. Mexican President Vicente Fox bragged, "In southern Mexico, we are establishing the same conditions as Guatemala or China. Maquiladoras do not have to leave Mexico. We can offer them the same level of competitiveness." But even in the desperately poor Mexican South wages aren't low enough to attract the maquiladoras abandoning northern Mexico. According to Rolando Gonzales, president of the Maquila Industry Export trade association, "instead of going south, they are going to China."[9] So are jobs from Taiwan, South Korea, Singapore, Thailand, Central and South America, and Japan.[10] In 2001, Taiwan had the steepest drop in GDP in the half century since records first were kept as "tumbling electronics exports slashed companies' profits and accelerated their flight to China, where costs are lower."[11]

The race to the bottom is forcing nations to trade away their entire systems of worker protection and job security. Even in the rich countries of Europe and North America, workers' economic security has been eroded. Economic insecurity is the face of globalization in daily life.

FROM GLOBALIZATION TO UNILATERALISM

The movement for globalization from below arose in the context of elite efforts to create new global rules and to impose common global corporate interests through institutions such as the WTO, the IMF, and the World Bank. Opponents argued that these rules favored the strong against the weak and the rich against the poor. They fought against such rules and for ones that would lead to greater economic and social justice.

The United States was a leader in the rule making, and the rules generally incorporated special benefits to the U.S. government and to U.S.-based corporations. However, the Bush administration has initiated a policy that has been dubbed "unilateralism," in contrast to the rule making that characterized the previous era of globalization. In the past, as a German official put it in the *New York Times,* Washington determined its national interest in shaping international rules, behavior, and institutions. "Now Washington seems to want to pursue its national interest in a more narrowly defined way, doing what it wants and forcing others to adapt."[12]

From its inauguration in January 2001, the Bush administration undermined one effort after another to address world problems on an international basis. It skipped out on the Kyoto Protocol on global warming, scuttled efforts to control biological weapons, refused to support an international war crimes tribunal, withdrew from efforts to limit nuclear proliferation, and renounced the Anti-Ballistic Missile Treaty.

After the September 11, 2001, attacks on the United States, the Bush administration called for a coalition against terrorism but in fact pursued a still more unilateralist policy. This was embodied in Bush's January 2002 proclamation that the United States confronted an "axis of evil." As Secretary of State Colin Powell explained, "we can't have our national interest constrained by the views of the coalition [that supported the U.S. war in Afghanistan]."[13] U.S. unilateralism is also evident in its global economic policy. In the IMF, for example, it has subordinated even neoliberal principles to short-term national policy, dictating the abandonment of Argentina, while calling for massive loans to Turkey as an ally in the "war against terrorism." Although the United States gives lip service to free trade, the Bush administration has embraced unilateral protectionism, as evidenced in its protection of the U.S. steel industry and the protectionist commitments it made to win passage of its "fast-track" trade authority.

FROM GLOBALIZATION TO GLOBALIZED REPRESSION

The advocates of globalization from above once projected a benign future in which free trade and economic cooperation would bring peace and stability. Instead we are seeing an escalation of war, preparation for war, and political repression.

U.S. unilateralism is rapidly setting the tone for a global war of all against all. Its justification for its attack on Afghanistan—that it was "harboring terrorists"—was repeated almost word for word by India, Israel, Russia, and China as they announced their own attacks on political enemies at home and abroad. The use of the "right of self-defense" as a justification for a unilateral decision to attack any country one accuses of harboring terrorists provides a pretext that all national leaders can now use to make war against anyone they choose in complete disregard of international law. Many will echo the Italian officials who recently proclaimed that "like George W. Bush they have the right to put their national interests first."[14] The catastrophic consequences can be seen in the Israeli "incursion" into the Palestinian territories.

The Bush administration's 2002 arms budget will be larger than the next nineteen largest arms budgets of other countries put together.[15] Its escalating rhetoric, from the "War against Terrorism" to the "axis of evil," has provided a model for belligerence and potentially for nuclear conflict from India and Pakistan to Israel and Palestine. This militarization of conflict has been justified by the terrorist attacks against the United States, but as a *New York Times* editorial pointed out, "Bush is using the anti-terrorism campaign to disguise an ideological agenda that has nothing to do with domestic defense or battling terrorism abroad."[16]

Another popular claim of globalization from above was that it was bringing democracy and human rights to the world. But according to a global survey by Human Rights Watch, "the anti-terror campaign led by the United States is inspiring opportunistic attacks on civil liberties around the world. . . . Some countries, such as Russia, Uzbekistan, and Egypt, are using the war on terror to justify abusive military campaigns or crackdowns on domestic political opponents. In the United States and Western Europe, measures designed to combat terrorism are threatening long-held human rights principles."[17] In place of global democratization, we are seeing globalized repression, including racial profiling, wiretapping, and military tribunals.

Meanwhile, global capitalism has replaced democracy with kleptocracy. The Enron scandal has shown that crony capitalism dominates the politics of the United States. The collapse of Argentina has led its population to conclude that virtually every political force and institution, from the supreme court to the political parties, are irredeemably corrupt. Citizens are reaching similar conclusions all over the world.

As globalization from above has become less and less defensible, its proponents have turned in desperation to smearing their critics. U.S. Trade Representative Robert Zoellick, for example, has linked opposition to U.S. trade policy to the terrorist attacks on the United States. "On September 11, America, its open society, and its ideas came under attack by a malevolence that craves our panic, retreat, and abdication of global leadership. . . . This president and this administration will fight for open markets and free trade. We will not be intimidated by those who have taken to the streets to blame trade—and America—for the world's ills."[18] (Before going to work for the government, Zoellick received $50,000 in advisory fees from Enron and had stock holdings of between $15,000 and $50,000.[19])

Globalization from above has failed—and will continue to fail—to provide what people need and want: safety, well-being, and a secure long-term future. Militarism, war, and repression will not save globalization from above. They will only further demonstrate its failure.

GLOBAL SELF-ORGANIZATION FROM BELOW

As globalization from above has grown more destructive, the constructive achievements of globalization from below in the two years since the Battle of Seattle have been impressive. An incredible range of movements and concerns that once seemed unrelated or even antagonistic have learned to cooperate in the face of corporate-led globalization from above.

Activists around the world have forged a new internationalism with a global vision. They have developed organizational forms—ranging from global advocacy networks and temporary affinity groups to global forums—to share ideas and coordinate actions over vast areas with a minimum of hierarchy. They have rediscovered the hidden power of people to force change by withdrawing their consent from established institutions. They have educated hundreds of millions of people around the world about the problems of globalization. They have established themselves as a global opposition force and supplanted right-wing nationalists as the leading critics of globalization. They have put the advocates of globalization from above on the defensive and forced a major change in the rhetoric, if not yet the reality, of global institutions.

The most dramatic expressions of globalization from below have been the demonstrations challenging international elite gatherings from Melbourne to

Prague, from Quebec to Manila, and from Washington, D.C., to Genoa. But these demonstrations are only the visible tip of a movement composed primarily of grassroots organizing and people-to-people cooperation across national borders.

The World Social Forum (WSF) in Porto Alegre, Brazil, has emerged as a global assembly for globalization from below's discussion and networking. In 2002, the second WSF brought together 51,300 participants, including 15,230 delegates representing 4,909 organizations from 131 countries.[20] The program for its workshops, demonstrations, and other events ran 151 tabloid pages. Its slogan, "Another World Is Possible," has flung open the discussion of global alternatives. Although some complain that the WSF has not produced a blueprint for global social reform, its emphasis on pluralism and diversity manifests the spirit of a movement that seeks a future based on open global dialogue, not decisions imposed by a new elite.

PROLIFERATING LILLIPUTIANS

The Lilliput strategy, in which grassroots groups cooperate across national borders to outflank corporations and other centers of power, remains at the core of globalization from below. The campaign to make drugs for AIDS patients available at a reasonable price in poor countries provides a leading example.

Writer Esther Kaplan describes a packed meeting in a stultifying room in a former church in North Philadelphia, "an area of falling-down porches and abandoned storefronts," of a group that might be expected to find the global economy a rather remote concern—recovering drug addicts. But John Bell of ACT UP/Philadelphia, a former war veteran with AIDS, was recruiting for a "Stop Global AIDS march." He began, "Hi. My name is John, and I'm an addict and an alcoholic." According to Kaplan, "as he went on to talk about his gratitude for his lifesaving med[icine]s, it seemed only natural that he'd invite the 100 or so assembled to stand up for HIVers worldwide who don't have access to the same meds." A few weeks later, twelve packed buses from Philadelphia rolled up in front of the United Nations, turning the Stop Global AIDS march into "an energetic African-American protest rally." According to Bell, they were "making the connections between local and global in terms of health care and AIDS. We have been preparing people to be not only U.S. citizens, but citizens of the world."[21]

An international coalition including Doctors Without Borders and religious networks around the world generated thousands of letters to drug companies and the U.S. government demanding that they stop using patent laws to restrict the sale of AIDS drugs in poor countries. And there were some results. In April 2001, a front-page article in the *Christian Science Monitor* titled "Drug Firms Yield to Cry of the Poor" reported that "39 international pharmaceutical companies unconditionally withdrew a lawsuit against the South African government aimed at barring the country from importing cheap anti-AIDS drugs." And in June 2001, the *Financial Times* reported, "The U.S. government . . . dropped its complaint against Brazil's patent law at the World Trade Organization, dealing a fresh blow to the leading global pharmaceutical companies' business in the developing world."[22]

Before the November 2001 meetings of the WTO in Doha, Qatar, AIDS activists, NGO representatives, and third world officials met and drew up a declaration stating that nothing in the WTO rules covering patents could prevent governments from safeguarding public health.[23] Daniel Berman of Doctors Without Borders reported the results from Doha:

> Since Seattle there has been a seismic shift. Two years ago many developing countries felt they were powerless against the will of the wealthy countries and their drug companies. Here in Doha more than 80 countries came together and negotiated in mass. It was this solidarity that led to a strong affirmation that TRIPS [Trade Related Intellectual Property Rights] "can and should be interpreted in a manner to protect public health." In practical terms, this means that countries are not at the mercy of multinationals when they practice price gouging.[24]

NEW FORMS OF GRASSROOTS SELF-ORGANIZATION

Popular resistance to the devastation caused by neoliberal policies in Argentina has revealed new possibilities for mass direct action against globalization from above. With 35 percent of workers unemployed or underemployed, a militant movement known as the *piqueteros,* a large proportion of them unemployed women, began blocking highways and then negotiating with the authorities for subsistence programs and public works employment. "They don't delegate any leaders to go downtown. They make the government come to the highways, and the people there discuss what they should demand and what they should accept."[25]

The example of the *piqueteros* spread to a more and more disgruntled population. Discontent came to a head as the government accepted even greater austerity demands from the IMF and imposed a state of siege to suppress popular protest. On the night of December 19, 2001, "people from all over the capital had taken to the streets to bang pots and pans, a traditional symbol of protest in Latin America, and to march on Congress and the presidential palace." The next day, "spontaneous street demonstrations" forced President Fernando de la Rúa to resign.[26]

That in turn led to the emergence of a new organizational form. "A bunch of us who met during the march that night decided that what we were doing should become a permanent, directed effort and not just a one-time thing," a participant recalled. "We wanted the fall of de la Rúa to mark the beginning of something, not the end." Out of the demonstrations grew "a new and increasingly assertive civic movement known as the 'self-convened neighborhood assemblies.'" Argentines are now "meeting after work and on weekends not just to vent their wrath at politicians but to organize and debate solutions to the country's crisis." Most neighborhoods in cities and towns across the country have their own assembly. "The movement is largely unstructured, with individual units communicating through web sites, and deliberately informal, with members ranging from middle-aged professionals in La-coste shirts to students with spiked hair and nose rings." A nationwide outdoor assembly brought groups together from all over the country. They decided that "they would continue to sponsor weekly protest meetings [at] the presidential palace."[27]

The convergence of the unemployed picketers and the newly impoverished middle-class *cacerolazo* pot-and-pan bangers has been embodied in the slogan *Pi-quete y cacerola, la lucha es una sola*—"pickets and pans, same struggle."[28] A leading newspaper editorialized that "a country cannot work in a state of permanent popular deliberation" and warned that "such mechanisms of popular deliberation" as the neighborhood assemblies "present a danger, since because of their very nature they can develop into something like that sinister model of power, the 'soviets.'"[29]

The people of Argentina have shown that popular movements can force even repressive and neoliberal governments to halt ruinous debt servicing. But when the government of one country abandons neoliberal policies, it faces devastating reprisals—as are already being planned against Argentina. A possible next step might be the kind of international solidarity sometimes referred to as a "debtors' cartel," "debtors' union," or "debtors' united front." If a number of debtor countries threatened to stop servicing their debts simultaneously, they would pose a devastating threat to global financial stability and thereby change the global balance of power. Such a strategy could become a prime weapon of popular movements demanding that the third world be freed from the chains of debt slavery.[30]

ISOLATING U.S. UNILATERALISM

The unilateralism of the Bush administration poses a barrier to nearly every initiative attempted by the global justice movement, from global warming agreements and protection of human rights to affordable AIDS treatment and sustainable development for poor countries. However, that unilateralism is provoking a reaction. According to *New York Times* columnist Thomas Friedman, "Europeans have embraced President Bush's formulation that an 'axis of evil' threatens world peace. There's only one small problem. President Bush thinks the axis of evil is Iran, Iraq, and North Korea, and the Europeans think it's Donald Rumsfeld, Dick Cheney, and Condi [Condoleezza] Rice."[31]

European Union (EU) officials warn of a rift opening up between Europe and the United States wider than at any time during the past half century. Chris Patten, the EU commissioner for international relations, said that it is time that European governments spoke up and stopped Washington before it goes into "unilateralist overdrive." He added, "Gulliver can't go it alone, and I don't think it's helpful if we regard ourselves as so Lilliputian that we can't speak up and say it." Patten called on Europe's fifteen member states "to put aside their traditional wariness of angering the United States and to speak up, forging an international stance of their own on issues ranging from the Middle East to global warming."[32]

Such a response—at both the governmental and grassroots levels—can begin to isolate the Bush administration's ideological agenda. For example, immediately after the United States rejected a modified version of the Kyoto climate accord, 178 countries went ahead and accepted it. (There is no contradiction between such action at the top and a more grassroots approach: After other governments accepted the accord, the city of Seattle announced that it would unilaterally abide by it and committed to cutting its carbon emissions by more than the required percentage.)

THE CONVERGENCE OF PEACE AND JUSTICE

Globalization from below is grounded in an understanding that no community or country can solve its economic problems by trying to beat out others—that the result of such competition is instead a race to the bottom in which all lose. It argues that the world's people and environment will suffer unless a global people's movement imposes rules on countries and corporations to block the destructive effects of that competition. It calls for worldwide cooperation to protect human and labor rights, the environment, and people's livelihoods.

This same kind of understanding is now being applied to global conflict. The September 11 attacks on the United States show that the era is over in which nation-states—even the world's single military superpower—can protect their people. So does the catastrophic escalation of violence in Israel and Palestine and the potential for nuclear conflict between Pakistan and India. There is no longer such a thing as national security; security must be global to be secure. Broad human interests require limits on the use of violence by anyone in the world, whether they initiate their attacks from caves in the wilderness or war rooms in national capitals.

When Israeli tanks charged into the West Bank in March 2002, they were met by another invasion. More than 500 courageous nonviolent activists, known as "the internationals," poured into Ramallah and other Palestinian towns to serve as "human shields" to protect Palestinians. Many of them, including the noted French farm protester Jose Bove, were veterans of the global justice movement. Observers indicated that they may have played a role in limiting some attacks on Palestinian communities and in preventing the total destruction of the Palestinian Authority headquarters. They represent a new level of direct intervention in international conflicts by global movement activists.

BEYOND "ANTIGLOBALIZATION"

The many strands that came together to form globalization from below were initially united by little beyond their opposition to globalization from above. But their common interests go far deeper than that. They share a common interest in putting the world on a safer, saner, and less destructive path than global elites currently offer. Therefore, globalization from below is less and less presenting itself as a movement against globalization. Lori Wallach of Public Citizen observed at the WSF that calling the movement "anti-global" only plays into the hands of the corporate elites. "Better we say what we are for. We are *for* democracy, diversity, and equity."[33] At a simultaneous "Another World Is Possible" rally in New York, Columbia University student Yvonne Liu of Students for Global Justice met cheers when she said, "We are not an antiglobalization movement. We are against *corporate-led* globalization. We are a global justice movement."[34]

Globalization from above is certainly doing its part to encourage a worldwide backlash in favor of globalization from below. A survey sponsored by the World Economic Forum found that nearly one in two citizens and majorities in half of the twenty-five countries surveyed "support people who take part in peaceful demonstrations against globalization because they are supporting my interests."[35]

Some Questions for the Future

Because globalization from below is developing so rapidly, and because the conditions to which it must respond are changing so fast, it has new questions posed to it almost daily. Here are a few questions for the next round of discussions:

How deep is the division between the United States and the other countries that once composed the "Washington Consensus"? How should the movement for globalization from below relate to that split?

As globalization from below moves beyond economic questions to become increasingly involved with international political and military conflicts, how does it avoid becoming a pawn of one or another side in such conflicts or an inadvertent vehicle for racial and ethnic bigotry and hatred?

As globalization from below is increasingly smeared as resembling or aiding terrorism, what needs to be done to clarify the differences between its methods and those of terrorism?

What are the implications of U.S. unilateralism for the IMF, World Bank, WTO, and other international economic institutions? Does it require rethinking of issues regarding their reform and/or abolition? Does it open new opportunities for transnational initiatives in regional agencies or those specialized in particular areas like environment, labor rights, or rural development?

What is the significance of the emergence of new grassroots organizational forms like the neighborhood and unemployed councils in Argentina? Can they provide an alternative means for mass political participation? Can they link with other aspects of globalization from below?

While what was once labeled the "antiglobalization movement" is increasingly asserting its global character, there is a strong awareness of the problems of organizational forms that go beyond the national, indeed, even beyond the local level. What forms of organization beyond the local level are appropriate and acceptable?

How can the "network of networks" that makes up globalization from below organize itself to maximize coordination and mutual support, minimize unnecessary duplication and division, and still provide an open, freely developing framework in which all can put forward their ideas and proposals?

How should globalization from below envision the process of change? Is it like a series of national reforms? A series of national revolutions? A world revolution? The taking over of corporations by those they affect? The formation of a democratic world government? Or something unlike any of these?

Globalization from above is leading millions of people around the world to organize on their own and others' behalf. While globalization from above may self-destruct through its own internal contradictions, its failure does not guarantee that another, better world can be realized. That depends on the commitment, integrity, wisdom, and unity of those who are forging globalization from below.

NOTES

1. Louis Uchitelle, "Foreign Executives Reject American Optimism Over Economic Recovery," *New York Times,* February 3, 2002, p. 16.

2. Joseph Stiglitz, "A Boost That Goes Nowhere," *Washington Post,* November 11, 2001, p. B1.

3. For our analysis of the origins of contemporary globalization in the crisis of the 1970s, see Jeremy Brecher and Tim Costello, *Global Village or Global Pillage: Economic Reconstruction from the Bottom Up,* 2nd ed. (Boston: South End Press, 1998), Chapter 3, "The Dynamics of Globalization."

4. Quoted in Lee Sustar, "How IMF Policies Led to Disaster," *Socialist Worker,* Vol. 389 (January 11, 2002), p. 7. Available online at http://www.socialistworker.org/389Pages/389_06_IMFInArgentina.shtml.

5. Alan Cowell, "Scandal Draws Critics Wherever Enron Went," *New York Times,* February 3, 2002, p. 27.

6. Human Rights Watch, "Enron: History of Human Rights Abuse in India." Available online at www.hrw.org/press/2002/01/enron 012302.htm.

7. Richard W. Stevenson, "Enron Received Many Loans from U.S. for Foreign Projects During the 1990s," *New York Times,* February 21, 2002, p. C10.

8. Ginger Thompson, "Fallout of U.S. Recession Drifts South into Mexico," *New York Times,* December 26, 2001, p. C1.

9. Ibid.

10. William Greider, "Pro Patria, Pro Mundo," *The Nation,* Vol. 273 (November 12, 2001), p. 22; William Greider, "A New Giant Sucking Sound," *The Nation,* Vol. 273 (December 31, 2001), pp. 22ff.

11. Bloomberg News, "Taiwan: Economy Slumps" *New York Times,* February 23, 2002, p. C2.

12. Steven Erlanger, "Bush's Move on ABM Pact Gives Pause to Europeans," *New York Times,* December 13, 2001, p. A19.

13. Quoted in David E. Sanger, "U.S. Goal Seems Clear, and the Team Complete," *New York Times,* February 13, 2002, p. A18.

14. Melinda Henneberger, "Italy Cooling on Europe, and 2 Aides Explain Why," *New York Times,* February 17, 2002, pp. 1, 13.

15. Seumas Milne, "Can the US Be Defeated?" *The Guardian* (London), February 14, 2002, p. 21.

16. Editors, "The Axis-of-Inefficiency Budget," *New York Times,* February 5, 2002, p. A24.

17. "Anti-Terror Campaign Cloaking Human Rights Abuse," *Human Rights News,* January 16, 2002. Available online at www.hrw.org/press/2002/01/wr2002.htm.

18. Robert B. Zoellick, "American Trade Leadership: What Is at Stake," speech at the Institute for International Economics, September 24, 2001, Federal News Service.

19. Dana Milbank and Glenn Kessler, "Enron's Influence Reached Deep into Administration," *Washington Post,* January 18, 2002, p. A1.

20. Clarinha Glock, "World Social Forum: Peace, Health and Little Violence," Inter-Press Service/Terraviva. Available online at www.ipsnews.net/terraviva/05_peace.shtml. Terraviva presented extensive daily coverage of the WSF.

21. Esther Kaplan, "The Mighty ACT UP Has Fallen: The Philadelphia Story," *POZ* (November 2001), pp. 28–33.

22. Rena Singer, "Drug Firms Yield to Cry of the Poor," *Christian Science Monitor,* April 20, 2001, p. 1; Geoff Dyer, David Pilling, Vanessa Valkin, and Frances Williams, "US Climbs Down Over Brazil's Patent Law," *Financial Times,* June 26, 2001, p. 8.

23. Editors, "The Urgency of Cheaper Drugs," *New York Times,* October 31, 2001, p. A14.

24. "How to Save Lives Without Even Trying," *Frontline* (India), Vol. 18 (November 24–December 7, 2001).

25. James Petras, "You Have to Take Action from Below," *Socialist Worker,* Vol. 389 (January 11, 2002), pp. 6–7. Available online at http://www.socialistworker.org/389Pages/389_06_PetrasInterview.shtml.

26. Larry Rohter, "Roused by Economic Crisis, Argentina's Middle Class Finally 'Gets Involved,'" *New York Times,* February 3, 2002, pp. 1, 8.

27. Ibid. See also Marcela Valente, "Argentina's Rebellion in the Neighborhoods," InterPress Service, February 14, 2002.

28. Jordi Martorell, "Argentina: National Workers' Assembly Meeting—A Big Step Forward." Available online at http://www.marxist.com/Latinam/argentina_ant_meeting0202.html.

29. *La Nacion,* February 14 and February 17, 2002, quoted in Martorell, "Argentina."

30. For a fuller discussion of this strategy, see "Debtors of the World, Unite!: Does 'Globalization from Below' Open New Possibilities for Resistance?" *International Socialist Review,* Vol. 19 (August–September 2001), pp. 116–121; see also www.villageorpillage.org.

31. Thomas L. Friedman, "Crazier Than Thou," *New York Times,* February 13, 2002, p. A31.

32. Jonathan Freedland, "Patten Lays into Bush's America: Fury at President's 'Axis of Evil' Speech," *The Guardian* (London), February 9, 2002, p. 1.

33. Marc Cooper, "From Protest to Politics: A Report from Porto Alegre," *The Nation,* Vol. 274 (March 11, 2002), pp. 11–16.

34. Liza Featherstone, "A Recovered Movement," *The Nation,* February 4, 2002. Available online at http://www.thenation.com.

35. "People around the World Increasingly Favour Globalization but Worry about Jobs, Poverty and Environment," World Economic Forum, February 1, 2002. Available online at www.weforum.org/site/homepublic.nsf.

15

Geography Financialized

RANDY MARTIN

Driving down a gleaming new superhighway, a stretch limo speeds by a sign that reads "Globalization kills." Indeed it does. But the more difficult question for those who did not make it into the limousine could readily be "How is globalization lived?" When globalization is simply another means of spreading misery, it is treated as history made behind people's backs. But if such conceptions of history excise from consideration the very political agency they seek, it is important to grasp how globalization offers, however unevenly, ways to participate in its promised journey. The culture of globalization would then entail understanding what people make with what is done to them.[1]

The ascent of financial capital has been a hallmark of integrating and disintegrating world markets. In the course of the past thirty years, finance has become not only capital for others but a way of constituting the self. Finance has gotten personal as people are invited to manage their own fate by deciding how to borrow and invest. As millions engage in this process, finance no longer belongs only to the bankers but organizes terms under which people are forced to live together and understand their prospects. This incorporation of money management into daily life can be termed financialization, which is the idiom in which globalization is lived.

The yarn of financialization has been spun as a kind of great cloak that would offer shelter to all. However, it does not share the universal ambitions of other self-anointed civilizing missions, however unctuous they may be. This is not to say that Enlightenment aspirations come to a screeching halt the minute the perquisites of finance walk through the door. It is not simply that the reign of finance yields winners and losers but that it at once justifies why the latter need not be considered while it continues to rely upon the bereft for its success. Geographic thought assumes that very different phenomena are brought together within a common space. The earth trundles along with its eruptions and fissures unfolding across the millennia, but ways of imagining the planet shift at a faster pace.

Financialization, too, augurs a reconfigured geography, certainly not anything utterly new, but it places new pressure on a familiar landscape. This emergent spatial principle conflates the internal geography of class with the external geography of nations. That both the inside and the outside obey a Trinitarian scheme (rich, middle, poor—first, second, third world) only increases the confusion, as the new divisions encamp on existing partitions.

THE POOR GET MORE

None of the triumph connected to the great nineties boom in which financialization blossomed speaks to those left off the bandwagon. In the 1960s expansion, elimination of poverty could be considered a sign of good faith in the universality of progress. Between 1959 and 1973, poverty rates in the United States were cut in half, from 22.4 percent to 11.1 percent. In the nineties, the reduction came late and was miserly by comparison. Not until 1999 did poverty fall below what it had been at the peak of the prior business cycle (1989), and although poverty was on the rise between 1989 and 1995, it fell by only one percentage point (14.1 to 13.1) in the second half of the 1990s so that the remarkable nineties actually had higher rates of poverty than the previous decade.[2] Beyond questions of redistribution of wealth, the very shape of how expansion relates to population was being reconfigured.

The more limited vision of what can count as gain is captured by Andrew Leyshon and Nigel Thrift's phrase "geographies of financial exclusion."[3] If exclusion is indeed part of the system, then the issue may be less who can gain access than who accesses gain. When a standard risk calculus is applied to the poor, money becomes more expensive for them to borrow because of longer terms for payment, less collateral, and lower future wealth—all determinants of loan risk likely to result in default. Lacking property, poor people are more likely to borrow to supplement wages, to pay medical bills, to make ends meet. Yet the likelihood of a negative outcome is increased by exorbitant interest rates. Michael Hudson found inner-city check-cashing outlets in the United States that charge up to 2,000 percent annual interest on short-term loans. He has identified a "poverty industry" that takes in hundreds of billions of dollars a year. Such a lucrative market is not left to community-based entrepreneurs. Hudson reported, "More and more, the merchants who profit from the disadvantaged are owned or bankrolled by the big names of Wall Street—Ford, Citibank, Nationsbank, BankAmerica, American Express, Western Union. Lesser known Wall Street companies are also grabbing a piece of the action. Add up all the businesses that bottom-feed on the 'fringe economy' and you'll come up with a market of $200 to $300 billion a year."[4]

One thing that the large consumer credit houses possess is the means to badger people in default. In practices that eventually led to a class-action lawsuit, the conglomerate ITT had collection agents who called an unemployed woman with a

$2,000 loan "and her friends and relatives night and day, at one point demanding that she send them her unemployment benefits."[5] Bad credit forms its own penal colony that, far from disconnecting people from the attentions of finance, renders indebtedness a total institution. Hardship debt burden is pegged at 40 percent of annual income, a distinction that increases as income lessens. In 1998, for example, amidst the cornucopia of a boom economy, 2.1 percent of those households with annual incomes of $100,000 or more were in the high debt burden category, whereas of those taking in less than $10,000, 32 percent were so designated.[6] Financial troubles bring intensified relations, however unwanted it may be. Redlining, declined credit, and other forms of exclusion bring added scrutiny and opportunity for disciplinary contact with financial regimens.

Poverty results in not a lack of but an excess of attention, both for those subject to it and for the general morality tales that are drawn from those who give up privacy for public demonstration of need. If the universal promises of progress are to be abandoned or renegotiated, the financially excluded cannot be invisible but must be placed on display through novel approaches to their self-management. What is touted as newfound independence for the poor rests upon different lines of dependency on vouchers, credits, and small loans connected to the various programs of reform. This is not to deny the material improvements that may ensue from even the most hard-nosed approaches to disciplining the poor. The logic is that the poor must find their own way and therefore cannot stake a claim on the huge masses of wealth that the financial expansion generated for its own.

The dependency involved is part of the gendering of poverty and translates across the seas into the special place of women in the emerging industries of microcredit. This approach to managing poor populations erases the boundary between first and third worlds and is characteristic of the new geography.[7] Without doubt the partition had served the constituents differently. The self-designation of third world was meant to open opportunities for development through nonalignment and in that regard was not inconsistent with the universalist aspirations of progress. Since socialist nations outside of Eastern Europe and the Soviet Union could also be part of the third world, as China and Cuba were, the term could make reference to a postcolonial world where the critique of capitalist imperialism translated into support for various revolutionary movements.

For that intersection of the North and West said to constitute the first world, the distant third was a source of cheap labor and materials to help subsidize government transfers to citizens who could all count themselves as beneficiaries of global inequalities. The emerging global alliance of women that received some organizational attention at the 1995 Beijing Conference on Women speaks to a condition that cuts against the presumption of citizenship-aligned privilege.[8] Certainly it was always true that working people sent to war against each other shared more of life's conditions than those doing the sending, but the belief in the righteousness of the nation and the privileges of citizenship served as a palliative.

With financialization's more parsimonious state, the case is tougher to make

that the interests are so clearly apart and that with abandonment of welfare enti-
tlements, sticking with the state is such a good bet for the citizens of the North.
No wonder military planners are so concerned about body counts when they de-
ploy soldiers in the former third world. High casualty rates may bring unwelcome comparisons with what the state now offers in exchange for the ultimate
sacrifice. Combat, we are told, remains the preserve of men. That reserves for
women the demonstration of what the new entente can yield. The fully financialized benefit from the powers of anonymous ownership through securitization
(the bundling of titles to consumer items like cars or homes that are then sold as
stock would be). In contrast, poor women are to lift themselves out of poverty
through the disciplining effects of local powers.

One vehicle has been the advent of the Village Bank, a microfinance institution backed by a government, a nongovernmental organization (NGO), or a private bank. Unlike the state or development agencies, these banks operate through
"peer pressure,"[9] in which village authorities ensure that debts are repaid. This has
led to violence and abuse against women otherwise deemed good credit risks. Such
baleful consequences have been documented in studies of the initial model of these
banks, the Grameen Bank of Bangladesh.[10] These findings should give pause to
those advocates of communitarian solutions to the anomic conditions of the modern world. There is no reason to assume that microcredit has the same consequences everywhere, but at the very least, this should introduce more caution than
has been the case in assuming that local, interpersonal attachments can circulate as
a kind of universal good. Although it is impressive that such practices have touched
millions, far larger is the number of people who are left out of the small business
assumptions of producing goods for exchange that cannot be readily applied to
subsistence agriculture or waged work.

The ambitions of microcredit know no bounds. It means to be as at home
with the poor in Oakland as with the poor in Bangalore and, by so doing, to alter
the way in which poverty at a world scale becomes part of global finance.[11] In the
1980s, the global poor fell into that vast trench of the "unbankable," which was
how then CEO of Citicorp, John Reed, regarded four-fifths of the planet's population unworthy of his attention.[12] Today this perception no longer holds. In 1997,
the first Microcredit Summit was organized with the goal of creating a poverty-free
planet by 2025 through the extension of entrepreneurial activity. By 1999, microcredit had been extended to more than 23 million clients, 75 percent of whom
were women. According to the summit's annual report, "experience shows that
women are a good credit risk, and that woman-run businesses tend to benefit family members more directly than those run by men."[13]

As some studies of the Grameen Bank suggest, being a good credit risk may
not be good for women. Far from creating self-sufficiency, the global initiative
for microcredit, were it to succeed, might more readily increase dependency. On
the other hand, there is no doubt that the project is being taken seriously by national leaders, such as Mexico's own head entrepreneur, President Vicente Fox,

who hosted the 2001 Latin American summit in Puebla with a plenary theme of "Working Towards Institutional Financial Self-sufficiency While Maintaining a Commitment to Serving the Poorest Families." Presently, through egrants.org, it is possible to make "donations" to the summit online. Can securitization of the poorest be far behind? Under the old geography, citizens of the first world consumed overseas goods made cheap by labor kept at bay by repressive states. The new arrangement indentures women who may risk a beating to maintain their good credit rating for overseas investors. Past development schemes rested upon the large-scale infusion of first-world industrial products to create urban centers of cheap labor. In contrast, the financialization of the poor can proceed with comparatively little investment. Bamboo stools can be made without advances in public health or infrastructure, although deforestation of bamboo stands may prove a problem. The risks to secure labor and materials would be borne by women but offer investment opportunities for others, converting their debt into a life-threatening situation that George Caffentzis has called a "productive crisis."[14]

The solution to the pathologies of poverty's high risk can be found in the former third world. The poor enter into bondage, where stigma is traded for low risk.[15] The price of low risk that microcredit advertises is low return. In this, the poorest entrepreneurs may be lifted out of poverty but not into the embrace of the higher returns that financialization promises. These contradictions are not lost on the women who are the objects of these schemes.[16] The world summits meant to manage them have become unwitting conduits for the articulation of new critiques and demands, as the financiers have found wherever they try to meet, be it Seattle, Washington, Prague, Ottawa, Göteborg, Genoa, or New York. The WTO, IMF, G8, World Economic Forum (WEF)—the conveners of these various meetings— are not one organization, but they have been melded into a single ruling interest by the protests. What is typically presented as the disruptive antics of a few privileged anarchists from the Ruckus Society needs to be linked more directly to the global conversion of poverty into lines of credit that lead from the villages of Bangladesh to the mobile encampments of the World Bank.

The World Bank has already signaled its retreat from the large-scale development projects it had helped to underwrite only a few years back, and microcredit speaks to the economics of its embrace of "localization" ("sharing responsibility for raising revenues") as a way forward.[17] Such shared responsibility is supposed to issue from greater cultural understanding of how customs and traditions can be invoked to involve people in the bank's proposals. The celebrations of the local are the refraction in cultural terms of development's own retooling for the world. Far from letting institutions off the hook, their meetings embrace a kind of global mediation of the local that they have claimed to champion.

In addition to criticizing the closed-door arcane nature of world finance, the protesters point to the instability of financializing populism itself. The better organized and prepared the protesters become and the more extensive the affiliated groups (the protest for the Genoa meeting in July 2001 listed 700), the more the heads of state seem to take up the agenda of the streets as their own (debt relief, environmental protection, human and labor rights), even as they disavow the legitimacy of the protesters. What might have once been restricted to technical deliberations has now been recast in more ambitious terms.

Although risk management for the poor is organized at the local level, it circulates globally with unexpected political consequences. Microfinance is dangled before the global poor so that they might identify themselves as entrepreneurs and not as laborers or part of a surplus population. Credit is easier to distribute than land, but it has a delocalizing aspect. By lumping the poor together across nations and regions, the World Bank and the various financial summits that emulate it help to define a new geographic continuity, a shared space of risk, that as much organizes a chain of command that leads to their door as it applies self-management to stem the need for development. Among the nearly 3 billion people living on less than $2 a day, there is still plenty of room for exclusion, but the presence of so many entrepreneurs around them is somehow supposed to lift their boats as well.

It would be foolish to think that the mere presence of a global space of poverty would wipe out national, regional, or subnational affiliations.[18] Just as globalization has reinforced certain national affinities, so too the nation-state's indifference to incorporating all within its borders tears violently at any conception of homogeneous global space, even of the poor or disenfranchised. What financialization of the poor has done is to make poverty something other than lack of necessities. It is both a means of gain for others (which it always has been) and a principle of association in its own right (which it has been only spasmodically). The geographic interest of the poor lies in the gap between the claims of an interest in eliminating poverty and the dependence upon it. Equally, this interest is torn between its transcendence of any juridical boundary and its complete delineation of persons according to their access to credit and category of risk.

GIRDLING THE MIDDLE

The financialization of daily life turns out not to be for everyone, or more precisely, it becomes the means through which people become measurably different. Before the world's poor broke up the party, socializing ownership seemed to make room for all. Instead, we need to imagine the space that girdles the middle of the globe. Those at the midriff of this terrestrial orb have experienced unprecedented population growth rates. The question is whether there is enough space in the bulge to center the world's aspirations. If the middle has lost its utopian promise, from where does the vision spring to excite people about the new hegemony of finance? More often than not, hope is laid at the door of technology. Unlike previous incarnations of technological salvation, the present one seems poorly equipped to do the job. Many are the approaches to the historical evaluation of technological change. The proliferation of computers that drive financialization have been assessed in terms of their increases to overall productivity and their compression of social time and space. The spread of computers is also credited with foregrounding knowledge and information in industrial production and reconfiguring the relations between culture and nature as machine functions become intrinsic to human expression.[19]

The paradox identified for progress, namely, that the more its measures advance, the farther away it appears as an ideal, seems apt for the myriad pronouncements of technological revolution as well. It is possible to track the dissemination of computers and Internet connections globally and evaluate obstacles to access and encroachments to privacy. For example, by dint of personal computer ownership alone, U.S. households possess about a third of the world's total, while almost half of the Internet users reside in North America.[20] China, on the other hand, a nation comprising one-fifth of the world's population (1.2 billion), has an estimated 40 million personal computers and 7 million Internet users as of late 1999.[21] It is easy to say that all this could change in the next few years, but the question is, how does one assess this difference? Excluding Japan, in the Asia-Pacific region there is now an Internet user population of almost 13 million who generate nearly three-quarters of a billion dollars worth of exchange. By the year 2004, users are projected to be at 100 million and revenue is expected to top $87.5 billion.[22] This reflects dramatic growth, but highly uneven development.

Appraising the subjective state that results from a new technology, however, is a more daunting exercise. It is not as if the technology produces a singular experience that could be used as a benchmark for future changes. Rather, the claims for how technology will affect life need to be assessed in their own terms. The power of technology to dazzle, to bewilder, to reveal a future better than the present rests more on its powers of spectacle than productivity. Whether in advertising, television, or film, the public has been flooded with a marketing intensity unrivaled for other home appliances. When compared with diffusion of the telephone, the refrigerator, or the automobile, the dissemination of computers has been more rapid. As a picture of life idealized, the computer has had a tougher time, though not by want of exposure. It seemed that from the 1980s on, few Hollywood movie products were without a computer in one scene or another. Perhaps the redundancy of one screen on another canceled the little one out, but the familiar clacking of keys and cursory movement hardly signify kinetic or dramatic excitement.

If not a revolution, the information reform, at its simplest, makes two promises: to make communications faster and to bring them closer. Speed is calibrated most prosaically with a constant, in this case the eighteen-month turnaround for doubling the power of microprocessors, a marketing strategy elevated to the status of a "law" named for Intel cofounder Gordon Moore. Each generation of Pentium chip has accelerated processing capacity to the point where images can move across the screen at the rate they would on television. E-mail communication is more encumbered by the speed of typing (or speaking) than by rates of transmission. Even assuming that what people craved was speed, the computer replaces the experience of a body hurtling through space with the fixed message on the screen, and it is more likely to engender frustration at the expectation of instantaneous exchange than to register the pleasure of having connected more quickly than previously possible.

Where speed is most germane to financial markets is in the turnaround time for transactions. There is some interval of time between the placement of a stock trade and its actual settlement or payment. In 1995, the industry standard shifted from five days to three days. The new initiative, slated for completion by 2004 and considered the most ambitious to date, is called T + 1 and aims to realize a trade within one day. By decreasing turnaround time, not only does the rate of accumulation increase, but the risk exposure is diminished. For example, in 2000, roughly $375 billion in trades was outstanding on a daily basis, so that within any three-day cycle, more than $1 trillion was unsettled. At the present rate of expansion of trading volume, exposure would reach nearly $3 trillion dollars by 2004. If a company's share price plummets or there is general market volatility of the sort tied to the Asian or dotcom meltdowns, millions of dollars can be lost in hours. T + 1 intends to synchronize information exchange globally and approach real-time processing of stock transactions.[23] The ability to respond to and profit from risk should increase accordingly. Although the sums of money involved are staggering to consider, the speedup is most likely to affect the working conditions of the 772,200 employees of the securities industries.[24] They can expect to experience volatility in a way that few others can.

In terms of propinquity, interactivity and the intimacy of mediated space would seem to take live interaction as its model rather than its object of transcendence. In an effort to create a sense of brandable permanence amidst product volatility, simplicity and user friendliness are presently the watchwords of Web design, not dazzle or extravagance. No longer exotic, the Web means to become a quotidian workhorse through which corporate logos and identities provide the intimacy that bridges public and private, home and work. The entertainment functions of the Web are pornographic both in content and by formal design (or its absence). The proliferation of pornography was already well underway with the videocassette, and the self-expression of everyday designers and chatters could be considered a kind of libidinal excess that helps to swell the spaces of the private precisely when they are matters of such public interest.

Yet far from progress's ideal of the autonomous individual, this highly mediated self unfolds with an eye ever over the shoulder. The financial correlate is that online investment allows you to become more intimate with your money, or more precisely, to live transactions as a kind of intimacy. A recent Morgan-Stanley television ad invites you to "move your money" through corporate affinity. The camera pans a line of men's shoes waiting to be shined until it pauses on an elegant women's pump. The voice-over beckons, "Welcome to the new old boys club. Less old, less boys." Visually, what starts as a penchant for shoes allows all to rub shoulders. Corporate comfort this, and not the reminder that you'll have to click to get it. The computer screen intimacy may aspire to the suspended disbelief of the proscenium theater's fourth wall, which, to create its closeness, must make itself disappear—a spectacle of closeness that erases itself.

Whatever its prejudices, this vision of the future is very different from ones of the recent past based on the spectacular images of growth and consumption. Critics like Jean Baudrillard made a career of announcing and bemoaning the spectacle. In *The Consumer Society,* originally published in 1970, Baudrillard spoke of the "miraculous status of consumption" and the "vicious circle of growth."[25] For Baudrillard, perpetual growth through the accumulation of a profusion of objects is the route to a profaned affluence, a society without myth or history other than further consumption. Just as the retreat from the principle that growth must anchor a market economy has not stopped practical concern that GDP continues to increase annually (only to maintain a slightly lower rate of 2.5 percent versus 5 percent), so too the disenchantment with consumerism has done nothing to curtail real consumption.

Although the myths of growth and consumption have fallen, it is not so easy to pull open the curtain and reveal the truths that the wizard wanted to keep secret. Transparency and low rates of inflation are concepts that still garner affirmation in polls, but the wholesale production of a mythos, if far less measurable, has been shaken at its foundations. For all the work that financialization demands, even for all the wealth it delivers to its remade middle, it has produced a regimen of discipline without a prescriptive pleasure. Margaret Thatcher, who did as much as anyone to issue in the reign of finance, was fond of saying, "There is no alternative" (or TINA). Tiny Tina is now grown up and still she sees no future for herself.

Though it is intended as such, the abdication of any utopian promise to market life should not be taken as a general attribute of humanity. TINA is self-referential and simply leaves the field wide open for others to enter their accounts. The massive advertising campaign unleashed under "The Fall of Communism" did little to explain what had been or what was to come, but it certainly meant to get capitalism off the hook of needing to promise any dramatic life transformation. That financialization is decidedly not a utopian project makes plain how the market delivers its wants and amasses wealth without answering the question of what it is for. If the middle was once all about insulated security, a safe perch from which to view a world of possibility, the domestically intrusive labor of self-managed finance is vulnerably exposed in a way that no office of homeland security could remedy.

FINANCIAL VISIONS?

How then are we to think of the wealth that finance has wrought? During the 1990s, records were broken for the longest period of continuous economic expansion and the longest and largest bull market. Besides the vinyl shards of broken records, what is there to show for it? How do we begin to assess the historical significance of this accumulation of wealth. The booms of the 1920s and 1960s were explosive times in many respects, and the 1990s seem tame in comparison, at least in tone. The twenties ushered in consumer society with great fanfare. The sixties advanced the social economy as a palliative to more radical demands. The nineties consummation of finance had a certain celibacy about it, given all the excess in our midst. The magnitude of prosperity seemed to be in inverse proportion to any ambition for what to do with it. Of course, the magnitude of the boom is only apparent after the fact; the news that we were living through boom times, so loudly proclaimed in earlier eras, remained muted. Perhaps the most staggering statistic of all is that $17 trillion was raised in the securities markets during the 1990s—more than was generated in the prior 200 years. More than two years after the boom went bust (in March 2000) and corporate scandals exposed profit inflation strategies to drive up stock prices, $10 trillion of that wealth remained. The very magnitude of this wealth stood as an object for all to see. But where was the vision?

This conspicuousness of wealth has been very different from the conspicuous consumption of a century before, insofar as it has appeared to be the consequence of a miraculous or virtuous economy and not the virtue of individuals who loomed larger than life. As far as presentation is concerned, Bill Gates is conspicuous for his ordinariness. George Soros has written diatribes against the evils of global capitalism. As two of the most public figures of financializing wealth, Gates and Soros deserve some further attention.

First, it is worth seeing how the trade group for finance, the Securities Industry Association, in its annual "briefing book," speaks of the virtue of the wealth it seeks to promote:

> Savings and investment fuel capital formation, economic growth, and job creation. Businesses and governments draw from the savings pool to invest in new factories and equipment, develop new technologies, build and repair infrastructure, and train and educate the nation's workforce. This investment, in turn, increases productivity, generates additional economic activity, and boosts employment. Then incomes increase, and improvements in the standard of living occur. The U.S. government can help perpetuate this positive cycle by helping Americans save and invest, which in turn, enlarges the pool of capital available.[26]

As a vision, this one certainly has the benefit of being comprehensive yet succinct. It also embraces the idea of wealth begetting wealth, the virtuous "cycle" it seeks to promote. Although "improvements in the standard of living occur," these too are caught up in the circular movement of wealth whose advance is self-justifying as being more of the same. Hardly a recipe for nirvana. Nor is it clear how to exit the merry-go-round. Above all, the endless cycling denies the opportunity to stand back and ask the question, "What is all of this wealth for?" The unprecedented accumulation would seem to ask for no less, especially when it has become easier to put a price tag on vaccinating the world's population or supplying clean drinking water.

If $17 trillion is thought of as a single aggregate of wealth, as money that could be raised for some purpose beyond its parceled distribution into more factories, then a discussion of what futures are possible might look very different. Mutual funds broadly indexed to the whole stock market point in this direction, toward ownership of not just productive capacity but speculative capacity. While the speculative lacks the spectacular to make of it a vision, such longings to make things whole may produce more ungovernable nostalgia than active intervention. The immediacy of socialized wealth presses into the present the question of what might be done differently, as a function of existing abilities and decisions rather than idealizations of a world freed from the shackles of this one.

By forcing the future into the present, financialization imposes a gargantuan scale onto a framework of management. If poverty can be erased by making everyone an entrepreneur, why can't entrepreneurialism be ousted for the cooperation on which it rests, and why can't that cooperation be what is extended by wealth rather than the other way around? The dull cycle of success that the Securities Industry Association commends to us might be successfully broken if the powers to decide how to invest wealth were taken seriously. Up to now, this power has been reserved for the successful. Perhaps it's time to see what they have in mind.

Bill Gates may have been in a better position to speak disinterestedly about the future before Microsoft was brought to court for playing unfairly with competitors in the new economy. His two exercises in futurology, *The Road Ahead* (1995) and *Business @ the Speed of Thought* (1999) are nonetheless unabashedly self-promotional. The claims of the earlier book that companies like IBM and Apple "have had an immense amount of our cooperation and support" may ring a bit hollow now.[27] Gates will certainly not be the last businessperson to write himself as the future, and his prognostications, including a high volume of consumer online trading, look, only six years on, a lot like the present. In this respect, the future is effectively at hand for Gates, and it is a well-functioning marketplace, which he terms "friction-free capitalism," that seamlessly converts information into transactions:

> Capitalism, demonstrably the greatest of the constructed economic systems, has in the past decade clearly proved its advantages over the alternative systems. The information highway will magnify those advantages. It will allow those who produce goods to see, a lot more efficiently than ever before, what buyers want, and will allow potential consumers to buy those goods more efficiently. Adam Smith would be pleased. More important, consumers everywhere will enjoy the benefits.[28]

Although technology may be revolutionary, capitalism is only getting closer to the older model posited by its master. Gates's talent is being synoptic, not inventive. He transcribes the values of a technology onto business, and of business onto society. "If the 1980s were about quality and the 1990s were about reengineering, then the 2000s will be about velocity."[29] We move from efficiency to speed as an end in itself, just as the new technologies promise. But when the gains of the Web lifestyle are realized, they will become invisible, taken for granted.[30] Again, the future is backward looking, a "town square for the global village of tomorrow."[31] In bespeaking the digital age, Gates gives a nod to inequality ("mitigate the challenges such as privacy and haves-versus-have-nots")[32] and to democracy ("Citizens in every culture must engage on the social and political impact of digital technology to ensure that the new digital age reflects the society they want to create").[33]

The moment of mitigation and democratic reflection passes within a few lines. Business makes history, one we should all eagerly await: "As tough and uncertain as the digital world makes it for business—it's evolve rapidly or die—we will all benefit. We're going to get improved products and services, more responsiveness to complaints, lower costs, and more choices. We're going to get better government and social services at substantially less cost."[34] Faster is more, and more is better. Quantity is quality. This is conventional enough logic for marketing a product, but how well does it sell the future? And what kind of future is it that looks so strikingly familiar? What's good for Microsoft is good for GM, but who else gets to be part of the "we"? So long as the company giveth, all is possible: "If companies empower their employees to solve problems and give them potent tools to do this with, they will always be amazed at how much creativity and initiative will blossom forth."[35] Yes, employers will be amazed at how much money their workers can make for them through schemes to get more labor power out of workers (like reengineering), but just how amazed will the workers be when they are laid off or their stock options turn to powder, or their creativity belongs to someone else? Alas, that's the last line of the book, and from Gates, at least, we may never know.

George Soros might be considered a self-anointed philosopher-king. Soros, whose money is made in speculation and arbitrage, wants the world to listen to him, and his many books and the Soros Foundation are devoted to that end. Soros is not short on visions of global transformation, and he takes the characteristics of the financial markets to be isomorphic with history as such—and he proposes a theory to explain both. He also sees his speculative activity as testing his ideas about history. In *The Alchemy of Finance* (1987), he argues that there is a reflexive relation between investor bias (thinking) and economic fundamentals (reality) that animates the markets.[36] In *Underwriting Democracy* (1991), he borrows the idea from chaos theory of "far-from-equilibrium conditions," used to describe the physics at the origin of the universe, to counter the notion that conditions in any given environment tend toward equilibrium. He then distinguishes three permutations of equilibrium: "dynamic equilibrium (open society); static disequilibrium (closed society); or dynamic disequilibrium (revolution or the boom-bust pattern familiar from financial markets)."[37] As historical referents, open and closed are Cold War terms for West and East, and Soros deploys them according to ideological convention. Open society is the ideal and is one "determined entirely by the decisions of its members."[38]

While Soros would be loath to admit it, such a definition would be at home in many socialist writings, although for him "decision" refers to the kinds of contractually regulated choices one finds in market transactions taken by individuals. That a state of static disequilibrium could suddenly become dynamic may cast doubt on how static it was in the first place. Indeed, Soros's grand trinity would soon have to devolve to its third boom-bust revolution as a general condition, as dynamics become increasingly destructive. A Hungarian emigré to the West in the 1950s who gave up his passion for philosophy to pursue economics, Soros assumes his accumulated wealth is a principal historical agency that abets revolution, by which he means the Soviet demise. He intends for his foundation to use its goal of creating an open society as a "comparative advantage, which we can exploit."[39]

Soros is pioneering venture philanthropy, which, rather than supporting existing institutions or projects, becomes the principal mechanism for the aims it seeks to accomplish. Although the foundation operates as a nonprofit organization, change is won through competition and exploitation of circumstances just as fully as beating the market. "My original objective has been attained: the communist system is well and truly dead. My new objective is the establishment of an open society in its stead. That will be much harder to accomplish. Construction is always more laborious than destruction and much less fun."[40] At the time, Soros was unconcerned with the human costs of the destruction he was helping to wreak, so sure was he that those who would enjoy the new choices and alternatives in the East outweighed those who had lost theirs. At least he was having fun. On Soros's agenda at the time (and later) was the marshaling of aid from the West to absorb the Soviet alliance. This would have demanded reflection on how the surplus wealth of capitalism might best be deployed. Looking back, Soros pined, "The West did not believe in open society as a universal idea."[41]

The failed openness of the West does not dim Soros's faith. Although he decries the market fundamentalism of a Thatcher or Bush that led the West to lose Russia, he also would have profited handsomely had foreign aid helped make viable his $2 billion acquisition in 1997 of Svyazinvest, the telecommunications holding company. At the time, he "felt that Russia needed foreign investment more than philanthropy."[42] The more disequilibrium reigned in global finance as in 1997 and 1999, the more Soros advocated comprehensive regulatory approaches, like an international central bank. As the risk on his positions subsided, he could retreat on these ideas for new financial and political architectures that were "far too radical."[43] Nonetheless, at a time when the financiers are treated as the few individuals entitled to speak for the many, he insists on an international-ist perspective that would increase foreign aid and strengthen institutional frame-works. He envisions a partnership between investment-interested civil society groups like his own and government initiative, led by a United States that could "recognize our fallibility" and "participate in forming rules by which we are will-ing to abide."[44] Although Soros wrote this before George W. Bush came to office, the antipathy with which U.S. foreign policy now regards the world makes Soros's remarks seem far too radical once again. At some point we might expect more to be made out of the antinomy between the Bush regime's promotion of venture philanthropy to usurp government functions and the ungovernable demands of the premier instance of this type.

When philanthropy ventures outside official foreign policy or stands in for popular opinion, it comes close to that ideal of civil society (a sphere of activity in-dependent of state or market). But if civil society requires the kindness of private wealth, its public freedom is rather tightly tethered to personal interests. The new philanthropy, like microfinance, has no obligation to be universal in its reach, but this only underscores the social limits to the visions of the future that finance yields. At the same time, there is something unsettling in the confidence that the personal accrual of wealth can solve the world's problems. However worthy, the ex-penditures of Gates appear remarkably unambitious in scope compared to Rocke-feller, Ford, or Carnegie. Soros is a bit different. If Soros is to be taken at his word, it was finance itself that led him to support revolution. One can certainly argue about which revolution to support and what kinds of global institutionality it would be most useful to implement. However, what is most salient is how the en-gagements with global finance open different routes out of the Cold War morass by posing the question of what to do with the world's wealth and its capacity to re-design society.

Waiting for philanthropy to come is hardly a prudent strategy for those in need of financial support. The idea that only the rich have access to surplus wealth has been revised by acolytes of human capital. Human capital takes the model of accumulated wealth and claims that anyone can be valued for what they have or could amass over time. It makes of the self a portfolio. Artists are the preferred ex-ample for illustrating the concept. Picasso tossed out a sketch in minutes but val-ued it in terms of the years it took him to acquire the ability to do so. David Bowie issued fifteen-year bonds for $55 million against future royalties and concert rev-enues.[45] The Bowie bonds were held by Prudential Insurance of America. Were they to be securitized and traded, Bowie would become the first fully financialized self. It is convenient for the models of human capital that the exemplars already possess substantial capital of the conventional sort.[46]

Just as securitization presents the specter of replacing individually held prop-erty with social property and treating pooled finance as wealth for any purpose available on demand (liquidity), a securitized incomes market presents labor's futures in a new key. Pooling the potential income of all who labor and treating it as a force in common makes explicit the interdependencies of those who generate value upon each other. All would be invested in these labor markets and presumably trade upon the fortunes and misfortunes that others incurred. An individual's labor would be bonded to others in a manner that would make it difficult to speak of that person's fate, interest, activity, creativity, or expansion as a thing unto itself. Whereas the artist was once the romantic symbol of the self-contained individual, the same figure could be deployed to advertise the individual's replacement. In the 1970s, management guru Peter Drucker got quite nervous at the thought of workers holding pensions and effectively owning corporations.[47] Extending this ownership to labor's collective capacity in itself would no doubt send him into orbit.

While many variants of shareholder and stakeholder value take up the socialization of ownership through various forms of securitization, their most typical impulse is to equate ownership with personalization. Illustrative here is Jeff Gates's *Ownership Solution,* which offers a communitarian spirituality of personal responsibility "to evoke a breakthrough to a capitalism that fosters a more mindful living."[48] Like the Grameen Bank example, the moral commitments of local control that ensure a "community without communism" can, through its intolerance, exclusions, and invocations of selected traditions, narrow the imagination of what politics are available to us.

In light of the rush to propose a final solution, it may be more useful to acknowledge that the political and organizational expressions of the financialization of labor have yet to assert themselves. However, were they to do so, potential scenarios for wealth produced and held in common would expand dramatically. Making everyone a capitalist, entrepreneur, or risk manager assumes that what can be generalized is the exploitation of each over all, that the wealthy individual is the model of success that all should emulate. If both labor and capital are socialized to the point where we were forced to confront them as funds for more profound mutual engagement, we can draw upon the intricacy of interaction that greatly opens up who and what we can be for one another. The values attributed to capital, to technologies, to wealth could then rightfully be integrated into questions about what kind of future we want to create. This would draw upon finance's means without embracing its ends, engendering a state of immeasurable risk, a departure from expectations whose rewards bore no price. Whatever course is charted for the world, this new geography nestles in the body of the present.

NOTES

1. This turn on Marx's phrase for history comes from labor historian Herbert Gutman. See his *Power and Culture: Essays on the American Working Class* (New York: Pantheon, 1987).

2. Lawrence Mishel, Jared Bernstein, and John Schmitt, *The State of Working America, 2000/2001* (Ithaca: Cornell University Press, 2001), p. 288.

3. Andrew Leyshon and Nigel Thrift, "Geographies of Financial Exclusion: Financial Abandonment in Britain and the United States," in *MoneySpace: Geographies of Monetary Transformation* (London: Routledge, 1997), p. 228.

4. Michael Hudson, "The Poverty Industry," in *Merchants of Misery: How Corporate America Profits from Poverty,* ed. Michael Hudson (Monroe, Maine: Common Courage Press, 1996), p. 2.

5. Eric Rorer, "Shark Bait: How Some Consumer-Finance Companies Make a Killing Off People Who Badly Need Money," in *Merchants of Misery: How Corporate America Profits from Poverty,* ed. Michael Hudson (Monroe, Maine: Common Courage Press, 1996), p. 31. Rorer notes that in California between 1985 and 1993, the number of licenses issued for lending to those considered marginal credit risks rose from 1,942 to 5,008.

6. Mishel, Bernstein, and Schmitt, *The State of Working America, 2000/2001*, p. 281.

7. For a critique of the development approach to thinking about the third world, see Arturo Escobar, *Encountering Development: The Making and Unmaking of the Third World* (Princeton: Princeton University Press, 1995), and Colin Leys, *The Rise and Fall of Development Theory* (Bloomington: Indiana University Press, 1996).

8. The conference brought together representatives from governmental and non-governmental organizations through a UN-sponsored event. Available online at http://www.igc.org/beijing/ngo/ngodec.html.

9. Stuart Rutherford, *The Poor and Their Money* (New York: Oxford University Press, 2000), p. 88.

10. Aminur Rahman, *Women and Microcredit in Rural Bangladesh: Anthropological Study of the Rhetoric and Realities of Grameen Bank Lending* (Boulder: Westview Press, 1999), p. 149. Rahman's critique is at odds with many otherwise sunny accounts. See, for example, Helen Todd, *Women at the Center: Grameen Bank Borrowers After One Decade* (Boulder: Westview Press, 1996); and Susan Holcombe, *Managing to Empower: The Grameen Bank's Experience of Poverty Alleviation* (London: Zed, 1995).

11. For an overview of some expressions of microfinance internationally, see Maria Otero and Elisabeth Rhyne, *The New World of Microenterprise Finance: Building Financial Institutions for the Poor* (West Hartford, Conn.: Kumarian Press, 1994).

12. Quoted in Richard J. Barnet and John Cavanagh, *Global Dreams: Imperial Corporations and the New World Order* (New York: Touchstone Press, 1994), p. 383.

13. Lise Adams, Anna Awimbo, Nathanael Goldberg, and Cristina Sanchez, eds., *Empowering Women with Microcredit: 2000 Microcredit Summit Campaign Report,* available online at http://www.microcreditsummit.org/campaigns/report00.html.

14. C. George Caffentzis, "The Fundamental Implications of the Debt Crisis for Social Reproduction in Africa," in *Paying the Price: Women and the Politics of International Economic Strategy,* ed. Mariarosa Dalla Costa and Giovanna F. Dalla Costa (London: Zed Books, 1995), pp. 15–41.

15. For a treatment of how risk tolerance differentiates the financial terrain among various global sites of poverty, see F. J. A. Bouman and Otto Hospes, *Financial Landscapes Reconstructed: The Fine Art of Mapping Development* (Boulder: Westview Press, 1994).

16. For an overview, see Rae Lesser Blumberg, Cathy Rakowski, Irene Tinker, and Michael Monteon, eds., *Engendering Wealth and Well-Being: Empowerment for Global Change* (Boulder: Westview Press, 1995). Gayatri Chakravorty Spivak has identified what she terms "globe-girdling movements" as the primary political effect of the new formations; see, for example, her essay "Supplementing Marxism," in *Whither Marxism: Global Crises in International Perspective,* ed. Bernd Magnus and Stephen Cullenberg (New York: Routledge, 1995), pp. 109–120.

17. The World Bank, *Entering the 21st Century: World Development Report, 1999/2000* (New York: Oxford University Press, 2000), p. 3.

18. For a revealing look at the case of Assam in the vise of Indian governmental antipathy and global human rights discourse, see Sanjib Baruah, *India Against Itself: Assam and the Politics of Nationality* (Philadelphia: University of Pennsylvania Press, 1999).

19. Some of the broader social entailments of new technologies are discussed in Manuel Castells, *The Information Age: Society, Economy and Culture,* 3 vols. (Malden, Mass.: Blackwell, 1996–1998); Mark Poster, *What's the Matter with the Internet?* (Minneapolis: University of Minnesota Press, 2001); and Patricia Ticineto Clough, *Autoaffection: Unconscious Thought in the Age of Teletechnology* (Minneapolis: University of Minnesota Press, 2000).

20. Outlook 2000, *New York Times,* December 20, 1999, p. C21.

21. Even the idea of the Internet is beyond the reach of most Chinese. The venerable firm of George Gallup, employed to find out how many sino-citizens had heard of the new technology, got an affirmative response from only 14 percent of their respondents. See Mark Landler, "An Internet Vision in Millions: China Start-Ups Snare Capital as Auction Fever Boils Up," *New York Times,* December 23, 1999, pp. C1, C4.

22. The forecasts come from the International Data Corporation, which bills itself as the "Global IT information resource" (at $1,500 per report). Available online at www.idc.com/AP112999PR.htm.

23. Elizabeth Rives, ed., *Powering the Global Economy: Securities Industry Briefing Book.* Available online at http://www.sia.com/publications/pdf/BBchapter1.pdf, p. 14.

24. Ibid., p. 13.

25. These are chapter titles from Jean Baudrillard, *The Consumer Society: Myths and Structures* (London: Sage, 1998). The visual display of goods as a substitute for direct participation is an argument made by Guy Debord in *Society of the Spectacle* (Detroit: Black and Red, 1983).

26. Rives, ed., *Powering the Global Economy,* p. 43.

27. Bill Gates, with Nathan Myhrvold and Peter Rinearson, *The Road Ahead* (New York: Viking, 1995), p. 182.

28. Ibid., p. 183.

29. Bill Gates, with Collins Hemingway, *Business @ the Speed of Thought: Using a Digital Nervous System* (New York: TimeWarner, 1999), p. xviii.

30. Ibid., p. 132.

31. Ibid., p. 131.

32. Ibid., p. 414.

33. Ibid.

34. Ibid.

35. Ibid., p. 415.

36. George Soros, *The Alchemy of Finance: Reading the Mind of the Market* (New York: John Wiley & Sons, 1987).

37. George Soros, *Underwriting Democracy* (New York: Free Press, 1991), p. xv.

38. Ibid., p. 204.

39. Ibid., p. 128.

40. Ibid.

41. George Soros, *Open Society: Reforming Global Capitalism* (New York: Public Affairs, 2000), p. 237.

42. Ibid., p. 245.

43. Ibid., p. 276.

44. Ibid., p. 356.

45. The examples are from Stan Davis and Christopher Meyer, *Future Wealth* (Boston:

Harvard Business School Press, 2000), pp. 21 and 47. The book is a brief for individual securitization as an image of replacing wage labor with selves valued as tradable commodities.

46. Robert J. Schiller, *Macro-Markets: Creating Institutions for Managing Society's Largest Economic Risks* (Oxford: Clarendon Press, 1993), p. 52.

47. Peter F. Drucker, *The Unseen Revolution: How Pension Fund Socialism Came to America* (New York: Harper and Row, 1976).

48. Jeff Gates, *The Ownership Solution: Toward a Shared Capitalism for the 21st Century* (Reading, Mass.: Perseus Books, 1998), p. 295.

16

Globalization, Trade Liberalization, and the Higher Education Industry

CLYDE W. BARROW

The term *globalization* is now widely used to capture a variety of economic, cultural, social, and political trends that are extending the boundaries of numerous institutions beyond established national borders (Steger, 2002; Waters, 1995; Leyton-Brown, 1996, 11). Higher education is not exempt from the impacts of globalization despite the fact that most college and university faculty still view their institutions as oases of cultural and intellectual autonomy (Barrow, 2001, 1990a). Yet, as early as 1918, the sociologist Max Weber (1946, 131) concluded that the image of the ivory tower was already "fictitious," because colleges and universities are in reality "state capitalist enterprises." Like similar enterprises in other sectors of the public economy, such as aviation, utilities, the postal service, and passenger rail transportation, the higher education sector has been partially privatized over the past two decades (Newson and Buchbinder, 1988). More recently, however, new initiatives have been launched to incorporate these newly privatized enterprises into the world trading system.

The liberalization of trade in "higher education services" has been quietly negotiated in multilateral trade meetings on both a global (WTO) and a regional (EU, NAFTA) basis. The major trade agreements have potentially enormous impacts on higher education throughout the world, but few students, faculty, or administrators are even aware of provisions in the major trade agreements that directly affect their institutions and professions. Thus, a necessary first step in evaluating the potential impact of globalization on higher education is to simply clarify how the major trade agreements promote the commodification and marketization of higher education by incorporating it into the world trading system as just another industry.

THE HIGHER EDUCATION SERVICES INDUSTRY

College and university employees, especially faculty, are unaccustomed to thinking about higher education as an "industry," despite the dominance of corporate rhetoric and business practices in higher education for almost a century (Barrow, 1990b). The corporatization of the university is now receiving a great deal of attention from scholars in numerous fields (Shumar, 1997; Scott, 1983; Slaughter, 1990), but leading corporate executives and government officials in the advanced capitalist countries have long articulated the goal of constructing an integrated and "socially efficient" capitalist *system* that subordinates every sphere of social activity to the imperatives of the modern corporation (Habermas, 1970, 90–100; Haber, 1964).[1] In the United States, as early as 1910, the Carnegie Foundation for the Advancement of Teaching (CFAT) launched the first higher education reform movement with a declaration that "the industrial world is coming more and more to feel that all work is done under certain broad principles, and that the application of these principles to one industry is little different from their application to any other" (Cooke, 1910, 26; Barrow, 1990b, ch. 3). Since that time, an ever increasing number of business and political leaders have come to reject the claim that teaching and scholarship are somehow different from other kinds of labor or that higher education should be treated differently than other business enterprises.

The status of higher education in this worldview is perhaps best captured by the industrial classification systems developed by most countries to collect data and monitor trends in employment, wages, business vitality, and international trade. The United States adopted its first Standard Industrial Classification (SIC) System in 1939 and periodically revises this classification system to account for changes in the structure of the economy (Executive Office of the President, 1987).[2] Every business establishment in the United States—both public and private—is assigned one or more SIC codes based on Division (e.g., manufacturing), Major Group (e.g., textile mill products), and Industry Group (e.g., spinning mills). An establishment's Division is identified by a single letter code (A–J). Its Major Group is identified by a 2-digit numeric code (01–99) and its Industry Group is identified by a 3- or 4-digit numeric code (001–9999). Educational Services is classified in Division I (Services) as Major Group 82 (see Table 16.1). Educational Services includes seven industry groups:

- 8221 Colleges, universities, and professional schools
- 8222 Junior colleges and technical institutes
- 8231 Libraries
- 8243 Data processing schools
- 8244 Business and secretarial schools
- 8249 Vocational schools, not elsewhere classified
- 8299 Schools and educational services, not elsewhere classified

TABLE 16.1 U.S. Standard Industrial Classification: Higher Education Services

SIC Code	Year 2000	Total Employment	Number of Establishments	Total Payroll
DIVISION I: SERVICES				
Major Group 72	**Personal Services**			
Industry Group 724	Barber shops			
7241	Barber college*	102	34	$1,839,780
Industry Group 729	Miscellaneous personal services			
7299	College clearinghouses*	624	92	$9,649,450
Major Group 82	**Educational Services**			
Industry Group 822	Colleges, universities, and professional schools	2,326,753	9,385	$86,179,971,000
8221	Colleges, universities, and professional schools			
	Colleges, except junior			
	Professional schools, e.g., dental, engineering, law, medical			
	Theological seminaries			
	Service academies (college)			
	Universities			
8222	Junior colleges and technical institutes	608,502	2,225	$16,434,436,000
	Community colleges (junior)			
	Junior colleges			
	Technical institutes			
Industry Group 823	Libraries	151,359	6,520	$3,290,902,000
8231	Libraries			
	Centers for documentation			
	Circulating libraries			
	Lending libraries			
	Libraries, printed matter			
	Rental of books			
Industry Group 824	Vocational Schools	31,768	3,371	$1,421,348,000
8243	Data processing schools			
	Computer operator training			

(continues)

TABLE 16.1 *(continued)*

SIC Code	Year 2000	Total Employment	Number of Establishments	Total Payroll
	Computer repair training			
	Computer software training			
	Data processing schools			
8244	Business and secretarial schools	14,418	543	$354,921,000
	Court reporting schools			
	Secretarial schools			
8249	Vocational schools, not elsewhere classified	66,890	3,941	$1,931,513,000
	Aviation schools (excluding flying instruction)			
	Banking schools (training in banking)			
	Commercial art schools			
	Construction equipment operation schools			
	Correspondence schools			
	Nursing schools, practical			
	Real estate schools			
	Restaurant operation schools			
	Trade schools			
	Truck driving schools			
	Vocational apprenticeship training			
	Other vocational schools			
Industry Group 829	Schools and educational services, not elsewhere classified			
8299	Schools and educational services, not elsewhere classified	209,091	22,760	$5,453,871,000
	Art schools, except commercial			
	Automobile driving instruction			
	Baton instruction			
	Bible schools, not operated by churches			
	Ceramics schools			
	Charm schools			
	Civil service schools			
	Continuing education programs			
	Cooking schools			

(continues)

TABLE 16.1 (continued)

SIC Code	Year 2000	Total Employment	Number of Establishments	Total Payroll
	Diction schools			
	Drama schools			
	Finishing schools, charm and modeling			
	Flying instruction			
	Hypnosis instruction			
	Language schools			
	Modeling schools, clothes			
	Music schools			
	Personal development schools			
	Reading schools			
	Speed reading courses			
	Student exchange programs			
	Survival schools			
	Tutoring			
	Vocational counseling, except rehabilitation counseling			
Major Group 87	**Engineering, Accounting, Research, Management, and Related Services**			
Industry Group 874	Management and public relations services			
8748	Business consulting services, not elsewhere classified (includes):*	52,361	10,261	$3,000,542,250
	Economic consulting			
	Educational consulting, except management			
	Test development and evaluation services, educational or personnel			
	Testing services, educational or personnel			
Total	**All Higher Education Services**	3,461,868	59,132	$118,078,993,480
	Higher as percentage of all U.S. industries	2.7%	0.7%	2.6%
U.S. Total	**All Industries**	129,925,813	7,899,243	$4,585,814,470,000

Source: U.S. Bureau of Labor Statistics, ES-202 Series, Covered Wages & Employment.
Note: *Estimate. The 4-digit ES-202 does not allow a precise measurement, since the higher education services are aggregated with other services.

One can also find other postsecondary educational services scattered across other industry groups such as barber colleges (7241), college clearinghouses (7299), educational consulting (8748), test development and evaluation services (8748), and educational testing services (8748). When viewed from the perspective of a simple economic impact analysis, the U.S. higher education services industry has more than 59,000 business establishments, which account for nearly 3.5 million jobs or 2.7 percent of total U.S. employment. The higher education services industry accounts for approximately $185 to $200 billion in annual output (sales) (U.S. Department of Commerce, 2002a). The annual output of the U.S. higher education services industry is larger than the gross national product of 110 countries (World Bank, 1999). Moreover, these estimates do not include the numerous economic spin-offs generated by postsecondary education such as textbook, computer, and software sales, printing and photocopying services, professional travel, or the private management of campus bookstores, food services, and even dormitories. Nor do these estimates include the growth of in-house and contract-based educational activities by "corporate universities," which are operated as training divisions within established corporations (e.g., Motorola University).

Thus, like many other service industries, such as financial services, engineering, and accounting, the higher education industry has emerged as an important element of U.S. economic vitality not merely through the indirect impact of its manpower training and technology transfer on overall business productivity but as a major industry in its own right. In fact, higher education services has displaced many traditional primary industries and manufacturing industries in terms of its relative importance to the U.S. economy. Higher education services now account for a larger share of U.S. gross domestic product than forestry, fishing, coal mining, the manufacture of tobacco products, railroad transportation, and motion pictures, to name a few (U.S. Department of Commerce, 2002a).

Yet, traditional colleges and universities are now merely one of many potential service providers in this growing industry. Despite the partial privatization of revenue streams and auxiliary operations (Barrow, 2000), 70 percent of U.S. colleges, universities, and professional schools (SIC 8221), as well as 70 percent of junior colleges and technical institutes (SIC 8222) are still state or local government enterprises (again, see Table 16.1). Publicly owned higher education enterprises account for 62 percent of total employment in industry group 8221 and 93 percent of total employment in industry group 8222. These two industry groups alone account for $68.8 billion in annual public payroll or a little more than 58 percent of the higher education service industry's total annual payroll. Furthermore, even "private" higher education institutions in the United States remain heavily dependent on state and federally funded student financial aid programs (tuition subsidies) and federally funded research contracts to support their operations. Moreover, with approximately 30 percent of college and university faculty belonging to unions, higher education is one of the most densely unionized industries in the United States (Barrow, 2000). Thus, at a time when traditional institutions of higher education are more and more perceived as a burden on public budgets instead of a social investment, they are also increasingly viewed by business and political leaders as inflexible public monopolies that have proven particularly resistant to the market imperative.

The segmentation and modularization of the higher education industry has made it possible to parcel out various components of the larger industry and to operate them as separate private enterprises (e.g., dormitories, food service, bookstores, continuing education, virtual universities, research centers, etc.).[3] However, to the degree that multilateral trade agreements incorporate higher education into the world trading system, local resistance to further privatization can be circumvented and displaced beyond the reach of state, local, and even national political systems. In fact, public higher education enterprises are increasingly subject to the rules of international trade, which is creating new opportunities for additional private sector competition from new types of higher education service providers.

THE WORLD TRADE ORGANIZATION

There are a variety of trade and economic policies established by each of the world's 190 countries, including tariffs, import quotas, foreign exchange rationing, domestic monetary policies, and many other national laws that affect international trade. There are also numerous bilateral and multilateral agreements between countries that establish an international legal framework limiting tariff protection, prohibiting certain trade policies (e.g., export subsidies), providing safeguard measures (e.g., antidumping), and establishing dispute resolution procedures (e.g., binding arbitration) (Whalley, 1989, 7). Although higher education has generally been perceived as exempt from the globalizing impacts of trade liberalization, the international market for global higher education is already conservatively estimated to be $30 billion or equivalent to 3 percent of the total services trade in the OECD countries (Larsen et al., 2001, 1).

The General Agreement on Tariffs and Trade (GATT) has long been the most important trade agreement governing the global economic system.[4] It was established by twenty-three countries in 1947, including the United States, Canada, Great Britain, Western Europe, Japan, Australia, and New Zealand, and was institutionalized through a secretariat, which provided technical assistance, dispute settlement, and enforcement of the agreement among member nations. Article I of GATT establishes most-favored-nation (MFN) status as the trading system's basic principle of nondiscrimination against imports on the basis of national origin. The principle of nondiscrimination requires each country participating in GATT to grant other parties to the agreement no less favorable treatment than is granted to the country receiving the most favorable treatment under its national trade laws. If a member country decides to grant the imports of one country better or more favorable treatment than required by GATT, the better treatment is automatically extended to goods imported from all countries that are parties to GATT (Graham, 1996, 46).

GATT has provided the framework for eight rounds of multilateral trade negotiations since the end of World War II, and on November 9–13, 2001, the Doha, Qatar, ministerial meeting agreed to initiate a ninth round of negotiations. The ninth round will undoubtedly place greater emphasis on trade in services than has been the case previously. The first round of GATT negotiations in Geneva (1947) resulted in significant tariff reductions among the twenty-three advanced industrial countries that initiated the agreement. Subsequent negotiations failed to produce any significant breakthroughs until the Kennedy Round (1963–1967), which agreed to a single tariff-cutting formula that led to a 35 percent overall reduction in the average tariff level among participating nations. The Tokyo Round (1973–1979) resulted in another 34 percent reduction in average tariff levels. By the early 1980s, the average tariff on most *goods* imported by the advanced industrial countries was under 10 percent, although GATT permitted higher tariffs for import-sensitive areas such as agriculture, textiles, and apparel (Schott, 1994, 60). In the Tokyo Round, governments also began negotiating new and improved rules on the use or removal of nontariff barriers (NTBs) (Whalley, 1989, 9).[5]

The first seven rounds of multilateral GATT negotiations mainly liberalized trade in goods among the developed countries. There was very little trade liberalization by developing countries attributable to GATT during this time, since most developing countries retained import substitution strategies that relied on high tariffs, import licensing, foreign exchange rationing, and balance-of-payment restrictions as allowed under GATT's Article 18-B. Furthermore, international trade in services, a key growth sector in the new postindustrial economies, was not covered by previous iterations of GATT.

However, by the mid-1980s, many developing countries unilaterally abandoned import substitution policies or moved toward trade liberalization through a variety of bilateral and regional trade agreements negotiated with other developing countries. This movement was stimulated partly by dissatisfaction with the results of import substitution strategies, the Latin American debt crisis, and a growing conviction that the export-oriented policies of the Asian "tigers" and "dragons" were proving more successful in promoting economic growth (Whalley, 1989, 15–16, 32). In reaction to the perceived movement toward "closed regionalism" by Europe, Japan, and the developing countries, the United States pressed for the Uruguay Round (1987–1994). After seven years of negotiations, the Uruguay Round culminated in the World Trade Organization (WTO) treaty, signed in Marrakesh, Morocco (April 1994), which became effective on January 1, 1995. The Uruguay Round cut the developed countries' tariffs by an average of 38 percent and lowered their average tariff on imported goods to only 3.9 percent (Schott, 1994, 9, 61). Meanwhile, the WTO's membership has grown to include 144 of the world's 190 countries (WTO, 2002).

THE GENERAL AGREEMENT ON TRADE IN SERVICES

The Uruguay Round also established a framework for trade liberalization in services that has the potential to extend the WTO treaty's provisions to large sectors of the "postindustrial" economy, which were not covered by previous versions of the agreement. The General Agreement on Trade in Services (GATS) is the first multilateral (global) agreement to establish guidelines governing international trade and investment in the service sector. The GATS covers service industries that "conduct international transactions either by sending highly skilled personnel, technical information, or currency across national borders or by performing services for foreign entities through affiliates located overseas" (USITC, 1994, IX-5). This definition includes education, finance, insurance, travel, film rentals, payments by governments abroad, business and professional services (e.g., legal, engineering, management, and information systems), telecommunications, and payments on franchises, patents, copyrights, trademarks, broadcast rights, and other intangible property rights.

The GATS is fully integrated into the World Trade Organization, which has established a Council for Trade in Services to oversee the implementation of trade agreements on services, to monitor ongoing negotiations within the GATS framework, and to organize working groups on outstanding issues involving trade in services. The General Agreement on Trade in Services consists of three major components: (1) a framework of rules intended to discipline government regulation of trade and investment in services; (2) a set of schedules, where each WTO member can commit itself to apply these rules to specific service sectors, subject to defined exceptions; and (3) a series of annexes and ministerial decisions that supply additional sector-specific detail and identify follow-up activities required by the schedule (WTO, 2001c, 6). The framework for trade in services obligates WTO members to respect fifteen general principles that apply to all services except those supplied "in the exercise of government authority."[6] The GATT's most fundamental principles, including transparency of laws and regulations, recognition of operating licenses and qualifications to practice a profession, and most-favored-nation treatment, are extended to the service sectors. Governments can exempt themselves from the MFN obligation on a sector-by-sector basis, but the exemption is not to exceed ten years (2004) and is subject to review within five years. Other basic GATT principles, including market access and national treatment, are binding only if a member country commits itself to a particular principle in a designated service sector.

Once a country commits itself to a principle within a service sector, it may choose to apply that principle to one or more of four modes of supply: commercial presence, consumption abroad, cross-border supply, and presence of individuals. *Commercial presence* includes corporations, joint ventures, partnerships, representative offices, branches, and other legal entities constituting foreign direct investment. *Consumption abroad*, often referred to as "movement of the consumer," occurs when a service is delivered outside the territory of the member making the commitment (e.g., tourism, ship repair, study abroad). *Cross-border supply* occurs when a service supplier is not present within the territory of the member country where the service is delivered (e.g., services delivered through telecommunications, mail, international transport, e-commerce or Internet sales, distance learning). The *presence of individuals* refers to natural persons who are service suppliers or employees of a service supplier who travel to another country to provide a service in that country (e.g., an engineering consultant).

A country may also include "horizontal commitments" in its schedule, which limit a principle's applicability to trade in a limited number of service subsectors, or it may be specific to only one mode of supply across a broad range of service sectors and subsectors. Once a country has made a partial or complete commitment on market access or national treatment, the other GATS rules automatically apply to that sector. Most of the initial commitments on education services submitted by individual countries regarding market access and national treatment are "standstill" commitments, which promise to not impose new trade restrictions on foreign service providers. WTO members have made fewer commitments to liberalize markets in education services than in any other service sector except energy services (WTO, 1998a, 10). Therefore, GATS at this time merely provides a framework for trade liberalization in education services (USITC, 1994, IX-5–6). However, the United States, Australia, and New Zealand have each made proposals that indicate their intention to press for further liberalization in the next round of WTO negotiations (WTO, 2000, 2001a, 2001b).

The WTO's horizontal classification of education services consists of five categories: Primary Education, Secondary Education, Higher Education, Adult Education, and Other Education Services (WTO, 1991; 1998b, 1, 25–26). The GATS is likely to have its most significant impact on trade in higher education, adult education, and other education services, since the agreement exempts trade in "services supplied in the exercise of governmental authority." It is widely accepted that primary and secondary education are covered by this exemption, although countries can choose to allow foreign competition in this sector (WTO, 1998b, 4; WTO, 2000). By 1998, the EU bloc and twenty-nine additional countries had made commitments in the education services sector with 21 commitments on primary education, 23 on secondary education, 21 on higher education, 20 on adult education, and 12 on other education services (WTO, 1998b, 10).[7]

INTERNATIONAL TRADE IN
HIGHER EDUCATION SERVICES

Higher education services are traded mainly through student mobility across national borders (consumption abroad), and therefore the largest current source of receipts for international higher education services is student fees paid to attend traditional colleges and universities in host countries. Nearly 1.5 million students study abroad, and this number is continuing to grow each year. The ten leading "exporters" of higher education services by consumption abroad are the United States, France, Germany, United Kingdom, Russian Federation, Japan, Australia, Canada, Belgium, and Switzerland (WTO, 1998b, 20). The competitive advantage of the OECD countries in the global market for higher education services is evident in the fact that collectively they receive more than 80 percent of the 1.5 million international students who study abroad each year (Skilbeck and Connell, 1996, 73).

Consequently, as low-wage manufacturing operations relocate to the developing countries, government and business leaders in many of the OECD countries are starting to see higher education as one of a few knowledge-intensive export industries with a positive balance of trade. The OECD countries' individual trade strategies are reinforced by the World Bank's higher education policy, which promotes the development of higher education in those countries that already enjoy a competitive advantage in that sector (World Bank, 1995, 23–24; World Bank, 1994). The World Bank's calculation is that the economic value of higher education, and its contribution to national economic growth, increases with the level of technological development and as countries achieve universal primary and secondary education. Thus, despite an increasing number of postsecondary graduates in the postindustrial societies, the available evidence suggests that rewards to higher education for individuals and society are still increasing in the developed countries (Davis, 1992). This correlation alone provides a significant rationale for continuing investment in higher education in the OECD countries (World Bank, 1995, 43).

However, at a time when many of the OECD countries have surplus capacity in their higher education systems, the World Bank (1995, 2–32) finds that on a global scale "the demand for higher education is in general increasing faster than the supply." Most of the global demand for higher education is being generated outside the OECD, particularly in East Asia, South Asia, the Middle East, and Latin America. Hence, from a global perspective, the World Bank sees the problem as one of matching surplus capacity to unmet demand. The increased export of higher education services by consumption abroad can partially meet this demand, but it also requires that additional higher education capacity be transferred to areas of high demand, but without the large public capital investment that would be necessary to replicate world-class higher education systems in areas that cannot afford them.

Moreover, the structural adjustment policies of the World Bank and the International Monetary Fund (IMF) grant priority to investment in primary and secondary education, because its estimated rate of return on social investment is higher in countries that have not yet achieved universal literacy. Thus, these policies, coupled with the developing countries' preferential investment in elementary and secondary education, institutionalize a global asymmetry in the provision of higher education services and privilege the developed countries as suppliers of higher education services. In this respect, higher education is becoming an increasingly important service export for the OECD countries in terms of attracting foreign students, scholars, and international research grants to higher education institutions, but also through the export of higher educational services directly to foreign countries (commercial presence, presence of individuals, and cross-border supply). Thus, economic globalization, trade liberalization under GATS, the pursuit of competitive advantage, and the educational investment policies of international organizations are each promoting a market-based strategy designed to shift excess demand for higher education in the developing countries into the OECD countries and to privilege the OECD countries as providers of higher education services in the rest of the world (OECD, 2002a).

The United States, especially, is aggressively promoting further liberalization of trade in higher education services (WTO, 1998b, 2000). The United States currently commands about one-third of the total world market in higher education services by consumption abroad, which makes it the leading exporter of higher education services by a considerable margin. The United States exported nearly $10.3 billion in education services in 2000 and recorded a trade surplus in education services of $8.2 billion (U.S. Department of Commerce, 2002b). This makes education the fifth-largest traded service in the United States, and it is one of the few industries where the United States consistently records a trade surplus.

The U.S. political leadership openly views multilateral and regional free trade agreements as mechanisms for strengthening the country's global competitive advantage in services and high technology.[8] The Clinton administration promoted free trade as a mechanism for raising living standards in the United States "by ensuring that more Americans are working in areas where the United States is comparatively more productive than its trading partners" (Office of the United States President, 1997, 21). For example, while U.S. exports boomed during the 1990s in areas where trade agreements were reached, the more important fact is that wages in the jobs generated by the export of U.S.-made goods and services were 13 percent to 16 percent higher than the national average. This relationship between the export sector and high wages has made exports a critical part of the U.S. strategy for creating high-wage, knowledge-intensive jobs, because exports allow U.S. firms to expand production in high-productivity sectors where they have a competitive advantage. The President's Council of Economic Advisors observes that the United States is especially well positioned to benefit from trade liberalization in the developing countries of Asia and Latin America because it is a major exporter of the capital goods, agricultural products, consumer goods, and commercial services in demand in these countries (Office of the United States President, 1997, 21–27, 238–239, 242–248).

However, U.S. dominance in the higher education sector is already being challenged by the governments of Japan, Australia, New Zealand, Canada, and the European Union, which are pursuing foreign student recruitment strategies as part of an aggressive higher educational services export policy. The U.S. position in the world market for international students is already being affected by increased global competition and regional economic integration elsewhere in the world. The effect of increased competition is evident in the fact that the U.S. share of the international student market has been decreasing since the mid-1980s (Davis, 1995, 79; Lambert, 1995, 22).

The European Union has adopted a policy to promote "academic mobility" among member countries with the explicit goal of improving its economic competitiveness in comparison to the United States, Japan, and the emerging economies of the Far East (Davis, 1995, 29). Under the European Community Action Scheme for Mobility of University Students (ERASMUS), European universities have established interuniversity agreements for credit and credential equivalency, program articulation, and tuition and fee payments (OECD, 1996; Baumgratz-Gangl, 1996; Lambert, 1995, 35).

Within the Asia-Pacific Economic Co-operation (APEC) Forum, Japan established the goal of increasing foreign student enrollment in its universities from 45,000 in 1991 to 100,000 by the year 2000. With 53,847 foreign students in 2000, Japan fell far short of this goal, but it is drawing more students from China, Korea, and Taiwan, which have been among the largest U.S. markets for foreign students and scholars. Similarly, Australia is actively recruiting Asian students into its universities and has successfully increased foreign student enrollments from 16,075 in 1985 to 47,834 in 1995 (Davis, 1995, 78, 182; Lambert, 1995, 22–23). New Zealand has also been exceptionally active in the export to Asia of education services, which are now are the fourth-largest services export for that country (WTO, 2001b, 2). As Japanese, Australian, and New Zealand programs draw significant numbers of Asian students into those countries, the number of Asian students coming to the United States is declining for the first time in two decades. Thus, as the OECD's major players in the global higher education market begin to cannibalize each other, particularly the United States, in a near zero-sum game, they share a common interest in finding ways to increase the size of the global higher education market by opening markets with growing or unmet demand for higher education.

In this respect, it is important to note that the official national and international trade data on higher education exports dramatically underestimate the actual levels of cross-border educational services that are already occurring, because official trade statistics measure only consumption abroad, that is, the tuition, fees, and living expenses of students attending foreign colleges and universities (Chamie, 2000; OECD, 2002b; Whichard, 2000). The official statistics on trade in higher education services, which include those of government agencies and international organizations such as the United Nations, simply do not include those areas of trade in higher education where the greatest future growth is likely to occur over the next decade. The official statistics do not capture fees paid by students enrolled in most forms of electronic or distance education (cross-border supply), the fees paid by students receiving instruction in their home country from foreign providers (commercial presence), or those being instructed in their home country by visiting foreign teachers or trainers (presence of individuals) (WTO, 1998b, 7). The official trade statistics also do not capture the international trade in higher education services conducted by for-profit educational institutions (e.g., language institutes) or by corporate education and training facilities in foreign countries (commercial presence), because these activities are recorded by the host countries as part of the gross "domestic" product, rather than as foreign trade (WTO, 1998b, 1). Thus, it is literally impossible at present to develop any reasonably accurate measure of the total international trade in higher education services. However, no one disputes that it is growing and that further liberalization under GATS will accelerate the growth of this new global industry.[9]

TOWARD A GLOBAL MARKET IN HIGHER EDUCATION

The proponents of further trade liberalization in higher education services frequently point to the fact that trade data on the industry is lagging real-time developments precisely because the delivery of higher education services is undergoing a global structural transition. Higher education is branching out into *new institutions,* such as for-profit education and training facilities as well as corporate-sponsored universities. Perhaps the best-known for-profit university is the University of Phoenix, which was established in 1976 to help adult learners earn a college degree or professional certificate without disrupting their career or personal life. The University of Phoenix offers bachelor's, master's and doctoral degrees, as well as professional certificate programs in several areas, including business, administration, accounting, management, technology management, information systems, education, counseling, and nursing. The University of Phoenix offers classes at 110 "campuses" and "learning centers" in the United States, Canada, and Puerto Rico, and via the Internet. The University of Phoenix is now one of the United States's largest private accredited universities with 107,842 enrolled students (University of Phoenix, 2002).

In 1988, there were 400 corporate "universities" in the United States; by 1997 this number had increased to 1,600. It is estimated that 250,000 full-time and 500,000 part-time instructors work for corporate universities, which is approximately equal to the total professorial staff employed by traditional colleges and universities in the United States. Motorola University, which was founded in 1981, now provides instruction to approximately 100,000 students annually, and only 22 percent of its enrolled students are Motorola employees. Motorola University's main "campus" is in Schaumburg, Illinois, but the institution operates thirty sites in nineteen countries, including Brazil, South Africa, China, and Germany (Robinson, 1999, 1–2).

The new for-profit and corporate universities have typically provided "training" and, to a lesser degree, professional certification rather than advanced "theoretical" education. In 1997, UNESCO's International Standard Classification of Education (ISCED) was modified to capture this distinction by incorporating two levels into its definition of tertiary/higher-level studies: "advanced theoretical professional" and "practical/occupational" (UNESCO, 1997). However, this distinction was breaking down as soon as it was adopted, because corporate and profit-making universities have been placing pressure on traditional higher education institutions to compete in this new domestic and international market. In response to these competitive pressures, many traditional nonprofit public and private universities, such as MIT, George Washington University, Temple University, the University of Maryland, the University of Florida, SUNY–Stony Brook, and Georgia State University, to name a few, have created for-profit entities that provide nontraditional education services in both domestic and international markets. These developments are already blurring the distinction between public and private higher education institutions and between their status as nonprofit or for-profit corporations (Slaughter and Leslie, 1997). The demarcation between institutions providing advanced theoretical higher education and practical/occupational certification is becoming equally blurred as evidenced by the fact that several prestigious public and private universities are member institutions of the United States's National Committee for International Trade in Education (NCITE) alongside the American Physical Therapy Association, the American Council for Construction Education, and the International Federation of Nurse Anesthetists (NCITE, 2002).[10]

The emergence of for-profit and corporate universities does not begin to exhaust the possibilities for international commercial presence and the presence of natural persons in the global higher education marketplace. Many of these institutions, including traditional colleges and universities, are seeking authorization to open branch campuses in foreign countries as either wholly owned subsidiaries or majority-owned foreign affiliates (MOFAs) (e.g., Temple University in Japan) (USITC, 1995, 4-3).[11] Others are seeking authorization to license franchises or brand names in foreign countries. Thus, in addition to study abroad, there are a variety of new mechanisms for delivering higher education services to foreign countries, including the following:

- Public higher education institutions are using their "independent" privately incorporated nonprofit foundations as fiscal agents for the delivery of courses, programs, and services that are liberated from state accounting and budgeting regulations.
- Public and private higher education institutions are establishing for-profit corporations to provide certain auxiliary services, which are better served by U.S. for-profit tax law than nonprofit status (e.g., bookstores, continuing education, management training, and executive development centers). Once these entities are extended overseas, they seek comparable or nondiscriminatory tax treatment in foreign countries.
- Freestanding programs are being established that operate outside the country of the supplier (e.g., an MBA school) (commercial presence).
- Branch campuses are being established at which a degree-granting entity is the child of a home institution (commercial presence).
- Operations are being franchised; that is, a third party is used to give a degree—such as a computer company delivering a university computer science degree in a foreign country (commercial presence).

- Twinning arrangements are set up in which a degree is obtained through study in more than one country through an agreement between two institutions of higher education (consumption abroad).
- Professors are giving courses abroad for transferable credit, and consultants are supplying certificated training courses abroad (presence of natural persons).

Moreover, both public and private campuses find for-profit tax status the most reasonable corporate vehicle when delivering higher education services in foreign countries that do not operate under the same tax laws (which raises issues about discriminatory tax treatment, repatriation of profits, etc.). Similarly, as with other transnational enterprises, commercial presence in a foreign country raises questions about national treatment, nontariff barriers (e.g., licensing), and "discriminatory" subsidies to domestic enterprises. A report by the WTO Secretariat (1998a, 9) suggests that as GATS is applied more widely to the higher education sector the resulting growth "in internationally traded education services is likely to have a profound impact on the higher education system of some countries and the economics of education."

In addition, higher education is also developing *new methods of delivery*, such as distance learning via the Internet, radio, and television. The United Kingdom's Open University began with a domestic focus, but its operations have expanded into the developing nations of Asia, such as Thailand and Singapore, and more recently into the United States. In the United States, the Open University has established a formal alliance with the Western Governors University to create a unique and politically powerful public-private joint venture that is allied with several major corporations and was supported enthusiastically by the Clinton-Gore administration (Robinson, 1999, 2). Although the University of Phoenix and the Open University are among the best-known pioneers in this field, U.S. higher education institutions have stampeded into the distance learning market with brandname products such as the New Jersey Virtual University, the Michigan Virtual University, the SUNY Learning Network, and UMass Online.

On an even larger scale, the World Bank has financed the development of the African Virtual University (AVU), established in 1997, which is a consortium of OECD colleges and universities that have partnered to deliver professional programs to students enrolled at higher education institutions in seventeen sub-Saharan countries. By 2001, more than 24,000 students had taken courses through AVU in technology, engineering, business, and science. AVU provides access to an online digital library with more than 1,000 full-text journals. The AVU has received glowing endorsements from the *Harvard Business Review, Time Magazine,* and the BBC ("The African Virtual University," 2001).

Finally, higher education is branching out into *new activities,* such as educational support services, management consulting, tutoring, student abroad facilitation, degree transfer and course transfer clearinghouses, and educational testing services. These "other education services" include the following:

- the sale of e-learning courseware and technical support services,
- the sale of proprietary materials such as books, courseware, multimedia packages, or testing, along with associated services,
- study abroad facilitation (payment of fees, visas, course transfer, housing arrangements),
- the sale of intellectual property, such as the licensing of the personal name of academic "superstars,"
- the sale of course packages or distance learning modules,
- the licensing of copyrights on new materials such as course software.

Thus, even though few countries have made GATS commitments on higher education services at the present time, the most recent proposals submitted to the WTO's Council on Trade in Services by the United States, Australia, and New Zealand suggest that further liberalization will be pressed hard in the next round of WTO negotiations with potentially enormous impacts on the global higher education market.[12] The WTO's Council on Trade in Services, the OECD, individual governments, and private associations such as NCITE have each identified numerous barriers to international trade in higher education that will certainly be addressed in the next round of WTO negotiations.

BARRIERS TO GLOBAL TRADE IN HIGHER EDUCATION

The United States, Australia, and New Zealand are the leading competitors in the lucrative Asian higher education market, so each has an obvious interest in promoting further trade liberalization in this sector. The United States is unequivocal in stating that its proposal for liberalizing trade in education services "is to help create conditions favorable to suppliers of higher education, adult education, and training courses" (WTO, 1998b, 2). The U.S. trade policy has targeted education services "as a growing industry" internationally, where it has exceptional competitive advantages in many of the fastest-growing segments of the market such as "the provision of management or technical training (including language training) and skills upgrades for current members of the workforce. The need for such education is particularly acute in high-technology industries including medical services, computer services, and flight training schools" (WTO, 1998b, 2).

Moreover, the major suppliers of international higher education argue that further liberalization will also benefit the consumer countries. The U.S. proposal argues that the "availability of these education and training services can help to develop a more efficient workforce, leading countries to an improved competitive position in the world economy" (WTO, 1998b, 3). The New Zealand proposal observes that international "trade in education services provides benefits to participating economies at the individual, institutional, and societal level, through academic exchange, increased cross-cultural linkages, and technology transfer"

(WTO, 2001b, 1). Australia views "the liberalisation of trade in education services primarily as a means of providing individuals with access to a wide variety of educational options," which in "qualitative and quantitative terms are not otherwise available in the country of origin" (WTO, 2001a, 1–2). For government officials in many developing countries, this may well be an attractive option. The liberalization of trade in education promises to bring state-of-the-art higher education, skills training, and educational infrastructure to poor countries through foreign direct investment instead of the massive social investments that would be necessary to build a world-class higher education system at public expense. The global option in higher education thus frees up limited resources for investment in other areas such as social welfare and K–12 education, where governments are likely to receive favorable treatment from the World Bank and IMF.

Consumption Abroad

Most of the recorded trade in higher education occurs through consumption abroad, and hence, measures restricting the mobility of students will likely receive a great deal of attention in the next round of WTO negotiations. Direct restrictions on consumption abroad generally take the form of immigration requirements and foreign currency controls, but the United States's "new war" on terrorism may well impede significant movement on this issue. However, there are many indirect barriers to student mobility, such as the difficulty of translating degrees obtained abroad into national equivalents and the denial of government employment to persons holding degrees from foreign countries. Hence, the WTO Secretariat is particularly interested in moving toward a series of agreements on standards for professional training, licensing, and accreditation, which would significantly liberalize trade through consumption abroad by making foreign-earned degrees more portable (WTO, 1998a, 8). It is widely recognized that a multilateral agreement on such standards has the potential to disadvantage domestic institutions of higher education in developing countries, which lack the physical facilities, libraries, personnel, and public financing to compete against better-financed private, corporate, or other foreign institutions.

Commercial Presence

There are still numerous barriers to trade in higher education through commercial presence, including the inability of foreign-based institutions to obtain national licenses in many countries (e.g., Greece, Japan) or to be recognized as a degree/certificate-granting educational institution. In some countries, there are measures limiting direct investment by foreign education providers (e.g., equity ceilings), nationality requirements for owners, needs tests, restrictions on recruiting foreign teachers, the existence of government monopolies, and high subsidies for local institutions.[13] These restrictions significantly limit the ability of transnational higher education institutions, in whatever form, to obtain market entry in many countries. The United States is particularly concerned about commercial presence restrictions, such as limitations on the type of legal entity, participation of foreign capital, and establishment of for-profit institutions, needs tests, accreditation and licensing requirements that can be used to obstruct the commercial presence of a foreign-based higher education institution. The U.S. position is that restrictions on commercial presence should be "liberalized to the greatest extent" in the next round of multilateral negotiations (WTO, 1998b, 2).

On this point, the United States has made numerous complaints on behalf of Temple University about the Japanese Ministry of Education's refusal to recognize affiliates of U.S. higher education institutions as "universities," which prohibits them from granting degrees and excludes their graduates from government employment (WTO, 1998a, 8). Local hiring requirements limit the ability of transnational higher education institutions (HEIs) to obtain a competitive advantage through the use of foreign instructors with Ph.D.s by requiring that local instructors be hired to teach courses. Some countries require a local partner in the enterprise or prohibit voluntary exit and repatriation of profits from a joint venture. Many countries are concerned that lifting investment restrictions will allow transnational corporations to purchase local higher education institutions and to license or franchise brand-name institutions (e.g., MIT) that will offer degrees that are indistinguishable from a degree obtained at the "real" institution.

Presence of Natural Persons

The United States allows natural persons of any nationality to teach at its institutions of higher education (HB1 visa), and it recently raised the ceiling on the number of visas granted to persons in this and related areas. Thus, it is pressing to remove restrictions on the presence of natural persons, such as nationality conditions (citizenship), restrictions on length of stay, payment of taxes, and needs tests (i.e., that no qualified citizen is available for the job). These conditions are already part of the North American Free Trade Agreement (NAFTA), which went far beyond the WTO in terms of liberalizing trade in services and foreign direct investment among the three NAFTA partners. The United States, Australia, and New Zealand are each seeking to ease visa restrictions and foreign currency controls that impede the movement of natural persons engaged in delivering educational services abroad.

Cross-Border Supply

Many countries are concerned that lifting restrictions on the cross-border supply of educational services will allow transnational corporations or foreign higher institutions to offer online degrees (e.g., Endicott College in Mexico) that are indistinguishable in form from a degree obtained in the institution's home country. However, aside from quality controls, many countries impose restrictions on the use and import of teaching and other educational materials. The Middle East is particularly onerous in restricting the electronic transmission of materials (e.g., radio, television, Internet), primarily for political and cultural reasons. Russia prohibits the importation of many medical textbooks and films as illicit pornography.

A GLOBAL FUTURE FOR HIGHER EDUCATION

There is a strong and deepening opposition to globalization among progressive social forces, which include organized labor, consumer advocates, environmental groups, feminists, students, leftist intellectuals, and many other groups. The intensity of this opposition cannot be underestimated following the "Battle of Seattle," particularly since that confrontation was followed by large demonstrations against the World Bank and IMF in Washington, D.C., and by a violent confrontation in Genoa, Italy. For this reason, however, it is important to note that not only is "globalization" a process, but it is a policy. Globalization is a set of agreements and decisions about how citizens and businesses will interact with each other across national boundaries, and these agreements are institutionalized in international organizations such as the WTO, the World Bank, and the IMF. These international institutions are political organizations and hence the question for educators is whether higher education will play its traditional role as outside critic of this process or violent opponent of the process, or will be an engaged participant in the development of the multilateral trade policies that will affect higher education in the coming decades. These strategies are not either/or choices, since the latter strategy will require educators to "kick in the door" of these organizations and to demand of their own governments that they participate in the negotiations that affect their institutions.

This is new political territory for most academics, who are unaccustomed to the language, the protocols, and dispute resolution procedures of multilateral trade agreements. Nevertheless, there are some indications that the nascent global upheaval of the past two years, combined with the concerns of many individual governments, is causing the proponents of trade liberalization in higher education to moderate some of their positions. The WTO Secretariat is now concerned that "in the rush to become market-oriented, universities might be distracted from their educational missions," while "flows of people and exposure to new ideas can arguably have a challenging impact on the structure of relatively fragile societies and touch on cultural sensitivities" (WTO, 1998a, 9). The WTO Secretariat has even responded to members' concerns that the global commodification of higher education is being used to prod traditional colleges and universities "to look for alternative [i.e., nongovernmental] sources of funds" when it is questionable on purely economic grounds "whether higher education can be profitable for private investors without public subsidies" (WTO, 1998a, 9; cf. Sauve and Stern, 2000).

The concerns of many countries about the GATS's potential to subordinate domestic education priorities to the rules of international trade liberalization have also moved the most aggressive market leaders in this sector to at least soften their positions on trade liberalization. The United States recently clarified an earlier position against "subsidies" (i.e., public funding) for higher education by declaring "that education to a large extent is a governmental function" under GATS (WTO, 2000, 1). The United States still insists that because "most countries permit private education to coexist with public education," it should be subject to the GATS regime, but the latest U.S. proposal for further negotiations on trade in education services accepts the principle that "that private education and training will continue to supplement, not displace, public education systems" throughout the world (WTO, 2000, 1).

This position is being advanced with even greater vigor by Australia and New Zealand, which are the only other countries to submit proposals on education services for the next round of WTO negotiations. New Zealand's proposal to the WTO argues that "international trade in education services can provide a means of supplementing and supporting national education policy objectives," rather than subverting them (WTO, 2001b, 1). Similarly, the Australian proposal acknowledges "the importance of education in the preparation for life as a citizen, the transmission of values and culture, and development of national well-being," and accordingly, it recognizes "that governments must retain their sovereign right to determine their own domestic funding and regulatory practices/measures" (WTO, 2001a, 1). Therefore, the Australian proposal goes furthest in accepting the principle that the upcoming "education services negotiations should not prevent Member countries from providing public funds for education to meet domestic policy and regulatory objectives" (WTO, 2001a, 3). Like its partners, Australia "views the liberalisation of trade in education services primarily as a means of providing individuals in all countries with access to a wide range of educational options," including government-funded public higher education institutions (WTO, 2001a, 1).

It is still much too early to judge the impact of globalization and trade liberalization on higher education, particularly since the current commitments to WTO schedules are limited to a few countries. Nevertheless, multilateral trade liberalization has the potential to transform higher education into an increasingly privatized commodity that is traded on world markets under the same rules that apply to coal and automobiles. There are powerful social forces seeking to create global markets that will push colleges and universities in this direction, and these forces include corporate universities, for-profit universities, the administrations of many public and private higher education institutions, and government trade delegations. These social forces often patently dismiss higher education's "noneconomic" role in the transmission of localized cultural and intellectual traditions, its role in promoting equal opportunity, citizenship, democratic leadership, and public service. Perry Robinson has observed that many leaders of the movement for trade liberalization in higher education regard it "as simply one industry among others that must face the discipline of the market," and hence, they "are hostile to university traditions, the professorial authority and control of instruction and curriculum, and increasingly view universities as institutions that must yield to the demands of the market that views education as worker training" (Robinson, 1999, 2).

Thus, as trade in higher education services becomes a higher priority in the next WTO negotiations, there are at least three major political and cultural issues that ought to concern those with a direct stake in higher education's mission in the next century. Despite the financial allure of foreign direct investment in higher education, a rapid transnationalization of "the industry" has the potential to overwhelm weaker and less developed systems of public higher education in the developing countries (Currie and Newson, 1998). Motorola University alone is larger than the entire higher education systems of many countries. It is not too far-fetched to suggest that the financial power of U.S. higher education institutions—always in search of new revenue streams—could create global franchises comparable to McDonald's, Coca-Cola, and Kentucky Fried Chicken. UMass–Buenos Aires or California State–Puebla are not unrealistic consequences of trade liberalization.

Second, the globalization of higher education has the potential to marginalize the transmission of national and local culture and to subordinate democratic citizenship to the purely profit-maximizing goals of transnational enterprises and their educational support units. This process of marginalization and subordination is directly linked to the privatization of higher education, including the private subsidiaries of nominally "public" universities. Finally, the corporatization of colleges and universities inevitably leads to a loss of faculty control and governance. It also raises many other issues about the changing class status of the professoriat on a global level, including the adequacy of current organizations to address the issues associated with globalization. And so, as always, we confront the question, What is to be done?

NOTES

1. Offe (1984, 257) notes that "the systems-theoretical approach is an adequate tool of analysis because it corresponds to the way the managers of the system conceive it."

2. The North American Industry Classification System (NAICS) has replaced the U.S. Standard Industrial Classification (SIC) system. NAICS was developed jointly by the United States, Canada, and Mexico to provide comparability in statistics about business activity across North America. The International Standard Classification of Education was created by UNESCO in 1976 to provide global comparability of education statistics, and it was revised in 1997 (UNESCO, 1997).

3. One of the most commonly cited examples of a virtual university is the Western Governors' University, which was founded by seventeen governors of western U.S. states but also includes private sector partners such as IBM, AT&T, Cisco, Microsoft, and International Thomson. The WGU is an independent, nonprofit, accredited, degree-granting entity that does not employ a teaching faculty or develop any of its own courses. The WGU purchases "academic content" from faculty "providers" employed by other private and public universities (WTO, 1998a, 5).

4. The full text of the original treaty as amended through 1966 can be accessed at http://pacific.commerce.ubc.ca/trade/.

5. The OECD (1996, 11–12, 59–63) defines nontariff barriers to trade as "border measures other than tariffs that may be used by countries, usually on a selective basis, to re-

strict imports." Approximately 20 percent of world trade encounters nontariff barriers, and the trade coverage of these measures was tending to expand as tariff barriers were lowered under GATT. The United Nations Conference on Trade and Development (UNCTAD) identifies 72 different types of NTBs in its classification scheme. NTBs include volume-restraining measures (e.g., prohibitions and quotas), import authorizations (e.g., licensing, health and safety standards, technical standards, censorship), price controls (e.g., minimum prices, antidumping actions), and other barriers such as subsidies to domestic producers, favorable tax treatment for import sensitive industries (Laird and Yeats, 1990, 4, 17–19), and anticompetitive practices by private firms (Hay, 1996; Janow, 1996; Warner, 1996).

6. The principles are most-favored-nation treatment, transparency without requiring the disclosure of confidential information, increasing participation of developing countries, economic integration so as not to prevent entrance into labor market integration agreements, domestic regulation, recognition, monopolies and exclusive service suppliers, business practices, emergency safeguard measures, payments and transfers, restrictions to safeguard the balance of payments, government procurement, general exceptions, security exceptions, and subsidies.

7. The commitments in higher education are by Australia, Congo RP, Costa Rica, Czech Republic, European Community, Hungary, Jamaica, Japan, Lesotho, Lichtenstein, Mexico, New Zealand, Norway, Panama, Poland, Sierra Leone, Slovak Republic, Slovenia, Switzerland, Trinidad and Tobago, and Turkey (WTO, 1998b, 21).

8. The United States has consistently recorded a trade deficit in goods since 1971, but it has recorded a trade surplus in services during the same period. For example, in 2000, the United States had a $452.2 billion trade deficit in goods, but a $76.5 billion trade surplus in services (U.S. Department of Commerce, 2002b, Table 1, p. 39). Despite the overall trade deficit in goods, the United States has recorded an average trade surplus of approximately $30 billion annually in "high technology" since 1989 (U.S. Department of Commerce, 2000).

9. The OECD acknowledges that its estimate that $30 billion is traded annually in higher education services "is undoubtedly an underestimate of the current level of trade in educational services," because it captures only consumption abroad. Consequently, the OECD convened the first "Experts' Meeting on Statistics and Indicators in Education Services" on December 13–14, 2001 (in Paris) to initiate a discussion about how to improve data collection and develop a more reliable picture of the size and main trends in trade in educational services worldwide (OECD, 2002b).

10. The National Committee for International Trade in Education Services is a membership/advocacy organization created in 1999 to advise the Office of the U.S. Trade Representative on the upcoming round of WTO negotiations on GATS (NCITE, 2002).

11. The Japanese Ministry of Education does not recognize affiliates of U.S. higher education institutions as "universities" in Japan and restricts the granting of "university degrees" to domestic institutions. Students of foreign affiliates do not qualify for student transportation passes or government financial assistance, and their graduates cannot obtain employment with the Japanese government (WTO, 1998a, 8).

12. The United States, France, Germany, and Great Britain command most of the world consumption abroad market in higher education services. However, Australia, which ranks seventh in consumption abroad, and New Zealand have aggressively entered the Asian market through commercial presence, cross-border supply, and the presence of individuals.

13. The expanding role of foreign direct investment (FDI) in the global economy is directly relevant to the problems of commercial presence. In 1997, 151 changes in FDI regulatory regimes were made by 76 countries and 89 percent of these changes created a more favorable or liberalized environment for FDI (UNCTAD, 1998, xix).

Works Cited

"The African Virtual University: Education for the Knowledge Age." 2001. Available online at http://www.avu.org.

Barrow, Clyde W. 2001. "What Is to Be Undone? Academic Efficiency and the Corporate Ideal in American Higher Education." *Found Object,* No. 10 (Spring), pp. 149–180.

———. 2000. "Strategic Planning and Institutional Restructuring in U.S. Higher Education: The Challenge to Faculty Unions." *Estudios del Hombre,* No. 12, pp. 145–162.

———. 1990a. "Styles of Intellectualism in Weber's Historical Sociology." *Sociological Inquiry,* Vol. 60 (Spring), pp. 47–61.

———. 1990b. *Universities and the Capitalist State: Corporate Liberalism and the Reconstruction of American Higher Education, 1894–1928.* Madison: University of Wisconsin Press.

Baumgratz-Gangl, Gisela. 1996. "Developments in the Internationalization of Higher Education in Europe," in *Academic Mobility in a Changing World* (pp. 103–128), ed. Peggy Blumenthal, Craufurd Goodwin, Alan Smith, and Ulrich Teichler. London and Bristol, Penn.: Jessica Kingsley.

Chamie, Mary. 2000. "Current Status and Latest Development of the Manual on Statistics of International Trade in Services." Paper delivered at the APEC Seminar on Statistical Reporting on Service Trade, held at Tianjin, P.R. China, August 14–17, 2000. Available online at www.apecsec.org.

Cooke, Morris L. 1910. *Academic and Industrial Efficiency.* CFAT Bulletin, No. 5. Boston: Merrymount.

Currie, Jan, and Janice Newson, eds. 1998. *Universities and Globalization: Critical Perspectives.* Thousand Oaks, Calif.: Sage Publications.

Davis, S. J. 1992. "Cross-Country Patterns of Change in Relative Wages." *NBER Macroeconomic Annual, 1992.* Cambridge: MIT Press.

Davis, Todd M., ed. 1995. *Open Doors, 1994–1995: Report on International Educational Exchange.* New York: Institute of International Education.

Executive Office of the President. 1987. *Standard Industrial Classification Manual.* Washington, D.C.: Office of Management and Budget.

Graham, Edward M. 1996. "Investment and the New Multilateral Trade Context," in *Market Access After the Uruguay Round: Investment, Competition and Technology Perspectives* (pp. 35–62). Paris: OECD.

Haber, Samuel. 1964. *Efficiency and Uplift: Scientific Management in the Progressive Era, 1890–1920.* Chicago: University of Chicago Press.

Habermas, Jurgen. 1970. *Toward a Rational Society.* Boston: Beacon Press.

Hay, Donald A. 1996. "Anti-Competitive Practices, Market Access and Competition Policy in a Global Economy," in *Market Access After the Uruguay Round: Investment, Competition and Technology Perspectives,* pp. 81–100. Paris: OECD.

Janow, Merit E. 1996. "Public and Private Restraints That Limit Access to Markets," in *Market Access After the Uruguay Round: Investment, Competition and Technology Perspectives* (pp. 101–122). Paris: OECD.

Laird, Sam, and Alexander Yeats. 1990. *Quantitative Methods for Trade-Barrier Analysis.* Washington Square, N.Y.: New York University Press.

Lambert, R. D. 1995. "Foreign Student Flows and the Internationalization of Higher Education," in *International Challenges to American Colleges and Universities* (pp. 18–41), ed. Katherine H. Hanson and Joel W. Meyerson. Phoenix, Ariz.: American Council on Education/Oryx Press.

Larsen, Kurt, Rosemary Morris, and John P. Martin. 2001. *Trade in Education Services: Trends and Emerging Issues,* OECD Document CERI/CD/RD(2001)6. Paris: OECD Centre for Educational Research and Innovation.

Leyton-Brown, David. 1996. "Political Dimensions of Regionalization in a Changing World," in *Academic Mobility in a Changing World* (pp. 7–19), ed. Peggy Blumenthal, Craufurd Goodwin, Alan Smith, and Ulrich Teichler. London and Bristol, Penn.: Jessica Kingsley.

National Committee for International Trade in Education (NCITE). 2002. "Welcome to NCITE." Available online at www.tradeineducation.org/general_info/intro.html.

Newson, Janice, and Howard Buchbinder. 1988. *The University Means Business: Universities, Corporations, and Academic Work*. Toronto: Garamond Press.

Offe, Claus. 1984. *Contradictions of the Welfare State*. Cambridge: MIT Press.

Office of the United States President. 1997. *Economic Report of the President*. Washington, D.C.: Government Printing Office.

Organization for Economic Cooperation and Development (OECD). 2002a. "About Trade in Education Services." Available online at http://www.oecd.org.

———. 2002b. "Statistics and Indicators on the Main Trends in the Internationalisation of Post-Secondary Education and Training." Available online at http://www.oecd.org.

———. 1996. *Indicators of Tariff and Non-Tariff Barriers*. Paris.

Robinson, Perry. 1999. "Transnational Higher Education and Faculty Unions: Issues for Discussion and Action." Paper delivered at Education International Higher Education Conference, held in Budapest, Hungary, September 23–25. Available online at www.aft.org/higher_ed/reports.

Sauve, Pierre, and Robert M. Stern, eds. 2000. *GATS 2000: New Directions in Services Trade Liberalization*. Washington, D.C.: Brookings Institution Press.

Schott, Jeffrey J. 1994. *The Uruguay Round: An Assessment*. Washington, D.C.: Institute for International Economics.

Scott, Barbara Ann. 1983. *Crisis Management in American Higher Education*. Westport, Conn.: Praeger Press.

Shumar, Wesley. 1997. *College for Sale: A Critique of the Commodification of Higher Education*. London: Falmer Press.

Skilbeck, Malcolm, and Helen Connell. 1996. "International Education from the Perspective of Emergence World Regionalism: The Academic, Scientific, and Technological Dimension," in *Academic Mobility in a Changing World* (pp. 66–102), ed. Peggy Blumenthal, Craufurd Goodwin, Alan Smith, and Ulrich Teichler. London and Bristol, Penn.: Jessica Kingsley.

Slaughter, Sheila. 1990. *The Higher Learning and High Technology: Dynamics of Higher Education Policy Formation*. Albany: State University of New York Press.

Slaughter, Sheila, and Larry L. Leslie. 1997. *Academic Capitalism: Politics, Policies, and the Entrepreneurial University*. Baltimore: Johns Hopkins University Press.

Steger, Manfred B. 2002. *Globalism: The New Market Ideology*. Lanham, Md.: Rowman and Littlefield.

United Nations Conference on Trade and Development (UNCTAD). 1998. *World Investment Report, 1998: Trends and Determinants*. New York and Geneva.

United Nations Education, Scientific, and Cultural Organization (UNESCO). 1997. *International Standard Classification of Education, ISCED 1997*. Available online at http://www.uis.unesco.org/en/pub/isced/ISCED_A.pdf.

United States Department of Commerce, Bureau of Economic Analysis. 2002a. *Industry Accounts Data: Gross Domestic Product by Industry, 1994–2000*. Available online at www.bea.gov/bea/dn2/gpoc.htm.

———. 2002b. *Industry Accounts Data: U.S. International Services: Cross-Border Trade & Sales Through Affiliates, 1986–2000 (Table 5.15—Other Private Services, 2000)*. Available online at www.bea.gov/bea/di/1001serv/intlserv.htm.

_____. 2002c. *Survey of Current Business.* Washington, D.C.: Government Printing Office.

United States Department of Commerce, Bureau of the Census. 2000. "U.S. Trade Balance with Advanced Technology, 1989–2000." Available online at http://www.census.gov/foreign-trade/balance/c0007.html.

United States International Trade Commission (USITC). 1995. *General Agreement on Trade in Services: Examination of Major Trading Partners Schedules of Commitments,* USITC Publication 2940. Washington, D.C.

_____. 1994. *Potential Impact on the U.S. Economy and Industries of the GATT Uruguay Round Agreements,* USITC Publication 2790. Washington, D.C.

"University of Phoenix." 2002. Available online at http://www.phoenix.edu/index_flat.html.

Warner, Mark A. A. 1996. "Public and Private Restraints on Trade: Effects on Investment Decisions and Policy Approaches to Them," in *Market Access After the Uruguay Round: Investment, Competition and Technology Perspectives* (pp. 123–142). Paris: OECD.

Waters, Malcolm. 1995. *Globalization.* London: Routledge.

Weber, Max. 1946. "Science as a Vocation," in *From Max Weber: Essays in Sociology* (pp. 129–156), ed. Hans H. Gerth and C. Wright Mills. New York: Oxford University Press.

Whalley, John. 1989. *The Uruguay Round and Beyond.* Ann Arbor: University of Michigan Press.

Whichard, Obie G. 2000. "United States Statistics on Trade in Services." Paper delivered at the APEC Seminar on Statistical Reporting on Service Trade, held at Tianjin, P.R. China, August 14–17, 2000. Available online at www.apecsec.org.

World Bank. 1999. *1999 World Development Indicators.* Washington, D.C.: World Bank.

_____. 1995. *Priorities and Strategies for Education: A World Bank Review.* Washington, D.C.: World Bank.

_____. 1994. *Higher Education: The Lessons of Experience.* Washington, D.C.: World Bank.

World Trade Organization (WTO). 2002. "The Organization: Members and Observers." Available online at http://www.wto.org/english/thewto_e/whatis_e/tif_e/org6_.htm.

_____. 2001a. "Communication from Australia: Negotiating Higher (Tertiary) Education, Adult Education, and Training (01-4716)." Geneva: Council for Trade in Services.

_____. 2001b. "Communication from New Zealand: Negotiating Proposal for Education Services (01-3215)." Geneva: Council for Trade in Services.

_____. 2001c. *GATS: Fact and Fiction.* Geneva: Secretariat.

_____. 2000. "Communication from the United States: Negotiating Proposal for Education Services (00-5552)." Geneva: Council for Trade in Services.

_____. 1998a. "Education Services: Background Note by the Secretariat (98-3691)." Geneva: Council for Trade in Services.

_____. 1998b. "Communication from the United States: Education Services (98-4048)." Geneva: Council for Trade in Services.

_____. 1991. "Services Sectoral Classification List: Note by the Secretariat (91-0074)." Geneva: Secretariat.

17

Vagabond Capitalism and the Necessity of Social Reproduction

CINDI KATZ*

The phrase *vagabond capitalism* puts the blame for vagrancy and dereliction where it belongs—on capitalism, that unsettled, dissolute, irresponsible stalker of the world. But it also suggests a threat that lies at the heart of capitalism's vagrancy, that an increasingly global capitalist production can shuck many of its particular commitments to place, most centrally those associated with social reproduction, which is almost always less mobile than production. At worst, this disengagement hurtles certain people into forms of vagabondage; at best, it leaves people in all parts of the world struggling to secure the material goods and social practices associated with social reproduction. Insisting on the necessity of social reproduction provides a critical arena—as yet undertheorized—within which many of the problems associated with the globalization of capitalist production can be confronted.

In this chapter I hope to delineate in a systematic fashion what is entailed in the accomplishment of social reproduction and what is at stake when social repro-

....

*An earlier version of this chapter was presented as the 2001 *Antipode* Lecture at the annual meetings of the Royal Geographic Society/Institute of British Geographers in Plymouth, England. (It also appears, with some changes, in *Antipode*, Vol. 33, No. 3, 2001. Permission to republish is gratefully acknowledged to Blackwell Publishing.) I am grateful to Jane Wills for inviting me and to *Antipode* for sponsoring my visit. My thanks to the audience for their stimulating and thoughtful questions. And as ever, my appreciation to Neil Smith, who months ago pushed me to rethink situated knowledge.

This chapter is dedicated with love to the memories of James Blaut and Graciela Uribe-Ortega, two of the most spirited, imaginative, and determined liberation geographers I have ever known. Their revolutionary energy, quick and sharp political insights, and willingness to fight for equality, justice, and freedom at great personal cost will always be an inspiration.

duction gets unhinged from production, as is now the case in many parts of the world. These concerns will be illustrated with a brief discussion of what might be conceptualized as a "rescaling of childhood." The final part of the chapter develops the notion of "topography" as a critical methodology that can be drawn on to produce "counter-topographies" that provide means of imagining and developing a translocal politics opposed to globalized capitalism and other forms of oppression, especially around issues of social reproduction.

Globalized capitalism has changed the face of social reproduction worldwide over the past three decades, enabling intensification of capital accumulation and exacerbating differences in wealth and poverty. The demise of the social contract as a result of neo-liberalism, privatization, and the fraying of the welfare state is a crucial aspect of this shift. Children, among others, suffer from these changes as all manner of public disinvestments take place, including those in education, social welfare, housing, health care, and public environments as part of and in concert with a relative lack of corporate commitment to particular places. The flip side of the withdrawal of public and corporate support for the social wage is a reliance on private means of securing and sustaining social reproduction—not just the uncompensated caring work of families, most commonly women, but also a shunting of responsibility, often geographically, that has clear class, race, and national components. The social reproduction of a workforce of migrants, for instance, is carried out in their countries of origin, and when they are employed elsewhere, it generally represents a direct transfer of wealth from poorer to richer countries. Variable capital produced in one site and tapped in another is no less a capital transfer than the extraction of raw materials, debt servicing, and the like. Yet this transfer seems of no moment to most theorists of globalization. Social reproduction is the missing figure in current globalization debates. The omission is serious. Globalization cannot be understood without addressing the restructuring of social reproduction.

SOCIAL REPRODUCTION

Social reproduction, the messy and indeterminate stuff of everyday life, is also a set of structured practices that unfold in dialectical relation with production, with which it is mutually constitutive and in tension. It encompasses daily as well as long-term reproduction of both the means of production and the labor power to make them work. At its most basic level it hinges upon the biological reproduction of the labor force, both generationally and on a daily basis, through the acquisition and distribution of the means of existence, including food, shelter, clothing, and health care. According to Marxist theory, however, social reproduction is also much more than this, encompassing the reproduction of the labor force at a certain (and fluid) level of differentiation and expertise. This differentiated and skilled labor force is socially constituted. Not only are the material social practices associated with its production historically and geographically specific, but its contours and requirements are the outcome of ongoing struggle. Apart from the need to secure the means of existence, the production and reproduction of the labor force call forth a range of cultural forms and practices that, again, are geographically and historically specific, including those associated with knowledge and learning, social justice and its apparatus, and the media.

Many struggles over wages are inflected with and driven by redefining what constitutes an "adequately prepared" labor force. Under Fordism, such struggles led to advances for a large fraction of the working class that were not simply economistic. These advances were measured in terms of expanded educational opportunities and steadily increasing levels of educational attainment, a broader span of benefits available to workers, and a wider spectrum of social and cultural services and opportunities of which working people might avail themselves. Procuring such gains progressively redefined the contours of social reproduction and its contents, and each gain for labor increased the relative costs of labor for capitalists.

But workplace struggles were not the only source of change in defining the compass of social reproduction or the means of its attainment. Social reproduction is secured through a shifting constellation of sources encompassed within the broad categories of the state, the household, capital, and civil society. The balance among these categories varies historically, geographically, and across class. Whereas the U.S. union struggles of the mid-20th century forced capitalist firms to shoulder an increasing proportion of the responsibility for social reproduction *and* simultaneously expanded what was considered socially necessary social reproduction (through increased social benefits packages, expanded workplace training programs, and the like), earlier reformist activists associated with the Progressive Era in the United States forced the state to shoulder an increasing share of the costs of social reproduction and provide an expanded array of practices associated with it (see Marston, forthcoming). These reformer-propelled shifts could be observed in such things as social housing, expanded public health services, playground and park development, public education, and the institution of social welfare programs. Of course, the picture is really more complicated than this: Clear class interests riddled the progressive movement, reconfiguring a polyglot immigrant and working-class society into a white middle-class image, and the state got on board because these new arenas of practice also served capitalist interests. Nevertheless, the expanded role of the state and capital in securing social reproduction altered the nature and extent of household-based practices of social reproduction as much as it did those associated with civil society such as church-based orphanages, almshouses, private charities, settlement houses, and immigrants' and working men's and women's circles. Certainly neither arena was "put out of business"; but the ways in which households secured their reproduction were altered tremendously, albeit without substantially affecting the gender division of labor within the household, and the role of private charities shifted to other realms (still often associated with social reproduction broadly conceived), such as the support of cultural institutions and activities.

Social reproduction, like globalization, has political-economic, cultural, and environmental aspects, each of which has a bearing on the geographies of social reproduction and, by extension, children's geographies. The political-economic aspect of social reproduction encompasses, among other things, the reproduction of work knowledge and skills, the practices that maintain and reinforce class and other categories of difference, and the learning that inculcates what Pierre Bourdieu refers to as the habitus, a set of cultural forms and practices that works to reinforce and naturalize the dominant social relations of production and reproduction. It also includes the reproduction and maintenance of the forces and means of production. Whereas the former are reproduced through some amalgam of the household, civil society, and the state (largely through schools), the latter are primarily the purview of capital and the state.

The gender division of labor within the household, which is itself historically and geographically contingent, commonly presumes women's responsibility for most of the work of reproduction—including, for instance, child-rearing, food provisioning and preparation, cleaning, laundering, and other tasks of "home-making." With wealth and "development," an increasing number of such tasks are provided through the market or can be purchased, depending upon household circumstances and other socioeconomic factors. Prepared foods, domestic assistance, childcare services, and the like may, for some, lessen household work and "free up" time for participation in the paid labor force or other activities, but they do not alter gendered divisions of labor or the social relations of production and reproduction that undergird and are sustained by the marketing of some of the means of social reproduction. As feminist geographers who have studied the questions of social reproduction associated with childcare have made clear, the transnational migration of childcare workers of various types represents a subsidy of wealthier "first world" women (and, by extension, those who employ them) either by young women from other parts of the "first world" or, more commonly, by women from the global south whose own children are often left behind with relatives. These transnational exchanges enable the migrant women to not only work longer hours but also receive less compensation in the process (Rose, 1993; Pulsipher, 1993; see also Parreñas, 2001; Hochschild, 2000).

The state, of course, has its own hand in this process. As an example, consider the immigration policies in the United States and Canada that simultaneously admit lone women workers from certain poorer nations (mostly in the global south) and prevent their families from joining them. Various visa programs in both countries ensure a continuous supply of cheap domestic labor including nannies and other child-minders. But the state is involved in the political-economic aspects of social reproduction as well. From state subsidies for electrification, water supplies, and sewage treatment to schools and health-care services and the provision of a variety of goods and services associated with the "welfare state," the state has long been implicated in social reproduction. The varying roles of the state across history and geography also affect the balance between the various constituencies in terms of how social reproduction gets carried out. Recent trends toward privatization, for example, have created sharp distinctions between rich and poor households that affect the ways in which the work of social reproduction is accomplished, and by whom. In many places these shifts have had a particularly chilling effect on women, who, for the most part, continue to fill the gap between state and market in ensuring their households' reproduction and well-being.

There is a blurred boundary between these practices, which I associate with the political-economic aspect of social reproduction, and those involving its cultural aspect. In the latter category I include the cultural forms and practices associated with knowledge acquisition in relation to work and the workplace as well as the learning associated with becoming a member of particular social groups. All people are, of course, members of multiple and overlapping social groups, and social reproduction entails acquiring and assimilating the shared knowledge, values, and practices of the groups to which one belongs by birth or choice. Through these material social practices, social actors become members of a culture that they simultaneously help to create and construct their identities within and against. In the course of these activities, young people (and others) are both objects and agents, acquiring cultural knowledge and reworking it through the practices—intentional and otherwise—of their everyday lives. Here, too, households and their fluid gendered and generational divisions of labor have as much bearing on how cultural reproduction is enacted as on its contours and what it is socially understood to encompass. These relations are both the "medium and the message" of social reproduction, and their particular form is thus of important political-economic and sociocultural consequence.

Also included among the primarily cultural arenas of social reproduction are "the media," "mass culture," and the institutions associated with religious affiliation and practice. Within these broad arenas, "culture" is both produced and reproduced. In the interchange, the social relations of production and reproduction that characterize a particular social formation at a given historical moment and geographical location are encountered, reproduced, altered, and resisted.

Finally, apart from the cultural and political-economic aspects of social reproduction, there are the material grounds of reproduction—its environmental aspect. All modes of production produce and are enabled by particular political-ecologies. This fact is so obvious that it often goes unremarked, but the environmental toll of centuries of capitalist production, and its increasingly global nature, has been enormous. The widespread and serious environmental problems that are symptomatic of capitalist relations of production have received plenty of public attention, but generally not as problems of social reproduction. In some cases, environmental problems have been displaced from one region to another. Environmental racism and environmental forms of imperialism, entailing a geographical "fix" to political-ecological problems such as the siting of toxic-waste repositories or the location of noxious industries (often regulated out of wealthier or more privileged locales), have implications in common with those of the social relations that foster the transfer of migrant workers from poor to rich countries. In both cases there is a rejigging of the geography of social reproduction such that the costs of social reproduction—in one case environmental and in the other political-economic—are borne in a place other than where most of the benefits accrue. In other instances, environmental problems, or the political responses to them, have impeded continued production, and manufacturers and others have had to develop alternate means of producing that are sensitive to fostering a more "sustainable" environment. Such environmental protection is often keyed to sustaining production—a capitalist rendition of "sustainable development." These concerns and practices suggest the important role of the environment in social reproduction. Environmental degradation, if nothing else, undermines sustained productivity. In this regard, the particular toll of environmental degradation on children's bodies should be noted. Children, because of their size and rapidly developing constitutions, are particularly susceptible to environmental pollutants, whether airborne, in the food chain, or in the water supply (e.g., Satterthwaite et al., 1996).

But there are other environmental aspects of social reproduction as well. Those affecting children's everyday lives are of particular concern to me here. Social reproduction always takes place somewhere, and the environments for its enactment are integral to its outcomes. Disregard for the concerns of social reproduction is visible in the landscapes of neglect common in the urban areas of both industrialized and underdeveloped countries. These neglected and undersupported landscapes include, for example, schools, playgrounds, parks, and public spaces, as well as underfunded or disinvested housing, infrastructure, and service-provision sites. The settings in which children grow up speak volumes about their value as present and future members of society. A particularly horrifying example is the increase in prison construction at the expense of schools and playgrounds in the United States over the past two decades—an unmistakable reflection of the undervaluation of certain young people, particularly those of poor, working-class, minority backgrounds, in the wake of declining employment opportunities in manufacturing since the 1970s. Less extreme are the material manifestations of disregard that we witness in schools, parks, and playgrounds where children spend so much of their time. These geographies of children and childhood have clearly suffered under the relations of production and reproduction associated with globalization (see Katz, 1998a, 1998b).

GLOBALIZATION AND THE RESCALING OF CHILDHOOD

If these arenas and practices constitute the basics of social reproduction, how have they been restructured in the wake of globalization? And perhaps more to the point, how can globalized capitalism be re-cognized and reckoned with through addressing questions of social reproduction?

As many analysts of contemporary globalization have suggested, technological, financial, and regulatory changes have altered the intensity and parameters of globalization, so that there are now major financial markets and trade agreements outside of the traditional centers of capital investment and exchange. Driving the current round of globalization, however, is that beginning in the 1970s, production capital began to cross national borders with greater intensity, as the now-familiar combination of disinvestment in traditional industrial centers and foreign direct investment in areas of lower labor and other production costs was set in motion. At the same time, there has been a transnationalization of production so that all manner of products are produced globally in a literal sense (see Smith, 1997). While capital was certainly fluid in earlier periods—capitalists long have shifted their production sites from places of higher production costs to places of lower (labor and other) costs—capitalism has become even less dependent on any one place now that goods are produced in a cyborgian fashion across national boundaries that are increasingly meaningless. Meaningless, that is, unless you live someplace. And everybody does.

When reproduction is highly mobile but social reproduction necessarily remains place-bound, all sorts of disjunctures occur across space, across boundaries, and across scale—as likely to draw upon existing inequalities in social relations as to provoke new ones. The results for children coming of age are profound. Having examined shifts in the geographies and social relations of social reproduction in each of the realms I have delineated—the political-economic, the cultural, and the political-ecological—I can now conceptualize what might be termed a "rescaling of childhood." This discussion, which is necessarily schematic, draws on my readings of the environmental literature as well as on my work on children in the neo-liberal city of New York and on the privatization of public space there. It also draws on others' work concerning children and the media.

In the political-economic realm of social reproduction, disinvestments in public space have left children in poor and underserved neighborhoods with few opportunities for safe autonomous outdoor play. At the same time, the cultural realm of social reproduction has expanded its reach to many children—both those hounded indoors by the lack of play opportunities in their neighborhood environs and those previously outside the reach of the cultural productions of capital. In both of these realms—the public spaces of children's everyday lives and the cultural spaces afforded by mass media and the Internet—adults often exercise astonishing vigilance over children's activities and potential engagements as if micro-local individualist practices of parenting might be enough to protect children from both the predations associated with public disinvestment and the bounty offered by the wild expansion of electronic technologies that has paralleled it (see Katz, 2001b; Kinder, 1999).

Meanwhile, within the political-ecological realm of social reproduction there are well-known problems at global and smaller scales for which even Herculean parental acts at the household scale are inadequate. For instance, it is well documented that environmental pollutants that accumulate over time in adult bodies may be conveyed to children in mothers' milk—all efforts to control infants' and children's exposure to environmental toxins notwithstanding. I raise this issue not to provide yet another venue for fostering what I call "terror talk" concerning children, or the hypervigilance that both undergirds it and is its outcome, but to suggest—albeit schematically—that the intertwined political-economic, cultural, and political-ecological aspects of social reproduction, and the ways these impinge on the everyday lives of children in the global north (and elsewhere) under contemporary conditions, require a similarly interconnected and "scale jumping" response. Crudely put, regulating children's exposure to television while they are living in a toxic environment, or blithely wishing away global warming in a political-economy that offers few prospects to so many children coming of age, may provide some solace in the daily mayhem of "parenting," but it avoids the larger questions at stake and sublimates if not completely ignores the broader politics of social reproduction.

The issues relating to social reproduction are vexing and slippery; but the arena of social reproduction is where much of the toll of globalized capitalist production can be witnessed, so it is a fertile ground for launching responses to it. I will highlight three of these issues here. First, almost by definition, social reproduction (at a minimal level, at least) *must* be accomplished, and it is in the interests of all people to ensure this outcome, no matter what the circumstances are in which they find themselves. Thus the withdrawal of support for social reproduction on the part of the state, capital, and even civil society will be countered to whatever extent possible by household, familial, and individual efforts. One thing I have found both astonishing and heartbreaking in my work in both Sudan and the United States has been the myriad ways that capitalist production and its entailments have pushed people to the limits of their own resilience, and how willing capitalists have been to draw on that resilience for their own ends. Second, social reproduction is vexing because, again almost by definition, it is focused on reproducing the very social relations and material forms that are already so problematic. Social reproduction is precisely not "revolutionary," and yet so much rests on its accomplishment—including, perhaps paradoxically, oppositional politics. Third, the fact that the politics around social reproduction has a mushy constituency and an almost infinite number of locations makes for some powerful contradictions. Because virtually everyone is caught up in the material social practices and necessity of social reproduction, it is paradoxically hard to organize around. "Everyone" can be no one in particular. Likewise, its piecemeal and sprawling geography offers no particular site on which to organize. As fraught as workplace organizing may be, there *is* a there there. And yet it is precisely social reproduction's ubiquity that necessitates redress in the wake of the past twenty years of assault on its forms and practices.

In short, a politics focused around social reproduction reconnects culture, environment, and political-economy in opposition to capitalist globalization across a wide and differentiated terrain. The contest over which arena among the state, household, capital, and civil society bears responsibility for social reproduction under particular circumstances has proven not only durable but vastly variable depending upon historical circumstances and geography. And so the struggle continues, providing ripe grounds for expansion.

For instance, labor's gains in terms of social benefits and an expanded social wage under Fordist capitalism in the industrialized economies during the mid-20th century have been under assault. At the same time, the victories of U.S. progressive middle-class white women in getting the capitalist state to take responsibility for a host of programs associated broadly with social reproduction have been eroded by the "lean mean" hollowing out of the capitalist state under neo-liberalism. These shifts, associated with the globalization of capitalist production, can be seen at all geographic scales as well as transnationally. For example, there are common threads between so-called welfare reform in the global north (especially in the United States) and structural adjustment programs in the global south, and between the incarceration of 2 million people (three-quarters of whom are black men and boys) in the United States and the militarization of many parts of the world where similarly "excessed" groups of people have no secure work future.

Frances Fox Piven (1999) has suggested that capitalists and the capitalist state have retreated from commitments to the social wage because "they could." Obviously true. There has been little effective (or even ineffective) resistance to the mobility of capitalist production and the neo-liberal practices it fosters. Labor militancy was way down in the latter part of the 20th century, while in other arenas—for example, white feminist middle-class politics—the focus was elsewhere, on issues such as women's equality in the workplace and the public sphere. A major shift has occurred since Progressive Era women's demands linked domestic concerns with the broader arena of local, regional, and national government.

Clearly the early 21st century requires a new form of organizing, a new political agenda, and a new and more nuanced scale of practice. The demonstrations in Seattle, Prague, Pôrto Alegre, and elsewhere against the institutions associated with globalizing capitalist production make clear that there is plenty of organized opposition focused on its key institutions and corporations, and that many groups are working on these issues in sustained ways between the demonstrations. But I want to suggest that while concerns over social reproduction are at the heart of much of this opposition, they are almost never addressed as such. They should be. Redistributing responsibility for social reproduction back to capitalists and the state, transnationally and at all scales, would begin to recalibrate the costs and benefits of globalization in ways that would pinpoint its widely distributed costs and promulgate increased social justice and equality across classes, nations, localities, and genders. Indeed, making such a move would help revitalize a truly internationalist politics.

TOPOGRAPHIES AND COUNTER-TOPOGRAPHIES*

By way of conclusion, I want to discuss the notion of producing topographies as a means of moving this politics forward. I have developed this idea at length in another publication (Katz, 2001a). I sketch it out here because producing "topogra-

....

*The following section draws heavily on Katz (2001a), in which I develop a "topography" of globalization and discuss in greater detail the ideas on topographies and counter-topographies that are presented here schematically.

phies" and "counter-topographies" can be a way not only to reimagine a politics that redresses the toll of globalization but also to begin to build a practical response that is at once translocal and strategically focused. In other words, I am trying to imagine a political response that has the fluidity and breadth to cope with the vexing issues I raised earlier concerning organizing around social reproduction. I understand this is a tall order, and my idea is a modest one.

I am offering topographies, then, as a research strategy that might contribute to building a political response "that works the grounds of and between multiply situated social actors in a range of geographical locations who are at once bound and rent by the diverse forces of globalization" (Katz, 2001a, 1214). Such connections might be made around the fallout for social reproduction of the increasingly global nature of capitalist production. Topography, of course, is both the detailed description of a particular location and the totality of the features that constitute the place itself. Both topographies and topographical knowledge are produced, and an examination of *how* can reveal their interested nature. Topographies certainly provide deliberate, purposeful, and systematic (albeit partial) information at all geographic scales to the military, the state, and business. And it is topographical knowledge that provides the grist for Global Information Systems (GIS) and related spatialized databases that guide and inform resource extraction, public and private surveillance, military movements, and various forms of governance and domination. This list of practices only hints at how integrally important gathering and mapping topographical data are to both the endurance and the expansion of imperialist globalization and to enactments of domination and exploitation closer to home. The place-based knowledge produced as topographies sustains and enables the exercise of power at various geographic scales and can transcend the specificities of the locality in which it was gathered. Topographical knowledge is integral to maintaining and advancing uneven development. Given its importance to capitalists and those in power, topographical knowledge should be of interest to those who would counter such power.

Topographies produced to counter these impulses will provide thick descriptions of particular places that can get at the ways a process associated with, for example, the globalization of capitalist production, the prosecution of war, or the imposition of structural adjustment programs affect a particular place. They will allow us to look not only at particular processes in place but also at the effects of their encounters with the sedimented social relations of production and reproduction there.

Topographies, in other words, are thoroughly material. They encompass the processes that produce landscapes as much as the landscapes themselves, making clear the social nature of nature and the material grounds of social life. Their production also simultaneously turns on, reveals, and specifies the intricate relations among discrete places. Topography, in other words, offers a methodology for critically scrutinizing the material effects produced in multiple locations by the processes associated with such abstractions as globalization, global economic restructuring, and uneven development. They can provide grounds—literal and figurative—for developing a critique of the social and political-economic relations sedimented into space and for examining the range of material social practices through which place is produced.

I have underscored the materiality of topographies, but note that they also offer productive metaphoric entailments, and these, too, are central to why I think doing topographies of globalization or social reproduction may be useful. Making conventional topographies involves the detailed description of place but also requires measurements of elevation, distance, and physical or structural attributes that allow the observation of relationships across space and among places. In a similar way, topographies could be made to work in examinations of abstract but thoroughly material processes such as globalization or social reproduction. They could be used, for instance, to take stock of the movements of capital, labor, or cultural products among places, but also to look at the common and iterative effects of capitalism's globalizing imperative as they are experienced across quite different locales. Finding, demonstrating, and understanding these connections and what they give rise to are crucial to challenging them effectively.

If we can produce critical topographies that show selected traces of globalization on particular grounds, such as those associated with social reproduction, how can we connect what is discerned to other locations affected by global and other systemic processes in analogous ways? Drawing such connections enables the production of what might be thought of as "counter-topographies." The notion of counter-topographies picks up on and complements one of the key metaphoric associations of topography—the contour line. Contour lines connect places at a uniform altitude to reveal the three-dimensional form of the terrain. My intent in invoking them is to imagine a politics that retains the distinctness of the characteristics of a particular place but simultaneously builds on its analytic connections to other places along "contour lines" marking not elevation but, rather, a particular relation to a process—for example, the deskilling of workers or the retreat from social welfare. In this way it is possible to theorize "the connectedness of vastly different places made artifactually discrete by virtue of history and geography but which also reproduce themselves differently amidst the common political-economic and sociocultural processes they experience" (Katz, 2001a, 1229). Counter-topographies involve precise analyses of particular processes that not only connect disparate places but, in doing so, enable us to begin to infer connections in unexamined places in between. In topographic maps, of course, it is the measurement of elevation at selected sites that enables contour lines to be drawn without measuring every inch of the terrain. The connections reflect precise analytic relationships, not homogenizations. Not every place affected by globalizing capitalist production or consumption is altered in the same way, and the issues that arise from place to place can vary and play out differently depending upon the constellation of social relations encountered in the various locations.

Topographical analysis provides the wherewithal to critically assess these processes through scrutiny of the abrasions and solidarities they simultaneously make and alter between the material social practices through which place is produced and the social and political-economic relations embedded in space. By constructing detailed topographies at a range of geographic scales, one is able to analyze a particular issue such as the disinvestment in some aspect of social reproduction or the "warehousing" of those excluded from the possibility of employment, in and across place, with the issue defining a particular "contour line." One can imagine mapping places connected along a multitude of different contour lines, each marking a potential terrain of translocal politics.

In short, the political, theoretical, and methodological project I want to advance is one that constructs "counter-topographies" linking different places analytically in order to both develop the "contours" of common struggles and imagine a different kind of practical response to problems confronting them. It is the geographical imagination of topographies and counter-topographies that I find particularly compelling. If topography is predicated upon the inseparability between the description and the landscape itself, counter-topography works by drawing analytic contours between places typically encountered as discrete. Together they offer a means of building a vigorous and geographically imaginative practical response to contemporary globalization—processes that not only take such distinctions for granted but are more predatory insofar as they succeed in keeping apart places with common problems and shared interests.

Apart from geographical imagination, producing topographies and counter-topographies also draws on the insights, and works the grounds, of multiply situated knowledges. In this way, the project builds upon the Marxist and feminist insistence that those who are dominated, oppressed, and exploited have a privileged perspective on these processes and the workings of power and inequality that enable them (e.g., Marx and Engels, 1976; Hartsock, 1984; Haraway, 1988; Mohanty, 1988). Situated knowledge, of course, is premised in and draws on a particular and identifiable location vis à vis the relations of production and reproduction. The mobilization of such knowledge across space and scale offers the possibility of making political connections lithe enough to counter capital's maneuvers under conditions of globalization. But situated knowledge alone is not enough; the notion may even have begun to hobble our political imaginations.

Situated knowledge, like standpoint theory,

> assumes knowledge at a single point, the knowing subject, and the particularity of that subject's vision is both its strength and its downfall. If the brilliance of the idea of situated knowledge was in making clear that all seeing, all knowing was from somewhere, and that that somewhere was socially constituted, allowing for and occluding particular insights, the implications of sites underlying knowledge has produced other problems. (Katz, 2001a, 1230)

First, while situatedness implies location, it is one built upon the Marxist-feminist notion of standpoint and, thus, resides in a knowing subject. This idea, in turn, has parallels with the abstraction "subject position" (see Hartsock, 1984; Henriques et al., 1984; Katz, 2001a). But in topographic maps, a "subject's position in the landscape is a point, and therefore a space of zero dimensions" (Katz, 2001a, 1240). Dimensionality is evacuated by the language of position, site, and situation. Not coincidentally, this language has led to a politics that founders on "difference," or at least negotiates it so finely that it becomes more an end than a beginning. Even then, the dizzying resolutions to the problems that position raises for identity politics, such as intersectionality, mobile subjectivity, and multiple identities, tellingly continue to reside in the individual subject who must move, split, or multiply to be made sensible and sufficiently complex (e.g., Crenshaw, 1995; Fuss, 1991; Trinh, 1989). Second, there is an implicit (and fashionable) spatiality to situated knowledge, but while the term *situated* suggests somewhere, it is nowhere in particular. Its location is relational and abstract, lacking the grit (and problems) of a specific geography. Although the discourse of "sites" and "spaces" has been productive for making new political alliances or thinking about novel strategies of engagement—and I have participated in such endeavors myself—these political responses are weakened inasmuch as they fail to grapple with how specific historical geographies embody, reproduce, and fortify social relations of power and production (e.g., Anzaldua, 1987; Trinh, 1990; Bondi, 1993; Katz, 1992). "Finally, situatedness is simultaneously universal—everything is situated—*and* specific—to the point of being zero dimensional" (Katz, 2001a, 1230–1231). The insistence on situatedness assumes rather than explains or works out a politics predicated on extension and translation from the site or subject to the global, and that is a serious problem.

Topography, on the other hand, is by definition an historical examination of social process in three-dimensional space. Critical topographies assume that space carries and reinforces uneven social relations. Changing social relations requires (and propels) changing their material grounds. Topographies can illuminate these spatialized processes and draw out their connections across various geographics, potentially informing the imaginative politics of "jumping scale" and impelling a kind of rooted translocalism (see Smith, 1992; Marston, 2000). Working against the ways that globalizing capitalism extends and draws on the uneven power relations of gender, race, class, and nation in different historical geographies, it is a politics that at once makes clear and works off of the contours that connect different social formations and their disparate geographies. It asks what connections there might be among sweatshop Bangladesh, *maquiladora* Mexico, and the prison work camps of the United States, or among structurally adjusted Sudan, welfare-reformed Britain, and neoliberal Brazil. Doing topographies not only provokes such questions; it may provide the means for answering them in ways as variously grounded and abstract as the ties that bind these such seemingly different places and circumstances. A broadly topographical project might also develop analyses and solidarities at the nodal points between contour lines.

I have attempted to trace one such contour line between two of the places in which I have done field research among young people—a village in central Sudan that I call Howa and Harlem in northern Manhattan (e.g., Katz, 1998a). My research sought to examine and connect the sorts of displacements experienced by young people in both places in the face of broad-based disinvestments in their communities. In New York I looked at the effects on working-class children and teens of economic restructuring witnessed largely in the decline of manufacturing, paying particular attention to the retreats from the social wage seen in such things as the lopsided provision of educational resources and funding cuts in public housing, public open space, and health and social welfare, each of which became serious enough to spur calls for privatization from many quarters. This work was a counterpoint to my earlier and ongoing work in Howa, where I looked at economic restructuring in the form of a "development" project that undermined long-established means of reproducing local relations and means of production without providing compensatory or new investments in social reproduction to replace them. In both places, large fractions of young people coming of age were butting up against the limitations produced by these broad-scale political-economic shifts and their local fallout. For many of these young people, all bets for the future were off, leaving few guarantees of stable, let alone meaningful, employment in their adulthoods. Moreover, there are indications in both places, as elsewhere, that certain segments of the "excessed" population have been "warehoused" as a matter of state policy—in prisons (as well as in the army and even in universities) in the United States and in the army or quasi-governmental "people's militias" in Sudan. Yet people in Harlem and Howa have organized to rework a number of the conditions confronting them and, in some instances, to resist them outright. Their conscious efforts at change have been complemented and sustained by everyday practices that demonstrate often stunning resilience among the members of each community (see Katz, 2001a).

At first, I thought of the comparison between Howa and Harlem sequentially, as a way of studying the displacements and other shifts that children experience in the transition from what I somewhat crudely conceptualized as "an agricultural to an industrial economy and from an industrial to a postindustrial economy" (Katz, 2001a, 1232). But a "topographical" analysis forces a spatialized understanding of these issues as simultaneous and intertwined. In revealing the simultaneity of different kinds of disruptions, topographies respond to John Berger's extraordinary observation that now it is "space not time that hides consequences from us" (Berger, 1974; Soja, 1989). What I am arguing, then, is that if the disruptions in social reproduction in Howa and Harlem are localized effects of a common set of processes, among them the globalization of capitalist production, then the political mobilization to challenge such processes must have similar global sensitivities, even if its grounds are local. The interests raised here transcend the specificities of any particular locale, even if they have varying local forms, and thus differ from "place-based" politics. Nor is this project a matter of building coalitions among different locales, crucial as that is.

Because globalization as such is an abstraction that has multiple forms, struggles to counter it have to mobilize equivalent abstractions. But just as a capital-inspired globalization reworks the material grounds of social life, so must any response be resolutely material. Doing local topographies can provide just such a grounding. Building on their juxtaposition, counter-topographies can offer the sorts of abstractions needed to reimagine and rework globalization and its effects. Interweaving thick descriptions of local specificities, an analysis that follows abstract connections among disparate places, and a spark of insurgence, counter-topographies can inform a new geographically invigorated praxis. Perhaps such efforts can inspire and mobilize new kinds of internationalist solidarities at once specific and fluid enough to contain and counter the vagabond in all of the various locales it wants to call home.

WORKS CITED

Anzaldua, G. 1987. *Borderlands/La Frontera: The New Mestiza*. San Francisco: Spinsters/Aunt Lute Book Company.

Berger, J. 1974. *The Look of Things*. New York: Viking.

Bondi, L. 1993. "Locating Identity Politics." In *Place and the Politics of Identity* (pp. 84–101), ed. M. Keith and S. Pile. London/New York: Routledge.

Crenshaw, K. W. 1995. "Mapping the Margins: Intersectionality, Identity Politics, and Violence Against Women of Color." In *Critical Race Theory: The Key Writings That Formed the Movement* (pp. 357–383), ed. K. Crenshaw, N. Gotanda, G. Peller, and K. Thomas. New York: New Press.

Fuss, D., ed. 1991. *Inside/Out: Lesbian Theories, Gay Theories*. New York/London: Routledge.

Haraway, D. J. 1988. "Situated Knowledges: The Science Question in Feminism as a Site of Discourse on the Privilege of Partial Perspective." *Feminist Studies*, Vol. 14, pp. 575–599.

Hartsock, N. 1984. *Money, Sex and Power*. Boston: Northeastern University Press.

Henriques, J., Holloway, W., Urwin, C., Venn, C., and Walkerdine, V. 1984. *Changing the Subject*. London/New York: Methuen.

Hochschild, A. 2000. "The Nanny Chain." *The American Prospect*, Vol. 11, No. 4.

Katz, C. 1992. "All the World Is Staged: Intellectuals and the Projects of Ethnography." *Environment and Planning D: Society and Space*, Vol. 10, No. 5, pp. 495–510.

———. 1998a. "Disintegrating Developments: Global Economic Restructuring and the Eroding Ecologies of Youth." In *Cool Places: Geographies of Youth Cultures* (pp. 130–144), ed. T. Skelton and G. Valentine. London/New York: Routledge.

———. 1998b. "Power, Space, and Terror: Social Reproduction and the Public Environment." Unpublished ms.

———. 2001a. "On the Grounds of Globalization: A Topography for Feminist Political Engagement." *Signs: Journal of Women in Culture and Society*, Vol. 26, No. 4, pp. 1213–1234.

———. 2001b. "The State Goes Home: Local Hypervigilance of Children and the Global Retreat from Social Reproduction." *Working Papers in Local Governance and Democracy*, Vol. 3.

Kinder, M. 1999. *Kids' Media Culture*. Durham/London: Duke University Press.

Marston S. A. 2000. "The Social Construction of Scale." *Progress in Human Geography*, Vol. 24, No. 2, pp. 19–42.

———. Forthcoming. "A Long Way from Home: Domesticating the Social Production of Scale." In *Scale and Geographic Inquiry: Nature, Society, Method*, ed. R. McMaster and E. Sheppard. Cambridge, Mass.: Blackwell Publishers.

Marx, K., and Engels, F. 1976. *The German Ideology*. Moscow: Progress Publishers.

Mohanty, C. T. 1988. "Feminist Encounters: Locating the Politics of Experience." *Copyright*, Vol. 1, pp. 30–44.

Parreñas, R. S. 2001. *Servants of Globalization: Women, Migration and Domestic Work*. Stanford, Calif.: Stanford University Press.

Piven, F. F. 1999. "Welfare Reform and the Economic and Cultural Reconstruction of Low Wage Labor Markets." *City and Society, Annual Review*, Vol. 1998, pp. 21–36.

Pulsipher, L. M. 1993. "He Won't Let She Stretch She foot": Gender Relations in Traditional West Indian Houseyards. In *Full Circles: Geographies of Women over the Life Course* (pp. 107–121), ed. C. Katz and J. Monk. London: Routledge.

Rose, D. 1993. "Local Childcare Strategies in Montréal, Québec: The Mediations of State Policies, Class and Ethnicity in the Life Courses of Families with Young Children." In *Full Circles: Geographies of Women over the Life Course* (pp. 188–207), ed. C. Katz and J. Monk. London: Routledge.

Satterthwaite, D., Hart, R., Levy, C., Mitlin, D., Ross, D., Smit, J., and Stephens, C. 1996. *The Environment for Children*. New York: UNICEF/London: Earthscan Publications.

Smith, N. 1992. "Contours of a Spatialized Politics: Homeless Vehicles and the Production of Geographic Scale." *Social Text*, Vol. 33: 54–81.

———. 1997. "The Satanic Geographies of Globalization: Uneven Development in the 1990s." *Public Culture*, Vol. 10, No. 1, pp. 169–189.

Soja, E. W. 1989. *Postmodern Geographies: The Reassertion of Space in Critical Social Theory*. London/New York: Verso.

Trinh, T. M. 1989. *Women, Native, Other: Writing Postcoloniality and Feminism*. Bloomington/Indianapolis: Indiana University Press.

———. 1990. "Cotton and Iron." In *Out There: Marginalization and Contemporary Cultures* (pp. 327–336), ed. R. Ferguson, M. Gever, T. T. Minh-ha, and C. West. New York: New Museum of Contemporary Art/Cambridge, Mass.: MIT Press.

18

On the Global Uses of September 11 and Its Urban Impact

PETER MARCUSE

The attacks of September 11 on the World Trade Center had substantial impacts on urban life, not only in New York City but on aspects of globalization worldwide. The attacks did not bring about any change in direction but rather accentuated trends already under way, and their impacts lie more in the use made of them by political and economic leaders than in the actual damage caused by the attacks themselves. This chapter focuses on the impact on urban form and urban life and the ways in which the true nature of globalization was exposed by the use made of the attacks of September 11. First, it looks at the direct impacts of the attacks on New York City: the direct physical damage done to the World Trade Center and its surroundings, which, except for the loss of life and the traumatic impact on the individuals who experienced the attacks, was of limited extent and duration. Then it considers the impact of security measures taken in real and purported reaction to the events: the defensive measures realistically taken to provide security against terrorism, and the unrealistic measures implemented for quite other reasons. I then go on to examine the changes in urban form that have followed the attacks: changes in the patterns of segregation and citadelization in cities that were already in swing before the attacks but that have intensified thereafter. And finally the chapter examines the ideological ramifications of the use made of the attacks in the United States, in terms of local, national, and international policy: The September 11 attacks provided an ideological smokescreen for political and business leaders to pursue their own interests, using the cover provided by an ostensible "war against terrorism" and the need for "homeland security." The net result has been to further skew the benefits and costs of globalization, in ways increasingly visible at both the urban and the global level.

To be clear, the word *globalization* here means the use of technological advances, particularly in communications and transportation, in the service of the increased concentration of power and profit, with a resulting shift in the balance of power between labor and capital based on the greater mobility of capital and the changed role of labor.[1] It is typically considered to have mushroomed after 1970. It should properly be called "really existing globalization" to distinguish it from an alternative globalization in which technological advances might serve to promote a common improvement in the living conditions of all people and an equalization of life chances across the globe. Really existing globalization, then, is Davos globalization, not Porto Alegre globalization—imperial globalization, not democratic and just globalization. New York City is one of its key locations, and its impact on urban life and urban form is very visible there and reflects the process in general.

THE DIRECT IMPACT: THE PHYSICAL DAMAGE

The attack on the World Trade Center exposed a limited vulnerability of the global economic system and showed that the very physical heart of the global economic system could be badly damaged by a handful of zealous opponents. But the actual damage was far less than what was at first anticipated. Recovery from its immediate physical consequences (again, apart from the loss of life and individual trauma) was rapid.

Within a few days of the attack (one week for the New York Stock Exchange) the major businesses that were interrupted on September 11 were back in full swing, including the financial and globally oriented tenants of the World Trade Center itself, even though smaller businesses, mostly retail and service concerns, did not all recover as quickly, and some permanently went out of business. The firms that had offices in the World Trade Center or in neighboring buildings that were damaged or destroyed continued their activities elsewhere; some already had offices outside the financial district of Manhattan to which they simply moved the functions that had been damaged in the attack; other firms quickly rented available space in other parts of the metropolitan area. The issue was quickly portrayed as a challenge to the real estate industry, and the real estate industry was happy to deal with it. More than 6 million square feet of office space was vacant in Manhattan at the time of the September 11 attack. Indeed, the vacancy rate in office space in New York City is still high, more because of the economic downturn than because of September 11, and the vacancy rate in lower Manhattan is higher now, after the destruction, than it was before.[2] So loss of space from the attack was hardly a body blow to the office-based economy of the city. A decentralization of business activities (see below) that was already in progress was simply given further impetus.

The direct impact on the global economy was also negligible, as it turned out. The stock market dropped by 7.12 percent on the opening day of trading one week after the attack, but it began its recovery by October 2, and by November 13,

2001, it was back where it had been before September 11.³ International transactions were not significantly impeded; some New York traders had back offices in the New York metropolitan area that quickly took over key functions, and one of the largest switched its operations to its London office. It is perhaps a reflection of the relative unimportance of particular locations for the global economy that the actual interference caused by the loss of significant parts of a central node in the worldwide financial net was barely felt in most of the system.

THE REACTION: REAL AND PURPORTED NEEDS FOR INCREASED SECURITY

The impact on the handling of security in the global economy is another matter. Realistic concerns need to be distinguished from paranoia (real and manufactured), but there are grounds for realistic concern. Before September 11, security against opposition of the system of really existing globalization had been regarded as an issue that was first and foremost political. Labor opposition came either from the organized trade unions or from the unorganized protest of workers, landless farmers, and the unemployed; that is to say, opposition was grounded in economic interests, and the tools of opposition were consistent with the normal functioning of formal political democracy. Absent a major economic crisis, the system had seemed capable of handling such opposition. Trade unions were assimilated into a routine of more or less regulated collective bargaining. Economic protest expressed outside of such bargaining could be drawn into conventional political channels, where the limits of political democracy in representative form could control it. Control of the media, campaign finance practices, and the selling of a plausible ideology of market freedoms were sufficient, particularly after the collapse of the state socialist alternative, to ensure the continued protection of the system from serious disruption. Oppositional social movements and ideologically oriented criticism, whether focusing on poverty, urban issues, environmental quality, the concerns of women, or commitment to political democracy, seemed similarly susceptible to incorporation with the system. Insecurity caused by the individual activities of those excluded from the benefits of the system could be punished as crime, and protesters could be removed from threatening spatial proximity.

A physical and forceful attack on the home territory of the global economy was in the minds of few people before September 11. Physical security from frontal attack was seen as an aberrational issue; with the possible exception of Germany during the Bader-Meinhoff period,⁴ the concern of security against terrorism was not with challenges to the system itself, but rather with the irrational behavior of a limited set of persons and countries. Specific confrontations involving the use of terror were limited to a few countries: The divisions in Northern Ireland were reflected in bombings in London; Palestinian anger was reflected in suicide attacks in

Israel; and secessionist movements in Spain, Sri Lanka, and a few other countries caused eruptions of violence. But those were not seen as threats to the major powers and certainly not to the United States. The dangers were taken to be primarily in airplane hijackings by small groups of misguided fanatics.

September 11 changed this picture. In the United States, security has now become an issue in everyday life and has created what might be called a hassle effect that impinges on the efficient functioning of many parts of the economic system. Trucks are held up for inspection at border crossings and bridges and tunnels, making just-in-time inventory practices more difficult. Airplanes are considered dangerous places, and provisions for security cause delays and unpleasantness, increasing travel times and leading to less travel and less face-to-face communication. Restrictions on access to buildings annoy visitors and discourage tourism. Providing duplicate backup facilities in case of attack is expensive; the New York Stock Exchange is making a complete standby trading floor available in case its primary site becomes unavailable, and it cannot be used for any purpose short of an attack because to reveal its location might expose it also to attack. Increased security, from increased police presence to the installation of security and surveillance equipment, has become a significant cost both to the public treasury and to private businesses. Security businesses are among the fastest growing in the economy in terms of number of employees, but their contribution is a net cost to productive businesses; their services do not increase productivity.

Not all of the measures undertaken in the name of security against terrorism are really functional for that purpose. Some are clearly part of a campaign with quite ulterior motives, having to do with the consolidation of a conservative regime nationally and the expansion of U.S. power internationally. And some are the result of a mix of manufactured and real paranoia.

The restrictions on civil liberties, the closure of public spaces of protest, the ubiquitous use of surveillance technology, the hemming in of political demonstrations, the official obloquy heaped on dissent, all serve to support the established powers. If one accepts Jean Baudrillard's eloquent assessment of the attacks of September 11 as being aimed at the central symbols of the prevailing form of globalization,[5] a plausible interpretation and one presumably shared by the attackers, then providing extra security at train stations, public parks, Disneyland, water supplies, and city halls is unconnected with any real dangers revealed by the September attacks. Perhaps there is an element of conscious or unconscious manipulation here. If the attacks were in fact focused on the symbols of economic and military power, it could lead to a reexamination of the values of the system of really existing globalization, as suggested by Baudrillard. For those interested in protecting that system, it would then make sense to divert attention from such questions of power and to portray the terrorists as attacking liberty, or democracy, or the American people. Of course, it was *not* the Statue of Liberty that they attacked, however inviting a physical target it might have made. It is useful for those in charge to play down the actual symbolism and instead to make the entire population feel threatened and at one with the economic and military establishments of the most powerful state of the globe.

And at a less symbolic level, heightened security concerns about terrorism have been used to enhance U.S. military, political, and economic hegemony globally. I take up this issue in Part IV below.

THE URBAN IMPACT: CONCENTRATED DECONCENTRATION, CITADELIZATION, SEGREGATION

The attacks of September 11 have been used to produce a variety of responses within American cities. These responses have highlighted the relative weakness of local influences on global enterprises and global networks. They have changed the locational patterns of business enterprises, in the direction of decentralized concentrations. They have legitimated the further creation of citadels of the rich and have reinforced the segregation and ghettoization of the poor. They have been used to pour money from public coffers into the hands of the wielders of economic power. To take these points one by one:

Localization—the concrete, locally bound aspect of globalized activities—has been a recognized but controversial topic in debates about globalization for some time,[6] but it now proceeds with a difference. On one side, the argument goes, global networks, no matter how high-tech, need a physical infrastructure at their base in order to operate, and that infrastructure must be located in specific places. It is not cheap, and there are major economies of scale to be achieved in its concentration in a limited number of places. The so-called global cities achieve their status from those economies, as well as from the need of central decision makers to have available a social infrastructure, including both professional services and quality-of-life amenities, which also benefit from agglomeration economies. Face-to-face exchanges and business lunches still play a significant role in the key sectors of the global economy. Hence, the premier position of New York City, London, and Tokyo is not likely to change under present circumstances.

The other side of the argument holds that although there are both the physical and the social infrastructure requirements for efficient global functioning, the need that they be concentrated in a few places is not so great, and the choice of places for their location is broad. Modern communication and transportation technology permit significant decentralization, and many environmental amenities may be better found in dispersed locations than in concentrated central ones. Further, costs of congestion increase with concentration; travel time to work in New York is now the highest of any metropolitan area in the United States. Activities in virtual networks are an adequate substitute for may forms of direct presence; having transactions take place on a single trading floor in the New York Stock Exchange is already an anomaly among such exchanges. The lack of impact on the

system as a whole of the destruction of one spatial node, in the financial district of
New York City, has already been described. Further, although it is true that global
businesses need to have at least one foot on the ground at some local point, the
choices of what local point that should be are great. All localities together would
make an important player in the global discussion;[7] individually the reality of competitiveness (and its overblown ideological embrace) leaves them enfeebled. Major
business firms have shown themselves to be extraordinarily footloose: American
Airlines moved its headquarters from New York City to Dallas when doing so
suited its purpose, even though its chief executive had been a leader in New York
City's economic development program.

The weaknesses of the local allegiances of major businesses is even more visible at the intra-metropolitan level, particularly when metropolitan areas are fragmented among multiple local jurisdictions, as is the case in New York City. Since
the attacks of September 11 exposed the vulnerabilities, real or feared, of central
business district locations, the preexisting footloose character of business offices has
been illuminated and magnified. Before September 11, having the highest status
location, the most symbolic site, the most important address was a desiderata for
many global business firms. Today, precisely those characteristics have a negative
meaning also; they represent characteristics seen, rightly or wrongly, as creating a
prime target for attack. While all of the advantages of concentration mentioned
above remain, if those advantages can be achieved elsewhere than in one central location, that becomes very desirable. The developing and dominant pattern in the
future will thus, I believe, be one of *concentrated decentralization:* decentralized
away from a single location, but concentrated in a few nearby locations. They will
generally be in the same metropolitan area, at the same time as the likelihood of
dispersion to remote "nonglobal" locations is strengthened.

For New York City, the pattern is evident. The decentralization leads away
from the financial district, in which the World Trade Center was originally built to
reinforce it as a primary location for financial and global activities.[8] In part, it is to
Midtown Manhattan, already a dominant center for business and services, but it is
also to secondary locations of concentration within the metropolitan area:
Metrotech in Brooklyn, Jersey City and Hoboken across the Hudson River, and
Long Island City in Queens. And in a few cases, it is entirely out of the New York
area, for example, Charlotte, North Carolina.[9] But in all cases, it is to locations in
which similar activities are concentrated: decentralized concentrations.

And these decentralized concentrations have become citadelized. The decentralized concentrations of major financial and other business activities do not take
just any physical form but adhere to a predictable pattern, one established well before September 11 but reinforced after it. They are secured, walled, fortified, organized so as to be able to exclude the undesirable, the stranger, the discordant in
order to attract and admit only those having business there or those from whom a
profit can be made. If we use the distinctions I have elsewhere suggested between
citadels, enclaves, quarters, and ghettos,[10] then these are the growing citadels of the

global age, in which security measures control access by physical, but also by more subtle social and economic, means. They incorporate within their protected spaces, as did the World Trade Center and Battery Park City before them, everything needed in the course of everyday life: workplaces, shopping, restaurants, recreational facilities, entertainment. For users, travel paths to the outside are protected; subway stops and garages are within the enclosures, express buses go to the door, and at the extreme—São Paulo is a good example—even heliports provide access from the suburb directly to the roof of the citadel.

Several good studies exist of walled and gated communities,[11] and there has been much popular discussion of edge cities.[12] Both have been given a boost by the reaction to September 11. However, the point here is different. The citadels that are designed to deal with the new situation are oriented to protecting business activities, often including luxury housing for their participants, even when they are not averse to providing shopping opportunities or profitable entertainment for a broader clientele. They are designed to protect particularly the economic elite (and their professional servants and advisers) in finance and control functions in global concerns and global activities, although they also need to take into account the more temporally limited needs of their lower-class workers and suppliers. They may be individual buildings, unified larger-scale developments, or mega-projects, such as several in Jersey City or Brooklyn, sharply separated from their surroundings, or at the extreme, they may be entire sections of a city. The danger in lower Manhattan, for instance, is that the entire neighborhood/quarter may end up being planned as a citadel, with special security measures, a concentration of specialized facilities, both public and private, focused on the needs of the elite and the their professionals, managers, and technicians, and with rigidly controlled access by outsiders—including the likely use of racial and economic profiling to reinforce the class nature of the protection.

The search for secure citadels has to do directly with globalization, not merely with the dangers of terrorism, although those dangers bring it to the fore. For the practitioners of globalization, citadelization can now be justified as a reaction to a new vulnerability established by the attacks of September 11. Although increased walling and gating is not limited to those involved in global activities, it is sharpest for them. They are the ones who, for many years, have sought out the most visible, the most striking, the most recognizable and symbolic architecture, the most prominent sites, the most towering edifices. But those were exactly the characteristics singled out for attack on September 11 in New York, and those in similar locations fear a repeat occurrence. Thus, the vacancy rate in the Empire State Building rose sharply after the World Trade Center attack, the disadvantages of high floors were taken to heart in Kuala Lumpur and Chicago, and new projects no longer boast of their dominance and even downplay their identity, if they feel that it may make them more attractive as targets of terrorists.

While citadelization is in part a reaction to the vulnerabilities of globalization exposed after September 11, its roots go much deeper. Citadelization, walling, and barricading are an inherent aspect of really existing globalization.[13] They are in the nature of the beast itself, for the use of citadels follows from the segregationist tendencies implicit in globalization. Segregation is hardly a novelty introduced in 1970; some forms of segregation—the involuntary assignment of living space to a subordinate population group—have characterized virtually every society since the beginning of civilization.[14] The racial or ethnic identification of those being segregated makes it easier to execute that process and leads to the creation of traditional ghettos. But globalization has exacerbated the tendencies to segregation of earlier periods and has added a new wrinkle. The exacerbation comes from the increased inequality that is a feature of globalization today. Really existing globalization is, after all, at heart a technologically facilitated extension of the power of a few to dominate and exploit those with less power on a worldwide basis. It is almost a cliché today to say that the rich have become richer and the poor poorer, both among nations and within nations, and within cities as well.[15] Inequality in income and wealth in turn means spatial segregation, since the allocation of residential and business location is determined overwhelmingly by the market, by ability to pay. In Europe, with its history of greater governmental control of urban development, lacking the extreme racial history of the United States, and with a safety net with smaller holes than what remains in the United States, segregation is less than it is in the United States, although it is increasing.[16] Nevertheless, the forces that promote and benefit from the market are strengthened by globalization, governmental involvement for social purposes is weakened, and perceptions of race are heightened.

Globalization has also contributed a new wrinkle to the contemporary form of the ghetto, the excluded ghetto, the underside of the citadel. Globalization itself added a new pattern to the older processes of segregation: the exclusion of those ghettoized from the mainstream economy.[17] Unlike the older Jewish ghettos of Europe, for instance, where during the day the residents were important to the business life of the cities from which they were at night excluded,[18] in the new form of the excluded ghetto that involvement is broken off or at best takes place at the margins of the economy. Those outside the globalized economy today are simply not needed by it, in Zygmunt Bauman's words; their power to disrupt it is reduced to extreme measures, of which the attacks of September 11 are—in some ways—a symbol.[19] Hence, we have now an excluded ghetto, the exclusion of whose residents from mainstream employment is enhanced by the emphasis on citizenship, educational qualification, and background checks applicable to more and more jobs. September 11 is used to justify measures that extend a pattern already in place. To the extent that immigrants have been ghettoized even in the welfare states of Europe, the tighter controls on immigration imposed in the name of defense against terrorism will both restrict mobility in and out of the ghetto and control the opportunities of those within even more tightly.

The attacks of September 11 have further been used directly to produce public actions favoring the wealthy over the poor, to enhance the position of the citadel-dwellers rather than the ghettoized. Taking advantage of the general public concern for those hurt by the attack on the World Trade Center, government actions have been skewed further in a regressive direction. At least $20 billion dollars—$21.3 is the current estimate—will be flowing to New York City in the near future, and its expenditure is an indicator of how far the power of government is going to reinforce the position of those already entrenched in positions of economic power. And they are very aware of the possibilities. In particular, real estate interests have been active ever since September 11, lobbying city officials, the state, and New York's two senators about how much money is needed and for what. Robert Kolker, in *New York* magazine, describes one such important meeting:

> "Get the money now," Bill Clinton is chanting into a microphone, sermonizing before a parish of pinstriped suits. "Get the money now." [The meeting] is in Citigroup's packed Park Avenue auditorium with some of the city's top business leaders—mega-developer Jerry Speyer, billionaire financier Henry Kravis, real estate baron and publisher Mort Zuckerman, AT&T chairman Mike Armstrong, Lehman Brothers chairman Dick Fuld. . . . Looking on from the audience like proud parents are Hillary Clinton and Chuck Schumer, along with George Pataki's economic czar, Charles Gargano, and union chieftains Brian McLaughlin and Randi Weingarten. "Get the money now," Clinton repeats in his folksiest drawl. The terrorists aimed for the World Trade Center because they "think we're weak and selfish and greedy," he says, but that's no reason not to fight hard for that money.[20]

The meeting, hosted by the nation's largest bank, seems to have been successful in its financial targeting. The latest distribution of funds, announced as this was being written, by the city's deputy mayor for economic development, was described as follows:

> The state and city have begun to send letters offering the first of dozens of multimillion-dollar federal grants to some of the most important financial companies in the world, . . . candidates include the financial giants Merrill Lynch, American Express, Goldman Sachs and the Bank of New York; Aon, the insurance broker; and the law firms Thacher Proffitt & Wood and Pillsbury Winthrop." [Deputy Mayor Doctoroff] said the criteria used to award the grants included the number of employees and the likelihood that a company would relocate. Mr. Doctoroff added that some benefit packages would go to companies "that never had any intent to leave." Asked why, he said, "First of all, everyone lies about it," with companies threatening to leave even if they really would not go. Beyond that, he said, "It probably is appropriate for people who recommit to downtown to get some money."[21]

Overall, public investments have been concentrated in lower Manhattan to an astonishing extent: Of the $21.3 billion from the federal government now expected, the single largest chunk, $5.1 billion, is allocated to make up for the losses suffered by business enterprises as a result of the attack (presumably in addition to the $15 billion allocated to the airline industry). In addition, in the March 2002 "economic stimulus" package, there was set aside for the consequences of September 11 in New York some $15.05 billion to go to businesses, with only $746 million to go to programs directly benefiting workers.[22] As Doctoroff admitted, federal funds allocated to the city under the Community Development Block Grant program will also go to subsidize those willing to move to or continue to live in the affected area of lower Manhattan, regardless of their need for assistance.

By the same token, the governmental allocation of funds to those at the bottom end of the economic ladder are being severely curtailed. The holes in the safety net will be further enlarged, and the segregationist effect strengthened. September 11 provides some of the cover for this misallocation; the rest is attributed to the economic downturn. City-funded public education programs will be cut by $358 million, parks by $16.6 million, libraries by $39.3 million, children's services, including child care and foster care, by $128 million, the Empowerment Zone budget (for business development in Harlem and the Bronx) by $3.1 million, economic development outside lower Manhattan, in the capital plan, is cut $204 million, while $252 million is retained for the expansion of the stock exchange, although the exchange itself has shelved the plans for a new building. On the other hand, $18.1 million is cut from the Department of Cultural Affairs, although most of those involved see cultural activities as necessary for a lower Manhattan revival. The preexisting need for housing was estimated by housing advocates to be $10 billion, and their call was for $1 billion a year,[23] a call largely supported by the leading candidates for mayor before September 11. Now, however, the city budget has cut $418 million in capital expenditures for housing over four years and cut entirely a number of housing preservation programs.[24] Suggestions were solicited by the Lower Manhattan Development Corporation on the proposed use of the first $700 million of the $2.7 billion coming to it in Community Development Block Grant money to help deal with the effects of September 11. Yet, "the comments from major NYC antipoverty organizations that some portion be allocated to transitional employment and targeting job opportunities for disadvantaged New Yorkers were simply dismissed out of hand."[25] The idea of raising taxes seems anathema to businesspeople and most politicians, although solid progressive proposals that would provide long-term benefits at modest short-term cost are available.[26]

Putting all these public budgetary developments together, combined with the increased ascendance of both the ideology and the reality of the private market, the segregationist effects of really existing globalization will be strengthened, and the attacks of September 11 will be used as part of the political cover.

THE IDEOLOGICAL USE:
SMOKESCREEN FOR AN AGENDA

The attack on the World Trade Center has been made synonymous with terrorism and has been used to justify a variety of measures that have little to do with the real fear of terrorism but much to do with advancing an ideology and a set of practices related to the advancement of particular urban interests—interests that are tightly linked to the advancement of really existing globalization. In this sense, the events of September 11 provided a useful smokescreen for the pursuit of a variety of pre-existing agendas.

The attacks have in fact been used to legitimate a set of policies that directly contradict the conventional ideology of conservative business interests and their politicians. Global and multinational groups have long argued that they should be free of governmental restraints on their activities, and real estate interests at the local level, profiting generously from global demand, also see governmental action as negative. "Market, market, market," is the cry, both at the metropolitan level and in lower Manhattan. The globally competitive stature of New York City is the motor of its economy; nothing can be allowed to interfere with it. Lower Manhattan is the place where New York City's globally competitive stature is attained, goes the argument, and everything must be done to sustain its location there. And that then requires the governmental action that otherwise would be anathema to business interests.

In fact, the argument is dubious. The better argument is that it would be more beneficial in the long run for the city's economy to diversify, to be less dependent on the swings of the financial market, to maintain and expand its specialized manufacturing capacity, to foster and support its creativity in health care, the arts, social research, education, to pay more attention to the general quality of its public education and community services, to equalize the quality of life of its residents. And if one looked at what even the market was saying about the location of globally connected businesses in New York, one would not be led to encourage development in Lower Manhattan. Such businesses were already focusing on Midtown Manhattan even before September 11. The number of square feet of office space in Lower Manhattan before September 11 was 82,436,287; in Midtown it was 180,506,802.[27] The construction of the World Trade Center itself, in the early 1970s, was a move specifically designed to counter the market, not move with it.[28] David Rockefeller, as head of Chase Manhattan Bank, wanted to protect his bank's investment in real estate when it built its headquarters in Lower Manhattan; Nelson Rockefeller, his brother, as governor of New York, pushed through the acquisition of the property of the World Trade Center and its construction with public funds. Its tenants were initially provided not by the market but by governmental agencies, largely of the state. Today, like yesterday, the future of real estate in lower Manhattan depends not on the private market but on the willingness of government to subsidize locations there. The attacks of September 11 are being used as an ideological smokescreen to conceal that simple fact.

At the national level, the events of September 11 have been used to justify other measures in the United States that were also clearly part of a preexisting political agenda: expanded investment in military procurement, reduced spending on social welfare, restrictions on immigration, control over the press, and limitations on protest. The tactic has been, at least up to the time this was written, very successful; political opposition from what is theoretically the opposition party in Congress has been virtually nil, the media is largely uncritical of measures justified as part of the War on Terrorism, and public opinion polls show large majorities supporting the administration's policies.

At the global level, the attacks of September 11 have also been used to legitimate a set of policies directly contradictory to the pervasive ideological underpinning of really existing globalization that free trade, with a minimum of government intervention and ever reduced roles for national states, is the form of globalization that will best meet human needs. Simple economic logic, it is held, will inevitably lead the world to that conclusion. Yet the reality is very different, and the attacks of September 11 have been used as the ideological cover to conceal that fact. The banner has inscribed on it a "War on Terrorism." But terrorism is a tactic, not an entity; one can no more declare war on terrorism than one can declare war on armor or airplanes or propaganda or camouflage. It is only the particular user or users of the tactic that can be fought. But because the users of this particular tactic, terrorism, have one thing in common—that they are not in power and are challenging those in power—it is a tactic that the powerful will agree unanimously should be condemned. A "war" on terrorism is thus one that can be used by Russia to justify the treatment of Chechens, by Israel to justify the treatment of Palestinians, by Spain to justify the treatment of Basques, and by Mexico to justify the treatment of Zapatistas. The building of a coalition against terrorism, in which the military power of the United States is a central feature and its dominance on the international scene is legitimated, has more to do with the strengthening of existing power relations than it does with a real concern about the dangers of international terrorism. Recently, it was reported: "The Brazilian government has sent troops to reinforce the police surrounding a ranch occupied by more than 500 families of Brazil's Landless Movement (MST). The property is owned by President Fernando Henrique Cardoso's two sons. Agrarian Development Minister Raul Juggman has called the occupation an act of terrorism."[29]

The reality that the smokescreen of responding to the events of September 11 has been used to conceal is very different. This summary of the administration's true political agenda is all the more telling coming from the *International Herald Tribune* and William Pfaff, hardly a doctrinaire leftist critic:

This administration is making use of the September 11 tragedy to do what the neoconservative right has wanted for a long time, which is to renounce inconvenient treaties, junk arms control, build and test nuclear weapons, attack Saddam Hussein, and abandon multilateralist cooperation with international organizations and compromise with allies, all in order to aggrandize American international power and deal expediently with those who challenge it.[30]

He might only have added that it is the power not of the American people but of those already in power in America that is being aggrandized.

In terms of the discussion of globalization, the dependency of the global system on military force is now obvious, perhaps regretted, but not challenged. The justification for permitting unlimited license to financial operators worldwide—that their operations cannot be controlled by enfeebled nation-states helpless in the face of globalized transactions—appears hollow; the finances of Al Qaeda have been tracked through complex multinational banks and financial intermediaries, and steps taken to allow nation-states to monitor and control multinational flows of funds are increasingly effective. The Enron debacle in the United States has increased the support for further measures of control over "free market" transactions, and the fact that control measures are possible is hardly in doubt (even though no one has yet suggested bombing the Cayman Islands if they do not make disclosure of financial transactions within their boundaries).

The events of September 11 have thus been used as a smokescreen to cover policies serving the interests of those benefiting from globalization, whether at the local, the national, or the international level, and to conceal the extent to which the reality being pursued differs from its purported ideological rationale. At the local level, as seen in New York City, the already powerful forces of real estate and the global financial firms they see as their best market have been allowed an unimpeded influence over the development of the city, leading to a concentrated deconcentration and citadelization of business activities and furthering the segregation of the city. At the national level, the events of September 11 have been used, under the banner of security from attack, to marshal support for a neoliberal domestic agenda, to restrict protest, and to undercut opposition to its agenda. Internationally, the attacks have been used, under the banner of a coalition against terrorism, to consolidate the unilateral power of the United States, revealing inadvertently the primacy of military power and the nation-state in the maintenance of a global economy. In each case, the contrast between the ideology of really existing globalization and its reality is stark; the smokescreen developed around September 11 cannot long cover the discrepancy. The skewed impact of really existing globalization has been strengthened by the ideological use of September 11, and the task of opposition has been made more difficult but also more necessary.

NOTES

1. The best recent general discussion of issues of globalization is William K. Tabb, *The Amoral Elephant: Globalization and the Struggle for Social Justice in the Twenty-First Century* (New York: Monthly Review Press, 2001).

2. *New York Times*, Real Estate, January 6, 2002, Section 11, p. 1.

3. Interestingly, the day after the first attack on the World Trade Center, on February 26, 1993, with the bomb in the basement garage, the Dow went up 0.17 percent, and six months later it was up 8.41 percent. On the other hand, the day after the Pearl Harbor attack, the Dow went down 3.5 percent, and six months later it was down by 9.48 percent.

4. The somewhat parallel activities of the Weather underground in the United States were never taken seriously by the establishment.

5. Speech by Jean Baudrillard, University of Vienna in Vienna, Austria, March 14, 2002.

6. See, for instance, Kevin Cox, ed., *Spaces of Globalization: Reasserting the Power of the Local* (New York: Guilford Books, 1997), particularly the contribution of Erik Swyngedouw in that volume.

7. Some of the proposals of the UN-sponsored Habitat II in Istanbul, for instance, point in this direction. "Conference [Habitat II] Hears More Wordplay than Substance." CUPReport, Center for Urban Policy Research, Rutgers University, Winter 1996, pp. 3, 5. Marcuse, Peter. 1996. "Slouching towards Istanbul: U.S. Further Isolates Itself at Habitat II." *Planners Network*, September, pp. 1–2.

8. Robert Fitch, *The Assassination of New York* (London: Verso Press, 1993).

9. TIAA-CREF, the largest pension fund in the United States, now has 4,600 employees in New York City, 1,320 in Denver, and 597 in Charlotte, North Carolina. Their planned expansion will be overwhelmingly in Charlotte, hardly a global city. Telephone information, TIAA-CREF, November 12, 2001.

10. Peter Marcuse, "The Enclave, the Citadel, and the Ghetto: What Has Changed in the Post-Fordist U.S. City?" *Urban Affairs Review*, Vol. 33, No. 2 (November 1997), pp. 228–264.

11. Edward J. Blakely and Mary Gail Snyder, *Fortress America: Gated and Walled Communities in the United States* (Cambridge, Mass.: Lincoln Institute of Land Policy, and Washington, D.C.: Brookings Institution Press, 1995).

12. Joel Garreau, *Edge City: Life on the New Frontier* (New York: Doubleday, 1991).

13. Peter Marcuse, "After the World Trade Center: Deconcentration and Deplanning," *Quaderns d'arquitectura i urbanisme*, No. 232, pp. 38–44.

14. Peter Marcuse and Ronald van Kempen, "The Divided City in History," in Peter Marcuse and Ronald van Kempen, *Of States and Cities: On the Partitioning of Urban Space* (Oxford: Oxford University Press, 2002).

15. Edward N. Wolff, *Top Heavy: A Study of Increasing Inequality of Wealth in America* (Washington, D.C.: Economic Policy Institute, 1996).

16. Peter Marcuse and Ronald van Kempen, *Of States and Cities: On the Partitioning of Urban Space* (Oxford: Oxford University Press, 2002).

17. Ulrich Beck, *What Is Globalization?* (Malden, Mass.: Blackwell, 2000); Peter Marcuse, "Space and Race in the Post-Fordist City: The Outcast Ghetto and Advanced Homelessness in the United States Today," in *Urban Poverty and the Underclass* (pp. 176-216), ed. Enzo Mingione (Oxford: Blackwell, 1996).

18. Richard Sennett, *Flesh and Stone: The Body and the City in Western Civilization* (New York: W. W. Norton, 1994).

19. This is not the place to enter into an extended discussion of the causes of September 11, but there is no doubt that feelings of exclusion from the benefits of globalization played at least a supportive role.

20. "The Power of Partnership," *New York*, November 26, 2001.

21. Charles V. Bagli, "Wall St. Giants Offered Grants for Staying Put," *New York Times*, March 21, 2002.

22. Comprehensive data are very hard to come by. The most useful compilation and breakdowns I have seen are by David Hoffer for Reconstruction Watch, a joint project of the Fiscal Policy Institute and Good Jobs New York. The breakdown in the text is strictly mine.

23. See their web site at http://www.housingfirst.net/platform.html.

24. These figures come from the Independent Budget Office's Analysis, March 2002, available online at http://www.ibo.nyc.ny.us/iboreports/march2002full.pdf.

25. Draft, Labor/Community/Advocacy Network to Rebuild New York, March 28, 2002.

26. See, for instance, the suggestions of the City Project at http://www.cityproject.org/.

27. *New York Times*, Real Estate, January 6, 2002, Section 11, p. 1.

28. See Fitch, *The Assassination of New York.*

29. Tom Gibb, BBC Brazil correspondent, "Landless Movement Occupies President's Estate in Brazil," cited in portside@yahoogroups.com, March 25, 2002. To provide context, the story goes on: MST leaders say they want the farm given to landless families. They say they occupied the farm after the authorities refused to discuss demands to be given other areas of land and to have electricity and water connected to existing MST settlements. The Landless Movement has for years been campaigning for major land reform in Brazil, where the distribution of wealth is one of the most unequal in the world. The government has been using divide and rule tactics, giving out land to other peasant organizations, and doing its best to discredit the confrontational tactics used by the MST. At the same time, it is still relatively common for leaders of the Landless Movement to be murdered, cases that the police usually fail to solve.

30. William Pfaff, "Unleashed by Sept. 11: Free at Last for a Global Power Play," *International Herald Tribune*, March 15, 2002, p. 6. What Pfaff says critically, others are beginning to say approvingly; thus the editorial features editor of the *Wall Street Journal* quotes the title of Patrick Buchanan's "America, A Republic, not an Empire" and says he has it exactly backward. In *Warrior Politics: Why Leadership Demands a Pagan Ethos* (New York: Random House, 2001), Robert D. Kaplan argues, approvingly, that the United States is carrying on a tradition of Empire dating back to Rome, but more widely and more effectively—and that's a good thing. See Emily Eakin, "All Roads Lead to D.C.," *New York Times*, March 31, 2002, p. 4.

19

Globalization and the Need for an Urban Environmentalism

ANDREW LIGHT*

Little Sally *"I don't think many people are going to come to see this musical, Officer Lockstock."*
Officer Lockstock *"Why do you say that, Little Sally? Don't you think people want to be told that their way of life is unsustainable?"*
Little Sally *"That, and the title's awful."*

URINETOWN: THE MUSICAL

The 2001 Broadway hit *Urinetown* may well be remembered as the first "Malthusian musical."[1] The plot takes place in an unnamed city, sometime in the not too distant future. In this possible world a water shortage has become so dire that private toilets have been outlawed and people are required to use public amenities for relief ("twenty years we've had this drought, and our reservoirs have all dried up . . . it's a privilege to pee"). Of course, this also being a savvy antineoliberal musical, the public amenities are owned by a private company—"UGC: Urine Good Company"—which has been in collusion with the state legislature for years to impose a system of draconian laws outlawing public urination and defecation, thereby forcing desperate people to pay to use UGC's toilets. Ostensibly the laws were passed for the public good, to overcome what are referred to throughout the performance as the early "stink years," when water scarcity, combined with a lack of central control, led people to quite literally soil the commons. But even

....

*My thanks to Heather Gautney, Jonathan Burston, and Jim Sheppard for helpful conversations and critical comments on this chapter, which substantially improved it. My biggest debt of gratitude, though, is to Susan Barbash and Eric Katz, who generously gave me their beach house for a month, where this, and many other things, were finally completed.

though the public good is behind the creation of this new scheme of regulation, UGC grows richer and richer with each passing year as dubious rate increases for use of public amenities are bribed through the legislature. In a twisted version of "ecological modernization" theories, like those propagated by Ulrich Beck, UGC becomes the universal global corporation that makes money off the environmental crisis. Those who choose to pee for free in violation of the laws are sent away by the play's narrator and chief of police, Officer Lockstock, to "Urinetown," assumed to be some sort of hellish prison colony.

Much of the action of *Urinetown* takes place in two settings: the corporate headquarters of UGC, referred to early on as a shining tower on the hill, and at the most dire of the public amenities (number nine) in the poorest district in town. Even though these two places are presented as being in the same city, they are clearly worlds away. At amenity number nine each announcement of a rate increase for usage of the facility causes more and more desperation among the chorus, dubbed in the script as simply, "The Poor." Eventually, a hero emerges, Bobby Strong, one of the toilet attendees. Seeing the misery around him, he seizes control of UGC's facilities and opens up amenity number nine for free use. He goes on to lead the poor folk of the district in a nascent resistance against the corporatized state. As the second act begins, Bobby is seen trying to rally other poor amenity districts to their cause. But rather than moving the people forward into a bright new future, he is arrested and sent away to Urinetown, which turns out to mean that he is simply thrown off the top floor of UGC headquarters to his death. Fear not however; the daughter of the head of UGC, Hope Cladwell, picks up the cause of the now martyred Bobby and leads the people in an overthrow of UGC and the creation of a new welfare state founded on an affirmation of personal and local freedom. Unfortunately, the new regime is long on spirit and heart and short on regulation. Before the play ends we learn that it has permitted overuse of dwindling water resources and thus worsened the environmental crisis beyond any hope of recovery. One by one, members of the cast start dying off, recognizing, as Lockstock says in his final remarks to the audience, that their town was Urinetown all along—inhabited only, we can assume, by corpses. In a rousing finish with the now deceased cast, Lockstock holds up a copy of *On Population* and shouts, "Hail Malthus!"

If one were looking for a better artistic production to inspire serious thinking about the consequences of globalization, Stephanie Black's documentary *Life and Debt* (2001) would be a better choice. But I start with this brief description of *Urinetown* for a reason; for whether it intended to or not, this farce locates the site of struggles over local environmental sustainability and global corporate power in a city, an anytown, which could remind us that the front lines of most decisions about the environmental consequences of collective consumption will be in those places where people live together.

But why is this important? The principal reason is that the rise of environmental awareness in the North has brought along with it an antiurbanism that sees cities as the root of our environmental ills rather than a source of their solution. At worst, cities represent the technological hubris of humans foolish enough to think they are now independent from nature, if not an outright embodiment of human domination over the natural world. By instead of focusing environmental awareness and activism almost exclusively on preservation of wild areas and the biodiversity of species, Northern environmentalists risk irrelevance or, worse, the propagation of unsustainable lifestyles by ignoring cities as the place where the correlation of issues of justice and protection of the environment will be decided.

Many environmental social scientists and historians, including William Cronon, Mark Dowie, William Shutkin, and David Schlosberg, have pointed to this urban gap in environmentalists' theories, practices, and organizations. The purpose of this chapter is to add another voice to rectifying this lacuna in the context of discussions of globalization. In what follows I will first provide a brief assessment of the criticisms of antiglobalization advocates concerning global environmental issues over local community priorities, second, make a case for why the environment of the city is an environment worthy of attention to environmentalists wishing to respond to such criticisms, third, briefly offer a model of urban citizenship, which includes a component entailing a range of obligations toward the urban environment that may answer some of the globalization critics of Northern environmental concerns, and finally fourth, offer an example of how the city can serve as a unique site for environmental participation, if not ecological citizenship, and as a more realistic site of environmental concerns in the face of global pressures.

As predicted in the excerpt cited at the start, most of the buzz over *Urinetown* was over its name. But as a casual observer, I was most distressed at the lack of discussion of the subject matter itself. Was this simply because of the absurd central conceit of the plot? One wonders, for surely there is something to Lockstock's suggestion—why would people come to a show to be told, even metaphorically, that their way of life was unsustainable? Perhaps only if they either didn't believe the message or didn't take it seriously. Helping people to take this message seriously should be of central concern to environmentalists today.

GLOBALIZING ENVIRONMENTAL
PRIORITIES OR LOCALIZING RESISTANCE?

Daily we are confronted with global environmental problems that challenge our ability to understand their local implications and our part in either causing or mitigating them. Daily we are either given reasons not to worry about these problems or, more commonly, confronted with trade-offs that require us to set them aside. Global warming is an ideal example. Fifteen years ago there was clear disagreement in the scientific community on the existence of anthropogenically caused global warming. Today there is near unanimity that the planet is heating up and that the consequences will be dire, especially for poorer countries in the South. The primary cause of global warming has been Northern industrialization. So, even if a case can be made that Southern countries are currently producing or will soon produce greenhouse gases in excess of their Northern neighbors (which is one of the arguments by the Bush administration for its refusal to sign the Kyoto Accords, which do not include China and India), such relatively recent consequences of industrialization pale in comparison to the cumulative effects of Northern production and consumption patterns over the years. Therefore, even if, as some economists and policy analysts would have it, the negative effects of global warming can either be absorbed by Northern economies or even turn out to be a net economic benefit, the North still has an almost unquestionable responsibility to mitigate warming trends so that the South does not suffer further to sustain our patterns of consumption and production.[2]

But even though the ethical case for a global covenant cutting greenhouse gases is virtually unassailable in almost every moral framework, the method of fulfilling such an obligation is less than clear. How should the responsibilities for cutting greenhouse gases be distributed, and how should these responsibilities be balanced with rights of national self-determination? The Bush administration in the United States remains adamant that the market should be used to solve this problem. Cutting greenhouse gases cannot be allowed at the expense of decreases in economic productivity or expectations in consumption. Worse still, since the terrorist attacks of September 11, environmental politics in this country has degenerated into calls for more defensive postures against any international agreement that would require sacrifice of quality of life as a matter of patriotism and national pride. If we increase mileage per gallon standards on sport utility vehicles, then the terrorists win.

Such sentiments are, of course, ridiculous. Climate change is a global problem that cannot be solved through the initiatives of individual state actors regulating corporations, global or not. International agreements are necessary, which will require both a restriction on production of greenhouse gases across the board and the development of new methods of industrialization in the South that will not recreate whatever problem we may solve through the restriction of Northern consumption. Furthermore, if a country as massive in either industrial output or population as the United States or China opts out of such an agreement, then we cannot hope to achieve any lasting solution to this problem.

Does the critique of globalization help or hinder the case for a strong international response to such issues beyond the empty parochial rhetoric that dominates such debates in the United States? It is beyond the scope of this chapter to provide a more thorough assessment of the merits of the literature on globalization and the environment.[3] My view, however, is that the relevance of such discussions is at least mixed. Those inveighing against "globalization," too often a vacuous category of analysis referring to everything and nothing, ask us to remember that many problems passed off as "global" are in fact attendant only to the needs of a particular local—the local needs of Northern power brokers and their elite counterparts in the South. By asking Southern countries to set aside their own needs in order to meet Northern priorities, figures such as Wolfgang Sachs and Vandana Shiva argue that the South is recolonized, again serving only as a repository of resources to make Northern overconsumption possible. Sachs, for example, sees environmentalists' language of "sustainability" to be only a cover for the retreat of environmentalism into a mere managerial ethic, no longer willing to take on the power of the corporate state but instead degenerating into a shrill call for tinkering around the edges.[4] For Shiva, the language of the global is used to justify a new green imperialism of North over South, masking Northern interests as global and shunting aside authentically local priorities. We must instead "democratize the global" and make it truly local again: "*Every* local community equipped with rights and obligations constitutes a new *global* order for environmental care."[5]

No doubt there is something to these criticisms. For example, once the United States has deforested its own old growth timber preserves, why is it now a "global" priority for Brazil to preserve its rainforest? Northerners might claim that the Amazon rainforest is needed just in order to mitigate the effects of excessive CO_2 production and that without those forests, we may all suffer ill effects. But Brazilians might quickly reply: Where were such international concerns when U.S. forests were being depleted at such a rapid rate? Why must we restrict our own needs in order to satisfy yours when you were not restricting your own needs to help satisfy ours? An alternative might be to claim that we are all "global environmental citizens" and the rainforest is a universal trust for us all. But besides largely falling on deaf ears, such arguments ignore the lack of responsibility we have historically demonstrated for the poor in countries forced to live in substandard conditions because of pressures to export resources to the North at the expense of local self-sufficiency. Sachs, Shiva, and others do make a good case that the creation of new regimes for global environmental regulation often wind up only justifying and extending the relative affluence of the North without compensation to the South. For this reason, Shiva argues that the "global" in "globalization" (her actual phrase is "global reach") "is a political, not an ecological space."[6]

But if the meaning of "globalization" in the context of environmental problems is simply that it designates a new form of colonialism, which is transparently unjust, then we need not create a new category of analysis in order to understand it. What we are calling here "globalization," at least on the environmental end of this discussion, is just the environmental arm of an old pattern of domination. Such a suggestion must be wrong, however. It is undeniable that there are many environmental problems that are global in scope and that require international agreements, which we may as well call "global solutions" or agreements with a "global reach." The fact of the existence of environmental problems that not only cross but transcend borders means that globalism has an ecological and not just a political dimension. One may decry those who Larry Lohmann calls "green globalists" as simply trying to "reinforce the dominance of a single industrial pattern," but one must be careful not to confuse such a political ideology with the recognition of the global integration of many critical ecological systems.[7]

But where does this leave us with respect to North-South environmental relations? Though there are certainly many counterexamples to the contrary, it is true that with each passing year we understand more the consequences of our past patterns of industrialization. Although 19th-century industrialists and the states that supported them may have known that they were exploiting labor (or rather disagreed that what they were doing was "exploitation" though still understood that this was an issue of some contention), it would be incredulous to claim that they could foresee the full potential consequences of their actions on the global environment. Does this consideration get northerners off the hook or justify globalizing environmental concerns at the expense of local southern priorities? Certainly not. But it does require us to bite the bullet on the need for some form of transnational regulation, or at least on joint incentive schemes, to mitigate those environmental problems that no state can hope to solve by itself. And given the pressures to create institutions for global governance, is there not some reason for environmentalists across all borders to try to influence those structures, which may transcend the narrow vision of some local politicians and policy makers?

Take the closely related example of genetically modified foods. If one were to embrace a wholesale rejection of GM foods under all circumstances (a position, by the way, that I would not endorse), there is just as strong a case to be made for supporting the creation of international trade agreements governing their production as to rejecting such agreements. Given how unlikely it is that many states already predisposed to license the creation or distribution of such products will strongly regulate these industries themselves, perhaps only an international convention can protect those of us who wish to opt out of this particular version of industrialization.[8]

To suggest that environmentalists should simply reject "globalization" in any form is naïve and, I would argue, irresponsible. Too often when reading antiglobalization critics of environmental priorities I see much by way of criticism and little by way of concrete alternative recommendations for how local sovereignty can be maintained and respected while at the same time raising awareness of, let alone addressing, those environmental issues that clearly are global in scope and that will require global compacts for remediation. Complaints about globalization ought not to degenerate into the latest in a series of litanies against occult dominant "forces" without anything by way of an alternative. It is a tune of hopelessness and desperation that winds up too often celebrating the most trivial signs of resistance to state or corporate power while the world burns. If every local community is to constitute a global order as Shiva tells us, how do we propose to coordinate and resolve conflicts among those localities when we must? Do we simply accept that some localities will be more powerful and hence able to externalize the costs of their environmental decisions downstream on their weaker neighbors? Strengthening local environmental priorities is no doubt a step in the right direction, but more important, I think, is to help people understand that how they come to treat and hopefully respect their own environment will have a direct effect on solving those problems that transcend local boundaries, however they are drawn. Otherwise, the celebration of locality becomes simply an empty rhetorical move against global actors.

Let us go back to the example that opened this section, global warming. Many antiglobalization advocates have focused on environmental problems like global warming by pushing for tighter controls on firms that are more responsible than others for producing greenhouse gases. But even if such regulations were successfully put into place, the problems associated with global warming would not simply go away. These problems would need to be mitigated and eventually remediated. So, aside from the question of how state and corporate actors should respond to such a clear environmental threat, an even more difficult issue is motivating individuals to take it up as a matter of their own concern. This is the terrain, after all, where actual people constituting "the local" will have the opportunity to confront such problems. If it is true that Northern countries have a clear moral or political obligation to cut their production of greenhouse gases, then how will individual citizens come to see it as part of their responsibility to press for the fulfillment of those obligations? Even further, will such citizens ever come to actively play a part in stopping the unsustainable consumption patterns that led to this problem to begin with? How can we expect states to shoulder their responsibility for such global environmental problems without pressure from their respective citizens or from affinity groups able to generate enough influence to force their hand? At bottom there can be little hope of reaching (and, perhaps more importantly, maintaining over time) any kind of international agreement on such issues without citizen interest, let alone action. No doubt critics like Shiva would agree.

But the key issue then becomes one of scale. Problems that are too big may surpass our ability to take them seriously in a moral sense, as we may think that our individual contribution to them is negligible and our responsibility accordingly limited. Global warming, and its myriad consequences, occurs at a scale beyond the comprehension of most of us, and so the problem seems far off, distant, and easy to ignore. Those consequences that matter are not just that we'll have a few warmer winters on occasion but that the future that we will not see will be much worse off than the conditions we have experienced in our lifetime. And even if the magnitude of the problem can be understood, what are we supposed to do about it? It is like someone pointing to one of the great Egyptian pyramids and telling us to "do our part and move it a foot to the left." Why would we have to do this and where would we possibly start? Confronted with the responsibility of helping to mitigate the consequences of global warming, and hopefully forestalling its worst effects, are we simply to opt out of the economic system that gives us precious few choices not to consume massive amounts of fossil fuels in the course of our lives? Are only the environmental saints among us the ones who are truly resisting globalization?

Antiglobalization critics of global environmental priorities are at least right about one thing: There is no progress on any transboundary problem unless there is first attention to local circumstances. Market incentives or state power are insufficient as a tool for motivating people either to press for a change to the infrastructures in which they live or to take personal responsibility for helping to resolve environmental problems. But we need to be more specific and more precise about what kind of relationships on the local level we are trying to engender and which arrangement of localities in relation to each other are both equitable and feasible as a foundation for taking on the challenge of global environmental problems. My argument in what remains of this chapter will be that one way of creating a sense of environmental awareness, sensitive to issues of justice and fair distribution of environmental harms and benefits, is through a recognition that the places where most of us live—cities—are an environment worthy of our attention not only in itself but as a first step in a causal chain to attending to the environmental problems that transcend localities. Unfortunately, like the reception of many to *Urinetown,* cities are not usually taken very seriously on the reform agendas of many environmentalists. Worse still, many in the environmental community are content to look at cities only as sources of disvalue, compared to the natural resource conservation issues more traditionally thought to be the foundation of a healthy environment. If environmentalists interested in the power of the local saw as a priority the encouragement of an ethic of responsible environmental citizenship close to home, I believe they would make a more substantial contribution to the creation of an international constituency to press for more responsible governance of global environmental problems.

URBAN ENVIRONMENTS AND THE ECOLOGICAL FUTURE

Too often when I am attending conferences on environmental issues, a well-meaning colleague stands up and unloads a litany of predictions of increasing trends to urbanization as proof of our dire environmental future. The details of such predictions are without a doubt a bit unsettling. The next quarter century, according to the United Nations, will see an "urban population explosion" of staggering proportions. The urban population of the developing world will double to 4 billion people, or 80 million people per year. This is equivalent to the world adding an additional Germany, Vietnam, or Colombia plus a South Africa every year, a Los Angeles every month, a Pittsburgh or Hanoi every week. By 2015, there will be 400 cities with populations exceeding 1 million people in developing countries, twice as many as in the 1990s, packing in twice the proportion of the third world's population. The urban population of India alone will grow to approximate the total population of the United States, Russia, and Japan combined, while China, now two-thirds rural, will become predominantly urban by 2025. Large city growth will be sustained, continuing from 1990 to 2015, at unprecedented increments (Lagos,

16.9 million; Bombay, 14 million; Dhaka, 13.2 million; and Karachi, 11.4 million), each city equivalent to the New York metropolitan area.[9]

There is no doubt that unchecked population growth, in and of itself, is a problem. But what exactly would happen if more than half of the world's population lived in cities? The claim seems to be that we would see an extrapolation of the worst environmental consequences that are assumed to be the result of urban dwelling: increased production of pollutants, increased fuel costs for transportation of food into cities, and loss of public land. The common assumption behind such analysis is that cities separate us from nature. And more people living in cities spells an environmental disaster because of this separation. So if we are to come to understand "the local" as a site of resistance to false moves toward environmental globalization, and also as a first step toward a more equitable approach to global environmental issues, then cities are the wrong locale on which to focus. Cities are part of the environmental problem, not part of the solution. We would do better to try to reverse trends toward global urbanization.

William Rees is often cited as one well versed in such concerns and satisfied with such conclusions. Rees, a Canadian geographer, is best known for his development of "ecological footprint" analysis. Ecological footprints are extrapolated maps of the environmental impacts of urban areas created with the help of Geographical Information Systems. These maps help to track the full ecological burden of cities on the environment by spatially representing as a "footprint" the resources required from surrounding land to sustain an urban population and the direct environmental harms produced by cities in the form of waste generated. The point of such maps is to demonstrate that the environmental stress caused by cities is far greater than the actual physical borders of the city.[10] Evocative figures are derived from this analysis, such as the claim that the ecological footprint of London is larger than the entire island of Britain.

Here is a point, however, where we can begin to retake some of the ground against cities in an environmental context and make a case for reframing environmental concerns around an urban dimension. One thing that is critical to remember is that ecological footprint analysis gives us not simply a representation of the impact of cities on the environment per se but a representation of the impact of cities on the environment as a function of the impact of a concentrated population relative to a given rate of consumption. The ecological footprints of cities in developing countries are always smaller than those of first-world cities with a comparable population. The environmental problem that is revealed here is more precisely the unsustainable consumption patterns of people in the North. And importantly, it is not really the unsustainable consumption patterns of only urban dwellers that is implicated in this analysis but the unsustainable consumption patterns of northerners in general. Footprint analysis provides a good indicator of unsustainable consumption patterns and a very helpful spatial metaphor to assist Northern urbanites in understanding the larger ecological consequences of their consumption patterns on the global commons. But perhaps more importantly, it also helps to

demonstrate the unjust distribution of resources between North and South. Ecological footprint analysis is therefore arguably a critique of unsustainable populations rather than cities themselves, absent evidence to the contrary, which can be
used as a method of helping to rectify the unjust ideology of globalization identified by Sachs and his colleagues.

Nonetheless, Rees and other advocates of this technique often use footprint
analysis as the linchpin of a general urban critique, which in recent years has grown
louder as global population has shifted toward cities. In a short editorial in the
Chronicle of Higher Education, Rees suggested that the increased urbanization predicted for the coming century is evidence of humanity's "technological hubris."
"Separating billions of people from the land that sustains them is a giddy leap of
faith with serious implications for ecological security."[11] Urbanization, we are told,
removes people spatially and psychologically from the land. Cities create more in-
tensive use of croplands and forests to sustain urban populations, and more
hectares of productive land are then relied upon to sustain the populations of rich
countries (presumably especially in cities). Most alarmingly, says Rees, in a world
of "rapid change," cities are unsustainable because they are susceptible to adverse
environmental changes and political instability in rural areas.[12] Political turmoil in
a countryside can cut off urban populations from their sources of food, fuel, and
other natural resources. Wouldn't it be better then for those interested in mitigating the unfair advantages of northerners over southerners to encourage people to
live in places less separated from their means of subsistence?

As it turns out, the evidence here is, at best, mixed. There is actually no reason
to believe that cities themselves are making it easier for populations to grow, even
though most cities do contain a demographic bulge at the critical childbearing ages
of 15–29. In the South, population is more likely to grow at a slower rate in cities
because there is less need to replace children who die young in order to maintain
family labor strength (for example, to work a farm). So, Rees's worries about urban
populations, except for the strategic concern he mentions at the end, are all claims
that apply generically to any population growth in the North, not just growth in
cities. The convention of using the ecological footprint to critique cities amounts
to little more than the old wine of population worries in the new bottles of GIS
data.[13]

What then about the strategic worries that Rees raises? Is it the case that urbanization is unwise for ecological reasons because surrounding lands may become
politically unstable? Perhaps. Thomas Homer-Dixon has argued that environmental problems are more likely to create political violence in rural areas than in urban
areas.[14] At the same time, Homer-Dixon reports that, empirically, urban violence
(at least political violence) does not necessarily increase with rural-urban migration. The extent to which urban advocates should worry about this consideration
is unclear.

How then are we to evaluate the environmental worries of Rees and others
about the demographic shift toward cities? Setting aside for the moment Rees's

vague charge of "technological hubris," does the move toward cities necessarily herald a new stage of environmental disaster? I don't think so. In fact, I would go so far as to argue that we should be very thankful that the demographic shift is toward urbanization rather than away from it. Without that shift, I would be very skeptical that we had a hopeful environmental future at all. Densely populated cities, even without a concentrated attempt at conservation efforts, consume less energy than rural areas or regions that sustain human populations alongside wilderness areas, *all other things being equal.*

For example, studies of the conservation gains made during the late 1970s and early 1980s in the United States show that more urbanized states tend to consume less energy per capita than less urbanized states. The lowest consumption rate went to New York state (215 BTUs on average) because so many residents live in New York City apartments (sharing walls and hence sharing heat) and do not own cars (nor regularly use them if they own them). The highest consumption rate went to Alaska, with 1,139 BTUs on average, five times as much energy consumed as a New Yorker. While surely climatic differences in part explain this gap, other states with high individual consumption rates included states with more comparable weather patterns. Aside from New York, the lowest consumption rates included Rhode Island and Massachusetts, other highly urbanized states containing relatively substantial proportions of shared-wall housing stock.[15]

Although this study reports on only one variable of measuring energy costs and savings, we should note how important a variable it is. Transportation costs for food and other goods are remarkably similar in most parts of the country. Most Americans now consume hothouse tomatoes from California (or some other equivalent region); the amount of energy expended to bring food to Montana or Manhattan is, per capita, comparable. Each consumer dollar spent in the United States also entails the consumption of some quantity of petroleum, but consumption is no greater on average in large urban areas than in suburbs, small towns, or most rural areas. The same is true of most production. The energy savings from effective public transportation and dense housing stock are arguably the most important structural differences between cities like New York and other residential areas in the United States, again, so long as everything else remains equal. If less densely populated areas were to undertake more substantial energy conservation measures, then perhaps these comparisons would change. Unfortunately, however, this is not happening, and at least in the United States, the federal government has failed to pass any incentive measures to make energy consumption more sustainable across the board. Assuming that population increases and consumption rates remain constant, moving away from density becomes one of the single biggest hurdles for achieving environmental sustainability. It is the suburbanization of cities and the flights of populations to the countryside that must be dissuaded.

No matter what other problems they have, densely populated cities get around the lack of environmental leadership on energy conservation by creating and encouraging an infrastructure where residents do not actively have to decide to change their lifestyles or priorities in order to live sustainably. The infrastructure it-self makes it irrational to live otherwise—it is a bad use of resources for a middle-income family in New York City to buy a sport utility vehicle, given the ease and availability of public transportation and the high costs of keeping such an auto-mobile in the city. So, if living lightly on Earth is indicative of environmental re-sponsibility, then surely Manhattanites are doing more for global environmental priorities than their counterparts in Colorado. If some sort of environmental con-sciousness raising is required for environmental responsibility, then one should be fearful that such a change in consciousness will not happen soon enough, or on a great enough scale, to forestall the worst consequences of the cumulative impact of humans on the planet. We should therefore nurture those forms of life that are structurally more sustainable. Of course, development of an explicit environmen-tal consciousness would be better for urbanites, too. But if global environmental problems are to be justly addressed by attention to local priorities, environmental-ists must stop inveighing on cities as such (rather than rightly criticizing sprawling Northern cities such as Atlanta and Houston) as the source of our ills.[16]

URBAN ECOLOGICAL CITIZENSHIP

If Shiva is right and every local community must come to constitute a new order for environmental care, then it is arguably the case that those locales that make a potentially larger impact on the environment must be included as a focus of our environmental concern, if not made a priority, as those large local impacts accu-mulate as global environmental problems. A focus on cities will also help us to imagine ways of motivating potentially larger numbers of people to consider the connection between how they live their everyday lives and our collective environ-mental future. So as not to put too much pressure on already stressed rural inhab-itants to conform to global environmental priorities, we must encourage those more responsible forms of urban infrastructure that will make the most of the en-vironmental advantages of dense forms of urbanization. In order to do this we must tackle environmental problems in cities head-on.

Northern environmentalists have not typically done this. Mark Dowie, in his excellent survey of the recent history of the environmental movement, points out that the image of the environmentalist as backpacker and tree-hugger has persisted throughout the history of environmentalism in the United States. Although many see this focus as more a tendency of the so-called first wave of environmentalists at the turn of the century (for example, John Muir and his followers), even the sec-ond wave of environmentalism, which got off the ground in the 1960s and 1970s, embraces this wilderness focus: "Environmentalism means wildlife protection and wilderness conservation, while the environmental movement is identified with the Sierra Club and similar organizations."[17] David Schlosberg confirms Dowie's find-ings and argues that the recent rise of the environmental justice movement has been in direct relation not only to the perceived lack of minority representation on the boards of major environmental groups but also to the focus of these groups. The "more telling complaint centered on the movement's focus on natural resources, wilderness, endangered species and the like, rather than toxics, public health, and the unjust distribution of environmental risks," exactly those issues that are of interest to low-income communities and communities of color, largely in urban areas.[18]

There are many potential ways to try to achieve the goal of refocusing the environmental agenda on urban issues. As a moral pluralist, I would claim that, in principle, there is no one single lens through which we may discern the natural values of cities and the connection of this range of values to the normative reasons that we may have for protecting or conserving the larger natural world. But again, taking a cue from Shiva, the importance of cities in a more responsible environmentalism must prioritize the connection of people to their locality in the broader global context of environmental problems. From the way that I have set up the range of issues here, a model of citizenship as both urban and ecological is one good candidate for helping us to reframe global environmental questions. The reason, however, is not just out of my own predilections. It stems from a description of what a city is. A city is not just a place; it is an environment in which humans live in proximity to each other, either in a thin or thick community (or if you prefer more technical language, either in an "instrumental" or "constitutive" community).[19]

The classical citizenship model of obligation may be uniquely well suited to contextualizing urban environmental concerns because cities are places where humans confront the advantages and disadvantages of living together. Citizenship, conceived along Aristotelian (or "republican") lines, identifies a normative role for residents of a place, articulating a range of obligations they have to each other for the sake of the larger community in which they live. On this account, citizenship is not satisfied merely by voting, nor is it a minimal legal category that one is either born into or becomes naturalized into. It is instead an "ethical citizenship," or a concept of "citizenship as vocation," where citizenship is a virtue met by active participation at some level of public affairs.

Following a discussion of this issue by Richard Dagger, we need not catalogue all of the possible activities of a responsible citizen here so much as realize that "what matters is that these activities set him or her apart from those who regard politics as a nuisance to be avoided or a spectacle to be witnessed."[20] Dagger and other republican theorists are quick to admit that this sense of citizenship is steadily in decline, if not dead on arrival, in some sectors. Yet it does remain a powerful place to orient such discussions, since its resuscitation is not beyond hope and holds much promise; such a model has a language of moral responsibility that still resonates widely in many cultures. It is, as Dagger notes, something that we do care to have concern and disagreements about. It is a ground that many outside of the academy still see as relevant to their lives and fortunes. Adding an environmental component to a classical republican model of citizenship becomes then the conceptual basis for a claim that the "larger community" to which the ethical citizen has obligations is inclusive of the city as space, place, and environment, as well as people. Any resource demands placed on the environment of cities is a demand that cannot be isolated from the needs of one's neighbors, both those in neighboring communities and, I would argue, those in the larger world. So, an urban environmentalism must focus at least as much on encouraging bonds of care or empathy with one's fellow urbanites (at least inclusive of their needs for clean air, water, open space, etc.) as it must focus on finding the normative source of bonds of care for nature or natural processes themselves.

If our goal is to come up with a conception of ecological citizenship and then expand that to an urban ecological citizenship with global implications, or a civic environmentalism, how do we begin? First, we start by articulating a notion of citizenship that is, as much as possible, intrinsically ecological. Such a conception of citizenship should not be too far off for us, especially if, as just mentioned, we stick to a classical republican idea of citizenship, in particular one considered as an urban citizenship. Dagger has already given us sound reasons why an urban citizenship would need to be concerned with environmental issues, forming a civic environmentalism. Using the example of urban sprawl, Dagger argues that republican citizens would need to fight sprawl because it threatens both the environmental and civic fabric of a city: A sprawled city will exacerbate the demise of civic associations that are necessary for the development of an urban citizenship.[21] Conjoining environmentalism to urban citizenship by making environmental concerns one of, in Dagger's terms, the "virtues of citizenship" may help to ameliorate this problem.

Discussions of citizenship cannot occur without an understanding of civic space. It goes without saying, I expect, that New York, and most other global cities, stand little chance of becoming a new agora at the level of their formal municipal boundaries. Even the early-20th-century language among urbanists of center and periphery does not capture the spatial dimension of the modern metropolis, where yesterday's suburb has become an identifiable and independent unit of potentially significant civic engagement today. It is important then to aim our understanding and expectations of urban citizenship at a continually updated picture of the scale of city life today that seems most conducive to a more robust conception of citizenship. Following from comments made at the end of section one, an environmental citizenship that identified the locus of citizen responsibilities at a global scale would be one that very few people would reasonably embrace. Instead, ecological citizenship, like any more robust notion of citizenship, must first be grounded in the environmental needs of one's local environment.

Recognizing this problem, some urbanists focus on grand symbolic spaces, such as the development of the Potsdamer Platz in Berlin as a locus of what it means, in some substantive sense, to be a Berliner. But even such heralded imagined urban centers are not much help to the project of grounding an urban citizenship that will have anything other than mere symbolic meaning. In New York, for example, spaces of meaningful democratic interaction cannot be encompassed only in symbolic spaces such as Central Park or, perish the thought, the now Disneyfied Times Square. These are not the spaces of democratic interaction where responsibilities to others as part of the whole are acknowledged. They are sites of play, leisure, and, increasingly, tourism—a home more to the visitor than the citizen. A ground for citizenship must be found at a smaller scale where citizens can know and interact with each other. One reason is that it is only at such a scale, as Dewey put it so well, that engagement and access to authority is possible by citizens in relation to each other. Reading Dewey's *The Public and Its Problems,* and bemoaning the descent into particularism in urban studies, Thomas Bender puts the point this way:

> A larger public, what [Dewey] called "the Great Community," is built upon the habits and accomplishments of *local publics.* Urban critics tend to focus on the diversity of public space and publics. Diversity is important; but so too are access to political institutions and the opportunity to give voice to public concerns. . . . I am proposing a public that is a public not because of mere propinquity, however important that is, but *because they propose to do something together.* The essential quality of what I call the "local" public is not, as we are inclined to think, sameness; it is accessibility to networks of informal power and to institutions of formal politics.[22]

I would add to this only that local public spaces also provide access to others as having shared lives, rather than serving only as symbolic representations of bonds of community. This access is necessary to ground a morally motivating empathy between citizens, which is arguably necessary to make civic obligation coherent to individuals who might not otherwise see such obligations as in their best interests.

It seems at least plausible to me that citizenship in today's global metropolis must at least in part be a necessary function of the ability to engender civic obligation at a smaller scale within the metropolis. Dagger agrees, proposing that a small, stable, and well-defined city, in civic republican terms, is in the range of 100,000 to 250,000 people. In turn, the goal of his republican-liberal citizenship when it comes to larger metropolitan areas is to enact political structures that decentralize them to create, in Bender's terms, "local publics." "The number of these [structures] would vary with the population of the city, but we might imagine that a city of 1,000,000 would be divided into 20 districts of roughly 50,000 each, with each district subdivided into 10 wards. The wards and districts would have their own councils, elected by and from their residents."[23] Whether Dagger is right about such figures will be largely an empirical issue. Nonetheless, he is not the first to argue that some reduced scale of civic association, if not governance itself, is a necessary condition to thicken citizenship.

One word of caution though: To argue that civic association should be made possible at a local scale is not to say that an argument for urban citizenship means that all power for deciding the distribution or outcome of local public resources should be turned over solely to the local public. Such a suggestion would be absurd. Encouraging people to engage in the virtuous activity of participating in their local parent-teacher associations does not entail the claim that local PTAs should make all decisions concerning the fate of local schools. Clearly, we would want a variety of regulatory actors to step in to ensure that a consistent range of quality across districts is maintained for teacher training, classroom resources, and so forth. These sorts of considerations of equality cannot be ensured by divesting all power to local publics in the name of increasing citizen participation virtues. The argument then is more simply that all levels of regulation are better when they are mediated through a robust form of local participation, be it in decisions over schools or other public amenities such as environmental regulation.

Even if Dagger's alternative for defining local publics is unfeasible, then at a minimum, the incorporation of environmental issues into discussions of citizenship would serve as a reason to bring local publics back together rather than give them reasons to ignore each other's needs. After all, one advantage of ecosystemic issues is that they actually are important across the bounded communities of local publics no matter how they are drawn, and they can serve to bring together differing publics in collaborative ventures for mutual benefit. This may not get us anything like a definitive argument for citizenship as the preferred model for a more responsible global environmentalism, but it does point to an interesting way in which the active task of conjoining civic environmentalism to urban notions of citizenship can avoid the descent of urban citizenship into the fractured polarizing of a plurality of locales pitted against each other.

Examples of civic environmentalism would include both the resistance to forms of urban growth that degrade civic involvement (such as Dagger's proposed opposition to sprawl) and common projects of preservation and restoration of vital natural areas in urban areas that cross a variety of communities. I want to close with an appeal for a specific parameter on such projects, namely, that they maximize opportunities for citizen participation in the local environment as a way of creating opportunities for expressing an urban ecological citizenship that can more specifically help us to imagine the implications of a call for a "new global order for environmental care."

RESTORATION AS REENGAGEMENT
RATHER THAN RESISTANCE

I hope that critics of the politics of globalization will see my suggestion that environmentalism be reoriented to be inclusive of urban issues as friendly with their priority of making more room for the local in discussion of global environmental issues. The reason again is not simply because the patterns of globalization do not always fit each local agenda (or in general do not fit Southern contexts) but because thinking about our local environment as a basis for broader notions of environmental responsibility is more tangible than an abstract environmentalism focusing on global issues that are difficult to understand. Recall my worries in section one concerning global warming. The problem is not simply understanding the science of the effects of generations of production of greenhouse gases. The problem is how to motivate people to take the findings of this science seriously enough to either change their own lifestyles or lobby their governments to do something about it. Though I do not have the space here to make this argument fully, I would contend that we are less likely to get to the point of motivating sufficient numbers of people to take such problems seriously if we continue propagating the notion that environmental problems are something that occur "out there," beyond the scope of our local habitus. Encouraging an urban ecological citizenship would help to overcome this problem both by making the local environment a site of civic responsibilities as well as creating opportunities for people to physically connect with the land around them or, as Dewey reminded us, to actually do something together. Once such connections are made, I would maintain that people will be more likely to be able to understand the global environmental scope of many aspects of their everyday lives.

For this reason, the first and most important goal of the development of an urban ecological citizenship involves the stimulation of public participation in the maintenance of natural processes. Why? I believe that a direct participatory relationship between local human communities and the nature they inhabit or are adjacent to, including urban natural areas, is a necessary condition for encouraging people to protect natural systems and landscapes around them rather than trading the future of these environments for short-term monetary gains from development. In this way, people can see how important local involvement is in tackling those problems that truly are global.

If I am in a normative and participatory relationship with the land around me, I am less likely to allow it to be harmed. But this does not mean that a relationship with nature is participatory only if it leads participants to make sacrifices for nature. It means only that such participation is a necessary condition for protecting nature as a foundation of ecological citizenship. Why? One reason is that rules governing environmental protection, like other laws governing common resources, are often violated where there is no clear motivation to enforce them. If all environmental legislation was mandated from above, be it from one's own state or from a global regime, and local populations had no reason to take an interest in environmental protection, then little would motivate citizens not to abstain from free rides or engage in other acts of violation of environmental regulations. This problem has been proven over and over again in the history of environmental legislation. Most recently we have seen this in several well-publicized examples in the developing world where drawing lines around an area and declaring it a national park or wilderness has done little to ensure environmental protection of the site. Deane Curtin provides a telling account of some of these cases, including the failing attempt by the Nepali government to create the Chitwan National Park, despite the needs of local communities to collect firewood.[24]

For reasons such as these, I am tempted to gauge the relative importance of different environmental practices in terms of their ability to engender a more participatory relationship between humans and the nature around them. Examples of such participatory activities abound. But even though their prudential benefit has been well documented, I am not certain that their moral and political implications have been fully appreciated. One activity that will bring this set of issues out for us here is restoration ecology, a practice whose greatest headway so far, in terms of serving as a conduit for public participation in nature, has been in urban areas.

Restoration ecology is the practice and science of restoring damaged ecosystems, most typically ecosystems that have been damaged by anthropogenic causes. Such projects can range from small-scale urban park reclamations to huge wetland mitigation projects. On two common indicators of the importance of environmental activities—number of voluntary person-hours logged on such projects and amount of dollars spent—restoration ecology is revealed to be one of the most important on the North American environmental agenda, and in most other developed countries as well. In the United States, for example, the cluster of restorations known collectively as the "Chicago Wilderness" project in the forest preserves surrounding the city typically attracted several thousand volunteers per weekend to help restore the native oak savannah ecosystems that have slowly become lost in the area.[25] As the turnover rate for volunteers is high and many of these projects have been going on for decades, the total number of people in Chicago who have participated in these restorations, or at least know about them, is significant.

In general, restoration makes sense because on the whole it results in many advantages over mere preservation of ecosystems that have been substantially damaged by humans. Restoration is an institutional practice that is of top concern to governments, businesses, NGOs, and research universities. But I think if we were to focus on the fact that restoration is taking place and chalk that up to proof of the importance of the sort of environmental issues that will motivate the development of an ecological citizenship, we would miss something quite important. The fact that landscapes are being restored is not nearly as important as the ethical choices involved in the process of completing those restorations. Seen as an environmental practice, it is easy to focus only on the landscapes, the end products of restoration. I would argue however that we need to think about what values are produced in that practice and how those values can best be used in the broader, long-term project of creating a sustainable society at a more global scale.

Up to this point, my concern with restoration has focused on the value of public participation in restoration projects as a positive pragmatic outcome of such activity.[26] But many restorations are either contracted out to private landscape design firms or completed by paid city employees, with only minimal input from local citizens. However, when citizen volunteers participate in restorations, then they become, in the sense I have described above, an important generator of the forms of responsibility associated with ecological citizenship. Participatory practices get us better restorations because they create the sorts of relationships with nature that I just suggested were a necessary condition for long-term environmental sustainability. Those restorations that are not produced by volunteers do not capture this participatory value and do not necessarily help the long-term project of creating communities committed to the protection of their local environments.

Sociological evidence on the Chicago restorations suggests that participants in restoration projects are more likely (as one might expect) to adopt a benign attitude of stewardship and responsibility toward nature as a result of such interactions with nature. The reason appears to be that participants in restoration projects learn about the hazardous consequences of anthropogenic impacts on nature because they learn in practice how hard it is to restore nature after it has been damaged. This same research suggests that participants take the lessons of restoration with them on the road. When restorationists visit preserved areas, such as national parks or wilderness areas, they are more likely to act as responsible environmental citizens while in those places.[27] The more interesting ethical issue then becomes how to guarantee or promote this value of participation in restoration projects. In terms of the values represented in the practice of restoration, there is a strong moral and political claim inherent to the practice for having more local participation in restoration projects as a sort of schoolhouse for environmental responsibility and as a means of stimulating more democratic environmental practices, which in turn become occasions for educating citizens on their global environmental responsibilities.[28]

This sort of analysis gets us both short-term and long-term goals. In the short term we want to encourage laws that would mandate local participation in restoration projects that are publicly funded (something like a right of first refusal for local communities and neighborhoods) on the assumption that local participation in all restorations is part of the overall criteria for what counts as a good restoration.[29] In the long term we want to focus our attention as environmentalists on those areas most likely to generate such foundations for ecological citizenship, namely, those geographical areas that are most amenable to public participation in restoration. Larger rural restoration projects, such as the multimillion-dollar projects undertaken by the U.S. Army Corps of Engineers to de-channalize rivers, are too unwieldy for significant voluntary efforts, but urban restorations, such as the Chicago projects, are perfect for serving this purpose. It seems perfectly reasonable to assume that the massive public participation generated in Chicago was directly linked to the location of the city in relation to the restorations.

There are of course no theoretical guarantees. Still, we are more likely to be able to engage people in the connection between their everyday lives and a problem as difficult to grasp as global warming if we can first provide them with opportunities to engage physically in their local environment. For as they come to care about their local environment, which they can also actively help to heal, and see this as a way of being a good community citizen, they should be better able to see how the outcome of larger global environmental questions affects that landscape that they have come to care about. Whether they go on to then care about the "global environment" is anyone's guess. Nonetheless, local ecological citizens will still have a good reason, and hopefully a morally motivating reason, to be concerned about environmental problems outside of their local community and will be more likely to have a stake in the outcome of those problems. And although we can't expect that all citizens will come to connect with their local environment through such practices, the fact that some will make this connection will more likely create a local constituency lobbying for attention to both local and global environmental concerns.

Although restoration ecology and other participatory projects in local environments, such as community gardening and other forms of urban stewardship, are no panacea for all environmental ills, they are concrete programs that can be used to strengthen the sense of cities as environments worthy of protection that are integrated into larger global ecological systems. Does this suggestion mean that we will not have a need for forming strong international agreements on global environmental problems? Certainly not. But it is at least one way to encourage a localism that engages with the environment as something much more than a site for resistance to an ambiguous global enemy.

NOTES

1. Mark Hollman and Greg Kotis, *Urinetown: The Musical*. Original cast recording. New York: RCA Victor, 2001.

2. See Peter Singer, *One World: The Ethics of Globalization* (New Haven: Yale University Press, 2002).

3. Those seeking a more thorough discussion of the range of issues concerning globalization and the environment should consult at least the following: Ronnie D. Lipschutz, *Global Civil Society and Global Environmental Governance* (Albany: SUNY Press, 1996); Paul Wapner, *Environmental Activism and World Civic Politics* (Albany: SUNY Press, 1996); Roger Gottlieb, *Environmentalism Unbound* (Cambridge, Mass.: MIT Press, 2001); Arthur P. J. Mol, *Globalization and Environmental Reform: The Ecological Modernization of the Global Economy* (Cambridge: MIT Press, 2001).

4. See Wolfgang Sachs, "Global Ecology and the Shadow of 'Development,'" in *Global Ecology: A New Arena of Political Conflict*, ed. Wolfgang Sachs (London: Zed Books, 1993).

5. Vandana Shiva, "The Greening of the Global Reach," in *Global Ecology*, op. cit., p. 155; emphasis in original.

6. Ibid.

7. Larry Lohmann, "Resisting Green Globalism," in *Global Ecology*, op. cit., p. 160.

8. See, for example, some of the considerations raised by Paul B. Thompson in "The Environmental Ethics Case for Crop Biotechnology," in *Moral and Political Reasoning in Environmental Practice*, ed. Andrew Light and Avner de-Shalit (Cambridge, Mass.: MIT Press, forthcoming in 2003).

9. Figures derived from *World Urbanization Prospects* (New York: United Nations Press, 1996). My thanks to Michael Cohen at New School University for calling my attention to these numbers in his preliminary draft of a new report of the panel on Urban Population Dynamics for the National Academy of Sciences Committee on Population.

10. See William E. Rees and Mathis Wackernagel, *Our Ecological Footprint* (New York: New Society, 1995).

11. William E. Rees, "Life in the Lap of Luxury as Ecosystems Collapse," *Chronicle of Higher Education*, July 30, 1999, p. 1.

12. Ibid., p. 2.

13. Although I have never carried it out, since first reading the literature on ecological footprints, I have always wanted to run a GIS experiment where the population of New York City is emptied out more equitably into the surrounding regions. It seems doubtful that the astounding forest regeneration that Bill McKibben and others have celebrated in upstate New York would be sustainable without the existence of a population concentration device as effective as the city.

14. Thomas F. Homer-Dixon, *Environment, Scarcity, and Violence* (Princeton: Princeton University Press, 1999), pp. 155ff.

15. Allen R. Myerson, "Energy Addicted in America," *New York Times*, November 1, 1998, Week in Review, p. 5.

16. For a sustained argument for why environmental ethicists, at least, have not heretofore focused much on cities in their work, see my paper, "The Urban Blind Spot in Environmental Ethics," *Environmental Politics*, Vol. 10, No. 1 (2001), pp. 7–35.

17. Mark Dowie, *Losing Ground: American Environmentalism at the Close of the Twentieth Century* (Cambridge, Mass.: MIT Press, 1996), p. 6. For a nice summary of the common supposition that American environmentalism contains three waves from turn-of-the-century reformers to today's interest groups (often accused of being coopted by the business community), see David Schlosberg, *Environmental Justice and the New Pluralism* (Oxford: Oxford University Press, 1999).

18. Schlosberg, *Environmental Justice and the New Pluralism*, p. 9.

19. See Richard Dagger, *Civic Virtues: Rights, Citizenship, and Republican Liberalism* (Oxford: Oxford University Press, 1997), p. 49.

20. Richard Dagger, "Metropolis, Memory, and Citizenship," in *Democracy, Citizenship, and the Global City*, ed. Engin F. Isin (London: Routledge, 2000), p. 28.

21. See Richard Dagger, "Stopping Sprawl for the Good of All: The Case for Civic Environmentalism," *Journal of Social Philosophy*, forthcoming, 2002.

22. Thomas Bender, "The New Metropolitanism and a Pluralized Public," *Harvard Design Magazine*, Winter/Spring (2001), p. 73; my emphasis.

23. Dagger, *Civic Virtues*, pp. 167–168.

24. Deane Curtin, *Chinnagounder's Challenge: The Question of Ecological Citizenship* (Bloomington/Indianapolis: Indiana University Press, 1999).

25. See William K. Stevens, *Miracle Under the Oaks* (New York: Pocket Books, 1995).

26. Andrew Light and Eric Higgs, "The Politics of Ecological Restoration," *Environmental Ethics*, Vol. 18 (1996), pp. 227–247.

27. See the essays in Paul Gobster and Bruce Hull, eds., *Restoring Nature: Perspectives from the Social Sciences and Humanities* (Washington, D.C.: Island Press, 2000).

28. See Andrew Light, "Ecological Restoration and the Culture of Nature: A Pragmatic Perspective," in *Restoring Nature: Perspectives from the Social Sciences and Humanities*, op. cit., pp. 49–70; and Light, "Restoration, the Value of Participation, and the Risks of Professionalization," in *Restoring Nature: Perspectives from the Social Sciences and Humanities*, op. cit., pp. 163–181.

29. I make a more thorough argument for this point and evaluate more of the sociological evidence on the value of restoration in "Restoring Ecological Citizenship," in *Democracy and the Claims of Nature*, ed. Ben Minteer and Bob Pepperman Taylor (Lanham, Md.: Rowman & Littlefield, 2002), pp. 153–172.

20

Argentina and the End of the First World Dream

CARMEN FERRADÁS

It is early in the morning in Argentina and a newsman seems to be involved in a routine similar to those performed by colleagues in most metropolitan areas of the world: He is reporting the state of the roads and recommending the best itineraries to reach downtown areas. But this newscast has an interesting twist that you would not find in similar European or North American television programs. The reporter is anticipating the daily chaos that has become part of the everyday experience of the Argentina of the New Millennium: He is mapping the planned road closings that will follow the various demonstrations for the day as well as the chosen *piquete* sites. The reporting covers Buenos Aires, the capital city, and suburban areas, but similar forms of collective action may be encountered at different sites of the national territory.

In fact, some of these forms of popular protest have originated outside the capital city. The piquetes have become one of the most popular forms of protest in contemporary Argentina. The original piquetes were the same as the picket lines in North American labor history; workers on strike would form them to stop scabs from entering the factories. In a nation where factories and employment are increasingly becoming a thing of the past, the piquetes have come to metaphorically express the profound spatial, cultural, and social transformations triggered by neoliberal policies. Piquetes as a refurbished form of protest had first appeared in socioeconomic regions excluded in the recent economic restructuring. They popped up in places that flourished when national development and import substitution strategies were favored—in localities where formerly state-run energy companies reigned; in company towns, now virtually ghost towns where the major employer went out of business; and in rural areas that used to enjoy government agricultural subsidies sustaining industrial development and urbanization processes. Unemployed workers and impoverished rural producers now sometimes camp for days at the entrances of bridges and major highways to cut off circulation of goods and of the few people still involved in production. While the old piqueteros inhibited entrance to work, and used their right to strike, to stop work, the piqueteros of today are asking for the right to work, by demanding that the government provide more *planes trabajar*, a working program created by the state to meet the basic needs of those pushed out of the labor force. Thus, while the old forms of picketing challenged production, current forms challenge circulation and consumption. Cutting off roads and international bridges spatially challenges the dominant principle of this global and neo-liberal era: the market.

The piqueteros are the first casualties of neo-liberal economic policies, but they are not alone in their protest. They have recently been joined by *caceroleros*, the latest victims of the Argentine economic collapse. The caceroleros are predominantly middle-class men and women who beat pots and pans to express their rage and frustration with the recent economic measures that captured their peso or dollar savings, leaving them penniless.

My aim in this chapter is to examine the development of these various forms of protest, to analyze their points of convergence and disagreement, and to trace the linkages between current forms of social mobilization and previous forms of social protest. I argue that these mobilizations are dramatic enactments of the failure of two contradictory national projects no longer feasible under the current dominant neo-liberal model. I also explore the catalysts of a potential alliance among historically antagonistic class fractions under a unifying nationalist discourse. I propose that the recent betrayal of an unspoken contract between national and international elites with middle-class sectors might strengthen nationalist feelings and appeals, thereby facilitating temporary alliances.

ARGENTINA'S "UNIQUENESS:" FIRST-WORLD NATION OR SUBMERGING NATION?

Argentina is an odd country. Argentines and foreign scholars alike have often been puzzled by the contradictions inherent in a nation endowed with natural riches and a highly educated population but beset by fragile political and economic institutions. Today, most analysts still stress its "uniqueness" and "exceptionality" when they try to make sense of its debacle. At the turn of the twentieth century it was a desired destination to which European immigrants headed to accomplish their "American dream." Immigrants were enticed by the country's export boom experienced in the last decades of the nineteenth century. A great majority of these immigrants settled in Buenos Aires, where the population increased from 177,787 in 1869 to 1,575,814 in 1914. In the quinquennium from 1904 to 1909, this capital city of Argentina was the second-fastest-growing city in the Western world.[1] Population growth patterns paralleled economic growth, which was unevenly distributed: While the Pampean region flourished, the Interior remained stagnant, a pattern that, as we shall see, haunts the nation to this day.[2]

Economic studies throughout the first half of the last century used to depict Argentina as one of the ten richest nations of the world.[3] Argentines and outsiders alike bought into the myth that the country was unique among Latin American nations. A predominantly all-white population with a European demeanor; a large, highly educated, modern, and cosmopolitan middle class; a resource-rich territory that could potentially form the basis of national development—these were some of the catchphrases that people endlessly repeated to show how Argentina stood out from its Latin American neighbors. A hundred years later, all the optimism and euphoria displayed at the beginning of the 20th century have dwindled. At the turn of the 20th century, few countries could rival Argentina's prosperity; now, at the turn of the 21st century, few can rival its precipitous downfall.

Historically, Argentina has shown a striking ambivalence toward itself. It has fluctuated between a self-image highlighting its modernity and westernness and one that emphasizes its leadership role among third world nations.[4] The deployment of these contrasting self-images reflects the choices made by the government at specific political economic junctures. When in 1976 the military ousted Isabel Perón from power with the alleged purpose of bringing the "house back to order," official discourse emphasized, ad nauseam, Argentina's affiliation with the Christian Western Civilization. The so-called Proceso of National Reorganization (Process of National Reorganization) used this affiliation to legitimate the final crusade to discipline people as well as the economy. Both took a fatal toll. A quarter-century later, the majority of the population is finally realizing the far-reaching effects of the crusade in the name of Western values. Imbued with ideas about national security, the military rulers of the Proceso aligned themselves with the West and withdrew from earlier alliances with other third world countries. Economically and politically they rejected national-populist and socialist projects advocating protectionist and redistributive policies.

Ironically, in the late 1980s, President Carlos Menem, who came into power through the political party once led by Juan Domingo Perón, one of the most fervent advocates of a "third position," also distanced himself from these previous strategic alliances and instead proclaimed that he would put Argentina back where it belonged—among the first world nations. This would be accomplished, he promised, through a revolution in production. None of this happened. After leading the country for ten years, Menem left power when the country was experiencing an economic recession from which it has not yet recovered. His administration betrayed most of the historical banners of *justicialismo*, the movement initiated by Perón. Menem stopped promoting national industrialization, abandoned the party's support base—the Argentine working class—by opening the market and flexibilizing labor, and dismantled the social welfare system, one of the major pillars of former Peronist administrations. Argentine factories were either sold out to multinationals or closed down. The sale of government assets at the beginning of Menem's administration and the flux of fresh international loans helped create the illusion of economic recovery. While there were obvious signs of lack of investment, loss of competitiveness because of unrealistic exchange rates, widespread unemployment, and alarming health and poverty indicators, foreign economic analysts insisted on presenting Argentina as a success story. By the end of Menem's administration it was hard to conceal the obvious; even an organization like the World Bank, which used to be a strong supporter of the economic model, started to admit some problems. A confidential economic report was leaked to the press a few months before Menem left the presidency, in the middle of the political campaign to choose his successor. The document was produced by World Bank economists. Among other things, it said that poverty rose 37 percent from 1993 to 1997. Statistics dramatically confirmed what the majority of the people already knew: 13.4 million people, more than 36 percent of the population, lived below the poverty line and 3.2 million people, 8.6 percent of the total population, were mired in absolute poverty. In some regions, such as the Northwest, the Northeast, and the Cuyo region, more than 50 percent of the people were poor.[5] The report released other disturbing details of Argentina's social drama as well: Governmental expenditures on social issues had not caught up with poverty growth, and a significant amount of money theoretically allocated to meet the needs of the poor was benefiting families who were not among the neediest. Although not discussed in the report, most of this money probably went to sustain political clienteles.

Government officials discredited this study by raising the specter of the hyperinflation crisis of 1989, which pushed President Alfonsín out of office before he finished his mandate. They argued that if they had not applied the current economic model, the country would be in abject poverty. Menem had put the blame on the "four plagues of Egypt": climatic disasters as well as the Mexican, Russian, and Asian crises. Authorities never welcomed data confirming the deepening of the social crisis, including studies conducted by government agencies. On one occasion, the ministry of economy, unaware of feminism's plight in recent decades, suggested that a very prestigious woman sociologist should "go and wash dishes" after she publicized the research results of a study on poverty in Argentina. Subsequently, in 1999, another woman sociologist was removed from office after she released the alarming findings of a study conducted by a team of well-respected social analysts. This study showed that 45 percent of Argentine children were poor. It also reported that 68 percent of the people interviewed believed that the middle class was worse off than before.

An alliance of renegade Peronists, progressive independents, and the Radical Party won presidential elections, whereupon the ten years of *menemismo* dominance came to an end. The newly appointed president, Fernando de la Rúa, inherited a dismantled nation with a people who had become disillusioned and skeptical after years of corruption and failed economic policies. In 2001, poverty figures grew even worse; the majority of the productive sectors were operating at less than 50 percent of their capacity, and many of the remaining factories were closed for the last half of the year. Instead of being among a selected group of chosen rich nations, Argentina has recently achieved, after displacing Nigeria from first place, the unenviable position of having the highest *riesgo país* (country risk factor) in the world, a rating assigned by the investment bank JP Morgan. Daily changes in this indicator, which measures the surcharge paid by a local bond against a similar U.S. one, were anxiously followed by the entire population until the economy completely collapsed at the end of 2001. Argentines scrutinized this rating as if looking at a thermometer to check how ill somebody was or in much the same way children would check to see if the teacher had compassionately raised their grades. In fact, this was the way the population was encouraged to experience the crisis: The press reported (indeed, still reports) the "grades" assigned by international watchdogs to furnish a measure of the severity of the situation. For example, in an October 16 newspaper article entitled "For Standard & Poor Argentina Is Even Riskier Than Pakistan," the journalist explicitly said that the credit rating agency had lowered the "grade" of the country's debt for the fifth time that year, and that the country's debt was the worst in the world. Although most of the people did not really understand what this indicator was about, they obsessively checked it, seeking a magic sign of relief. Instead, throughout the last few months of 2001, the indicator kept jumping to unprecedented levels.

Instead of being a first world nation, as imagined, or an emerging nation, as some world organizations now euphemistically call those nations previously identified as "underdeveloped," Argentina could more properly be called a *submerging* nation. Unlike other nations that came close to being wrecked in recent years, such as the Asian Tiger countries, Russia, and Mexico, Argentina is drifting away, and this time nobody is coming to its "rescue." Analysts have advanced different interpretations for the current lack of support. The media suggest that economic watchdogs want to prevent "contagious" reactions from countries facing similar economic problems. They want others to recognize the dangers involved in deviating from economic orthodoxy. The North American economist Paul Krugman has also said that "Argentina is in the wrong place at the wrong time." Unlike others, he maintains that the current situation can be blamed not on local politicians or lack of fiscal discipline but, rather, on the current U.S. government's decision to "apply the theory of moral risk." Krugman was referring here to the United States's refusal to come to the rescue of investors who had risked their capitals in a country such as Argentina.[6]

Until quite recently, each time Argentina faced the possibility of not meeting its debt obligations, the IMF released some funds to prolong the agony. As Fidel Castro recently put it, "[T]he Argentines are like those prisoners who keep appealing against the death penalty, but the only thing they achieve is the postponement of their death; you were given the grace of not being executed immediately" (*Pagina 12*, October 10, 2001). But this last time, the emergency call was released in a new world economic context marked by the rise to power of a Republican president in the United States and by the dramatic events of September 11. Although it is prob-

ably premature to assess how these two factors might impinge on ongoing debt negotiations, recent developments suggest that we might be witnessing a shift in the
negotiating power of multilateral agencies vis à vis the United States and, to some
extent, the European Union. The controversy over a study conducted at the request
of the U.S. Congress and released by the press in March 2000 could provide a hint
of what we might now expect. The report was critical of the role played by the
World Bank and the IMF. It suggested that the IMF should limit itself to providing
aid during fiscal crises, providing statistical information, and giving advice to governments only when such advice was requested, and that the World Bank should
provide help only to the poorest countries and not to those with medium development. Democrats attacked the report on the grounds that it was neo-isolationist and
suggested that it might be used to condition IMF decisions regarding approval of
aid packages to specific countries. Republicans are said to favor bilateral relations,
and many are believed to question the granting of loans to debt-ridden nations.
Throughout the last months of 2001, Argentina desperately tried to avoid default-
ing on its debt obligations and waited for a wink from the United States to get some
support in the restructuring of the debt. Neither the wink nor the IMF assistance
ever materialized. By the end of December, its unmanageable economic crisis had
triggered unprecedented forms of social mobilization, which led to the resignation
of the democratically elected president and left the country in a political vacuum.
Under these extraordinary circumstances the country defaulted. Deserted by the financial powers, Argentina could not readily find a political or economic solution capable of easing the explosive social situation while complying with the draconian
conditions demanded by the IMF and the United States.

How has Argentina gotten into this terminal situation, and how is the population responding to it? To what extent can the nation-state maintain its legitimacy
if it sacrifices the social, economic, and political compromises that sustain and reinforce its power? In the following sections, I will examine how and why the population initially accepted the weakening of the state's economic power, thus inevitably impairing its ability to function in the social welfare and redistributive
roles necessary to ease class tensions. Furthermore, I will show how recent events
have corroded the government's ability to mobilize and unify the population
through the mobilization of national symbols and meanings.

MARKET MAGIC AND A WEAK STATE

When Argentina returned to democracy in 1983, President Alfonsín inherited a foreign debt that jeopardized the nation's ability to guarantee economic growth. Economic analysts speak about the development of an "economic war" in which the
state became an arena of confrontations between the various business factions and
the lending banks. Rampant inflation is attributed both to the lack of support from
powerful national sectors that withdrew export dollars from circulation and to the

pressure exerted by creditors on the demand of dollars and exchange rates. In an attempt to stop inflation, the government changed the national currency twice during a two-year period. And common folks, children included, rushed to buy dollars in the black market or purchased food as soon as they had received payment in cash as a strategy to beat inflation. By 1989, a crisis of hyperinflation had caused the value of the national currency to decline more than 200 percent in a single day. In the same year, the inflation rate reached an unequaled 4,923.6 percent. From one day to the next, Argentines' savings vanished and the purchasing value of their salaries dwindled. This dramatic economic collapse illustrates how easily people accepted new discourses that made the nation-state into a villain and embraced new economic policies that encouraged the dismantling of the developmentalist nation-state, already significantly transformed during the years of the military dictatorship.

Alfonsín left power a few months before completing his mandate, in the midst of a hyperinflation crisis. Menem was sworn in. He immediately embarked on a program of state restructuring to comply with creditors' expectations and conditions. His political and economic reforms were received with wide acclaim. Foreign and national analysts started to speak about a deep transformation of the political culture. Argentina, they said, was finally abandoning a history of social unrest to embrace a modern behavior; the new democratic nation was finally settling down. Many envisioned a stability of the body politic and of the economy under the rule of President Menem. Argentina was finally going from insolvency to growth, as the World Bank country study had stated.[7] An Argentine sociologist commended Menem's foresight in predicting the failure of all the various forms of nationalism, socialism, corporatism, and populism as well as the advent of a profound cultural change involving the redefinition of the relations between state and civil society and an entry into the great market of the world.[8] The Menem administration initially had the curious ability to make most people believe that there was no alternative but to privatize the state's assets in the name of efficiency and profitability and to open the Argentine economy to foreign investment. Even a socialist-oriented social scientist, Juan Carlos Portantiero, claimed that the return to democracy marked not only the end of a military regime but a "crisis of the state, the end of a model of inefficient capitalism, politically protected by subsidies financed through inflation, which also included some redistributive services as a precarious creole formula of an underdeveloped social welfare state."[9] Few voices anticipated the devastating effects of the subordination of the state to the economy, which would lead to widespread disenchantment with politics.

It is no surprise that the Convertibility Law, which established a parity between the peso and the dollar, was welcomed by the majority of the population. The law required the Argentine Central Bank to back its currency with gold or foreign currency. It created the illusion that the national currency was as strong as the dollar, halting speculation and the stampede in consumer prices. Depending on who did the analyzing, the economic phase initiated in the 1990s was either praised as a model of neo-liberal discipline (as many publications like *Forbes*, the

Wall Street Journal, and the *New York Times* attested until quite recently) or seen as the beginning of an inevitable fall. Many economists recommended that other countries should replicate Argentina's approach.

Social analysts saw some forms of investment as positive signs of recovery, when in actuality they reflected processes of deindustrialization, restructuring of labor, and decline of the national economy. Some pointed at investments in real estate in and around the capital city, at the construction of international hotels, and at the opening of supermarkets and shopping malls as indicators of a healthy economy and successful integration into the global economy. What these indicators dramatically expressed, however, were changes in Argentina's social structure and in the relationship between the capital city and the Interior (i.e., the provinces). Investment in real estate was mainly concentrated in the development of gated communities and the transformation of former ranches into weekend retreats or permanent homes for a reduced elite group that had profited from the restructuring of the economy.

Most of these neighborhoods were created in the Buenos Aires metropolitan area and in rural areas near the capital city. The investments themselves reflected the increased polarization in Argentina's social structure, which, until the 1970s, was characterized by a large middle class—one that comprised 40 percent of the total population. In the 1990s, the concentration of wealth was staggering: When the Convertibility Law went into effect, the richest fifth of the population earned 10.8 percent more than the poorest fifth; today, the richest fifth make 13.5 percent more, thereby controlling 53.9 percent of the national income.[10] While the rich retreated to gated communities or bought property in country clubs where they spent their weekend leisure time, the poor and the new poor—those excluded from the middle classes and working classes—were forced to move to slum neighborhoods, many of them adjacent to the enclosed neighborhoods of the rich. Downward mobility has become so common that one of these slum neighborhoods displays a sign reading "Welcome middle class." The new suburban enclaves created for the privileged few have augmented social tensions in the Buenos Aires metropolitan area and in former rural towns in Buenos Aires province, where unemployment has become rampant. These areas have witnessed violent food riots since December 2001.

The malls, the supermarkets, and the new real estate were created to meet the consumption demands of those able to link themselves with the newly "globalized economy." The malls and supermarkets, in particular, have put small factories and small merchants out of business; the parity between the peso and the dollar allowed them to supply their large businesses with imports purchased at very low prices, with devastating effects for small local businesses. Affordable imported goods temporarily created the illusion of well-being. People from all classes participated in a consumption frenzy. They spent beyond their means, enticed by commercials advertising cheap electronics, clothing, and foreign travel and tempted by accessibility to credit and the bogus stability of the Argentine currency. Very few realized that their consumption patterns were contributing to the erosion of the national industries and jeopardizing even their own sources of employment. Few also realized that under open-market conditions, the state could not easily regulate either national or foreign investors to guarantee the revenues necessary for the smooth reproduction of basic state apparatuses.

George Soros was one of the major foreign investors in the real estate ventures during this period. An article in the Argentine newspaper *Clarín* (May 24, 1999) claimed that he had become the major landowner in the country after acquiring all shopping malls, some of the major hotels, and other iconic real estate in the city of Buenos Aires.[11] European capital purchased most of the privatized state business and privately owned Argentine banks and factories. Initially, most of the population welcomed these changes as they bought into the dominant discourse asserting that Argentines could not efficiently run any business.

The economic transformation left an imprint in the spatial configuration of Argentina. The capital city now displays dilapidated former industrial areas and a few niches for leisure consumption by the very rich, many of them occupying former production sites. Privatization of railroads and airlines had condemned some areas of the nation to an inevitable death, because certain destinations were not considered profitable. While many global organizations and economic analysts complimented Argentina for its exemplary behavior in following directives for structural adjustment that included privatization of government assets, fiscal discipline, dismantling of the state apparatus, and decentralization, very few acknowledged that the Convertibility Law would negatively affect Argentina's competitiveness. Also rarely acknowledged were the social costs of the policies: the state's diminished responsibility for social security, the rise in unemployment, the bankruptcy of business, and the denationalization of banks.

The rise in social unrest and the prolonged recession have not, however, prompted many analysts to recognize the real sources of the current crisis. Rather, they place the blame on a corrupt state and corrupt provincial administrations. As we shall see, this explanation for the current crisis, embraced by international lending banks, foreign powers, and certain sectors of national interest, obscures the contradictions inherent in the current dilemmas of the Argentine political economy and impedes the search for solutions that would otherwise tackle the structural causes leading to Argentina's default.

These last years' corrective measures have pursued only "fiscal health" and the cutting of state expenditures to guarantee payments. One of the most blatant measures was passed in 1999, when the Ministry of Economy, following IMF instructions, drastically cut the national budget. Among the most affected areas was education. The government ordered a cut of $280 million. Meanwhile, the Ministry of Interior, in charge of security forces, maintained its budget intact, thus allowing the purchase of 250 patrol cars to enforce internal security. Security has become a highly contested issue. Poverty and unemployment, but also a corrupt police force, are some of the factors behind the tremendous rise in criminality.

Armed robbery and acts of violence are legitimizing the restructuring of the repressive apparatus of the state, one of the many outcomes of globalization. This issue is very problematic in a nation that has not yet recovered from the wounds left by the terrorist state of the 1970s and early 1980s. The contrast between the "policing" budget and the "education" budget did not pass unnoticed. School teachers' and university professors' unions, which have become some of the most vocal labor organizations after democratization, have called for public demonstrations against the cuts. The response of the population was massive and even festive, a common feature of many current forms of protest. Street representations and teach-ins in parks and subway stations, music recitals, and even ballet performances accompanied many of the education protests. The message was so powerful that the government had to back off after asking for permission from the IMF.

This was a temporary victory, however. In 2001, universities were facing closings because they did not have enough money to cover their basic operating costs. Today, some universities are unable to pay salaries, and it is unlikely that students will be able to finish out the academic year. Many research institutions, including those responsible for providing critical supplies for preventing the spread of infectious disease and covering the basic health needs of the population, can no longer operate. In January 2002, the government was forced to declare a food and health emergency. Hospitals have had to cancel vital surgery procedures and stop health prevention campaigns. Children faint in classes because they are malnourished. Schools have limited budgets to provide the only meals that children consume throughout the week.

The onslaught against the public education system, once the pride of the national body, stirred popular anger and was repudiated by large sectors of the population. During the Menem administration, a gigantic white tent erected in front of the National Congress, filled with fasting teachers, expressed public discontent with government educational policies. Middle- and upper-middle-class sectors turned to private instruction without realizing that the deterioration of public education would also impact them in the long run.

NATIONALISM AND POLITICAL DISENCHANTMENT

Although privatization was welcomed at the beginning, the loss of national icons such as banks and food manufactures to foreign investors, the crisis in education (one of the pillars of nation building), and the bankruptcy of the privatized Argentine Airlines have recently stirred various forms of patriotism, even among some elite sectors that once had been the major supporters of the free-market model. As the crisis deepened, sales of Argentine flags went up, attendance at the commemorations of national holidays increased significantly, and young folklorists and national rock musicians became more popular. Xenophobic reactions also intensified. These attitudes were often exacerbated by the media, state representatives, and co-opted labor leaders who previously blamed unemployment on undocumented foreign workers.

Nationalist feelings have deepened as well. After the food riots and massive demonstrations of December 2001, many store owners removed imported items from their shelves and displayed goods with labels specifying their Argentine origin. Internet messages championed the boycott of foreign-owned supermarket chains and encouraged citizens to patronize mom and pop stores. The myriad direct-action groups that mushroomed with the intensification of the crisis are using electronic messages to organize civil disobedience. Although the claims of these groups are multifarious, expressing differences in their social bases and the interests they represent, a common thread runs through them: They all appeal to the nation by using powerful unifying symbols such as the Argentine flag. Who will hegemonize this reemerging nationalist discourse, and how it will be mobilized and for what purposes, remains to be seen.

On the one hand, we see an increase in nationalism; on the other, we see complete disenchantment with politicians, state institutions, and the nation itself. In the last elections, citizens were encouraged, via the Internet, to express their disappointment with the political class by voting for their favorite cartoon characters or national heroes from earlier centuries. The response was outstanding: The so-called *voto bronca*, or anger vote, obtained the majority in the capital city (with more than 50.5 percent of the votes) and in other key electoral districts.

While some Argentines have expressed their disappointment with current political options by voting for Clemente, a cartoon character who cannot rob because he has no hands, or for San Martin or Rosas, two national icons of the nineteenth century, others have given up on the nation altogether and are joining the thousands trying to claim citizenship from a European nation to be able to migrate to the land of their ancestors. Many of those unable to trace their origins to other nations have opted to become undocumented migrants in the United States, the European Union, or even another Latin American nation. Journalists claim that 50,000 Argentines have emigrated to Miami in the last few years. As a clear indication of the withdrawal of U.S. endorsement of Argentina's inclusion among the selected group of first world nations, Argentines are no longer admitted without a visa. Moreover, deportation of Argentines from both the United States and Europe has increased following the country's fall from grace. These events have been a hard blow to Argentines' pride. The recent enlisting of young Argentine males and females in the Spanish armed forces and Argentine nationals' applications for visas to travel to Poland have also stirred national sentiments.

Meanwhile, some Argentines and foreigners alike refuse to accept that Argentina's first world aspirations can no longer be sustained. A Latin American president recently said that Argentina cannot easily collapse "because it has cows and wheat." But, ironically, not even these traditional exports are available to rescue the nation: The cows are prevented from crossing the border owing to the outbreak of foot-and-mouth disease, and the wheat has been lost in devastating floods.

The End of a Dream: Caceroleros, Piqueteros, and Neighborhood Assemblies

By the end of December 2001 it had become apparent that Argentina's economic situation was unmanageable. Economic measures shook the middle class in an unprecedented manner. Vast sectors of the population were already in disarray after watching their incomes shrink as the result of an unpopular governmental decision to cut salaries and pensions by 13 percent and to threaten bigger cuts if the national economy worsened. Many Argentines who until then had been supportive of the Convertibility Plan, and of structural adjustment measures advocated by multilateral banks, suddenly started to raise concerns about the running of the economy.

In a desperate attempt to avoid the collapse of the banking system, the national government initially decided to close banks and hold everybody's account hostage. In the weeks preceding these measures, the situation was already tense. For months, investors had been withdrawing their bank deposits as an expression of lack of confidence in government policies. Following the scandal over the collapse of Argentine Airlines, resentment against privatized companies intensified. A complex network of electronic communications invited people to boycott the telephone companies and to denounce their exorbitant rates, considered the highest in the world. These actions paralleled earlier ones taken against privatized electrical and water companies in which people questioned the quality of service, infuriated by the passivity—and complicity—of the state. All of these events contributed to the realization that the nation-state had ceased to take responsibility for the defense and representation of people's interests. The illusion that the state was operating as an arbiter among contested interests could not be maintained.

During the last weeks of 2001, Argentina was subsumed by a chaotic situation from which it has not yet recovered. Hungry women, men, and children begged for food at the doors of supermarket chains and small neighborhood groceries, and food riots erupted throughout the country.

This time, the poor were not alone. Enraged by economic measures that allowed the withdrawal of only minimal amounts of money and froze savings accounts in what metaphorically came to be called *el corralito* (the cattle pen), people of the middle classes started to beat their pots and pans in an outstanding and unsurpassed demonstration of civil disobedience. Rather than stopping the protest, the government decision to declare a state of siege ignited a tremendous social response. The city of Buenos Aires was overwhelmed by the deafening sound of kitchen utensils. People who had never before been involved in a demonstration took over the streets and walked to Plaza de Mayo, the privileged site of popular mobilization, chanting the motto "Que se vayan todos, que no quede ni uno solo" (We want everybody to leave, we do not want anybody to stay). This has become the rallying cry of the various forms of social action that have been operating since then.

The government lost all its legitimacy after declaring the state of siege and ordering the violent repression of the demonstrations. The democratically elected president resigned. A succession of presidents followed, further reflecting the anarchic situation.

Representatives of the legislative, judicial, and executive branches of the state became targets of *escraches*, a form of public exposé through which the people take justice in their hands by identifying those involved in wrongdoings. These tactics were first developed by human rights activists to ostracize individuals involved in human rights abuses during the dictatorship. They identified where former torturers lived and organized demonstrations around their homes to make neighbors aware of who these persons were. The escraches are a powerful form of social justice and criticism against the nation's juridical system.

Besides making claims from their apartment buildings and in the streets, the caceroleros have organized an intricate network of support through the Internet; they have even asked for a global *cacerolazo* (simultaneous beating of pots and pans). Some of them are in close connection with *asambleas barriales*, new neighborhood organizations that operate independently from political parties. The asambleas barriales have a horizontal form of organization in which all decisions are consensual. They gather both to solve local problems and to make claims at a national level. Representatives from the asambleas barriales gather periodically in a park to discuss strategies. Nearly 200 of these organizations can be found throughout the Republic, although the majority of them are based in either Buenos Aires or its metropolitan area.

Ever since these new forms of social mobilization emerged, the attitude toward the piqueteros has changed. Merchants and other middle-class individuals who used to lock stores and houses every time piqueteros organized a demonstration have recently offered them food and water, applauded, and even joined them in their march toward Plaza de Mayo. An elderly well-dressed lady was recently overheard commenting that they should unify their struggles because they were all victims of the same process. However, although different social classes might unify in specific circumstances, it is unlikely that they would conform a collective movement. They differ radically in their interpretations of the crisis and in the methodologies they adopt to express their discontent. Some of the caceroleros resent the breach of social contract between the government and civil society. Their anger is mainly a response to the loss of life savings. They feel betrayed by a government that welcomed their dollar deposits but then converted them to devalued pesos and now prohibits their retrieval. Banks, ATM machines, government officials, and the judicial system are the targets of their rage. The banks are now surrounded by gates and their windows have been covered. It is undoubtful, however, that the caceroleros would remain mobilized if they were allowed to recover their savings. Many of them also feel uncomfortable about recent alliances among piqueteros, neighborhood assemblies, leftist political parties, and human rights groups such as the Mothers of Plaza de Mayo and Hijos (the children of the disappeared). During

April 2002, these coalitions demanded the president's resignation and a breaking off from the IMF. While the unemployed and the more radicalized social sectors blame the crisis on the economic conditions imposed by multilateral banks with the complicity of corrupt government functionaries and powerful interest groups, some middle-class caceroleros have pointed the finger at local politicians. This discrepancy in the politics of blame is related to the different class positions involved. Whereas the piqueteros suffered the consequences of the neo-liberal model early in the process of structural transformation of the national economy, some of the caceroleros initially benefited from a stable economy, a cheap dollar, and accessibility to credit.

Even though there are obvious differences among the various protesters, the uncompromising position of the IMF in the present circumstances, encouraged by the United States, might create the conditions to forge new alliances unimaginable just a few months earlier. After Argentina defaulted and the Justicialista presidential contender in the last elections, Eduardo Duhalde, became the last president in a succession of failed attempts to fill the political vacuum created with the unfolding of the December crisis, the United States and IMF authorities warned Argentina not to isolate itself from the international community of nations. They were clearly threatening retaliation if the country opted for a national, populist solution and withdrew from the neo-liberal model. The media commented extensively on the parallels being established between the Venezuelan Chavez regime and the prospects of the Duhalde administration. Although Duhalde's first political statements hinted at the possibility that he would take a more independent path, it soon became clear that he was ready to negotiate an agreement with the IMF. The social costs of the conditions set by the IMF are enormous, however; any government that complies with its requirements is unlikely to be able to stay in power.

Indeed, the IMF insists that Argentina should undergo a fiscal reform, approve a bankruptcy law, deepen the opening of the market, reduce public expenditures, and develop a new financial system. To achieve fiscal reform and reduction of the public budget, the state is expected to decrease transfers to provincial governments, cut off public jobs, and stop the emission of various provincial bonds. Provinces are expected to collect more taxes and abandon payment with bonds, an impossible condition in places where there is no production and no employment. Furthermore, it is estimated that if these measures are enforced, 5 million more Argentines will be living in poverty. Changes in the finance system are aiming at restructuring the banking system and at imposing regulations that protect foreign banks. One of the most polemical suggestions is that litigation with foreign banks should be settled in international tribunals. This suggestion is fiercely opposed by the majority of the population, who witnessed the arrest of foreign bank managers as they were attempting to board planes with a cargo of millions of dollars to be taken out of the country. The insensibility of these measures, which are blind to the social realities of the nation, is encountering widespread resistance and might lead to an ungovernable situation. According to two recent surveys, the majority of the population believe that if Argentina reaches an agreement with the IMF, the situation would be either the same or worse. One of the surveys found that 75 percent of the population oppose negotiations with the IMF and want Argentina to have its own economic program.[12]

The behavior of the Indian envoy of the IMF mission to Argentina in 2002 confirmed that there is no sovereign state left. He directly negotiated with provincial governors in an improvised office in the Argentine Ministry of Economy without the mediation of any federal authorities. Global-oriented economists do not seem to see any conflict in this loss of decision-making power by a sovereign state. Two economists from MIT have gone so far as to propose that Argentina should temporarily give up its sovereignty in financial matters by leaving the control of the economy to foreign agents, including a council of foreign bankers.[13]

By insisting that the problem is exclusively political, by ignoring their own role in the development of the current crisis, by blaming the provinces for the bankruptcy of the nation, and by making statements that offend the national pride, foreign economists and government officials are demonstrating a diplomatic ineptitude that may cost them dearly. By attempting to pit the national government against provincial authorities, ill-advised economic experts are intensifying a confrontation that historically has divided the nation. And by making a mockery of sovereign power and transforming national leaders into beggars, foreign powers are encouraging isolationism and xenophobic feelings. The outcomes of such actions are unpredictable. They might unify the people behind the establishment of a more just and equitable society. Or they might encourage the development of right-wing nationalist authoritarian leaders. Indeed, Argentina is on a dangerous tightrope. The crisis is so acute that it would not be unthinkable for the whole nation to form a piquete.

NOTES

1. See D.C.M. Platt, "Domestic Finance in the Growth of Buenos Aires, 1880–1914," in *The Political Economy of Argentina: 1880–1946*, ed. Guido Di Tella and D.C.M. Platt (London: Macmillan, 1986), p. 2. With an annual growth rate of 5.8 percent, Buenos Aires in 1909 was second only to Hamburg (6.1 percent) and ahead of New York (5.7 percent).

2. According to David Keeling (1997, 231), approximately 70 percent of the country's agricultural production and 80 percent of the industrial production are concentrated in the Pampeana region.

3. For example, Jorge Garfunkel (1933, 144) asserts that in 1930, Argentina was the eighth economic power in the world measured in terms of per capita GDP.

4. In the context of the Cold War, President Perón strategically advocated a third world position. This position was identified as an anti-colonial struggle in which nations of the South distanced themselves from the United States as well as the Soviet Union, both constructed as empires. After Perón went into exile in 1952, a whole generation of young Argentines embraced Peronism; some joined armed groups such as Montoneros after reading the former president's writings and the work of authors, like John William Cooke (1968),

that inspired anti-imperialist nationalist sentiments. In 1973 Argentina joined the United Nations group of seventy-seven nonaligned nations.

5. Maximiliano Montenegro revealed these findings in an article for *Pagina 12* (April 30, 1999). The information is based on a report, "Poverty and Income Distribution in Argentina: Patterns and Change," prepared by economist Haeduck Lee.

6. See *Pagina 12* (April 26, 2002).

7. See *Argentina, from Insolvency to Growth: A World Bank Country Study* (Washington, D.C.: World Bank, 1993).

8. Ruben Zorrilla (1994), an Argentine sociologist, sees Menem's transformations as revolutionary, claiming that the retreat of the state unleashes the creativity of civil society, aided by the privatization process and open-market policies. In a similar vein, Keeling (1997) says that since 1990 Argentina has experienced the most significant period of change relative to the 1880s, and that Menem's policies will reinsert the nation into regional and global economic systems. In 1993, David Erro also predicted the resolution of the "Argentine Paradox" and suggested that it might be replaced by the "Argentine Miracle" under the visionary leadership of economist Domingo Cavallo.

9. See Portantiero (2000, 14).

10. A study by the National Institute of Statistics and Census (INDEC) also showed that 44.3 percent of Argentine children live in homes under the poverty line (*Clarin*, June 8, 1999).

11. According to this article, Soros invested $731 million in Argentina, making him the largest landowner in the country.

12. These surveys were conducted by Graciela Römer and Associates and Catterberg and Associates; see *Pagina 12* (April 15, 2002).

13. This proposal is cited in the Web publication "Rebelión," dated April 28, 2002 (http://www.rebelion.org/sociales/klein280402.htm). The related article by Naomi Klein originally appeared in *The Guardian Weekly*.

WORKS CITED

Cooke, John William. 1968. *La Revolución y el Peronismo.* Buenos Aires: Ediciones E.R.P.

Erro, David G. 1993. *Resolving the Argentine Paradox. Politics and Development. 1966–1992.* Boulder/London: Lynne Rienner Publishers.

Garfunkel, Jorge. 1933. "Economic Policy and Economic Performance: A Private Sector View of Regime Change," in *Argentina in The Crisis Years (1983–1990)*, ed. Colin M. Lewis and Nissa Torrents. London: Institute of Latin American Studies. Pp. 144–158.

Keeling, David. 1997. *Contemporary Argentina: A Geographical Perspective.* Boulder: Westview.

Platt, D.C.M. 1986. "Domestic Finance in the Growth of Buenos Aires, 1880–1914," in *The Political Economy of Argentina: 1880–1946*, ed. Guido di Tella and D.C.M. Platt. London: Macmillan, p. 2.

Portantiero, Juan Carlos. 2000. *El Tiempo de la Política. Construcción de Mayorías en la Evolución de la Democracia Argentina. 1983–2000.* Buenos Aires: Temas Grupo Editorial.

World Bank. 1993. *Argentina, from Insolvency to Growth: A World Bank Country Study.* Washington, D.C.: World Bank.

_____. 1987. *Economic Recovery and Growth.* Washington, D.C.: World Bank.

Zorrilla, Ruben. 1994. *El Fenómeno Menem.* Buenos Aires: Grupo Editor Latinoamericano.

21

The Globalization Movement
and the New New Left

DAVID GRAEBER

It's hard to think of another time when there has been such a gulf between intellectuals and activists, between theorists of revolution and its practitioners. Academics who for years have been in the habit of publishing essays that sound like position papers for vast social movements that do not in fact exist seem seized with confusion or, worse, dismissive contempt, now that real ones are everywhere emerging. It's particularly scandalous in the case of what's still, for no particularly good reason, referred to as the "antiglobalization" movement, a movement that has in a mere two or three years managed to completely transform the sense of historical possibilities for millions across the planet. In the United States, it's quite difficult to find a professional academic whose knowledge of it goes much beyond what might be gleaned from overtly hostile sources like the *New York Times;* then again, most of what's written even in progressive outlets seems to largely miss the point—or at least, to miss what participants in the movement really think is most important about it.

As an anthropologist and active participant in the movement—particularly, in the more radical, direct-action end of it—I might be able to at least clear up some common points of misunderstanding, though I cannot help but wonder how welcome some of this information might be. Much of the hesitation, I suspect, is based in a reluctance on the part of academics who have long fancied themselves radicals of some sort to come to terms with the fact that they are in fact liberals interested in expanding individual freedoms and pursuing social justice, but not in ways that would seriously challenge the existence of reigning institutions like state or capital. And even many of those who would, in fact, like to see revolutionary change might not feel entirely happy about having to accept the fact that most of the creative energy for radical politics is now coming from anarchism—a tradition that they have hitherto mostly dismissed with stupid jokes—and that taking this movement seriously will necessarily also mean an earnest and respectful engagement with it.

I am writing as an anarchist. This means that what follows will simplify a lot of things: For example, I won't be entering into the complex synergies between radical direct action groups and more reformist (and hierarchically organized) NGOs, though this has been the key to many of the movement's past successes. Still, if there is one aspect of the movement to highlight, surely anarchism is it. The very notion of direct action—with its rejection of a politics of protest (which would appeal to those in power to modify their behavior) in favor of efforts to physically intervene against power in a form that itself prefigures an alternative to its very existence—emerges directly from the libertarian tradition. In a certain sense, counting how many people involved in this or that aspect of the movement are actually willing to call themselves "anarchists," and in what sense, and in what contexts, is a bit beside the point.[1] Anarchism is the heart of the movement, its soul; from it has emerged most of what's new and hopeful about it.

What follows, then, is addressed primarily to those professional intellectuals who actually do feel there is something new and hopeful here. I'll start by trying to clear up what I think are the three most common misconceptions about the movement—our supposed opposition to something called "globalization," our supposed "violence," and our supposed lack of a coherent ideology—and then make a few suggestions about how we, as intellectuals, might think about reimagining our own intellectual practice in the light of all of this.

WE ARE NOT AN ANTIGLOBALIZATION MOVEMENT

The phrase "antiglobalization" movement is a coinage of the U.S. media, and activists have never felt comfortable with it. But in the United States, language is always a problem. Insofar as this is a movement against anything, it's against neoliberalism, which can be defined as a kind of market fundamentalism (or perhaps it might be better to say, market Stalinism) that holds there is only one possible direction for human historical development, and its secrets are held by an elite of economists and corporate flacks who must now be ceded all power once held by institutions with any shred of democratic accountability—through unelected treaty organizations like the IMF, WTO, and NAFTA. In Argentina, or Estonia, or Taiwan it would be possible to simply say this: "We are a movement against neoliberalism." But the U.S. corporate media is probably the most politically monolithic on the planet; here, neoliberalism is accepted as the basic ground of reality. As a result, the word itself cannot be used. Such issues can only be discussed with propaganda terms like "free trade" or "the free market." So American activists find themselves in a quandary: If one proposes to use "the 'n' word" in a pamphlet or press release, alarm bells immediately go off; one is being exclusionary, playing only to an educated elite. There have been all sorts of attempts to frame alternative expressions—we're a "global justice movement," we're a movement "against corporate globalization." None are especially elegant or quite satisfying, and as a result it is common in meetings to hear the speakers using the expressions "globalization movement" and "antiglobalization movement" pretty much interchangeably.

The phrase "globalization movement," though, is really quite apropos. If one takes globalization to mean the effacement of borders and the free movement of people, possessions, and ideas, then it's pretty clear not only that the movement itself is a product of globalization but that most of the groups involved in it—and the most radical ones in particular[2]—are in fact far more supportive of globalization in general than supporters of the IMF or World Trade Organization.

The real origins of the movement lie in an international network called People's Global Action, or PGA. The vision for such an "intercontinental network of resistance" was first laid out during the first Zapatista encuentro in Chiapas in 1996;[3] a formal structure was created the following year in Spain. From the start, PGA included not only anarchist groups and radical trade unions in Spain, Great Britain, and Germany but a Gandhian socialist farmers' league in India (KRRS), associations of Indonesian and Sri Lankan fisherfolk, the Argentinian teachers' union, indigenous groups such as the Maori of New Zealand and Kuna of Ecuador, the Brazilian landless peasants' movement (MST), a network made up of communities founded by escaped slaves in South and Central America, and any number of others. North America was for a long time one of the few areas largely unrepresented (except for the Canadian Postal Workers Union, which acted as PGA's main communications hub, now only partly replaced by the Internet, and a Montreal-based anarchist group called CLAC). It was PGA that put out the first calls for global days of action such as J18, and N30—the latter, the original call for direct action against the 1999 WTO meetings in Seattle.

Internationalism is equally reflected in the movement's demands. Here one need only look, for a particularly dramatic example, at the three planks of the platform of the Italian group Ya Basta!:[4] a universally guaranteed "basic income," a principle of global citizenship that would guarantee free movement of people across borders, and a principle of free access to new technology—which in practice would mean extreme limits on patent rights (themselves a very insidious form of protectionism). More and more, activists have been trying to draw attention to the fact that the neoliberal vision of "globalization" is pretty much limited to the free flow of commodities and actually increases barriers against the flow of people, information, and ideas. The size of the U.S. border guard, for instance, has almost tripled since the signing of NAFTA, which is hardly surprising; if it were not possible to effectively imprison the majority of people in the world in impoverished enclaves where even existing social guarantees could be gradually removed, there would be no incentive for Nike or The Gap to move production there to begin with. Given a free movement of people, the whole neoliberal project would collapse. This is another thing to bear in mind when people talk about the decline of "sovereignty" in the contemporary world. The main achievement of the state form in the last century or so has been the ability to establish a uniform grid of heavily policed barriers across the world, halting and controlling the free movement of peoples; nothing that has happened recently, even the occasional collapse of entities like Somalia or Afghanistan, has altered this because the ultimate meaning of the state system lies not in the control of a territory by any one (this could never, by definition, be absolute) but in the relations between them. It is precisely this international system of control that we are fighting against, in the name of genuine globalization.

These connections—and the broader links between neoliberal policies and mechanisms of state coercion (police, prisons, militarism)—have played a more and more salient role in our analyses as we ourselves confronted escalating levels of state repression. Borders became a major issue in Europe during the IMF meetings at Prague and later E.U. meetings in Nice; in North America, the FTAA summit in Quebec City—where invisible lines that had previously been treated as if they didn't exist (at least for white people) were converted overnight into lines of fortification against the movement of would-be global citizens demanding the right to petition their rulers. The three-kilometer "wall" constructed through the center of Quebec City to shield the heads of state junketing inside from any contact with the populace became the perfect symbol for what neoliberalism actually means, in human terms; the spectacle of the Black Bloc, armed with wire cutters and grappling hooks, joined by everyone from steelworkers to Mohawk warriors, tearing the wall down, became—for that very reason—perhaps the single most powerful moment in the movement's history.[5]

But here's the catch: It was powerful mainly for citizens of Canada, since they got to hear about it. In the United States, no one knew any of this happened. The choke-hold on information and ideas by the corporate media remains the greatest impediment to any real globalization. The obvious solution is to create our own media, and this has happened with remarkable speed; in the last year or so, a worldwide network of Independent Media Centers, run on anarchist principles, has sprung up in at least forty different countries worldwide, connected by the Internet. However, despite some remarkable triumphs (during Genoa, the IMC home page, www.indymedia.org, was getting more hits than CNN's), this is still but a faint challenge to those who control what gets put on television. The days of action in Genoa, for example, were kicked off by a 50,000-strong march calling for lifting all barriers to immigration in and out of Europe—a fact that went completely unreported by the international press, the same press that the very next day gave headline status to statements by George Bush and Tony Blair denouncing "protesters" for calling for a "fortress Europe."

There is one striking contrast between this and earlier internationalisms, however. The former usually ended up being about exporting Western organizational models to the rest of the world; in this, the flow has been, if anything, the other way around. Many, perhaps most, of the movement's signature techniques (consensus process, spokescouncils, mass nonviolent civil disobedience itself for that matter) were first developed in the global South. In the long run, this may well prove the single most radical thing about it.

"VIOLENT PROTESTERS" AND WORLD PEACE

In the corporate media, the word "violent" is invoked as a kind of mantra—invariably, repeatedly—whenever a large action takes place: "violent protesters," "violent protests," "violent clashes," "police raid headquarters of violent protesters." Such expressions are typically invoked when a simple, plain-English description of the acts that took place (activists holding hands blockading corners, a few throwing paint, one breaking a window, police beating them all with sticks and smashing dozens of their heads against walls) would probably convey that the only truly violent parties were the police. Again, the U.S. media invokes the term most insistently—this despite the fact that after two years of increasingly militant direct action, it is still impossible to produce a single example of anyone to whom a U.S. activist has caused physical injury. I would say that what really disturbs the powers that be is not the "violence" of the movement but its relative lack of it; governments simply do not know how to deal with an overtly revolutionary movement that refuses to fall into familiar patterns of armed resistance.

The effort to destroy existing paradigms is usually quite self-conscious. Where once it seemed that the only alternatives to marching along with signs were either Gandhian nonviolent civil disobedience or outright insurrection, groups like the Direct Action Network, Reclaim the Streets, Black Blocs and Tuti Bianci have all, in their own ways, been trying to map out a completely new territory in between. They're attempting to invent what many call a "new language" of civil disobedience, combining elements of what might otherwise be considered street theater, festival, and what can only be called nonviolent warfare (nonviolent in the sense adopted by, say, Black Bloc anarchists, in that it eschews any direct physical harm to human beings). Ya Basta! for example is famous for its tuti bianci or white overalls tactics, men and women dressed in elaborate forms of padding, ranging from foam armor to inner tubes to rubber-ducky flotation devices, helmets, and chemical-proof white jumpsuits. As this odd mock-army pushes its way through police barricades while protecting each other against injury or arrest, the ridiculous gear seems to reduce human beings to cartoon characters—misshapen, ungainly, foolish, largely indestructible. (The effect is only increased when lines of costumed figures attack police with balloons and water pistols or, like the "Pink Bloc," dress as fairies and tickle them with feather dusters.)

At the American Party Conventions, Billionaires for Bush (or Gore) dressed in high-camp tuxedos and evening gowns and tried to press wads of fake money into the cops' pockets, thanking them for repressing the dissent. None were even slightly hurt—raising suspicions among many that police are given aversion therapy against hitting anyone in a three-piece suit, let alone a tuxedo. This was, alas, not true of the Revolutionary Anarchist Clown Bloc, with their high bicycles, rainbow wigs, and squeaky mallets, who confused the cops by attacking each other (or the billionaires). They had all the best chants: "Democracy? Ha Ha Ha!" "The pizza united can never be defeated!" "Hey ho, hey ho—ha ha, hee hee!" as well as meta-chants like "Call! Response! Call! Response!" and—everyone's favorite— "Three Word Chant! Three Word Chant!"

In Quebec City, a giant medieval catapult lobbed soft toys and confetti at the FTAA meetings. Ancient-warfare techniques have been studied to adopt for non-violent but very militant forms of confrontation; there were peltasts and hoplites at Quebec City, and research continues into Roman-style shield walls, "turtles," and similar formations. Blockading has become an art form: If you make a huge web of strands of colored yarn across an intersection, it's actually impossible to cross; motorcycle cops get trapped like flies. There are Liberation Puppets that, when their arms are fully extended, can block a four-lane highway; snake dances and bicycle swarms can be a form of mobile blockade. Rebels in London last Mayday planned Monopoly board actions—Building Hotels on Mayfair for the homeless, Sale of the Century in Oxford Street, Guerrilla Gardening—only partly disrupted by heavy policing and torrential rain. But even the most militant of the militant— eco-saboteurs like the Earth Liberation Front—scrupulously avoid doing anything that would cause harm to human beings (or animals, for that matter). It's this scrambling of conventional categories that so throws the forces of order and makes them desperate to bring things back to familiar territory (simple violence), even to the point, as in Genoa, of encouraging fascist hooligans to run riot as an excuse to use overwhelming force against everybody else.

One can trace the origins of such forms to any number of directions. One could begin with the stunts and guerrilla theater of the Yippies or Italian "Metropolitan Indians" in the '60s. Alternately, one might consider the squatter battles in Germany or Italy or even the peasant resistance to the expansion of the Tokyo airport in the '70s and '80s. The latter marked perhaps a critical point of passage, the point where the governments of certain industrialized powers (all of them, interestingly, former Axis powers) had become so thoroughly demilitarized that it became possible for unarmed rebels not only to seize and defend territory against them but to engage in pitched battles that they were actually allowed to win— something that would, incidentally, be well-nigh inconceivable in the United States, where the populace is assumed to be armed. But it seems to me that here, too, the really crucial origins lie with the Zapatistas and other movements in the global South. In many ways, the Zapatista Army of National Liberation (EZLN) represents an attempt by people who have always been denied the right to nonviolent civil resistance to seize it—essentially, to call the bluff of neoliberalism and its pretenses of democratization and yielding power to "civil society." It is, as its commanders say, an army that aspires not to be an army any more. It is also about the least violent "army" one can possibly imagine. (It's something of an open secret that for the past five years, at least, they have not even been carrying real guns.) The

EZLN is the sort of army that organizes "invasions" of Mexican military bases in which hundreds of rebels sweep in entirely unarmed to yell at and try to shame the resident soldiers. Similarly, mass actions by the Landless Peasants Movement gain an enormous moral authority in Brazil by reoccupying unused lands entirely non-violently. In either case, it's pretty clear that if the same people had tried the same thing twenty years ago, they would simply have been shot.

However you choose to trace their origins, these new tactics are perfectly in accord with the general anarchistic inspiration of the movement, which is less about seizing state power than about exposing, delegitimizing, and dismantling mechanisms of rule while winning ever-larger spaces of autonomy from it. The critical thing, though, is that all this is possible only in a general atmosphere of peace. In fact, it seems to me that these are the ultimate stakes of struggle at the moment—a moment that may well determine the overall direction of the 21st century.

It is hard to remember now that (as Eric Hobsbawm reminds us) during the late 19th century, anarchism was the center of the revolutionary left; this was a time when most Marxist parties were rapidly becoming reformist social democrats.[6] This situation only really changed with World War I and, of course, the Russian Revolution. It was the success of the latter, we are usually told, that led to the decline of anarchism and catapulted communism everywhere to the fore. But it seems to me that one could look at this another way. In the late 19th century, most people honestly believed that war between industrialized powers was becoming obsolete; colonial adventures were a constant, but a war between France and England on French or English soil seemed as unthinkable as it would today. By 1900, even the use of passports was considered an antiquated barbarism.

The 20th century (which appears to have begun in 1914 and ended sometime around 1989 or '91) was by contrast probably the most violent in human history. It was a century almost entirely preoccupied with either waging world wars or preparing for them. It is hardly surprising, then, that the ultimate measure of political effectiveness became the ability to create and maintain huge mechanized killing machines, that anarchism quickly came to seem unrealistic. This is, after all, the one thing that anarchists can never, by definition, be very good at. Neither is it surprising that Marxist parties (already organized on a command structure, and for whom the organization of huge mechanized killing machines often proved about the only thing they were particularly good at) seemed eminently practical and realistic in comparison. And could it really be a coincidence that the moment the Cold War ended and war between industrialized powers once again seemed unthinkable, anarchism popped right back to where it had been at the end of the 19th century, as an international movement at the very center of the revolutionary left?

If so, it becomes clear what the ultimate stakes of the current "antiterrorist" mobilization are. In the short run, things do look very frightening. Governments who were desperately scrambling for some way to convince the public that we were terrorists even before September 11 now feel they've been given carte blanche; there is little doubt that a lot of good people are about to suffer terrible repression.

But in the long run, a return to 20th-century levels of violence is simply impossible. The September 11 attacks were clearly something of a fluke (the first wildly ambitious terrorist scheme in history that actually worked); the spread of nuclear weapons is ensuring that larger and larger portions of the globe will be for all practical purposes off-limits to conventional warfare. And if war is the health of the state, the prospects for anarchist-style organizing can only be improving.

Ideology, Consensus, and Direct Democracy

I can't remember how many articles I've read in the progressive press asserting that the globalization movement, while tactically brilliant, lacks any central theme or coherent ideology. These complaints seem to be the left equivalent of the incessant claims in the corporate media that this is a movement made up of dumb kids touting a bundle of completely unrelated causes (free Mumia, dump the debt, save the old growth forests). Even stranger are the claims—which one sees surprisingly frequently in the work of academic social theorists who you'd think might know better—that the movement is plagued by a generic opposition, rooted in bourgeois individualism, to all forms of structure or organization. It's distressing that two years after Seattle I should have to write this, but someone obviously should: In North America especially, this is a movement about reinventing democracy. It is not opposed to organization. It is about creating new forms of organization. It is not lacking in ideology. Those new forms of organization *are* its ideology. It is about creating and enacting horizontal networks instead of top-down structures like states, parties, and corporations, networks based on principles of decentralized, nonhierarchical consensus democracy. Ultimately, it aspires to be much more than that, because it aspires to reinvent daily life as whole. But unlike many other forms of radicalism, it has first organized itself in the political sphere—this mainly because that was a territory that the powers that be (who had put all their heavy artillery in the economic sphere) had largely abandoned.

Over the past decade, activists in North America have been putting enormous creative energy into reinventing their groups' own internal processes to create viable models of functioning direct democracy—drawing particularly, as I've noted, on examples from outside the Western tradition, which almost invariably rely on some kind of process of finding consensus rather than majority voting. The result is a rich and growing panoply of organizational forms and instruments—affinity groups, spokescouncils, facilitation tools, break-outs, fishbowls, blocking concerns, vibes-watchers, and so on—all aimed at creating forms of democratic process that allow initiatives to rise from below and attain maximum effective solidarity without stifling dissenting voices, creating leadership positions, or compelling anyone to do anything that they have not freely agreed to do. It is very much a work in progress, and creating a culture of democracy among people who have little experience in such things is necessarily a painful and uneven business, full of all sorts of stumblings and false starts, but—as almost any police chief who has faced us on the streets can attest—direct democracy of this sort can be astoundingly effective. And it is difficult to find anyone who has fully participated in such an action whose sense of human possibilities has not been profoundly transformed as a result. It's one thing to simply say "another world is possible." It's another to experience one, however momentarily.

Here, though, I mainly want to stress the relation of theory and practice this organizational model entails. Perhaps the best way to start thinking about groups like the Direct Action Network (DAN, or more explicitly anarchist versions of the same thing, such as the Anti-Capitalist Convergences, Global Action Networks, and Mobilization for Global Justice, which have begun cropping up everywhere from Chicago to the Philippines) is to see them as the diametrical opposite of the kind of sectarian Marxist group that has so long dominated the revolutionary left.[7] Whereas the latter puts its emphasis on achieving a complete and correct theoretical analysis, demands ideological uniformity, and tends to juxtapose the vision of an egalitarian future with extremely authoritarian forms of organization in the present, these openly seek diversity. Debate always focuses on particular courses of action; it's taken for granted that no one will ever convert anyone else entirely to their point of view.[8] The motto of such groups might as well be, "if you are willing to act like an anarchist now, your long-term vision is pretty much your own business" (which seems only sensible, since none of us really know how far these principles can actually take us or exactly what a complex society based on them would really end up looking like). Their ideology, then, is immanent in the antiauthoritarian principles that underlie their practice, and one of their more explicit principles is that things should stay this way.

This is how consensus works. The basic idea is that rather than voting, one tries to come up with proposals acceptable to everyone—or at least, proposals that no one finds profoundly objectionable. There are different sorts of process, some more formal than others, but the basic pattern is this: Someone states a proposal, and then the facilitator (the person who keeps the meeting moving) asks first for clarifying questions and then whether anyone has any "concerns." Often, at this point, someone might propose "friendly amendments" to the original proposal, or otherwise alter it, to ensure concerns are addressed. If skepticism seems widespread, a proposal might just be tabled or fused with a different proposal—compromises and creative syntheses are in every way encouraged—until one can finally get to the point of calling for consensus. At this point, the facilitator asks if anyone wishes to "stand aside" or "block." Standing aside is just saying, "I would not myself be willing to take part in this action, but I wouldn't stop anyone else from doing it." (Those who do so also get a chance to explain their conclusions to the group.) Blocking, however, is much more serious. A blocker is stating, in effect, "I think this proposal violates the fundamental principles or purposes of the group." It functions as a veto; any one person can kill a proposal completely by blocking it—although most groups also have ways to challenge whether a block is genuinely principled.

Consensus process obviously operates best on a small scale, though there are all sorts of techniques (careful use of agendas, timekeeping, etc.) to make sure meetings do not go on forever. Although all this is not nearly so unwieldy as one might think, it is unwieldy enough that the process itself encourages extreme decentralization of decision making. Much of it takes place on the level of affinity groups—small groups of, say, four to twelve people who know and trust each other, wherein the process can be much less formal and more "organic." Before large-scale actions like Seattle or Quebec City, there are always "spokescouncils," in which each affinity group selects a "spoke" empowered to speak for them and participate in the actual process of finding consensus (in theory, each group is arranged in a vast circle like the spokes of a wheel, with their spoke at the center, as they whisper back and forth deciding what to advise her). Before major decisions there are usually breakout sessions, where each affinity group comes to consensus on what position they want their spoke to take. Or break-outs might mean creating a series of smaller meetings to focus on making decisions or generating proposals on specific topics, which can then be presented for approval before the whole group when it reassembles (not as unwieldy as it might sound). Facilitators come armed with any number of different "tools" to help resolve problems or move things along if they seem to be bogging down: One can ask for a brainstorming session, in which people are only allowed to present ideas but not to criticize other people's, or for a nonbinding straw poll, where people raise their hands just to see how everyone feels about a proposal (to get a "sense of the room") rather than to make a formal decision. A fishbowl is used only if there is a profound difference of opinion: Two representatives for each side—one man and one woman—sit in the middle with everyone else surrounding them silently, and the four try to clarify exactly where the differences lie, before returning to work out some kind of solution or synthesis. Often there are "vibes watchers" to monitor whether anyone is feeling frustrated or excluded or to note whether people are getting bored or the energy is lagging. The arsenal of tools and techniques tends to expand with practice.

There is indeed something very new here, something potentially extremely important. Consider, for example, the principles behind consensus. One of the basic ones is that one always treats others' arguments as fundamentally reasonable and principled, whatever one thinks about the person making it. This creates an extremely different style of debate and argument than the sort encouraged by majority voting, one in which the incentives are all oriented toward compromise and creative synthesis rather than polarization, reduction, and treating minor points of difference like vast philosophical ruptures. I need hardly point out how much our accustomed modes of academic discourse resemble the latter—or even more, perhaps, the kind of sectarian reasoning that leads to endless splits and fragmentation, which the "new new left" (as it is often called) has so far managed almost completely to avoid. It seems to me that in many ways the activists are way ahead of the theorists here. The most challenging problem for us will be to create forms of intellectual practice more in tune with newly emerging forms of democratic practice rather than with the tiresome sectarian logic these groups have finally begun to set aside.

SOME FINAL DIRECTIONS

I want to end with some thoughts on how professional intellectuals might be able to contribute to this movement. If we are no longer going to play a role in the constitution of some kind of new vanguard (even a Gramscian one), what can we do? That is, *as* theorists.

Surely there is no one right answer to this question, but I'd like to suggest one possible direction, what I like to think of as the intellectual equivalent of a gift economy. It seems to me that one of our most important roles might be to tease out the possible moral and political implications of initiatives that arise from people who are organizing and taking action on the streets and then to shape them into more concrete ideas and visions that can be offered back to them. As gifts. By "gifts," here, I especially mean "in forms that are substantially detachable from the author's personality." This would actually involve a pretty major change in much of what passes for radical thought in the academy, since it would mean consciously rejecting the kind of intentionally arcane, mysterious declarations of high theory that even readers who actually can afford the requisite years of graduate education can never completely detach from the charisma of the (would-be) Great Thinker, because they can never quite understand them. Let me throw out a few examples of one form I think such intellectual exercises might take:

1. Organizations involved with direct action tend to combine a blanket refusal to enter into dialogue with what they consider inherently undemocratic ("evil") institutions together with standards of internal democracy so generous that it is considered a matter of principle to give everyone the benefit of the doubt for honesty and good intentions. Clearly, these are two sides of the same coin, and there is a certain kind of institutional morality implied here, one whose implications it would be helpful to elaborate. (Equally so, the fact that when such institutions fall into crisis, it is always when they have to confront structures of oppression—such as racism and sexism—which are embedded in individual dispositions as much as formal institutional arrangements.)

2. The fact that direct action and forms of organization surrounding it are essentially about experimenting with the creation of nonalienated forms of action raises all sorts of interesting questions about what we really mean by "alienation" and its broader implications for revolutionary practice. For example: Why exactly is it that even when there is next to no other constituency for revolutionary politics in a capitalist society, the one group most likely to be sympathetic to it consists

of artists, musicians, writers, and others involved in some form of nonalienated production? Surely there must be a link between the actual experience of first imagining things and then bringing them into being (individually or collectively) and the ability to imagine social alternatives—particularly, the possibility of a society itself premised on less alienated forms of creativity. One might even suggest that revolutionary coalitions always tend to rely on a kind of alliance between a society's least alienated and its most oppressed; actual revolutions, one could then say, have tended to happen when these two categories most broadly overlap. This would, at least, help explain why it almost always seems to be peasants and craftsmen—or even more, newly proletarianized former peasants and craftsmen—who actually overthrow capitalist regimes and not those inured to generations of wage labor. Finally, I suspect this would also help explain the extraordinary importance of indigenous people's struggles in the new movement. Such people tend to be simultaneously the very least alienated and most oppressed people on earth; now that new, global communications technologies have made it possible to include them in revolutionary alliances, it is well nigh inevitable that they should play a profoundly inspirational role in them.

3. Might it be possible to reimagine the very notion of human rights starting from this notion of nonalienated experience—particularly, from forms of directly democratic practice? If nothing else, seeing rights as emergent from such forms of practice (and the explicit notion of "rights" emerging, as a discourse, when the principles already immanent in certain forms of action become clearly articulated) would overcome the old problem of reconciling positive and negative rights, which never seems to get completely resolved.[9] If one starts from the assumption that fundamental human rights consist, say, of the right to full political participation in the affairs of one's community—or for that matter, to freedom of creative self-expression, or to freedom of sexual expression—then it becomes obvious that such rights cannot be exercised in the absence of a certain baseline life security, since one cannot meaningfully participate in the democratic life of one's community if one is paralyzed by fear of homelessness or death squads, or engage in free sexual expression if one has to sell one's body to get food. Most of what are usually seen as fundamental rights, positive or negative, could then be seen as already entailed by these more primary ones. One might even think of them as something in the nature of infra-rights. Direct action groups, or directly democratic community groups, could then be reimagined as groups whose political engagement with the world is aimed at addressing those forms of oppression that prevent the full realization of those principles and forms of experience already immanent in their own organization.

As I say, these are only suggestions (largely based on my own current intellectual projects). There are other groups of scholars—the Raisons d'Agir group in France, the Shifting Ground collective in Great Britain, numerous groups in Italy—who have been grappling with the same questions and finding rather different, if complementary, answers. At this point, the critical thing is simply to start asking. As I've said, none of us can really know how far these new, broadly anarchistic principles will actually be able to take us, or what new global syntheses might emerge. What matters is whether we are willing to find out.

NOTES

1. There are many who take anarchist principles of antisectarianism and open-endedness so seriously they are sometimes reluctant to call themselves "anarchists" for that very reason.

2. Anarchists, obviously, are opposed to the very existence of national borders in any form. But generally, direct action–oriented groups have highlighted this aspect far more than, say, the International Forum on Globalization, which is much more ambivalent.

3. "Not an organized structure; it doesn't have a central head or decision maker; it has no central command or hierarchies. We are the network, all of us who resist." Zapatista's Second Declaration of La Realidad, read by Subcomandante Marcos during the closing session of the First International Encounter for Humanity and Against Neoliberalism, August 3, 1996.

4. Which also appear at the end of Michael Hardt and Antonio Negri's book *Empire* (Cambridge, Mass.: Harvard University Press, 2000). Their history, in fact, represents an interesting case study in the migration of ideas back and forth between intellectuals and social movements. Most of them emerged from the experience of Autonomia in the 1970s, as refracted through the writings of authors like Paolo Virno, Franco "Bifo" Berardi, and Negri himself. I think it's important though to bear in mind that such ideas are not simply the product of individual heroic intellectuals, as academics (who by a rather elitist instinct like to give other academics as much credit as possible) almost always prefer to imply.

5. Helping tear it down was certainly one of the more exhilarating experiences of this author's life.

6. "In 1905–1914 the marxist left had in most countries been on the fringe of the revolutionary movement, the main body of marxists had been identified with a de facto nonrevolutionary social democracy, while the bulk of the revolutionary left was anarcho-syndicalist, or at least much closer to the ideas and the mood of anarcho-syndicalism than to that of classical marxism." See Eric Hobsbawm, "Bolshevism and the Anarchists," in *Revolutionaries: Contemporary Essays* (New York: Pantheon Books, 1973), p. 61.

7. It's not clear that anarchist groups in the traditional sectarian sense still exist in North America (though many that exist largely as intellectual positions, for instance Primitivists and Social Ecologists, have certainly not lost the habits of mutual condemnation typical of sectarian groups, I have never heard of anyone being purged from an actual organization for ideological reasons). Still, one can make a distinction between what I call capital-A anarchist groups, such as, say, the North East Federation of Anarchist Communists, whose members must accept a specific platform first developed in the 1920s, and that have some centralized features, and the small-a anarchists. The latter appear to be the real locus of historical dynamism right now, although many people have been experimenting with groups like NEFAC as a way to add a certain degree of ongoing structure to the looser confederations that tend to fade in and out around big actions, in a way that would carefully ensure that it does not collapse into vanguardism.

8. Consensus is much misunderstood. It's quite different from unanimity, in that it assumes diversity. Those objecting to a proposal have the option of either "standing aside," which means they don't think the proposal is a good idea and won't be bound by it personally, or "blocking it"—vetoing it—though blocks must be based in a group's founding prin-

ciples or reasons for being. Similarly, consensus, rather paradoxically, has proved the form of decision-making most appropriate for radical decentralization, if only because finding consensus in large groups is often so laborious a process that there's a strong incentive to keep decision-making among the lowest level possible.

9. I'm assuming most readers are familiar with the basic problem here. C. B. MacPherson first noted that bourgeois notions of human rights were basically negative, since they start from the notion that one owns one's person and property and can exclude others from intruding on it; efforts to expand on them have always seemed somewhat artificial. See C. B. MacPherson, *The Political Theory of Possessive Individualism.* (Oxford University Press, Oxford. 1962).

About the Authors

Stanley Aronowitz is a distinguished professor of sociology and urban education at the Graduate Center, City University of New York, where he has taught since 1983, and has been the director of the Center for the Study of Culture, Technology and Work since 1988. Formerly a steelworker, he was an organizer for the Amalgamated Clothing Workers (now UNITE) and the Oil, Chemical, and Atomic Workers. Aronowitz has continued his organizing and activist efforts as an elected officer of the Professional Staff Congress, AFT (American Federation of Teachers), and as the 2002 New York gubernatorial candidate for the Green Party. He is also the author or editor of twenty books, including *The Knowledge Factory* (2000), *The Last Good Job in America* (2001), and, as co-editor with Peter Bratsis, *Paradigm Lost: State Theory Reconsidered* (2002). His book on class in America, *Class Rules,* will appear in 2003.

Clyde W. Barrow is a professor of policy studies and director of the Center for Policy Analysis at the University of Massachusetts, Dartmouth, where he specializes in political theory and political economy. Barrow has published extensively on critical state theory, higher education policy, and American political thought. His most recent book is *More Than a Historian: Charles A. Beard's Political and Economic Thought* (2000). He has previously authored *Critical Theories of the State* (1993) and *Universities and the Capitalist State* (1990).

Peter Bratsis is a research fellow at the Hellenic Observatory, European Institute, London School of Economics and Political Science. Most recently, he has co-edited, with Stanley Aronowitz, *Paradigm Lost: State Theory Reconsidered* (2002).

Jeremy Brecher is a historian and the author of ten books on labor and social movements, including *Strike!* (1972), *Brass Valley* (1982), *Building Bridges* (1990), *Global Visions* (1993), *Global Village or Global Pillage* (1994), *History from Below* (1995), and *Globalization from Below* (2000). He is also a documentary screenwriter who has been awarded four Emmy Awards and the Edgar Dale Screenwriting Award. He produced the Emmy-nominated documentary "Global Village or Global Pillage?" Brecher has served as Fulbright Research Scholar at the University of Otago in New Zealand, and he received the Wilber Cross Award of the Connecticut Humanities Council as Humanities Scholar of the Year. For more information, visit www.villageorpillage.org.

Jeffrey Bussolini is a doctoral candidate in sociology at the City University of New York Graduate Center and in history of technology at the Ecole des Hautes Etudes en Sciences Sociales in Paris, France. He writes on the history of Los Alamos and on the sociology of science and technology. A long-time friend of Wen Ho Lee, Bussolini was active on his behalf as the eastern U.S. coordinator, with Christa Savino, of the Wen Ho Lee Defense

Fund and Justice for Wen Ho Lee. As such, he attended many of the federal court proceedings and organized with a number of groups on behalf of Dr. Lee.

Alex Callinicos was born in Zimbabwe in 1950. After studying at Oxford and the London School of Economics, he is now a professor of politics at the University of York (England), where he has taught since 1981. Among the books he has written are *Althusser's Marxism* (1976), *The Revolutionary Ideas of Karl Marx* (1983), *Making History* (1987), *South Africa Between Reform and Revolution* (1988), *Against Postmodernism* (1989), *The Revenge of History* (1991), *Theories and Narratives* (1995), *Social Theory* (1999), *Equality* (2000), and *Against the Third Way* (2001). He is also a columnist for *Socialist Worker* (London) and is active in the movement against capitalist globalization.

William DiFazio is a professor of sociology at St. John's University, author of *A Little Food and Cold Storage: Ordinary Poverty in New York City* (2003), co-author, with Stanley Aronowitz, of *The Jobless Future: SciTech and the Dogma of Work* (1995), and co-host of CityWatch, a weekly radio show on WBAI (99.5 FM) in New York City.

Carmen Alicia Ferradás is an associate professor in the department of anthropology and the director of the Latin American and Caribbean Area Studies at Binghamton University, SUNY. Her research interests are focused on critiques of development practice and environmentalism. She is currently conducting research on environmental struggles in the Triple Frontier of Mercosur. In addition, she has published *Power in the Southern Cone Borderlands: An Anthropology of Development Practice* (1998) as well as various articles examining development projects and the impact of neo-liberalism in the Southern Cone.

Heather Gautney is an activist and a doctoral student at the Graduate School and University Center at the City University of New York. She is also a fellow at the Center for the Study of Culture, Technology and Work, and a member of the editorial collective of the journal *Found Object*.

David Graeber is an activist and anthropologist based in New York, while teaching at Yale. He was a student of Marshall Sahlins at the University of Chicago and has conducted fieldwork in Madagascar—the result being a monograph (as yet unpublished) called "Catastrophe: Magic and History in Central Madagascar." More recently, he authored *Towards an Anthropological Theory of Value: The False Coin of Our Own Dreams* (2001). As an activist, he has worked with the New York Direct Action Network, Ya Basta!, People's Global Action, and the Anti-Capitalist Convergence. He is currently working on an ethnography of the direct action movement and a book of essays on the relationship between anthropology and anarchism.

Bruno Gullì is a Ph.D. candidate in comparative literature at the Graduate Center, CUNY. He also teaches history and philosophy in Brooklyn.

Michael Hardt is associate professor of literature at Duke University and **Antonio Negri** was a professor of political science at the University of Padua, Italy. They are co-authors of *Empire* (2000) and *Labor of Dionysus* (1994). Hardt is also the author of *Gilles Deleuze* (1993). Negri has written more than twenty books; among these, the one most recently published in English is *Insurgencies* (1999).

Cindi Katz is professor of geography in Environmental Psychology and Women's Studies at the Graduate Center of the City University of New York. Her work concerns social reproduction and the production of space, place, and nature; children and the environment; and the consequences of global economic restructuring for everyday life. She has published widely in edited collections and in journals such as *Society and Space, Social Text, Signs, Fem-*

inist *Studies, Annals of the Association of American Geographers,* and *Antipode.* She is the editor, with Janice Monk, of *Full Circles: Geographies of Gender over the Life Course* (1993) and recently completed *Disintegrating Developments: Global Economic Restructuring and Children's Everyday Lives* (forthcoming in 2003). She is currently working on two projects, one on "Retheorizing Childhood" and the other on the "Social Wage."

Andrew Light is assistant professor of environmental philosophy, director of the Environmental Conservation Education Program at New York University, and research fellow at the Institute for Environment, Philosophy, and Public Policy at Lancaster University (U.K.). He has authored more than fifty articles and book chapters on environmental ethics, philosophy of technology, and philosophy of film, and has edited or co-edited thirteen books including *Environmental Pragmatism* (1996), *Social Ecology After Bookchin* (1998), *Technology and the Good Life?* (2000), *Beneath the Surface: Critical Essays on the Philosophy of Deep Ecology* (2000), and *Moral and Political Reasoning in Environmental Practice* (2002). Light is also co-editor of the journal *Philosophy and Geography.*

Manning Marable, a professor of history and political science at Columbia University in New York City since 1993, is the founding director of the Institute for Research in African-American Studies. He has authored and edited nearly twenty books and anthologies, the last three of which are *Let Nobody Turn Us Around: Voices of Resistance, Reform, and Renewal: An African-American Anthology* (2000, with Leith Mullings), *Dispatches from the Ebony Tower: Intellectuals Confront the African American Experience* (2000), and *Black Leadership* (1998). Marable's books and anthologies in progress include *Race and Democracy* (Basic Books); *Freedom* (Phaidon Press, with Leith Mullings), *Freedom on My Mind: The Columbia Reader of African American History* (Columbia University Press, with Nishani Frazier and John McMillian), and *No Easy Victories: An Anthology of Black Radicalism, 1968 to the Present* (Verso, with Leith Mullings and Johanna Fernandez). He has also written more than 225 scholarly articles in academic journals and edited volumes throughout his teaching career beginning in 1974.

Peter Marcuse, a lawyer and urban planner, is professor of urban planning at Columbia University in New York City. He was majority leader of Waterbury, Connecticut's Board of Alderman (City Council), a member of its City Planning Commission, president of the Los Angeles Planning Commission, and, more recently, a member of Community Board 9 in Manhattan and co-chair of its Housing Committee. Before arriving at Columbia, he was in the private practice of law in Waterbury for more than twenty years and taught at UCLA as professor of urban planning. He is also co-editor, with Ronald van Kempen, of both *Globalizing Cities: A New Spatial Order of Cities* (1999) and *Of States and Cities* (2002). An early member of the Planners Network, he has remained active in its efforts to influence New York City planning in the aftermath of September 11. He is also on the editorial boards of a number of professional journals, and has been a consultant to local, state, and national governments on housing policy issues.

Randy Martin is professor of art and public policy and associate dean of faculty and interdisciplinary programs at Tisch School of the Arts, New York University. His recent books include *Financialization of Daily Life* (2002), and *On Your Marx: Relinking Socialism and the Left* (2001). He is also co-editor of the journal *Social Text.*

Michael Ratner is the president of the Center for Constitutional Rights in New York. He is currently involved in challenging constitutional violations in the wake of 9/11, including a habeas corpus petition on behalf of the Guantanamo detainees and a class action against the continued detention of noncitizen Middle Eastern men within the United States. In his previous work he has served as special counsel to Haitian President Jean-Bertrand Aristide to assist in the prosecution of human rights crimes, as legal director of the Center for Constitutional Rights, and as president of the National Lawyers Guild. He has also taught at Yale Law School, where he was the Skelly Wright Fellow, and is currently teaching international human rights litigation at Columbia Law School. Ratner is the author or co-author of numerous books and articles including *The Pinochet Papers: The Case of Augusto Pinochet in Spain and Britain* (2000), *International Human Rights Litigation in U.S. Courts* (1996), *Che Guevara and the FBI* (1998), and "How We Closed the Guantanamo HIV Camp: The Intersection of Politics and Litigation" (1998).

Corey Robin is an assistant professor of political science at Brooklyn College, CUNY. He has written for a wide variety of publications, including the *New York Times Magazine*, the *Times Literary Supplement, Lingua Franca*, the *Washington Post Book World, Dissent, American Political Science Review*, and *Social Research*. His article topics range from conservative intellectuals, the war on terrorism, and globalization to Montesquieu, Tocqueville, Hobbes, and modern political theory. His first book, *Fear: Biography of an Idea*, is forthcoming from Oxford University Press.

William K. Tabb teaches economics at Queens College and is on the political science faculty at the Graduate Center of the City University of New York. His recent books include *Unequal Partners: A Primer on Globalization* (2002), *The Amoral Elephant: Globalization and the Struggle for Social Justice in the Twenty-First Century* (2001), *Reconstructing Political Economy: The Great Divide in Economic Thought* (1999), and *The Postwar Japanese System: Cultural Economy and Economic Transformation* (1995). He is currently completing a new book, *Globalization Rules: Economic Governance for the World System*.

Ellen Willis is professor of journalism and director of cultural reporting and criticism at New York University. Her essays on politics and culture have appeared in numerous publications, including *The Nation, Dissent, Salon, Social Text*, and the *New York Times*. Her latest book, on the political culture of the 1990s, is *Don't Think, Smile! Notes on a Decade of Denial* (1999).

Index